Name	Class	Year

Canadian Students'

Guide to Language, Literature, and Media

Susanne Barclay
Judith Coghill
Peter Weeks

Contibuting Authors
Norm Olding
Don Quinlan

OXFORD
UNIVERSITY PRESS

70 Wynford Drive, Don Mills, Ontario M3C 1J9
oup.com/ca

Oxford University Press is a department of the University of Oxford.

It furthers the University's objective of excellence in research, scholarship, and education by publishing worldwide in

Oxford New York
Athens Auckland Bangkok Bogotá Buenos Aires Cape Town
Chennai Dar es Salaam Delhi Florence Hong Kong Istanbul Karachi
Kolkata Kuala Lumpur Madrid Melbourne Mexico City Mumbai Nairobi
Paris São Paulo Shanghai Singapore Taipei Tokyo Toronto Warsaw

with associated companies in Berlin Ibadan

Oxford is a registered trade mark of Oxford University Press
in the UK and in certain other countries

Published in Canada
By Oxford University Press

First published 2001

National Library of Canada Cataloguing in Publication Data

Barclay, Susanne
Canadian students' guide to language, literature and media

Includes index.
ISBN 0-19-541675-9

1. English language—Rhetoric. 2. Readers (Secondary). I. Coghill, Judith Ann, 1948– . II. Weeks, Peter. III. Title.

PE1121.B35 2001 808'.0427 C2001-930542-7

Printed and bound in Canada
This book is printed on permanent (acid-free) paper ∞

2 3 4—04 03 02 01

Cover design: Joan Dempsey
Text design: Valentino Sanna, Ignition Design & Communications
Editor: Karen Alliston

Text Credits

7–8 Susan Perly: "The Land." Reprinted by permission of the author; **11** David Mason, "Song of the Powers" from *The Country I Remember: Poems* (Ashland, OR: Story Line Press, 1996). Published by permission of the author and Story Line Press, Ashland, Oregon (www.storylinepress.com); **12** Gwendolyn Brooks: "We Real Cool" from *Blacks.* Reprinted by permission of the author; **20** Frances Cornford: "The Watch" from *Collected Poems* by Frances Cornford, published by Cressett Press. Reprinted by permission of The Random House Group Ltd.; **29–30** Adapted from *Easy Access: The Reference Handbook for Writers*, 2nd edition, by Michael Keene and Katherine H. Adams (Mountain View, CA: Mayfield Publishing, 1996/1999); **39** Excerpt from *Love in the Time of Cholera* by Gabriel García Márquez, translated by Edith Grossman (New York: Alfred A. Knopf, 1988). Reprinted by permission of Random House, Inc.; **40** Tom Wolfe: *A Man in Full*. pp. 503–504. Reprinted by permission of Farrar, Straus and Giroux, LLC; **41–44** Graham Greene, "I Spy" from *Collected Stories* (London: Random House, 1972). Copyright © 1972. Reprinted by permission of David Higham Associates; Annotations from *Literature, Criticism and Style: A Practical Guide to Advanced Level English Literature*, Revised Edition, by Steven Croft and Helen Cross (Oxford, Oxford University Press, 2000); **45** Two paragraphs from *The Bean Trees* by Barbara Kingsolver. Copyright © 1988 by Barbara Kingsolver. Reprinted by permission of HarperCollins Publishers, Inc.; **45–46** Excerpted from "Sonny's Blues" © 1957 by James Baldwin. Collected in *Going to Meet the Man*, published by Vintage Books. Copyright renewed. Reprinted by arrangement with the James Baldwin Estate; **47–48** Excerpt from Margaret Atwood *The Handmaid's Tale* (Toronto: McClelland & Stewart, 1986); **49** Excerpt from Michael Ondaatje *In the Skin of a Lion* (Toronto: McClelland & Stewart, 1987), p.54; **50–51** "The Jade Peony" by Wayson Choy from *The Jade Peony,* copyright © 1995 by Wayson Choy. Published in Canada by Douglas & McIntyre. Reprinted by permission; **52–56** R.K. Narayan "Forty-Five a Month"; **72–75** Wendy Lill, "The Fighting Days" from *The Fighting Days* © Wendy Lill 1985; Vancouver, Talonbooks; **77** Excerpt from *Overlaid* by Robertson Davies (Toronto: Samuel French, 1952). Reprinted with permission of Pendragon Ink; **77–78** Excerpt from *Largo Desolato* by Vaclav Havel, translated by Tom Stoppard. Copyright © 1987 by Tom Stoppard. Used by permission of Grove/Atlantic, Inc.; **79** Excerpt from "Lament for Harmonica (Maya)", *The Collected Plays of Gwen Pharis Ringwood*, Borealis Press, 1982. Reprinted by permission; **80–85** From *The Glass Menagerie* by Tennessee Williams, copyright 1945 by Tennessee Williams and Edwina D. Williams. Copyright renewed 1973 by Tennessee Williams. Used by permission of Random House, Inc.; **95** From *Death of a Salesman* by Arthur Miller, copyright 1949, renewed © 1977 by Arthur Miller. Used by permission of Viking Penguin, a division of Penguin Putnam Inc.; **95–96** Excerpt from *The Drum-Maker* by Kendel Hippolyte is reprinted by permission of the author; **97** From *Joe Turner's Come and Gone* by August Wilson, copyright © 1988 by August Wilson. Used by permission of Dutton Signet, a division of Penguin Putnam Inc.; **99–104** Valorie Bunce: "Account Balanced" from *Instant Applause: 26 Very Short Complete Plays*, (Winnipeg: Blizzard Publishing, 1994); **108–110** Adapted from *Easy Access: The Reference Handbook for Writers*, 2nd edition, by Michael Keene and Katherine H. Adams (Mountain View, CA: Mayfield Publishing, 1996/1999); **116–117** E. Annie Proulx, "Books a Dying Art? Don't Believe It" from *The New York Times*, 26 May 1994. Copyright © 1994 by The New York Times Co. Reprinted by permission; **120–122** Chief Dan George, "I Am a Native of North America" from *My Heart Soars*, (Surrey, BC: Hancock House Publishers, 1974). Reprinted by permission of Hancock House Publishers; **128–130** "What Literature Is For" from *Language in Thought and Action*, Third Edition, by S.I. Hayakawa, copyright © 1972 by Harcourt Inc., reprinted by permission of the publisher; **137–138** H. Northrop Frye: "Don't You Think It's Time to Start Thinking" from *Journal of Ontario Council of Teachers of English*; **140–141** From Tennessee Williams: *A Streetcar Named Desire*; Annotations and diagram p. 142 from *Literature, Criticism and Style: A Practical Guide to Advanced Level English Literature*, Revised Edition, by Steven Croft and Helen Cross (Oxford, Oxford University Press, 2000); **154–155** Sandra Shamas, "Pie-in-the-Sky-Guy" from *National Post*, 31 January 2001, reprinted by permission of the author; **157–158** Excerpts from Margaret Laurence: "Where the World Began" from *Heart of a Stranger* (Toronto: McClelland & Stewart, 1976), pp.23–26; **159** From *Zlata's Diary: A Child's Life in Sarajevo*, Zlata Fiilipovic, trans. Christina Pribichevich-Zoric, (London: Penguin Books, 1994), p.6; **163** Tom Honey: Letter to the Editor from *The Globe and Mail*, 6 February 2001; **164** "May 5" from *The Weight of the World: A Journal* by Peter Handke, translated by Ralph Manheim. Translation copyright © 1985 by Farrar, Straus & Giroux, Inc. Reprinted by permission of Farrar, Straus and Giroux, LLC; **164–165** Jack Kerouac: Excerpt from January 3, 1949, journal entry from *The New Yorker*, 22/29 June 1998; **165–167** Maria Said: "Half-Walls Between Us" from *Re: Generation Quarterly* 5.1 (pp.9–10). Visit www.regenerator.com for more articles and subscription information. © 1999 Maria Said. All rights reserved. Used by permission of the author; **168–170** Excerpt from *Long Walk to Freedom* by Nelson Mandela. Copyright © 1994 by Nelson Rolihlahla Mandela. By permission of Little, Brown & Company (Inc.); **170–171** V.S. Naipaul: Letter dated 22 November from *The New Yorker*, 13 December 1999, pp.69–70; **174–176** Adapted from *Easy Access: The Reference Handbook for Writers*, 2nd edition, by Michael Keene and Katherine H. Adams (Mountain View, CA: Mayfield Publishing, 1996/1999); **184–190** Sabine Jessen: excerpts from "Sheltering the Deep" (text only) from *Explore*, May/June 2000; **198–202** Dane Lanken: "Struck By Lightning" from *Canadian Geographic*, July/August 2000; **203** Excerpt from "Chile Faces Rainforest Dilemma" by Jimmy Langman from *The Globe and Mail*, 2 November 2000, reprinted by permission of the author; **204–207** Danylo Hawaleshka, "A Matter of Trust: Water is governed by a patchwork of regulations" from *Maclean's*, 12 June 2000. Reprinted by permission; **213–215** Clive Thompson, "Halt! Who Goes There?" from *Report on Business*, September 2000. Reprinted by permission; **216–220** Robert Sheppard, "We Are Canadian" from *Maclean's*, 25 Dec 2000/1 Jan 2001. Reprinted by permission; **249–254** "Eggs" (text only) from *Canadian Advertising Success Stories: CASSIES 99*, ed. David Rutherford, (Toronto: Canadian Congress of Advertising, 1999). Reprinted by permission of the the Canadian Egg Marketing Agency and Roche Macaulay & Partners; **284** ABC radio spot – Reproduced with permission of ABC Canada.

Visuals Credits

189 Reproduced with permission of Ivy Images; **194–195** Illustrations reproduced with permission of David Fierstein; **196–197** Reproduced with permission of Maclean's; **200–201** Lightning photos and map – Reproduced with permission of Canadian Geographic; **209–210** Reproduced with permission of Canadian Geographic Magazine; **262** Reproduced with permission of Energizer Canada; **270–273** Reproduced with permission of the National Post; **274** Reproduced with permission of Maclean's; **275** Reproduced with permission of Saturday Night magazine; **276** Reproduced with permission of Weider Publications; **278** Reproduced with permission of Leader Sports; **279** Associated Press; **282** Reproduced with permission of Andrea Dietrich; **286** *TV Guide* pages—Reproduced with permission of Transcontinental Publications; **288–289** Reproduced with permission of Frito Lay and BBDO Canada; **290** Reproduced with permission of Big Brothers and Big Sisters Canada; **293** Reproduced with permission of Transworld Snowboarding Magazine; *294*: Reproduced with permission of Snowboardermag.com; **297** Reproduced with permission of Finish Line and Lodge Design

CONTENTS

to the student

This reference handbook is designed to assist you in your study of English literature and language. You can use this book whether you are working alone or with others; and whether you are reading it in the classroom or outside of it.

Each chapter focuses on a particular genre. These include traditional genres—such as narrative, drama, and essays—as well as the more recent genres of media and business and technical writing. In every chapter you'll find interesting samples of texts from various time periods and cultures. Many are annotated to highlight key features that you will be able to study and then apply in your own work.

Each chapter is organized in a clear and consistent way under the following main headings.

Analyzing and Responding

- "*Checkpoint: Assess Your Knowledge*" features a selection from the genre followed by questions. We encourage you to read the selection and then respond to the questions. This will help you discover what you may need to learn about the genre.
- *Information about meaning, form, and style*. These sections include definitions, explanations, samples from professional writers (some of which are annotated), charts, and strategies.
- "*Checkpoint: Reassess Your Knowledge*" gives you another sample and another set of questions. Responding to these questions gives you the opportunity to apply what you've learned in the chapter.

Creating

- *Ideas about how to get started on your own original work*. You'll find suggestions about how to prepare and plan your creation, whether it's a poem, an essay, or a storyboard for a video.
- *Tips on revising and editing your work*. This includes the finer points of grammar, usage, and mechanics.

Presenting

- *Each genre lends itself to one or more styles of presentation*, whether it's a choral reading (poetry), readers' theatre (narrative texts), or storytelling (personal writing). This section begins by describing one approach, and how to put it into action.
- *Tips on how to present*, whether on your own, with a partner, or with a group. You'll also find checklists to help you remember all the important aspects.

You can work through a chapter systematically or dip into it as needed to help you complete an activity or clarify a point you may not be sure of. Use the handy contents page at the beginning of each chapter to help you find what you are looking for. Definitions of key terms are also boldfaced throughout the text so that you can spot them quickly as you scan a section. Once you become familiar with the organization and format, you will be able to navigate your way quickly through the book to find what you need just when you need it. Enjoy the opportunity to hone your analytical and creative skills.

to the teacher

The Canadian Students' Guide to Language, Literature, and Media is designed to encourage student involvement in their own learning. It is intended for students' independent use, but also lends itself well to individual or small-group study under the teacher's direction.

The Canadian Students' Guide is organized by genre. Each chapter features samples of the genre that model patterns or demonstrate the effective use of particular techniques. This "language in use" approach enables students to see what quality work looks like; as a result, students become better equipped to create their own works.

Each chapter begins with the first of two "checkpoints." This initial checkpoint—a sample of the genre followed by a list of questions—provides students with an opportunity to self-assess their knowledge and thus identify what more they may need to learn. Once they have worked their way through the chapter, students are provided with a second checkpoint in order to reassess their knowledge. This final assessment allows students the opportunity to integrate and apply their learning.

This approach to assessment reflects new thinking about the critical role of student involvement in their own learning. The work of Rick Stiggins in Student-Involved Classroom Assessment, for example, clearly demonstrates that, in order to improve, students must be involved in their own learning and begin to take responsibility for it.

Following the initial checkpoint, each chapter focuses on analyzing and responding to texts and is clearly organized into sections on meaning, form, and style—the key components of language and literature, as recognized in all provincial curricula. Although these components are initially studied in isolation, the final checkpoint gives students the opportunity to integrate them as they respond to the sample and accompanying list of questions.

The concept of "language in use" is also evident in how grammar, usage, and mechanics have been incorporated into the chapters. Grammar is best learned in context; that is, when students have a particular purpose for using these structures correctly and effectively. The work of such noted language teachers as Donald Graves and Lucy Calkins emphasizes the importance of teaching grammar in context, and knowing when and where in the writing process to teach it. Students learn best when they can access what they need at the moment they most need it. The reference section at the back of the book provides another means of giving students quick, easy access to aspects of grammar, usage, spelling, and vocabulary.

Understanding and analyzing works in a particular genre are key stages toward creating one's own. Once students complete the second, reassessment checkpoint in each chapter, they are given the opportunity to focus on creating their own work. Creation requires students to apply what they have learned and to develop their own style; it is frequently considered the highest level of demonstrated learning.

Each chapter concludes with a section on presenting works using approaches and techniques appropriate to the genre. The checklists that are included for both creating and presenting further bolster students' involvement in their own learning.

CHAPTER 1

poetry

Poems expect you to fill in the silences.
Michael Ondaatje

Poetry is a very concentrated form, and therefore the explosiveness of each word becomes much greater.
Margaret Atwood

Poetry is an echo, asking a shadow to dance.
Carl Sandburg

What is poetry? There are almost as many "definitions" of poetry as there are poets. One of the most obvious differences between poetry and prose is that most poetry is written in verse. But there are other aspects of style that we associate with poetry—the rhythm and rhyme of the lines, the careful choice and play of words, the use of powerful imagery. All these characteristics contribute to the richness of poetry.

A poem conveys meaning in many different ways and on many different levels. The full experience of a poem involves our minds, hearts, and various senses. Our eyes take in the grouping and spacing of lines on the page, our ears hear the particular patterns of sounds, our minds conjure up visual images created by the words, and our hearts respond to the powerful emotions evoked. We are engaged not only by the literal or surface meaning, but also by the meaning behind the words—the subtext.

LEARNING GOALS

- explore the meaning of poems
- develop the skills to write a poem
- examine poetic forms and stylistic devices
- present an effective choral reading of a poem

CONTENTS

Analyzing and Responding to Poetry

» CHECKPOINT: *Assess Your Knowledge*

the train

I like to see it lap the Miles—
And lick the Valleys up—
And stop to feed itself at Tanks—
And then—prodigious step

Around a Pile of Mountains—
And supercilious peer
In Shanties—by the sides of Roads—
And then a Quarry pare

To fit its Ribs
And crawl between
Complaining all the while
In horrid-hooting stanza—
Then chase itself down Hill—

And neigh like Boanerges—
Then—punctual as a Star
Stop—docile and omnipotent
At its own stable door—

Emily Dickinson

1. This poem is an excellent example of an extended metaphor. To what is Dickinson comparing the train? Identify the words and phrases that develop this metaphor. (Note: *Boanerges* is a Hebrew term meaning "Sons of Thunder." It's used to describe loud-voiced preachers and orators.)
2. How does the poet use rhythm to enhance the meaning of the poem?
3. Explain the poet's fascination with the train as suggested in the poem.
4. Explain the capitalization used in this poem.
5. How does the extensive use of the dash affect your reading of the poem?
6. What literary device is used in line 12? What is its effect?

Reading Strategies

When you first encounter a poem, read it aloud, if you can. Reading a poem aloud, either alone or in the company of others, will often help you to deepen your understanding of it. And it will certainly help you with stylistic elements such as rhythm and rhyme.

Decide why you think the poet created the poem.

Ask Yourself

- *What is the poem about?*
- *How is it written (i.e., what is its form, and what stylistic devices are used)?*
- *Why did the poet choose to write it this way?*

Developing Your Response

- *Jot down some thoughts about your answers, and find someone to talk with about your initial impressions of the poem.*
- *Read the poem several times more. Read slowly and attentively. Great poetry will reveal more and more with each reading. It's often necessary to read a poem many times before its meaning, form, and stylistic devices finally take shape in your mind.*
- *Create a question or two that you might have about the ideas in the poem. Note an image or language feature that impressed you. Talk with someone about these.*
- *Read other poems by the same poet.*
- *Read other people's responses to poetry. Sometimes understanding another's perspective will help you to broaden your own.*

Here is a representation of the key elements that combine to create the overall effect of a poem:

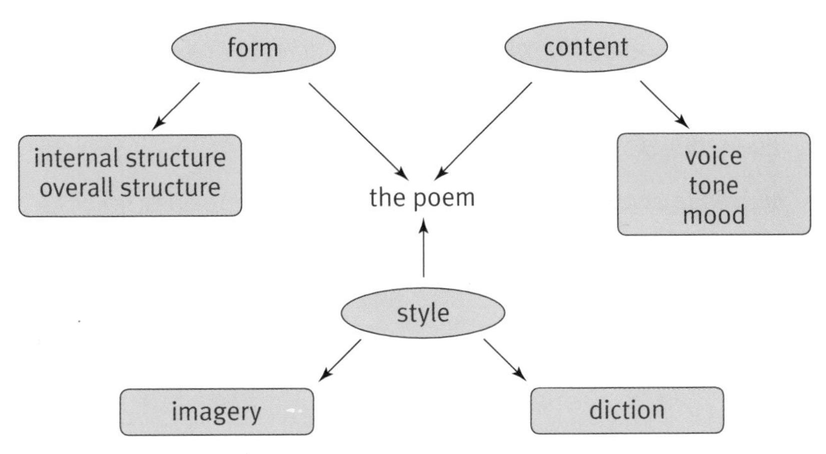

Understanding Meaning

CONTENT

The content of a poem is what it's all about: the ideas, themes, and storyline that it contains.

Begin to consider the poem by getting a general idea of its meaning. While this is only a superficial understanding, it will give you a framework on which to build a more detailed and complex response. Sometimes it is possible to respond to a poem without fully understanding every word or phrase. Sometimes meaning evolves as you continue to think and talk about a poem.

You will find that some poems are more difficult to interpret than others. Perhaps the poet uses difficult words that you don't understand. Or, perhaps the poem was written in a different historical, geographical, or social context, and so aspects of the language are unfamiliar to you. The poem could deal with concepts, ideas, or themes that are completely outside your experience. It may contain references that are difficult or obscure. For example, the poet might make a reference to classical mythology, or perhaps to the Bible. Finally, you might find that some of the imagery is difficult to understand, or that the very style in which the poem is written is difficult to decipher.

Here are some ideas that might help you come to a clearer understanding of a poem:

Tips on Understanding a Poem

- *Read the poem several times.*
- *Ask yourself questions about its meaning. Based on your prior knowledge and personal experience, try to use the parts of the text that you do understand as clues to help you find the answers.*
- *Consider how the poem's title influences its meaning.*
- *Highlight difficult words, phrases, and images.*
- *Look up words you don't know.*
- *You might need to consult classical dictionaries or encyclopedias for some references.*
- *Make sure to read the notes or glossary contained in the text.*
- *Read about the poet or the period in which the poem was written.*

VOICE, TONE, AND MOOD

It's important to consider how the meaning of a poem is affected by poetic voice, mood, and tone.

Poetic **voice** refers to the "speaker" of the poem. The poet may have created a character or other narrator through which to speak. The poetic voice could be expressing an emotion that the poet may or may not share.

The **tone** of a poem is projected through the poetic voice. It is created through diction, rhythm, rhyme, and use of imagery. There are obviously many different kinds of tone. The tone might be angry or reflective, melancholy or joyful, bitter or ironic. By picking up on the tone of a poem you'll be better able to understand its intended meaning.

Mood is the atmosphere that the poem creates. Very often tone and mood are closely linked, with a certain tone producing a certain mood. For example, if the poet uses a melancholy tone, it's unlikely that the mood of the poem will be bright and lively. Mood is created by a poet primarily through choice of words and imagery.

Look at the poem below. The annotations show you how tone and mood can be created, and how they influence our understanding of the poem.

the land

The land under this house
is weak, girl

audience—*young woman, perhaps visitor to town*

you can't tell by looking
at it
but, see
it's all mined out
under here
and we're after sittin on
a bridge over caves

voice—*diction suggests common folk; someone older*

Now the other week
old Cameron down the road
dropped clean out of sight
into a hole

Drivin along now
mind, not out to harm a fly
dropped twenty foot
down
clean out of sight

Had to bring MacNeil
the fire chief
down in town
to come haul'em out

But nobody was surprised, eh?

Look, years ago
Dominion Coal
dried up these here wells
mining all under the town
minin

ya, and there we were with no water

What did they do?

Well, I'll tell you what they did
brought a little truck around
every day
and every family got two buckets of water
whether they needed it
or not
Ha.

There's no support'all girl

Hell, no one was surprised
when old Cameron and his heap
went straight down

the company took it all,
see
whether they needed it or not.
Ha.

Susan Perly

tone—*conversational (interjections, rhetorical questions)*

repetition emphasizes significance of mining

mood—*angry, bitter (repeated "Ha" communicates frustration)*

Understanding Form

Form refers to the different ways in which poems can be structured. A poet doesn't simply use a certain form at random. It is carefully chosen, and has a direct bearing on its meaning.

A particular poetic form is achieved through its **internal structure**; that is, the way the lines are organized, grouped, or structured. This includes its rhyme and rhythm patterns as well as its division (or not) into stanzas. Form can also refer to the poem's **overall structure**, or thematic characteristics (for example, elegies focus on death as their theme). Some poetic forms are determined by text arrangement, others by their thematic characteristics, and some by both.

INTERNAL STRUCTURE

RHYME

How to Determine a Rhyme Scheme

In this nursery rhyme, the lines that rhyme with each other have each been given the same letter.

Old Mother Hubbard **a**
Went to the cupboard **a**
To get her poor dog a bone **b**
But when she got there **c**
The cupboard was bare **c**
And so her poor dog had none. **b**

The rhyme scheme, then, of "Old Mother Hubbard" is aab ccb.

Groupings Based on Rhyme

Poetry may be written in line groupings known as **stanzas**. These line groupings are often determined by the form of the poem or the rhyme scheme. They may also be based on the thought contained in the lines, similar to a paragraph in prose. There are many different kinds of stanzas; their names are determined by the number of lines they contain.

A pair of lines that rhyme is called a **couplet**. Sometimes a whole poem will be written in rhyming couplets. The couplet may also be part of a larger rhyme scheme. Rhyming couplets usually create a bold, assertive effect and convey a message or point of view. They are also used for comic effect or to put down an argument or character.

The final two lines of the sonnet "Shall I Compare Thee to a Summer's Day?" by William Shakespeare provide a classic example of the rhyming couplet:

> So long as men can breathe or eyes can see,
> So long lives this, and this gives life to thee.

A **triplet** is a series of three lines that share the same rhyme, such as in Tennyson's poem "The Eagle":

> He clasps the crag with crooked hand;
> Close to the sun in lonely lands,
> Ringed with the azure world, he stands.

A set of four lines that rhyme is called a **quatrain**. The rhyme schemes of a quatrain can be either abab, abcb, aaaa, or abba. The effect of a quatrain is usually of regularity and order.

This stanza from Tennyson's "In Memoriam" provides an example of the quatrain in the abba pattern:

> Be near me when my light is low,
>   When the blood creeps, and the nerves prick
>   And tingle; and the heart is sick,
> And all the wheels of being clow.

Six lines grouped together are called a **sestet**. Rhyme schemes will vary in this form. The last six lines of a Petrarchan, or Italian sonnet (named after the medieval Italian writer, Petrarch) provide an example of a sestet.

An eight-line stanza is called an **octave**. It might be formed by linking two quatrains together. Or, it might have a rhyme scheme that integrates all eight lines. The first eight lines of the Italian sonnet are called an octave.

This classic poem by William Wordsworth is an example of an Italian sonnet. The first eight lines of the sonnet form an octave, and the last six lines, a sestet.

> **Composed Upon Westminster Bridge, September 3, 1802**
> Earth has not anything to show more fair:
> Dull would he be of soul who could pass by
> A sight so touching in its majesty:
> This City now doth, like a garment, wear
> The beauty of the morning: silent, bare,
> Ships, towers, domes, theatres, and temples lie
> Open unto the fields, and to the sky,
> All bright and glittering in the smokeless air.

Never did sun more beautifully steep
In his first splendour valley, rock or hill;
Ne'er saw I, never felt, a calm so deep!
The river glideth at his own sweet will:
Dear God! The very houses seem asleep;
And all that mighty heart is lying still!

RHYTHM

While not all poetry contains rhythm, certainly the existence of a regular beat or **rhythm** is one of the basic differences between poetry and prose.

Rhythm is used by a poet to create a number of different effects. Rhythm gives poetry its feeling of movement and life. It can be used to emphasize a certain idea. It often contributes to the mood or tone of a poem. Just as the rhythms in music make it gentle and flowing, or harsh and discordant, or driving and forceful, so the rhythms in poetry create the same effects.

Poets use language to create rhythm in the following ways:

Syllable Stress

Language possesses natural rhythms that are built into every word and that we use automatically when we say those words. For example, when we say the word *happy*, we put the **stress** on the first syllable. There is indeed a rhythm in the word. The stress on a syllable is shown like this: háppy̆.

Emphatic Stress

Poets consider very carefully the order of words in a line and the natural rhythms of speech. Read aloud this stanza from "Song of the Powers" by David Mason, putting the emphasis on the different words in the line:

Mine, said the stone,
Mine is the hour.
I crush the scissors,
Such is my power.
Stronger than wishes,
My power alone.

Phrasing and Punctuation

The rhythm of a poem is influenced by factors such as word order and length of phrases. Punctuation marks, line and stanza breaks, and use of repetition also affect the rhythm. Read aloud "We Real Cool" by black American poet Gwendolyn Brooks, and you'll hear how the phrasing and punctuation emphasize the rhythm.

We Real Cool

The Pool Players
Seven at the Golden Shovel.

We real cool. We
Left school. We

Lurk late. We
Strike straight. We

Sing sin. We
Thin gin. We

Jazz June. We
Die soon.

Metre

Lines of poetry often follow a precise and regular pattern in the number of syllables and their stress or emphasis. Regular patterns of stressed and unstressed syllables are called **metres**. Identifying the metre of a poem is called **scansion**. In scansion, a ´ or a ¯ above a word indicates a stressed syllable, and a ˘ is used to show an unstressed one.

Metre is used to create an effect. The rhythm that most closely follows the patterns of natural speech is ˘ ´. This is called **iambic** metre. This metre is used by Shakespeare in his plays and sonnets. "Sonnet 29" shows us this rhythm:

˘ ´ ˘ ´ ˘ ´ ˘ ´ ˘ ´
When in disgrace with Fortune and men's eyes,
I all alone beweep my outcast state,
And trouble deaf heaven with my bootless cries,
And look upon myself and curse my fate

Blank verse is written in an iambic metre but does not have a rhyme scheme. The last three lines of Tennyson's "Ulysses" are an example of blank verse:

˘ ´ ˘ ´ ˘ ´ ˘ ´ ˘ ´
One equal temper of heroic hearts,
Made weak by time and fate, but strong in will
To strive, to seek, to find, and not to yield.

A metre that creates a sense of movement, and perhaps underlying tensions is ˘ ˘ ´. This metre is called **anapestic**.

Robert Browning used the anapestic metre in his poem "How They Brought the Good News from Ghent to Aix" to create a sense of movement:

Not a word to each other; we kept the great pace
Neck by neck, stride by stride, never changing our place.

By contrast, two stressed syllables (´´), called **spondaic** metre, creates a feeling of heaviness, resignation, or immobility. Poems are rarely, if ever, written entirely in spondaic metre. It is inserted only occasionally to provide emphasis and variety. This is illustrated in the first line of this nursery rhyme:

Hark, hark, the dogs do bark.

The **trochaic** metre (´˘), because it puts emphasis on the first syllable, adds emphasis and power to the words it stresses. A famous example of the use of the trochaic metre comes from Shakespeare's *Macbeth*:

Double, double, toil and trouble
Fire burn and cauldron bubble.

Finally, the **dactylic** metre, which consists of a stressed syllable followed by two unstressed ones (´˘˘), reflects the rhythm of a horse galloping—as is demonstrated in Tennyson's "The Charge of the Light Brigade":

Half a league, half a league,
Half a league onward

It's also used to create a sad, reflective, and sometimes heavy mood, as in this first line of Thomas Hardy's "The Voice":

Woman much missed, how you call to me, call to me

When scanning a line of poetry, the number of metric units is counted. One such unit is called a **foot**. The end of each foot is noted with a /. One foot per line is called a monometer, two a dimeter, three a trimeter, four a tetrameter, five a pentameter, six a hexameter, seven a heptameter, and eight an octameter.

A line of poetry written in iambic metre and containing five units or feet would thus be called **iambic pentameter**. A line with six units of dactylic metre would be called dactylic hexameter.

Try these ones out to see if you can successfully name them:

Tyger! Tyger! burning bright
In the forests of the night.
William Blake, "The Tyger"

Storm'd at with shot and shell,
While horse and hero fell,
They that had fought so well
Came thro' the jaws of Death
Back from the mouth of Hell,
All that was left of them,
  Left of six hundred.
      Alfred, Lord Tennyson, "The Charge of the Light Brigade"

Into the street the Piper stept,
  Smiling first a little smile,
As if he knew what magic slept
  In his quiet pipe the while;
      Robert Browning, "The Pied Piper of Hamelin"

More important than giving the rhythm a name is the ability to explain *why* you think the poet chose that particular rhythm structure. What effect is created? How is the reader's understanding of the poem affected by the poet's choice of a particular rhythm? Look at the above samples again and see if you can figure out why the poets made the choices they did.

OVERALL STRUCTURE

BALLAD

A **ballad** is a poem that tells a simple story in a straightforward way. The themes of ballads are traditionally tragic and often focus on physical courage and love. Many contain elements of the supernatural or fantastic. Little attention is paid to characterization and description, and action is largely developed through dialogue. The ballad usually concludes with a summary stanza.

The traditional ballad is written in four-line stanzas with a rhyming scheme of abcb.

The first and third line of each stanza have four accented syllables, and the second and third lines have three. The number of unaccented syllables will vary. The ballad will often have a refrain that appears throughout.

BLANK VERSE

Blank verse consists of non-rhyming lines written in iambic pentameter. This form of poetry is used in dramatic verse and is commonly found in long poems, whether dramatic, philosophical, or narrative. In fact, three-quarters of all English poetry is written in blank verse.

DRAMATIC MONOLOGUE

The **dramatic monologue** is a poem in which a character speaks to an identifiable but silent listener in a dramatic moment in the speaker's life. The circumstances surrounding the speech are clear by implication, and the reader gets deep insight into the character of the speaker.

ELEGY

An **elegy** is a meditative poem that is usually sad and reflective in tone. It is often inspired by the death of a particular person, but may also be a generalized observation or expression of a solemn mood.

EPIC

Epics are lengthy narrative poems. The main character is a figure of heroic stature, and of great historic or legendary significance. The setting is vast—covering great nations, the world, or the universe. The action consists of deeds of great valour requiring great courage and/or strength. Supernatural forces intervene from time to time in the action. The style of the writing is elevated, and the poet tells the story objectively.

In addition, certain conventions or devices are used. The poet opens by stating the theme, invokes a Muse to inspire and instruct, and begins the story in the middle of the action, leaving explanations to later portions of the epic. Included in the epic are catalogues of ships, warriors, and armies. The main characters give extended formal speeches. Epic poets often make use of epic similes—extended and elaborate comparisons of "epic" proportions.

FREE VERSE

The term **free verse** refers to any poem that does not have a fixed structure. This form of verse often does not have lines that are equal in length or in a regular metre, and often it does not rhyme. The rhythmical unit of free verse might be considered to be the stanza.

LAMENT

A **lament** is a poem expressing great grief.

LYRIC

A **lyric** is a brief, subjective poem expressing the poet's personal imaginings and emotions. Lyric poems come in a variety of rhythm patterns and may be expressed in rhymed or unrhymed verses. Subjectivity, imagination, melody, and emotion are the essential characteristics of lyric poetry.

SONNET

A **sonnet** is a lyric poem of fourteen lines in one of the following two forms.

1. The Petrarchan or Italian sonnet is usually written in iambic pentameter, and is divided into two parts:
   - The octave, consisting of the first eight lines with the rhyming scheme of abba abba, presents the narrative, states the proposition, or raises a question.
   - The sestet, consisting of the last six lines with the rhyming scheme of cde cde, cdc cdc, or cde dce, drives home the narrative by making an abstract comment, applying the proposition, or solving the problem.
2. The Shakespearean or English sonnet is divided into four parts:
   - Three quatrains, each with its own rhyme scheme: abab cdcd efef.
   - A concluding rhyming couplet: gg.

Consider how the rhythm, rhyme, and form of the following sonnet contribute to its meaning:

what lips my lips have kissed, and where, and why

What lips my lips have kissed, and where, and why,
I have forgotten, and what arms have lain
Under my head till morning; but the rain
Is full of ghosts tonight, that tap and sigh
Upon the glass and listen for reply,
And in my heart there sits a quiet pain
For unremembered lads that not again
Will turn to me at midnight with a cry.
Thus in the winter stands the lonely tree,
Nor knows what birds have vanished one by one,
Yet knows its boughs more silent than before:
I cannot say what loves have come and gone,
I only know that summer sang in me
A little while, that in me sings no more

Edna St. Vincent Millay

rhythm: iambic pentameter—flowing, gentle, suggests calm reflection

emphasis on words that suggest mood

abba

abba

octave remembering and saddened by lost loves

cde, dce

sestet—birds during summer represent youth, love; vanished birds, winter represent age, absence of love

Understanding Style

IMAGERY

An **image** is used to help us see, hear, taste, feel, think about, or generally understand more clearly what the poet is saying. Imagery is pictures through words. It allows readers to make the connection to their own emotional, intellectual, or spiritual experiences. So it's important to think about why the poet has used that particular image, and how it works in the mind of the reader.

A **literal image** provides a detailed description of the reality of the scene or situation. It allows us to see the scene or experience the situation more vividly. Beyond this, images can work in several different ways.

FIGURATIVE IMAGERY

Poets use non-literal or **figurative imagery** frequently. In figurative language, the thing being described is compared to something else with which it has something in common.

The most common figures of speech are simile, metaphor, and personification.

Simile

Similes are easy to identify because they make the comparison between the two things quite clear by using the words *like* or *as*. Chippewa poet Lenore Keeshig-Tobias uses a simile in "I Grew Up":

> I snuggled in the grass
> like a bug basking in the sun

Metaphor

The **metaphor** is like a simile in that it also creates a comparison; however, it does not use the words *like* or *as*. Often the metaphor describes the subject as being the thing to which it is compared. Notice how in the poem "To See the World in a Grain of Sand" William Blake uses a metaphor in every line:

> To see a World in a Grain of Sand
> And a Heaven in a Wild Flower,
> Hold Infinity in the palm of your hand
> And Eternity in an hour

Personification

Personification occurs when an inanimate object or idea is given human qualities or actions, as in "The Wind" by James Stephens:

> The wind stood up and gave a shout.
> He whistled on his fingers and
>
> Kicked the withered leaves about
> And thumped the branches with his hand
>
> And said he'd kill and kill and kill
> And so he will and so he will.

Apostrophe

Apostrophe occurs when a poet addresses a dead or absent person, or an abstract or inanimate object. Apostrophes are used frequently in odes and elegies. Wordsworth provides us with examples in the following lines from two poems:

> Spade! With which Wilkinson hath tilled his lands

And

> Milton! Thou shouldst be living at this hour

Hyperbole

Poets often use a figure of speech known as **hyperbole**, an overstatement or extreme exaggeration. In this speech from Shakespeare's play *Antony and Cleopatra*, Cleopatra describes the dead Antony:

> His legs bestrid the ocean; his reared arm
> Crested the world.

This exaggerated description isn't meant to be understood literally, but rather impresses the reader or listener with the heroic stature and power of Antony.

Metonymy

Metonymy is a figure of speech that replaces the name of one thing with the name of something else closely associated with it. A famous example is "The pen is mightier than the sword," whose literal meaning is that writing is more effective than fighting.

In this poem by John Dyer called "Grongar Hill," the words *cradle* and *grave* in the last line signify birth and death:

> A little rule, a little sway,
> A sun beam on a winter's day,
> Is all the proud and mighty have
> Between the cradle and the grave.

Paradox

Paradox is another example of figurative language. It's found in a statement or phrase that is apparently self-contradictory. The reader is forced to find a way or a context in which the statement could be true. The following line, from William Wordsworth's poem "My Heart Leaps Up," is an excellent example of paradox:

> The Child is father of the man.

Consider how that statement might be true.

Oxymoron

An **oxymoron** is similar to a paradox, in that it describes a contradiction. An oxymoron is generally compressed into two words or a short phrase. Terms like *bittersweet* or *living death* are examples of oxymoron. Look at this speech of Romeo's from *Romeo and Juliet* and see how many oxymorons you can find:

> Why then, O brawling love, O loving hate,
> O anything of nothing first create;
> O heavy lightness, serious vanity,
> Misshapen chaos of well-seeming forms,
> Feather of lead, bright smoke, cold fire, sick health,
> Still-waking sleep, that is not what it is!

Pun

A figure of speech known as a play on words is called a **pun**. A writer creates a pun by using a word that reminds us of other words of similar or identical sound but of different denotation. Often puns create humour, as in the pun on "arms" in this ballad by Thomas Hood entitled "Faithless Nellie Gray":

> Ben Battle was a soldier bold,
> And used to war's alarms;
> But a cannon-ball took off his legs,
> So he laid down his arms!

AURAL IMAGERY

Poets also create responses in the reader by using **aural images**, which have more of an impact on our sense of hearing than on our visual sense. The most common devices used to create aural images are alliteration, assonance, consonance, and onomatopoeia.

Alliteration

Alliteration involves the repetition of the same consonant sound at the beginning of each word over several words together. Coleridge uses the technique in this line from "The Rime of the Ancient Mariner":

> The fair breeze blew, the white foam flew,
> And furrow followed free

Assonance

Assonance involves the repetition of similar vowel sounds within the stressed syllables of a series of words to create a particular effect. In the "Ballad of the Long-Legged Bait," notice how Thomas's use of assonance creates a musical effect:

> The bows glided down, and the coast
> Blackened with birds took a last look
> At his thrashing hair and whale-blue eyes;
> The trodden town rang its cobbles for luck.

Consonance

Consonance is the repetition of the same consonant sounds in a series of words in which the vowel sounds are different. Consonance may occur in the middle or at the end of a series of words. Look at the above ballad again: *look* and *luck* are an example of consonance.

Onomatopoeia

Onomatopoeia occurs when the sound of the word reflects its meaning, for example *slithering* and *pluck*.

Consider how Frances Cornford uses onomatopoeia in "The Watch":

> I wakened on my hot, hard bed,
> Upon the pillow lay my head;
> Beneath the pillow I could hear
> My little watch was ticking clear.
> I thought the throbbing of it went
> Like my continual discontent.
> I thought it said in every tick;
> I am so sick, so sick, so sick.
> O death come quick, come quick, come quick,
> Come quick, come quick, come quick, come quick!

DICTION

Diction refers to the choice of words that a writer makes. Poetry is such a concise form that every word is considered thoughtfully.

All words have both denotations and connotations. **Denotation** is the meaning of a word as it's defined in the dictionary. Often a word can have several very different denotations. For example, look up the word *field* in the dictionary and you'll see that several different meanings are provided.

Words also have **connotations**. These are their additional, *implied* meanings. Writers make use of connotation all the time. In Shakespeare's *Romeo and Juliet*, for example, Romeo declares that Juliet "is the sun." We understand him to mean dazzling, warm, the centre of his universe, etc., because of the connotations we have of the word *sun*. We know as readers that he doesn't intend his statement to be taken literally.

When you are examining a poem, it's important to ask yourself why the poet chose the words he or she did.

Focusing on Diction

- *What words create particularly strong images?*
- *Are there types of words (e.g., action words, adjectives) that are used frequently?*
- *Are there patterns of monosyllabic or multi-syllabic words?*
- *Are words repeated?*
- *Are there words that are unexpected or out of place?*
- *Are there any internal sound structures in the words that are obvious?*
- *Are some words more obviously stressed than others? If so, why?*

Look at how the poet's choice of words in the following poem helps to create meaning:

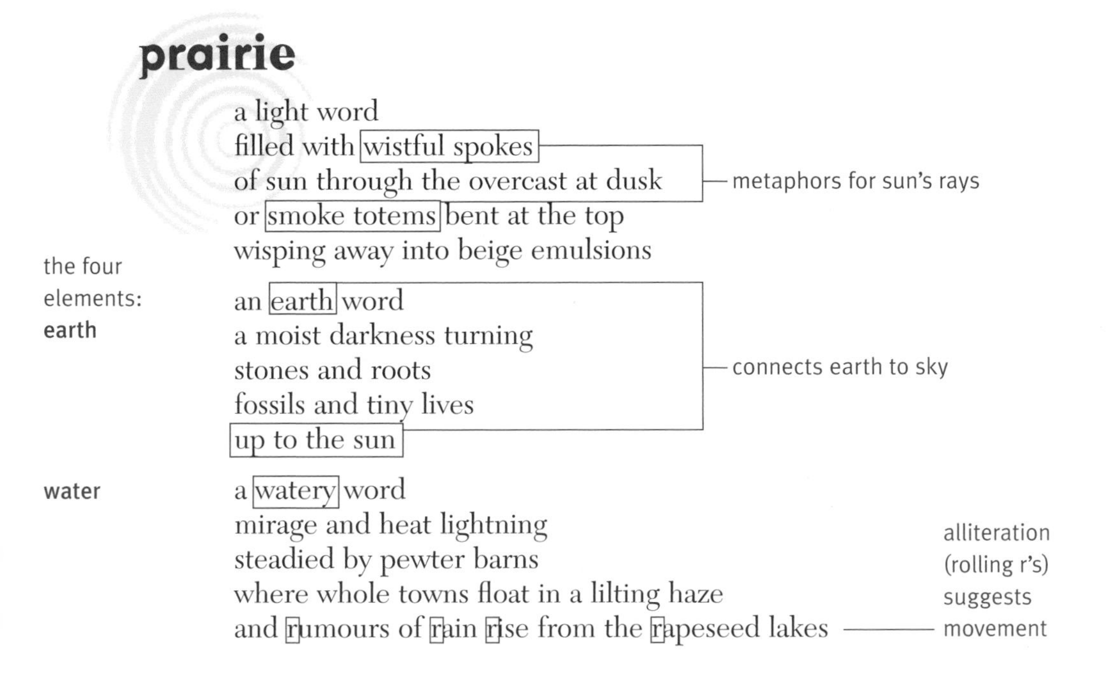
prairie
a light word
filled with wistful spokes
of sun through the overcast at dusk
or smoke totems bent at the top
wisping away into beige emulsions
an earth word
a moist darkness turning
stones and roots
fossils and tiny lives
up to the sun
a watery word
mirage and heat lightning
steadied by pewter barns
where whole towns float in a lilting haze
and rumours of rain rise from the rapeseed lakes
metaphors for sun's rays
the four elements:
earth
connects earth to sky
water
alliteration (rolling r's) suggests movement

fire

a flame shaped word
a ragged mane blowing for miles across dry grass — metaphor for fire suggests its movement
lighting the night like fired breath
out of the old testament — simile conveys its power

air

a word with air
in its belly that howls
for hours or days and dries
the memory of soft conversation
to wheatdust under the tongue

like the distance we've come
to stand here in the sky at the top of the world — communicates poet's feeling about the prairie

George Amabile

» CHECKPOINT: *Reassess Your Knowledge*

to autumn

I

Season of mists and mellow fruitfulness,
  Close bosom-friend of the maturing sun;
Conspiring with him how to load and bless
  With fruit the vines that round the thatch-eves run;
To bend with apples the moss'd cottage-trees,
  And fill all fruit with ripeness to the core;
    To swell the gourd, and plump the hazel shells
  With a sweet kernel; to set budding more
And still more, later flowers for the bees,
Until they think warm days will never cease,
    For Summer has o'er-brimm'd their clammy cells.

II

Who hath not seen thee oft amid thy store?
  Sometimes whoever seeks abroad may find
Thee sitting careless on a granary floor,
  Thy hair soft-lifted by the winnowing wind;
Or on a half-reap'd furrow sound asleep,

Drows'd with the fume of poppies, while thy hook
Spares the next swath and all its twined flowers;
And sometimes like a gleaner thou dost keep
Steady thy laden head across a brook;
Or by a cyder-press, with patient look,
Thou watchest the last oozings hours by hours.

III

Where are the songs of Spring? Ay, where are they?
Think not of them, thou hast thy music too,—
While barred clouds bloom the soft-dying day,
And touch the stubble-plains with rosy hue;
Then in a wailful choir the small gnats mourn
Among the river sallows, borne aloft
Or sinking as the light wind lives or dies;
And full-grown lambs loud bleat from hilly bourn;
Hedge-crickets sing; and now with treble soft
The red-breast whistles from a garden-croft;
And gathering swallows twitter in the skies.

John Keats

1. What lines and phrases in the poem suggest the poet's feeling about the autumn season?
2. Explain why you think Keats wrote this poem.
3. What is the rhyme scheme of the poem?
4. What is the rhythmic pattern found in this poem?
5. Do you notice any patterns in the structure of this poem? Can you explain these patterns as they relate to the meaning of the poem?
6. Why do you think Keats chose the poetic form and rhythmic structure he did?
7. Name and explain the figure of speech found in the first two lines of the poem.
8. Select another figure of speech in the poem and explain it.
9. Find an example of aural imagery in the poem and explain its effect.

Creating Poetry

Preparing and Planning

Getting an idea for a poem is sometimes difficult. Poetry is a very personal form of writing, and requires that the writer communicate feelings, insights, and experiences. So it's generally a good idea to write about something that's personally important or significant to you.

Ideas for a Poem

- *a memory that's connected to a particular person or place*
- *something that you experienced that was important to you*
- *something that happened to someone else that meant something to you*
- *an everyday occurrence of personal significance*

Brainstorming is a great way of coming up with ideas. The following chart demonstrates an example of how images and ideas for a poem can be generated.

	My Grandmother
domestic	*knits, bakes (her apartment—aroma of brownies) ...* *other smells: lavender, spaghetti sauce, Pond's face cream*
wise	*gives good advice to grandchildren (sometimes not welcome!)*
solitary	*lives alone, enjoys a good book (especially political biographies),* doesn't seem to mind being on her own (independent)
volunteer	*knits tiny caps for newborns ...* *wears floppy, old-fashioned hats herself*
colours	*likes soft, pale dresses—same as her rose-coloured oriental rugs and lemony wallpaper—calm, warmth*
loves a party	*especially when the younger grandchildren are there—maybe the old and the young have a special bond?*
funny	*often likes to say what she knows everyone else is privately thinking (ouch!)—soft murmur, but glinting eyes ... paradox?*
sharp	*loves to play cards—quick flap of shuffled deck, crack of poker chips ... likes high stakes!—maybe you're more carefree when you get older? maybe a connection here to her outspokenness? (you can express more because you no longer worry so much about what people think)*

Once you have your idea, as well as a sense of the images and thoughts connected with that idea, it's important to ask yourself: What is my purpose in writing this poem?

Establishing Your Purpose

- *to evoke an emotional response (e.g., empathy, laughter, sadness, anger, indignation)*
- *to tell a story*
- *to describe*
- *to explain*
- *to make fun of*
- *to teach*

Your purpose will determine many of the choices you make. Once you've settled on it, you can then ask yourself the following questions.

Meaning

- *What will the poem be about? Will it have a meaning that is embedded below the surface of the text?*
- *Will the poem be written in my voice, or will I create a persona with a point of view different from my own?*
- *Is my tone of voice angry, reflective, emotive, sarcastic, etc.?*
- *Is there a mood, such as sadness, gloom, or joy, that pervades the poem?*
- *To whom am I writing this poem?*
- *Where and when does this poem take place?*

Form

- *Is there a specific overall structure or form (e.g., ballad, sonnet, free verse) that I will use?*
- *Are there obvious ways that the poem can be internally divided into sections or stanzas, either by its layout or its meaning?*
- *Will my poem rhyme? If so, what rhyme scheme will I use, and will it be consistent throughout the poem?*
- *Will the rhythm of the poem be smooth and flowing, short and jerky, reflective of natural speech?*
- *Will the rhythm change at any point in the poem?*

Style

- *What kind of visual images or word pictures will I attempt to create?*
- *Will I use similes, metaphors, or personification?*
- *Will I use any aural devices, such as alliteration or onomatopoeia?*

When considering your answers to any of the above questions, remember to keep asking yourself *why*. Your answer must relate to the effect you're trying to achieve in your poem, or how you want to communicate the message of your poem. There should be a reason behind every choice you make.

Once you've written your poem, ask yourself the questions in the following checklist:

Checklist

- [ ] Is the meaning clear?
- [ ] Will the reader understand how I or the poetic voice I chose felt about what I was writing?
- [ ] Is there a mood or feeling created in my poem?
- [ ] Is there a poetic form that I used? Why or why not?
- [ ] Did I try to use rhythm or rhyme in my poem? If so, are both consistent?
- [ ] Did I choose the words I used carefully? Are the word choices I made the best ones possible? Did I try using any figures of speech or aural imagery?
- [ ] Does the title of the poem add something to the poem?

Revising and Editing

CHOOSING WORDS CAREFULLY

Appropriate and creative diction, or word choice, is crucial when writing poetry. Imagine if, instead of

> This City now doth, like a garment, wear
> The beauty of the morning: silent, bare,
> Ships, towers, domes, theatres, and temples lie
> Open unto the fields, and to the sky,
> All bright and glittering in the smokeless air.
>
> "Composed Upon Westminster Bridge"

William Wordsworth had written

> This city in the morning
> Is quiet and bare
> All the buildings
> Shine in the clean air.

Or if Gerald Manley Hopkins had written

> Thank God for spotted things
>   For the sky coloured reddish brown like a cow
>   For scales dotted on trout that swim;

instead of

> Glory be to God for dappled things—
>   For skies of couple-colour as a brinded cow;
>   For rose-moles all in stipple upon trout that swim;
>   "Pied Beauty"

Obviously, poets choose words with great care, with an eye and ear always to the effect.

You must help your readers see, hear, smell, taste, and feel by providing them with the most specific and detailed language that you can. Instead of describing a party as "nice" or "fun" or "great," help your readers feel as if they were at that midnight beach party under a sky full of northern lights, eating Four-Alarm chili, and listening to the sound of the harbour's foghorn with a jazz guitar in the background.

PUNCTUATING VERSE

Give careful consideration to the punctuation you use throughout your poem. Look at the punctuation in Thomas Hardy's poem "Hap":

> If but some vengeful god would call to me
> From up the sky, and laugh: "Thou suffering thing,
> Know that thy sorrow is my ecstasy,
> That thy love's loss is my hate's profiting!"
>
> Then would I bear it, clench myself, and die,
> Steeled by the sense of ire unmerited;
> Half-eased in that a Powerfuller than I
> Had willed and meted me the tears I shed.

> But not so. How arrives it joy lies slain,
> And why unblooms the best hope ever sown?
> —Crass Casualty obstructs the sun and rain,
> And dicing Time for gladness casts a moan ...
> These purblind Doomsters had as readily strown
> Blisses about my pilgrimage as pain.

Why does Hardy use a colon after *laugh*, a semi-colon after *unmerited*, a dash before *Crass*, and an ellipsis after *moan*? And what is the difference among the uses of the comma in the first line of the second verse?

Remind yourself of the rules for using the different punctuation marks and consider those rules when you are revising your own written poetry.

GRAMMAR, USAGE, AND MECHANICS

DASH

Consider the effect of the dashes that Emily Dickinson used in her poem at the beginning of this chapter. A **dash** is dramatic; it draws the reader's attention to a word or a phrase. It can signal a sudden change, or it can emphasize an introductory list or parenthetical material. It should be used sparingly—just in the situations mentioned here and not as a substitute for the semicolon or the colon—so that it doesn't lose its particular power.

Here are three examples of the uses of the dash:

1. The strong signal of a sudden change in thought or tone, a new direction in the sentence:

> I'm sure we will get our raises soon—or never.

2. Between an introductory list and the main part of the sentence. This construction leads the reader to consider an emphasized list and then apply it to the subject:

> Sly, cautious, clean nurturing—these traits of snakes receive little attention because most people think of snakes as dangerous and evil.

3. To emphasize an added explanation, illustration, or comment:

> Barrier islands—sandy areas that protect the mainland from storms—change location every ten to fifteen years.

ELLIPSE

The **ellipsis mark** (...) is sometimes used in poetry, particularly at the end of a line, to emphasize a thoughtful pause. The ellipsis after the word "moan" in Hardy's poem is a good example of this.

In prose writing, the ellipsis mark can also indicate a pause, as well as a reluctance to speak further, or an intentionally unfinished statement. If the omission follows a complete sentence, the ellipsis mark should be preceded by a period:

> He remembers many joyous moments from his marriage.... And too many fights over nothing.

> "I'm not sure how I feel...," she said. "Don't press me to decide."

> It's a bird.... It's a plane.... No, it's Superman!

In prose writing, ellipsis marks are also used to indicate that a word, phrase, sentence, full paragraph, or more has been left out of a quotation. (An ellipsis mark is not necessary to indicate that material preceded or followed your excerpt. Your reader will understand that the quotation, whether a few words or a few paragraphs, is part of a larger work.)

If the omission follows a sentence, its period precedes the ellipsis mark (making, in effect, four dots).

COMMA

Look at the places where Hardy uses a comma in his poem, and note how each of them affects the rhythm of the lines.

The following list pinpoints the ten situations in which a **comma** is necessary:

1. To set off introductory elements:

> *With her long hair flowing free*, Matina caught everyone's eye.

2. To set off nonessential (nonrestrictive) elements:

> Antonio called one man, *his father*, to share the good news.

3. To separate the independent clauses of a compound sentence:

> The newest mountain bikes are durable, *and* the best of them are also lightweight.

4. To separate coordinate adjectives:

> Hamed's computer is a *newer*, *faster* one than mine.

5. To separate three or more items in a series:

    Sam never dreamed that a subject like Latin American history could be so *complex, challenging, and interesting.*

6. To set off transitions, parenthetical elements, absolute phrases, and contrasts:

    Then, *his hopes dashed,* he ran for the bus without looking back.

7. To set off nouns of direct addess, tag questions, words such as *yes* and *no*, and interjections:

    Yes, *my friends,* we have had a fantastic time, haven't we?

8. To set off phrases of attribution, such as "she said," that identify the source of a quotation:

    "Let's head for the door," *Andre said* suddenly.

9. To separate the parts of dates, addresses, and numbers:

    We will leave on *May 5, 2001,* to visit *Saskatoon, Saskatchewan,* and some towns along the way.

10. To prevent confusion:

    The members of the winning team marched *in, in* no hurry to end their victory parade.

Presenting: Choral Reading

Poetry is meant to be heard. A very effective technique for presenting poetry is **choral reading.** Reading poetry aloud, as a group, allows you to experiment with elements of voice (tempo, volume, pitch, stress, and juncture), movement, and gestures. It also helps to deepen your understanding and enjoyment of poetry.

Select material with care. Some poems lend themselves better to choral reading than others. Discuss with your group the meaning of the poem and talk about the various ways of reading it that will allow you to bring out this meaning.

As a group, select appropriate arrangements or patterns for an oral interpretation. Consider the following patterns:

Choral Reading Patterns

- *unison (all read together)*
- *refrain (one person reads the narrative portion of the text while the rest of the group joins in the refrain)*
- *antiphonal (the group is divided into two or more subgroups, with each subgroup being responsible for a certain part of the selection)*
- *cumulative (groups of voices or individual voices are added to or subtracted from the choral reading, depending on the message or the meaning communicated by the selection)*
- *solo lines (individuals read specific lines in appropriate places throughout the group activity)*
- *line around (each line is taken by a different person in the group)*

Practise your readings several times, and talk about ways of improving phrasing and diction. Consider how you could make the selection more interesting.

Fine-tuning Your Presentation

- *Could you read quickly or slowly? (tempo)*
- *Where might it be louder? Softer? (stress and volume)*
- *Do you need high or low voices? (pitch)*
- *Where should you pause? (juncture)*
- *Which lines might be most effectively delivered by the whole group, by part of the group, or by individuals?*
- *Could you add simple movement to your reading, or perhaps some other visual element to make the presentation more interesting?*

After experimenting and practising your text, share your interpretation with the whole class or with one other group.

CHAPTER 2

narrative texts

'Oh! it is only a novel!' … only some work in which the greatest powers of the mind are displayed, in which the most thorough knowledge of human nature, the happiest delineation of its varieties, the liveliest effusions of wit and humour, are conveyed to the world in the best chosen language.

Jane Austen

Stories are not chapters of novels. They should not be read one after another, as if they were meant to follow along. Read one. Shut the book. Read something else. Come back later. Stories can wait.

Mavis Gallant

The two main types of narrative texts are novels and short stories. The **novel** includes such forms as fictional biography and autobiography; picaresque novels, which follow a central character on a journey comprising a series of adventures; novels of social manners, which use the character and the world they inhabit as a way of criticizing social mores or political systems; and science fiction. The **short story** is one of the most recent and most popular of fictional genres. It is a brief, well-told narrative with a limited focus, often restricted to one moment of crisis in a person's life.

LEARNING GOALS

- interpret narrative texts from various periods and cultures
- use a range of reading strategies for particular purposes
- analyze common narrative elements
- develop the skills to write a short story
- present an effective dramatic reading (readers' theatre)
- develop skill in the use of particular narrative devices
- use varied syntax and vocabulary

CONTENTS

Analyzing and Responding to Narrative Texts

» CHECKPOINT: *Assess Your Knowledge*

the story of an hour

Knowing that Mrs. Mallard was afflicted with a heart trouble, great care was taken to break to her as gently as possible the news of her husband's death.

It was her sister Josephine who told her, in broken sentences; veiled hints that revealed in half concealing. Her husband's friend Richards was there, too, near her. It was he who had been in the newspaper office when intelligence of the railroad disaster was received, with Brently Mallard's name leading the list of "killed." He had only taken the time to assure himself of its truth by a second telegram, and had hastened to forestall any less careful, less tender friend in bearing the sad message.

She did not hear the story as many women have heard the same, with a paralyzed inability to accept its significance. She wept at once, with sudden, wild abandonment, in her sister's arms. When the storm of grief had spent itself she went away to her room alone. She would have no one follow her.

There stood, facing the open window, a comfortable, roomy armchair. Into this she sank, pressed down by a physical exhaustion that haunted her body and seemed to reach into her soul.

She could see in the open square before her house the tops of trees that were all aquiver with the new spring life. The delicious breath of rain was in the air. In the street below a peddler was crying his wares. The notes of a distant song which someone was singing reached her faintly, and countless sparrows were twittering in the eaves.

There were patches of blue sky showing here and there through the clouds that had met and piled one above the other in the west facing her window.

She sat with her head thrown back upon the cushion of the chair, quite motionless, except when a sob came up into her throat and shook her, as a child who had cried itself to sleep continues to sob in its dreams.

She was young, with a fair, calm face, whose lines bespoke repression and even a certain strength. But now there was a dull stare in her eyes, whose gaze was fixed away off yonder on one of those patches of blue sky. It was not a glance of reflection, but rather indicated a suspension of intelligent thought.

There was something coming to her and she was waiting for it, fearfully. What was it? She did not know; it was too subtle and elusive to name. But she felt it, creeping out of the sky, reaching toward her through the sounds, the scents, the colour that filled the air.

Now her bosom rose and fell tumultuously. She was beginning to recognize this thing that was approaching to possess her, and she was striving to beat it back with her will—as powerless as her two white slender hands would have been.

When she abandoned herself a little whispered word escaped her slightly parted lips. She said it over and over under her breath: "free, free, free!" The vacant stare and the look of terror that had followed it went from her eyes. They stayed keen and bright. Her pulses beat fast, and the coursing blood warmed and relaxed every inch of her body.

She did not stop to ask if it were or were not a monstrous joy that held her. A clear and exalted perception enabled her to dismiss the suggestion as trivial.

She knew that she would weep again when she saw the kind, tender hands folded in death; the face that had never looked save with love upon her, fixed and gray and dead. But she saw beyond that bitter moment a long procession of years to come that would belong to her absolutely. And she opened and spread her arms out to them in welcome.

There would be no one to live for her during those coming years: she would live for herself. There would be no powerful will bending hers in that blind persistence with which men and women believe they have a right to impose a private will upon a fellow-creature. A kind intention or a cruel intention made the act seem no less a crime as she looked upon it in the brief moment of illumination.

And yet she had loved him—sometimes. Often she had not. What did it matter! What could love, the unsolved mystery, count for in face of this possession of self-assertion which she suddenly recognized as the strongest impulse of her being!

"Free! Body and soul free!" she kept whispering.

Josephine was kneeling before the closed door with her lips to the keyhole, imploring for admission. "Louise, open the door! I beg; open the door—you will make yourself ill. What are you doing, Louise? For heaven's sake open the door."

"Go away. I am not making myself ill." No; she was drinking in a very elixir of life through that open window.

Her fancy was running riot along those days ahead of her. Spring days, and summer days, and all sorts of days that would be her own. She breathed a quick prayer that life might be long. It was only yesterday she had thought with a shudder that life might be long.

She arose at length and opened the door to her sister's importunities. There was a feverish triumph in her eyes, and she carried herself unwittingly like a goddess of Victory. She clasped her sister's waist, and together they descended the stairs. Richards stood waiting for them at the bottom.

Someone was opening the front door with a latchkey. It was Brently Mallard who entered, a little travel-stained, composedly carrying his gripsack and umbrella. He had been far from the scene of the accident, and did not even know there had been one. He stood amazed at Josephine's piercing cry; at Richards's quick motion to screen him from the view of his wife.

But Richards was too late.

When the doctors came they said she had died of heart disease—of joy that kills.

Kate Chopin

1. Explain the irony of the ending of the story.
2. Identify one specific example of foreshadowing and explain its effectiveness.
3. Describe the character of Brently Mallard, making specific references to the story.
4. Identify the narrative viewpoint and explain how it is used effectively.

Reading Strategies

While you are reading a narrative text for an assignment, keep your specific purpose in mind. If, for example, your task is to compare the narrative structure in two novels, you would focus carefully on structure as you read.

It's always important, however, to gain a clear sense of the whole narrative text first. No one element operates separately from the others. Make sure the interpretation you offer of specific elements is consistent with the whole text.

Reading Strategy	Purpose
Read the novel quickly before you begin to study it.	You gain an overall impression (e.g., plot construction, characters) and can just enjoy it!
Do some research. Find out about the author and the location and period in which the novel is set.	Knowing something about the historical and social context in which the author lived and in which the novel is set can help you understand details that might otherwise seem strange or incomprehensible.
Keep a separate notebook or log for your work. Divide the notebook into sections for each of the major elements (plot, character, theme, setting, language, and style) or into those categories that you need for your work.	This will help to organize your thoughts as you read.

Reading Strategy	Purpose
Jot down observations as you read. Include appropriate quotations and page references. (See the "Reflective Reading Notes" chart for how you might organize these notes.)	You won't have to page through the book looking for those perfect quotations or examples; key references will be easy to locate when you come to write your essay or make your seminar presentation.
If you own the novel, annotate it so that you don't have to use a second notebook. Make your annotations clear and concise. (See the annotations to the short story "I Spy" on pp. 41–44.)	Annotation helps you to explore the text—you can record those tentative first responses and questions as you read. These notes will help you focus on the meaning and implications of individual words and phrases. You may find that you're able to collect the annotations that relate to one another (e.g., listing all references to "stone angel" in Margaret Laurence's novel of the same name in order to gain a clear sense of what this figure symbolizes).
You may wish to view one or two film versions of the novel. It's interesting to see the differences between earlier and later film versions of the same novel (e.g., Truman Capote's *Breakfast at Tiffany's*).	This can add another level of pleasure—you can discuss whether you think the film was true to the original text, what was changed, and whether these changes were an improvement over the novel. Watching a film version, however, is no substitute for reading the novel. Each director creates his or her own interpretation of the work, adding or omitting characters or leaving out or altering events (e.g., Patricia Rozema's film *Mansfield Park* is not an entirely faithful version of the novel; she has added various letters of Jane Austen's and created a feminist interpretation).

REFLECTIVE READING NOTES

Quotation/Phrase/Image (with page noted)	Context	Importance

Ways to Modify This Chart

- *Use one chart for key quotations only, another for key images, etc.*
- *Create one chart to document the thoughts, attitudes, and relationships of only one character.*
- *Use one chart for theme only and pull relevant quotes, images, and actions from other charts.*

Understanding Meaning

Meaning focuses on the main ideas or theme(s) of the narrative text. It's important to keep in mind all the elements of narrative as you read. In this way you'll be better able to interpret how the elements work together to develop overall themes and ideas.

INTERPRETING CHARACTER

TYPES OF CHARACTERS

Static characters are undeveloped, one-dimensional figures. They are known by one or more traits that remain constant throughout the story. Josephine in "The Story of an Hour" is a static character, in that all we really learn about her is that she's a caring person.

Dynamic characters are complex and realistic, and change or develop during the course of the narrative. Louise Mallard in Chopin's story is a dynamic character, in that she changes as the story unfolds.

Stereotypes are stock characters who often appear in particular genres. One stereotype often found in murder mysteries, for example, is the well-intentioned but fumbling police officer.

CHARACTER DEVELOPMENT

In a short story, characters are introduced economically. The depiction of characters and their relationships with each other is tightly focused. Characters aren't usually developed so much as revealed in a meaningful moment, which often constitutes the climax of the story. It takes only a very brief interlude, for example, for "The Story of an Hour" to reveal the true nature of a marriage that has lasted for years.

The first appearance of a major character in a novel usually involves an introductory "pen portrait." This often includes a physical description through which the attitudes and sense of the person begin to emerge. To help you track the character's development, it's helpful to identify three or four significant passages at different stages of the novel—

usually the beginning, middle, and end—in which the character is featured. These may be descriptive passages, moments of dramatic action, episodes where the character contrasts or is in conflict with others, or where he or she faces a decision.

Description: After the initial description the narrator builds up our knowledge with details as the story progresses. Key passages describe main characters or make us aware of how they change and develop.

Dialogue: We may discover a great deal about characters from their own speech, as well as through what other characters say about them.

Thoughts and feelings: The inner life of a character is revealed directly in the first-person voice or indirectly through third-person narrative.

Actions and reactions: How characters behave in various situations will inform our view of them.

Imagery and symbol: Characters may be described using simile and metaphor, or may be associated symbolically with a colour or an element. For example, in Emily Brontë's novel *Wuthering Heights,* Heathcliff is frequently linked with fire and the colour black.

Think about how the character is portrayed in the following introductory "pen portrait." What would you say is the narrator's attitude toward this character?

> He was the only one who knew how to react when the fugitive parrot appeared in the dining room at midnight with his head high and his wings spread, which caused a stupefied shudder to run through the house, for it seemed a sign of repentance. Florentino Ariza seized him by the neck before he had time to shout any of his witless stock phrases, and he carried him to the stable in a covered cage. He did everything this way, with so much discretion and such efficiency that it did not even occur to anyone that it might be an intrusion in other people's affairs; on the contrary, it seemed a priceless service when evil times had fallen on the house.
>
> He was what he seemed: a useful and serious old man. His body was bony and erect, his skin dark and clean-shaven, his eyes avid behind round spectacles in silver frames, and he wore a romantic, old-fashioned mustache with waxed tips. He combed the last tufts of hair at his temples upward and plastered them with brilliantine to the middle of his shining skull as a solution to total baldness. His natural gallantry and languid manner were immediately charming, but they were also considered suspect virtues in a confirmed bachelor. He had spent a great deal of money, ingenuity, and willpower to disguise the seventy-six years he had completed in March, and he was convinced in the solitude of his soul that he had loved in silence for a much longer time than anyone else in this world ever had.
>
> Gabriel Garcia Marquez, *Love in the Time of Cholera*

INTERPRETING SETTING

The imaginary world of the novel or short story varies widely in scope. The setting of a short story is usually narrowly defined; it may be as minimal as a room during a half hour in "The Open Window" by Saki (H.H. Munro). The setting of a novel may be as grand as London and Paris during the French Revolution in Charles Dickens's *A Tale of Two Cities*. But regardless of its scope, the setting is often more than simply the place where the story happens.

How Setting May Function

- *is important in itself*
- *is merely a backdrop to the action*
- *reflects the characters and their experiences*
- *symbolizes the ideas the writer wants to convey.*

In this excerpt, Ray Peepgass has come to see Martha Croker. From the description of her home seen through his eyes, what do you learn about him? about her?

> So she sent the maid off for some coffee and led Peepgass into some sort of den or library. It wasn't a big room, but every square inch of it looked as if it cost more than the sum total of Peepgass's possessions in Collier Hills. The Oriental rug ... the antique secretary at which she seemed to have been working ... the fabric on the walls ... the bookshelves ... the chintz-covered easy chairs ... and, above all, a charming bay that was set off from the rest of the room by a parabolic wooden arch and a sumptuous display of Victorian moldings that surrounded the bay's three big windows ... In the bay was a round rosewood Regency table with a pair of upholstered Regency dining chairs pulled up to it.
>
> "Let's sit by the window," said Martha Croker. "It's a nice place to have coffee."
>
> And, sure enough, it was. The windows looked out on a small formal garden, bursting with statice, delphinium, and peonies that seemed to have been created especially for the view from this one room. An ancient gardener, a black man, was down on his knees doing something with a trowel. He wore old-fashioned puttees, an article of dress Peepgass had never seen before, except in pictures of the World War I military. At the perimeter of the garden was a dense semicircle of boxwood bushes, mature ones, waist-high and grown together and immaculately clipped until they looked like a single fat green wall. Beyond the boxwood was an immense lawn, partly in open sunlight, partly in the shade of huge old trees, and everywhere bordered by carefully groomed shrubbery and beds of flowers.
>
> Peepgass gazed out the window and, without turning toward her, said, "It's absolutely beautiful, Martha." Something told him to tuck in as many Marthas as he could.
>
> Tom Wolfe, *A Man in Full*

IDENTIFYING THEME

The **theme** of a narrative is its message or main idea; for example, *pride, suffering*, or *hope*. Although a theme is a universal idea, each author will present a particular view of this theme. For example, in some works, *wisdom gained through suffering* is the message. In others, the theme may be *the wastefulness and tragedy of suffering*.

Themes are rarely stated directly in narrative text. You will need to carefully examine character, action, key image patterns, and repeated words or phrases to help you develop your understanding of the theme. Read the following story and its annotations. What would you say is its central theme?

i spy

sense of secrecy

sense of mystery, menace, potential danger

What is Charlie up to?

Charlie Stowe waited until he heard his mother snore before he got out of bed. Even then he moved with caution and tiptoed to the window. The front of the house was irregular, so that it was possible to see a light burning in his mother's room. But now all the windows were dark. A searchlight passed across the sky, lighting the banks of cloud and probing the dark deep spaces between, seeking enemy airships. The wind blew from the sea, and Charlie Stowe could hear behind his mother's snores the beating of the waves. A draught through the cracks in the window-frame stirred his nightshirt. Charlie was frightened.

"manly" to smoke Why?

But the thought of the tobacconist's shop which his father kept down a dozen wooden stairs drew him on. He was twelve years old, and already boys at the County School mocked him because he had never smoked a cigarette. The packets were piled twelve deep below, Gold Flake and Players, De Reszke, Abdulla, Woodbines, and the little shop lay under a thin haze of stale smoke which would completely disguise his crime. That it was a crime to steal some of his father's stock Charlie Stowe had no doubt, but he did not love his father; his father was unreal to him, a wraith, pale, thin, indefinite, who noticed him only spasmodically and left even punishment to his mother. For his mother he felt a passionate demonstrative love; her large boisterous

father doesn't bother with him

contrast with father

presence and her noisy charity filled the world for him; from her speech he judged her the friend of everyone, from the rector's wife to the "dear Queen," except the "Huns," the monsters who lurked in Zeppelins in the clouds. But his father's affection and dislike were as indefinite as his movements. Tonight he had said he would be in Norwich, and yet you never knew. Charlie Stowe had no sense of safety as he crept down the wooden stairs. When they creaked he clenched his fingers on the collar of his nightshirt.

At the bottom of the stairs he came out quite suddenly into the little shop. It was too dark to see his way, and he did not dare touch the switch. For half a minute he sat in despair on the bottom step with his chin cupped in his hands. Then the regular movement of the searchlight was reflected through an upper window and the boy had time to fix in memory the pile of cigarettes, the counter, and the small hole under it. The footsteps of a policeman on the pavement made him grab the first packet to his hand and dive from the hole. A light shone along the floor and a hand tried the door, then the footsteps passed on, and Charlie cowered in the darkness. At last he got his courage back by telling himself in his curiously adult way that if he were caught now there was nothing to be done about it, and he might as well have his smoke. He put a cigarette in his mouth and then remembered that he had no matches. For a while he dared not move. Three times the searchlight lit the shop, while he muttered taunts and encouragements. May as well be hung for a sheep, Cowardy, cowardy custard, grown-up and childish exhortations oddly mixed.

fear of discovery builds atmosphere of tension

mixture of adult and child

But as he moved he heard footfalls in the street, the sound of several men walking rapidly. Charlie Stowe was old enough to feel surprise that anybody was about. The footsteps came nearer, stopped; a key was turned in the shop door, a voice said: "Let him in," and then he heard his father, "If you wouldn't mind being quiet, gentlemen. I don't want to wake up the family." There was a note unfamiliar to Charlie in the undecided voice. A torch flashed and the electric globe burst into blue light. The boy held his breath; he wondered whether his father would hear his heart beating, and he clutched his night-shirt tightly and prayed, "O God, don't let me be caught." Through a crack in the counter he could see his father where he stood, one hand held to his high stiff collar, between two men in bowler hats and belted mackintoshes. They were strangers. "Have a cigarette," his father said in a voice dry as a biscuit. One of the men shook his head. "It wouldn't do, not when we are on duty. Thank you all the same." He spoke gently but without kindness; Charlie Stowe thought his father must be ill.

like Charlie clenching his nightshirt

fear, uncertainty

"Mind if I put a few in my pocket?" Mr. Stowe asked, and when the man nodded he lifted a pile of Gold Flake and Players from a shelf and caressed the packets with the tips of his fingers.

why this word? (much emphasis on cigarettes)

"Well," he said, "there's nothing to be done about it, and I may as well have my smokes." For a moment Charlie Stowe feared discovery, his father stared round the shop so thoroughly; he might have been seeing it for the first time. "It's a good little business," he said, "for those that like it. The wife will sell out, I suppose. Else the neighbours'll be wrecking it. Well, you want to be off. A stitch in time. I'll get my coat.

or the last!

the end of his family life

"One of us'll come with you, if you don't mind," said the stranger gently.

"You needn't trouble. It's on the peg here. There, I'm all ready."

The other man said in an embarrassed way, "Don't you want to speak to your wife?" The thin voice was decided, "Not me. Never do today what you can put off till tomorrow. She'll have her chance later, won't she?"

"Yes, yes," one of the strangers said and he became very cheerful and encouraging. "Don't you worry too much. While there's life …" and suddenly his father tried to laugh.

When the door had closed Charlie Stowe tiptoed upstairs and got into bed. He wondered why his father had left the house again so late at night and who the strangers were. Surprise and awe kept him for a little while awake. It was as if a familiar photograph had stepped from the frame to reproach him with neglect.

we see everything through Charlie's eyes

He remembered how his father had held tight to his collar and fortified himself with proverbs, and he thought for the first time that, while his father was boisterous and kindly, his father was very like himself doing things in the dark which frightened him. It would have pleased him to go down to his father and tell him that he loved him, but he could hear through the window the quick steps going away. He was alone in the house with his mother, and he fell asleep.

just like Charlie

something has happened to change Charlie's view

returns to the beginning

Graham Greene

Understanding Form

PLOT STRUCTURE

> 'The king died and then the queen died' is a story. 'The king died and then the queen died of grief' is a plot.
>
> E.M. Forster, *Aspects of the Novel*

In other words, a plot is more than just a series of events; these events are connected by cause and effect. The plot structure results from how the events are related.

Considering Plot Structure

- *List the key events in the narrative.*
- *Look at the order in which these events are recounted.*
- *Look at the* ***time structure*** *of the story. Is it told in chronological order, does it cut back and forth in time, are there flashbacks?* ***Flashbacks*** *—the shifting from the present to the past and back again—fill in missing background information that is relevant to the story or to the development of character and action.* ***Foreshadowing*** *—hints about future events—keeps an alert reader guessing about what might happen next. (If you miss some of these hints on a first reading, a rereading can give you the added pleasure of seeing how subtly the author has prepared you for the ending of the story or the revelation of character.)*
- *Look for any* ***details*** *or pieces of information that the writer omits or particularly emphasizes. Even the smallest of details may prove to be important!*
- *Identify the* ***key conflict****. This may be primarily an internal one (e.g., a battle with one's conscience), which could manifest itself in related external conflicts.*

- *Identify the **climax** or turning point of the story. This is the point at which the direction of the resolution of the conflict becomes clear. The climax in a short story frequently occurs close to or right at the end.*

BEGINNINGS

Beginnings and endings of narratives are particularly important. After all, if the opening doesn't capture the reader's interest, he or she may not continue. The opening must also clearly establish the direction of the narrative, particularly in a short story, where space is at a premium.

Possible Opening Strategies

- *The writer launches straight into the narrative.*
- *The scene is set using explicit background information.*
- *Rather than direct description, the writer uses suggestion or implication.*
- *The opening is direct and holds the reader's attention, perhaps capturing attention with a word or short phrase.*

Read the following beginnings. For each excerpt, how would you describe the author's strategy of pulling in the reader? How is this effective?

> I have been afraid of putting air in a tire ever since I saw a tractor tire blow up and throw Newt Hardbine's father over the top of the Standard Oil sign. I'm not lying. He got stuck up there. About nineteen people congregated during the time it took for Norman Strick to walk up to the Courthouse and blow the whistle for the volunteer fire department. They eventually did come with the ladder and haul him down, and he wasn't dead but lost his hearing and in many other ways never was the same afterward. They said he overfilled the tire.
>
> Newt Hardbine was not my friend, he was just one of the big boys who had failed every grade at least once and so was practically going on twenty in the sixth grade, sitting in the back and flicking little wads of chewed paper into my hair. But the day I saw his daddy up there like some old overalls slung over a fence, I had this feeling about what Newt's whole life was going to amount to, and I felt sorry for him. Before that exact moment I don't believe I had given much thought to the future.
>
> Barbara Kingsolver, *The Bean Trees*
>
> I read about it in the paper, in the subway, on my way to work. I read it, and I couldn't believe it, and I read it again. Then perhaps I just stared at it, at the newsprint spelling out his name, spelling out the story. I stared at it in the swinging lights of the subway car, and in the faces and bodies of the people, and in my own face, trapped in the darkness which roared outside.

> It was not to be believed and I kept telling myself that, as I walked from the subway station to the high school. And at the same time I couldn't doubt it. I was scared, scared for Sonny. He became real to me again. A great block of ice got settled in my belly and kept melting there slowly all day long, while I taught my classes algebra. It was a special kind of ice. It kept melting, sending trickles of ice water all up and down my veins, but it never got less. Sometimes it hardened and seemed to expand until I felt my guts were going to come spilling out or that I was going to choke or scream. This would always be at a moment when I was remembering some specific thing Sonny had once said or done.
>
> James Baldwin, "Sonny's Blues"

ENDINGS

It's often the ending that reveals the meaning of a short story and its significant theme. Short stories are known for focusing on a key moment in the life of the major character—a moment that causes a realization or a change in that character's life—and this moment frequently comes at the end. This is true of Kate Chopin's "The Story of an Hour" that introduces the chapter.

Short story writers are particularly fond of these twist endings. But the best writers ensure that, if they do use a twist ending, it's for a good reason; namely, to reveal something fundamental in the narrative as a whole.

Endings usually leave the reader with a feeling of satisfaction that the story is completed. This feeling can be generated through different means, of course. Writers choose to develop their plot in particular ways for particular effects, such as creating suspense, resolving problems, leading or misleading the reader, and leaving endings open to interpretation.

Considering Endings

- *Does the story have what you would recognize as a definite ending?*
- *How does the ending relate to the rest of the story?*
- *Does the writer draw attention to any specific points in the ending?*
- *How would* you *have ended the story?*

Understanding Style

Close reading and expert skills of analysis are required in order to determine the particular effects of the author's stylistic choices. A particular writing style results from the combination of decisions made about the following elements:

Narrative viewpoint/voice: the choice of first-person or third-person narrative or stream-of-consciousness

Diction and imagery: the selection of particular words rather than others; and the use of simile, metaphor, personification, and symbol. Look particularly for recurring images or patterns of imagery.

Narrative sentences and paragraphs: the use of sentences that are long or short, complete or incomplete, complex or simple

NARRATIVE VIEWPOINT

Critical to a clear and complete understanding of a story or novel is identifying the narrative viewpoint. Internal narrators are part of the story and use the **first-person** pronoun. They may be the major character, or a relatively minor or supporting character. External narrators are usually not characters in the story. They tell the story from an outside perspective using the **third-person** pronoun.

FIRST PERSON

Advantages	Limitations
Strengthens the illusion that the story is real; the reader becomes more involved and able to empathize with the character.	We see the other characters only through the eyes of this one character.
Because the narrator is a character in the story, the story becomes more complex. More is demanded of us as readers.	How far can we trust this character? Our ability to see and understand the other characters is limited or enhanced according to the first-person narrator's ability to see clearly, completely, and without bias. As well, we can't know directly of any events other than the ones the first-person narrator is involved in. The narrator may also intentionally deceive us.

In the following excerpt, the first-person narrator is living in a future society in which people are restricted to narrow, specific roles. She is a "handmaid," whose job is to breed to ensure the survival of her nation.

What more can you learn about her situation from what she reveals about her thoughts and feelings?

> A window, two white curtains. Under the window, a window seat with a little cushion. When the window is partly open—it only opens partly—the air can come in and make the curtains move. I can sit in the chair, or on the window seat, hands folded, and watch this. Sunlight comes in through the window too, and falls on the floor, which is made of wood, in narrow strips, highly polished. I can smell the polish.

> There's a rug on the floor, oval, of braided rags. This is the kind of touch they like: folk art, archaic, made by women, in their spare time, from things that have no further use. A return to traditional values. Waste not want not. I am not being wasted. Why do I want?
>
> A bed. Single, mattress medium-hard, covered with a flocked white spread. Nothing takes place in the bed but sleep; or no sleep. I try not to think too much. Like other things now, thought must be rationed. There's a lot that doesn't bear thinking about. Thinking can hurt your chances, and I intend to last. I know why there is no glass, in front of the water-colour picture of blue irises, and why the window only opens partly and why the glass in it is shatterproof. It isn't running away they're afraid of. We wouldn't get far. It's those other escapes, the ones you can open in yourself, given a cutting edge.
>
> So. Apart from these details, this could be a college guest room, for the less distinguished visitors; or a room in a rooming-house, of former times, for ladies in reduced circumstances. That is what we are now. The circumstances have been reduced; for those of us who still have circumstances.
>
> But a chair, sunlight, flowers: these are not to be dismissed. I am alive, I live, I breathe, I put my hand out, unfolded, into the sunlight. Where I am is not a prison but a privilege, as Aunt Lydia said, who was in love with either/or.
>
> Margaret Atwood, *A Handmaid's Tale*

Stream of consciousness is a variety of first-person narration. This technique represents the continuous flow of a character's sense perceptions, thoughts, feelings, and memories. It can be quite demanding for the reader, since it's usually unpunctuated and disjointed. It records, seemingly with no intrusion of the author, the character's internal thoughts. They jump from one to another with no logic other than the feelings, memories, and associations of the character's mind in a particular time and situation.

THIRD PERSON

Advantages	Limitations
Because the narrator is omniscient (all-knowing and all-seeing), we see and can relate events that may take place at different times, places, or even at the same time. We have a "fly on the wall" perspective.	Sometimes the author intentionally limits our view of a situation by filtering a scene or parts of a story through the eyes of one character for a particular purpose. See the excerpt from *In the Skin of the Lion*.
Characters' feelings are often described so that we can understand the events based on the perspectives of more than one character.	Distancing occurs as the characters' thoughts and feelings are described rather than expressed directly.

Advantages	Limitations
The story appears to be told without judgment so that we may form our own.	The story may appear to be told without bias, but the writer may use this apparent lack of bias to direct our sympathies in particular directions.

In the following excerpt, what can you infer about Patrick Lewis's state of mind from this third-person recounting?

> Now, in the city, he was new even to himself, the past locked away. He saw his image in the glass of telephone booths. He ran his hands over the smooth pink marble pillars that reached up into the rotunda. This train station was a palace, its niches and caverns an intimate city. He could be shaved, eat a meal, or have his shoes coloured.
>
> He saw a man with three suitcases, well-dressed, shouting out in another language. The man's eyes burned through everyone who at first received his scream personally. But the phrases were for angels in the air to assist him or for demons to leave him. Two days later Patrick returned to pick up his luggage from a locker. He saw the man again, still unable to move from his safe zone, in a different suit, as if one step away was the quicksand of the new world.
>
> Patrick sat on a bench and watched the tides of movement, felt the reverberations of trade. He spoke out his name and it struggled up in a hollow echo and was lost in the high air of Union Station. No one turned. They were in the belly of a whale.
>
> Michael Ondaatje, *In the Skin of a Lion*

An **intrusive narrator** is an omniscient narrator who, in addition to reporting the events of the story,

- offers further comments on characters and events
- sometimes reflects generally upon the significance of the story.

The intrusive narrator was used frequently by nineteenth-century novelists. This approach allows the novel to be used for general moral commentary on human life, sometimes in the form of brief digressive essays.

DICTION AND IMAGERY

Choice of words and the use of rhetorical devices are important aspects of a writer's style. Your analysis of diction and imagery must always be based on what the author is attempting to develop or reveal about character, setting, and theme.

Some Rhetorical Devices

- *personification (p. 50)*
- *metaphor (p. 51)*
- *simile (p. 50)*

In the following excerpt from Wayson Choy's *The Jade Peony*, the author's careful word choice and use of imagery contribute to the meaning of the text. How does the imagery contribute to the pathos of the grandmother's imminent death?

But it was the countless hours I spent with Grandmama that were my real education. Tapping me on my head she would say, "Come, Sek-Lung, we have our work" and we would walk up the stairs to her small crowded room. There, in the midst of her antique shawls, the old ancestral calligraphy and multicoloured embroidered hangings, beneath the mysterious shelves of sweet herbs and bitter potions, we would continue doing what we had started that morning: the elaborate windchime for her death.

"I can't last forever," she declared, when she let me in the secret of this one. "It will sing and dance and glitter." Her long fingers stretched into the air, pantomiming the waving motions of her ghost chimes. "My spirit will hear its sounds and see its light and return to this house and say goodbye to you."

words convey something mysterious, magical

Deftly she reached into the Safeway carton she had placed on a chair beside me. She picked out a fish-shaped amber piece, and with a long needle-like tool and a steel ruler, she scored it. Pressing the blade of a cleaver against the line, with the fingers of her other hand she lifted up the glass until it cleanly snapped into the exact shape she required. Her hand began to tremble, the tips of her fingers to shiver, like rippling water.

words convey preciousness

"You see that, Little One?" She held her hand up. "That is my body fighting with Death. He is in this room now."

personification of death emphasizes its reality and proximity

My eyes darted in panic, but Grandmama remained calm, undisturbed, and went on with her work. Then I remembered the glue and uncorked the jar for her. Soon the graceful ritual movements of her hand returned to her, and I became lost in the magic of her task: dabbled a cabalistic mixture of glue on one end and skilfully dropped the braided end of a silk thread into it. This part always amazed me: the braiding would slowly, very slowly, unknot, fanning out like a prized fishtail. In a few seconds the clear, homemade glue began to harden as I blew lightly over it, welding to itself each separate strand.

simile suggests expansion, release

Each jam-sized pot of glue was precious; each large cork had been wrapped with a fragment of pink silk. I remember this part vividly, because each cork was treated to a special rite. First we went shopping in the best silk stores in Chinatown for the perfect square of silk she required. It had to be a deep pink, a shade of colour blushing towards red. And the tone had to match—as closely as possible—her precious jade carving, the small peony of white and light-red jade, her most lucky possession. In the centre of this semitranslucent carving, no more than an inch wide, was a pool of pink light, its veins whirling out into petals of the flower.

"This colour is the colour of my spirit," she said, holding it up to the window so I could see the delicate pastel against the broad strokes of sunlight. She dropped her voice, and I held my breath at the wonder of the colour. "This was given to me by the young actor who taught me how to juggle. He had four of them, and each one had a centre of rare colour, the colour of Good Fortune." The pendant seemed to pause as she turned it: "Oh, Sek-Lung! He had white hair and white skin to his toes! It's true, I saw him bathing." She laughed and blushed, her eyes softened at the memory. The silk had to match the pink heart of the pendant: the colour was magical for her, to hold the unravelling strand for her memory…

A few days after that she died of the complications of pneumonia. Immediately after her death my father came home and said nothing to us but walked up the stairs to her room, pulled aside the drawn lace curtains of her window and lifted the windchimes to the sky.

I began to cry and quickly put my hand in my pocket for a handkerchief. Instead, caught between my fingers, was the small, round firmness of the jade peony. In my mind's eye, I saw Grandmama smile and heard, softly, the pink centre beat like a beautiful, cramped heart.

Wayson Choy

Annotations:

- words convey something mysterious, magical
- words convey preciousness
- metaphors suggest expansion, release, deepening
- repetition of "blushing towards red" suggests connection between grandmother and peony
- alliteration heightens effect
- echoes movement of silk thread used in windchime
- connection between the windchime and the releasing of the grandmother's spirit in death
- images of jade peony contrast with earlier "fanning out," "whirling out," perhaps suggesting distinction between life and death; jade peony is "alive" for Sek-Lung as enduring symbol of his grandmother

NARRATIVE SENTENCES AND PARAGRAPHS

Short sentences are often used to reflect fast-paced action or to create a sense of excitement or suspense. They are used in dialogue for the same purposes, as well as for humorous effect in comical exchanges.

Incomplete sentences are frequently used to show that the character is distracted, overcome by emotion, or losing his or her sanity.

Long sentences tend to be used for descriptive passages, for example when introducing a particular character or a setting. They may be used to convey an overall impression of a group of people in a large location.

The **narrative paragraph** is usually much looser and shorter than the expository paragraph. When dialogue is used, usually a new paragraph begins. This makes it clear to the reader who is speaking. Begin a new paragraph also when there is a change in time, place, or action.

» CHECKPOINT: *Reassess Your Knowledge*

forty-five a month

Shanta could not stay in her class any longer. She had done clay-modelling, music, drill, a bit of alphabets and numbers and was now cutting coloured paper. She would have to cut till the bell rang and the teacher said, "Now you may go home," or "Put away the scissors and take up your alphabets—" Shanta was impatient to know the time. She asked her friend sitting next to her, "Is it five now?"

"Maybe," she replied.

"Or is it six?"

"I don't think so," her friend replied, "because night comes at six."

"Do you think it is five?"

"Yes."

"Oh, I must go. My father will be back at home now. He has asked me to be ready at five. He is taking me to the cinema this evening. I must go home." She threw down her scissors and ran up to the teacher. "Madam, I must go home."

"Why, Shanta Bai?"

"Because it is five o'clock now."

"Who told you it was five?"

"Kamala."

"It is not five now. It is—do you see the clock there? Tell me what the time is. I taught you to read the clock the other day." Shanta stood gazing at the clock in the hall, counted the figures laboriously and declared, "It is nine o'clock."

The teacher called the other girls and said, "Who will tell me the time from that clock?" Several of them concurred with Shanta and said it was nine o'clock, till the teacher said, "You are seeing only the long hand. See the short one, where is it?"

"Two and a half."

"So what is the time?"

"Two and a half."

"It is two forty-five, understand? Now you may all go to your seats—" Shanta returned to the teacher in about ten minutes and asked, "Is it five, madam, because I have to be ready at five. Otherwise my father will be very angry with me. He asked me to return home early."

"At what time?"

"Now." The teacher gave her permission to leave, and Shanta picked up her books and dashed out of the class with a cry of joy. She ran home, threw her books on the floor and shouted, "Mother, Mother," and Mother came running from the next house, where she had gone to chat with her friends.

Mother asked, "Why are you back so early?"

"Has Father come home?" Shanta asked. She would not take her coffee or tiffin but insisted on being dressed first. She opened the trunk and insisted on wearing the thinnest frock and knickers, while her mother wanted to dress her in a long skirt and thick coat for the evening. Shanta picked out a gorgeous ribbon from a cardboard soap box in which she kept pencils, ribbons and chalk bits. There was a heated argument between mother and daughter over the dress, and finally Mother had to give in. Shanta put on her favourite pink frock, braided her hair and flaunted a green ribbon on her pigtail. She powdered her face and pressed a vermilion mark on her forehead. She said, "Now Father will say what a nice girl I am because I'm ready. Aren't you also coming, Mother?"

"Not today."

Shanta stood at the little gate looking down the street.

Mother said, "Father will come only after five; don't stand in the sun. It is only four o'clock."

The sun was disappearing behind the house on the opposite row, and Shanta knew that presently it would be dark. She ran in to her mother and asked, "Why hasn't Father come home yet, Mother?"

"How can I know? He is perhaps held up in the office."

Shanta made a wry face. "I don't like these people in the office. They are bad people—"

She went back to the gate and stood looking out. Her mother shouted from inside, "Come in, Shanta. It is getting dark, don't stand there." But Shanta would not go in. She stood at the gate and a wild idea came into her head. Why should she not go to the office and call out Father and then go to the cinema? She wondered where his office might be. She had no notion. She had seen her father take the turn at the end of the street every day. If one went there, perhaps one went automatically to Father's office. She threw a glance about to see if Mother was anywhere and moved down the street.

It was twilight. Everyone going about looked gigantic, walls of houses appeared very high and cycles and carriages looked as though they would bear down on her. She walked on the very edge of the road. Soon the lamps were twinkling, and the passers-by looked like shadows. She had taken two turns and did not know where she was. She sat down on the edge of the road biting her nails. She wondered how she was to reach home. A servant employed in the next house was passing along, and she picked herself up and stood before him.

"Oh, what are you doing here all alone?" he asked. She replied, "I don't know. I came here. Will you take me to our house?" She followed him and was soon back in her house.

Venkat Rao, Shanta's father, was about to start for his office that morning when a jutka passed along the street distributing cinema handbills. Shanta dashed to the street and picked up a handbill. She held it up and asked, "Father, will you take me to the cinema today?" He felt unhappy at the question. Here was the child growing up without having any of the amenities and the simple pleasures of life. He had hardly taken her twice to the cinema. He had no time for the child. While children of her age in other houses had all the dolls, dresses and outings that they wanted, this child was growing up all alone and like a barbarian more or less. He felt furious with his office. For forty rupees a month they seemed to have purchased him outright.

He reproached himself for neglecting his wife and child—even the wife could have her own circle of friends and so on: she was after all a grown-up, but what about the child? What a drab, colourless existence was hers! Every day they kept him at the office till seven or eight in the evening, and when he came home the child was asleep. Even on Sundays they wanted him at the office. Why did they think he had no personal life, a life of his own? They gave him hardly any time to take the child to the park or the pictures. He was going to show them that they weren't to toy with him. Yes, he was prepared even to quarrel with his manager if necessary.

He said with resolve, "I will take you to the cinema this evening. Be ready at five."

"Really! Mother!" Shanta shouted. Mother came out of the kitchen.

"Father is taking me to a cinema in the evening."

Shanta's mother smiled cynically. "Don't make false promises to the child—"

Venkat Rao glared at her. "Don't talk nonsense. You think you are the only person who keeps promises—"

He told Shanta, "Be ready at five, and I will come and take you positively. If you are not ready, I will be very angry with you."

He walked to his office full of resolve. He would do his normal work and get out at five. If they started any old tricks of theirs, he was going to tell the boss, "Here is my resignation. My child's happiness is more important to me than these horrible papers of yours."

All day the usual stream of papers flowed onto his table and off it. He scrutinized, signed and drafted. He was corrected, admonished and insulted. He had a break of only five minutes in the afternoon for his coffee.

When the office clock struck five and the other clerks were leaving, he went up to the manager and said, "May I go, sir?" The manager looked up from his paper. "You!" It was unthinkable that the cash and account section should be closing at five. "How can you go?"

"I have some urgent private business, sir," he said, smothering the lines he had been rehearsing since the morning: "Herewith my resignation." He visualized Shanta standing at the door, dressed and palpitating with eagerness.

"There shouldn't be anything more urgent than the office work; go back to your seat. You know how many hours I work?" asked the manager. The manager came to the office three hours before opening time and stayed nearly three hours after closing, even on Sundays. The clerks commented among themselves, "His wife must be whipping him whenever he is seen at home; that is why the old owl seems so fond of his office."

"Did you trace the source of that ten-eight difference?" asked the manager.

"I shall have to examine two hundred vouchers. I thought we might do it tomorrow."

"No, no, this won't do. You must rectify it immediately."

Venkat Rao mumbled, "Yes, sir," and slunk back to his seat. The clock showed 5:30. Now it meant two hours of excruciating search among vouchers. All the rest of the office had gone. Only he and another clerk in his section were working, and of course, the manager was there. Venkat Rao was furious. His mind was made up. He wasn't a slave who had sold himself for forty rupees outright. He could make the money easily; and if he couldn't, it would be more honourable to die of starvation.

He took a sheet of paper and wrote: "Herewith my resignation. If you people think you have bought me body and soul for forty rupees, you are mistaken. I think it would be far better for me and my family to die of starvation than slave for this petty forty rupees on which you have kept me for years and years. I suppose you have not the slightest notion of giving me an increment. You give yourselves heavy slices frequently, and I don't see why you shouldn't think of us occasionally. In any case it doesn't interest me now, since this is my resignation. If I and my family perish of starvation, may our ghosts come and haunt you all your life—" He folded the letter, put it in an envelope, sealed the flap and addressed it to the manager. He left his seat and stood before the manager. The manager mechanically received the letter and put it on his pad.

"Venkat Rao," said the manager, "I'm sure you will be glad to hear this news. Our officer discussed the question of increments today, and I've recommended you for an increment of five rupees. Orders are not yet passed, so keep this to yourself for the present." Venkat Rao put out his hand, snatched the envelope from the pad and hastily slipped it in his pocket.

"What is that letter?"

"I have applied for a little casual leave, sir, but I think ..."

"You can't get any leave for at least a fortnight to come."

"Yes, sir. I realized that. That is why I am withdrawing my application, sir."

"Very well. Have you traced the mistake?"

"I'm scrutinizing the vouchers, sir. I will find it out within an hour ..."

It was nine o'clock when he went home. Shanta was already asleep. Her mother said. "She wouldn't even change her frock, thinking that any moment you might be coming and taking her out. She hardly ate any food; and wouldn't lie down for fear of crumpling her dress...."

Venkat Rao's heart bled when he saw his child sleeping in her pink frock, hair combed and face powdered, dressed and ready to be taken out. "Why should I not take her to the night show?" He shook her gently and called, "Shanta, Shanta." Shanta kicked her legs and cried, irritated at being disturbed. Mother whispered. "Don't wake her," and patted her back to sleep.

Venkat Rao watched the child for a moment. "I don't know if it is going to be possible for me to take her out at all—you see, they are giving me an increment—" he wailed.

R.K. Narayan

1. Describe Venkat Rao, making specific references to the story. Would you say he is a man of strength or of weakness? Justify your decision.
2. Select one section of dialogue that you find particularly effective. Analyze and explain its effectiveness.
3. Explain the irony in the ending of the story.
4. State and explain the theme of this story in a thoughtful paragraph or two, using specific references.

Creating Narrative Texts

Preparing and Planning

The inspiration for your short story may come from any number of sources—even someone you've passed on the street who for some reason caught your attention. You may begin to imagine a life for that person; a story could start to take shape.

A writer's notebook is an excellent means of storing away perceptions, fragments of conversations, or your thoughts and opinions on any given topic. Having a small book that you can carry around with you and write in at any moment can provide a rich base for writing.

Generating Ideas for a Short Story

- *Start with a theme that you've studied; for example, the effect of a great fear upon an individual and how the conflict is resolved. Since some of the best writing comes out of our own experience, you might like to think about the theme of fear and how it has applied to your own life. Or think of a time when you were surprised or unhappy. Write down the situation. Describe it as clearly as you can, and include your own thoughts and emotions at the time. Develop an appropriate character sketch for the key character(s).*

- *Study a number of stories whose themes appeal to you, then choose a theme that you would like to write about. Study some stories with especially good background and description (perhaps selected from stories you've read in this course or earlier), and practise writing some descriptive settings of your own. Use the same approach to start thinking about character and plot, and soon ideas for your own story or stories may begin to emerge.*

- *Read short story anthologies or novels that deal with adolescent themes. You might identify the opposite of these themes in order to come up with your own (e.g., concern versus indifference, security versus anarchy). Then, to start filling in the rest of your story, think of different combinations of characters whose values and attitudes could be in conflict (e.g., parent–child, teacher–student).*

Important Planning Decisions

- *What is the key moment in the story? Does it occur in the last paragraph of the story or simply later in the story? Everything else must fit around this central moment of conflict and character revelation.*

- *What is the origin of this conflict? Where will your story begin in relation to this conflict? Remember that a short story isn't usually long enough to show all the events in a particular conflict. You must focus on the most significant moment and include only what you need of its earlier development.*
- *How will you tell the story? Chronologically? With flashbacks? With foreshadowing?*
- *Who is/are the main character(s)? A short story rarely has more than two main characters. Describe their main physical and personality traits. Are there any specific distinguishing characteristics (e.g., has a tattoo on the lower forearm, chews Wrigley's spearmint gum, is deathly afraid of cats or large open spaces)?*
- *What is the setting of the story? Will you need to research information about the location or the time period in order to describe clothing, street scenes, and societal customs, for example?*
- *What influence will the setting have on how the characters speak? Will you have any dialect or particular accent? Writing dialect well is tricky—trickier even than speaking it. Don't attempt it unless you're very familiar with it.*
- *Will the story have a significant amount of dialogue? More description and narration than dialogue? What's an appropriate balance for your story? Think about your reader when you're making decisions like this, as well as what's best for your story.*
- *From what narrative viewpoint will you tell the story? Will a character in the story narrate it? Which character? Why? What would happen if a different character narrated the story (for example, the antagonist)? Will the story be written in third-person limited or omniscient? Consider different possibilities to see how the story would be told differently. Consider also what theme you want to develop and therefore whose viewpoint might be the most advantageous.*
- *What figurative devices might complement the development of character, mood, and theme? Consider the use of symbol, metaphor, simile, personification, and imagery.*
- *What role might literary devices such as irony, contrast, pathos, and humour play in the story?*

Know your story structure well before you begin writing. Having a well-worked-out structure will help you focus on conciseness and subtlety. And remember that the best short stories have an element of surprise; for example, perhaps at the end of the story you could reveal something that will make your reader doubt his or her trust in your first-person narrator. The secret of a really good short story is to reveal just enough for the readers to figure it out—without you actually telling them!

Checklist

Creating a Short Story

- **Introduction:** Does it quickly and effectively engage the reader's interest? Does it harmonize with the general tone of the story? ❑
- **Conflict:** Is the conflict sharp enough to be interesting? Is it realistic? ❑
- **Plot line:** Does the story develop logically? Is there any event that could be removed so that the story could be told more economically? ❑
- **Narrative viewpoint:** Is it consistent? If not, then is the shifting viewpoint used effectively? Is there a more effective way of telling the story and revealing the theme? Does it assist the flow of the narrative? ❑
- **Characters:** Are they consistent? Sufficiently contrasting? Engaging? Have they been introduced and developed with clear, distinguishing characteristics? Are they sufficiently detailed to be realistic and not stereotypical? ❑
- **Atmosphere:** Are elements of surprise or humour or irony or suspense included for specific effects? ❑
- **Style:** Is appropriate diction used for each character and the time period and location of the setting? Has descriptive language been used where it can be most effective? ❑
- **Ending:** Does it leave the reader satisfied? Surprised? Does the story end soon enough? ❑
- **Title:** Is the title suggestive? Brief? Does it appeal to the imagination? Does it reveal too much? ❑

Revising and Editing

INCORPORATING QUOTATIONS IN DIALOGUE

When you write dialogue it's important to vary the way you incorporate quotations. This can add drama and heighten the effect of the exchange. Consider the following:

> She stood up. "I'm late," she noted matter-of-factly.
>
> He said slowly, in that laidback way of his, "Yeah, I'm late too."
>
> Gritting her teeth, she fought for control. "But I'm *so* late," she said evenly, "that it might mean trouble."

"What, are you saying you have more important things to do?" He sounded incredulous.

"Yes, I am!"

"Then," he replied, haughty now, "you had better go."

"Don't you get what I'm saying?" she sputtered. "I *have* to go!"

The Four Basic Methods

- *Write the speaker at the start of the quotation*
  John said, "______."
- *Write the speaker at the end of the quotation*
  "__________," said John.
- *Write the speaker in the middle of the quotation:*
  "__________," said John. "__________."

or

"__________," John said, "________________."

- *Do not name the speaker.*
  "____________."

SUBSTITUTIONS FOR "SAY"

"Say" can be overused in a short story. Here are some possible replacements:

agreed	hesitated	remarked
assented	implored	retorted
burst out	laughed	roared
coaxed	maintained	shouted
continued	mimicked	sighed
denied	murmured	smiled
echoed	nodded	stammered
exclaimed	pleaded	warbled
faltered	promised	warned
grinned	put in	whispered

DEVELOPING A WRITER'S VOCABULARY

Pay attention to all the verbs in your story. For example, try to substitute action verbs for forms of *to be* and *to have*. The new verbs will give life and movement to the story, partly because you'll find that the replacement verbs change the sentence structure. For example,

Original	**Revised**
Lear had many possessions that he gave away.	Possessing much, Lear gave much away.
He was tired and didn't think about what he was doing.	Fatigued, he acted without thought.

Having an extensive vocabulary is a must for a successful writer. The best writers choose exactly the right word for the context. Start to extend your vocabulary by looking up two unfamiliar words that you encounter each day. Make notes about them in your writer's notebook, and begin to use them in your speech and in your writing.

Look particularly for the **shades of meaning** or **nuances** in one word that might *seem* to mean the same thing as another. As well as the literal, or denotative meaning, always consider the connotative values or feelings associated with a word. For example, "home" *denotes* a place someone lives but also *connotes* feelings of safety, intimacy, and love. The word "house," on the other hand, does not carry these connotations. Words are more specific than we may realize.

GRAMMAR, USAGE, AND MECHANICS

CREATING VARIED AND INTERESTING SENTENCES

May in Ayemenem is a hot brooding month.

Arundhati Roy, *The God of Small Things*

Ten days after the war ended, my sister Laura drove a car off a bridge.

Margaret Atwood, *The Blind Assassin*

The small Catholic churches here are all the same, white clapboard drenched with snow or blistering under a northern sun, their interiors smelling of confessionals and pale statues of the Madonna.

David Adams Richards, *Mercy Among the Children*

Above the town, on the hill brow, the stone angel used to stand.

Margaret Laurence, *The Stone Angel*

By mistake Larry Weller took someone else's Harris tweed jacket instead of his own, and it wasn't till he jammed his hand in the pocket that he knew something was wrong.

Carol Shields, *Larry's Party*

All of the above are opening sentences of well-known Canadian novels. Notice the range and varying complexity of the sentence structures.

It is in the narrative form that you will generally find the most interesting and creative examples of finely crafted sentences. Writing narrative gives you the opportunity to develop the skill of creating your own varied sentences. But in order to experiment, you may need to reacquaint yourself with the essential building blocks of a sentence: clauses and phrases.

CLAUSES

A **clause** is a unit of words with a subject and a predicate, or an actor and an action. There are two kinds of clauses: independent or principal clauses and dependent or subordinate clauses.

An **independent** or **principal clause** can stand alone as a simple sentence. At the very least, it must have a subject (noun or pronoun) and a predicate (verb). The most basic simple sentence might be:

> John ran.

A simple sentence may also have a compound subject:

> John and Peter ran.

Most independent clauses or simple sentences, however, will also contain other descriptive words or phrases that extend the reader's understanding of the single idea.

> John, hurrying to be home in time for supper, ran furiously down the street.

Often two or more independent clauses or simple sentences are joined with a **conjunction** to make up a compound sentence. Writers create compound sentences to suggest that the two ideas contained in it are of equal value.

> Her mentor taught her about writing and her uncle introduced her to her first publisher.

Independent clauses are joined by words called **coordinating conjunctions**. There are only seven: *and*, *but*, *or*, *nor*, *for*, *so*, and *yet*.

Correlative conjunctions (*either … or, neither … nor, not only … but also, both … and*) also join words, phrases, or clauses.

> The boys and their parents are expected to participate in the fundraising event. *(coordinating conjunction joining equal parts of a compound subject in a simple sentence)*
>
> Not only the boys, but also their parents are expected to participate in the fundraising event. *(correlative conjunction joining equal parts of a compound subject in a simple sentence)*

All applicants for the position should have studied business at college or worked in a related field. *(coordinating conjunction joins two principal clauses in a compound sentence)*

All applicants for the position should have either studied business at college or worked in a related field. *(correlative conjunction joins two principal clauses in a compound sentence)*

When using correlative and coordinating conjunctions, it's important to make sure that the units on either side of the conjunction have the same grammatical form. Joining units with different grammatical forms is called **faulty parallelism**.

Faulty Parallelism	Revised
Ellen is not only an excellent dancer, but she is also a talented actress.	Ellen is not only an excellent dancer but also a talented actress.
Anil knows both clarinet and how to play the piano.	Anil knows both clarinet and piano.

Dependent or **subordinate clauses** also have a subject and a predicate, but cannot stand on their own. They depend on a principal clause for their meaning.

John ran furiously down the street because he thought he would be late for dinner.

"Because he thought he would be late for dinner" cannot stand alone as a sentence. The sentence requires the principal clause "John ran furiously down the street" in order for it to make sense. The subordinate clause does, however, have a subject "he" and a predicate "thought he would be late for dinner."

You can often identify subordinate clauses by the **subordinating conjunctions** or **relative pronouns** that introduce them. Here are some subordinating conjuctions: *after, because, in order that, although, before, in that, as even, if once, as if, even though, since, as soon as, how, so that, as though, if, than, that, until, where, though, when, wherever, unless, whenever, while*

Here are some relative pronouns:
that, whichever, whomever, what, who, whose, whatever, whoever, which, whom

Dependent or subordinate clauses are used in sentences either as nouns, adjectives, or adverbs. They are often named according to their use.

Subordinate noun clauses serve as subjects or objects/objective completions.

The adults had forgotten that rain can be fun.
What the children understood was awesome.

Subordinate adverb clauses modify or describe a verb, adjective, adverb, or entire sentence.

> When the rain stopped, things went slowly back to normal.
> No big changes had occurred where I live.

Subordinate adjective clauses describe a noun or pronoun.

> The weather radars had screens that were lit up green, gold, and red.
> The city, which had been dozing through another hot summer afternoon, shook itself into new life.

Some writers fail to distinguish between modifying clauses that are essential to the meaning of the sentence (restrictive clauses) and those that are not essential (non-restrictive clauses).

Restrictive clauses usually narrow or specify the meaning of the sentence in an essential way. They are almost always introduced with the word *that*. **Nonrestrictive clauses** are introduced by the word *which* and merely add additional information. Nonrestrictive clauses are set off by commas; restrictive clauses are not.

> The cemetery that contained the body of the famous poet was in France.
> The cemetery, which contained the body of the famous poet, was in France.

Think about what distinction the author is making in these two sentences.

A sentence that contains both an independent or principal clause and one or more dependent or subordinate clauses is called a **complex sentence**.

A sentence containing more than one principal clause and one or more subordinate clauses is called a **compound-complex sentence**.

PHRASES

A **phrase** is a group of grammatically related words. It differs from a clause in that it lacks either a subject or a complete verb.

> The raincoat, which was dripping wet, was hung on the rack. *(clause)*
> Dripping wet, the raincoat was hung on the rack. *(phrase)*

There are four types of phrases that serve as useful building blocks when crafting sentences.

Prepositional Phrases

A **prepositional phrase** consists of a preposition and its object (a noun, pronoun, and any modifiers).

Some common prepositions are:
about, concerning, regarding, outside, above, over, across, down, despite, against, except, excepting, since, past, after, during, through, among, along, for, throughout, around, from, to, as, in, toward, at, inside, under, underneath, behind, beneath, below, into, beside, near, before, until, between, on, like, unlike, of, up, off, upon, with, beyond, onto, within by, out, without

In addition, there are several prepositions of more than one word: *according to, due to, in spite of, along with, except for, instead of, aside from, in addition to, next to, because of, in front of, out of, by way of, in place of, with regard to*

Here are some examples of prepositional phrases:

> He climbed under the fence.
> The fire crept toward the subdivision.
> In the beginning, he was fearful of climbing the ropes.

Notice that three of these prepositions (*as, before, until*) have also been identified earlier as being subordinate conjunctions, used to begin subordinate clauses.

> Before the rain, the ground was dry. (*prepositional phrase*)
> Before the rain fell, the ground was dry. (*subordinate clause*)

A subordinate clause is distinguished from a phrase in that it contains a subject (*the rain*) and a predicate (*fell*). A phrase contains no predicate.

Gerund Phrases

A **gerund** is a verb form that ends in *ing* and functions as a noun.

> Parking in the city is impossible.
> She enjoys skating.
> They accused him of cheating.

A **gerund phrase** combines the gerund with a noun or adverb. Consider the following examples:

> Fixing shoes is a lucrative business.
> Sam enjoys hunting deer.
> Falling down can be painful and injurious.

Because a gerund has the value of a noun, a noun or pronoun used to modify it must be in the possessive case.

> Carol's wanting cake irritated her friend. *not* Carol wanting cake ...
> My stopping smoking was very difficult. *not* Me stopping smoking ...

Infinitive Phrases

An **infinitive** is the form of the verb preceded by *to*, e.g., *to run, to fly*. Infinitives can function as subjects, objects, and complements in sentences. Combined with their modifiers, they form infinitive phrases.

> To lean precariously out of a window is dangerous.
> I wanted to be madly in love by the time I was twenty.
> Peter intended to hitchhike all the way to Saskatoon.

Participial Phrases

A **participle** is the *ing* or *ed* form of a verb. A **participial phrase** serves as an adjective to describe a noun or pronoun. A participial phrase combines the participle and any modifying or completing words associated with it.

> Turning red with embarrassment, Joseph walked away.
> Slowly turning her head, she offered a coy smile.
> He left the stage, pleased with his performance.

Sometimes a participial phrase modifies a whole sentence rather than a single noun or pronoun. It is then called an **absolute phrase**.

> The storm having cleared the air, we decided to go for a walk after dinner.
> *(The absolute phrase explains the context for the subsequent action described in the rest of the sentence.)*

Make sure that you distinguish between an absolute phrase, which modifies a whole sentence, and a **dangling modifier**, which is an error in sentence structure because it does not describe anything in the sentence.

> Running quickly, the train was reached.

A **misplaced modifier** is also an error in sentence structure. Misplaced modifiers are phrases that are located closer to words they don't modify than to words they do. The results are often quite humorous.

> Hanging over the fireplace, Jack showed us his new painting.

Presenting Narrative Texts: Readers' Theatre

One way of presenting a short story is to dramatize it. This involves rewriting a key episode or telescoping the entire story into a shorter script and then reading it aloud in a dramatic way. **Readers' theatre** is one way to present a dramatic reading. Few actions or props are involved. Whether they sit or stand, readers communicate the plot, characterization, and theme through gestures, facial expressions, and voice qualities. Stories that have strong characters, well-developed conflicts, and distinctive language are particularly appropriate for readers' theatre.

Preparation

- *Discuss what section of the story will be scripted or whether the entire short story will be telescoped into a short script.*
- *Discuss the nature of the characters, conflict, and theme.*
- *Work with a group to select parts of dialogue and details that are most important to carry the narrative line.*
- *Write each character's dialogue from the story. Adapt the narrative viewpoint to provide background information about the setting and characters or to connect events in the story.*
- *The rewriting process requires some time, patience, and effective compromise to arrive at a finished product of high quality.*
- *Once the script is in place and agreed upon, each reader assumes the role of one of the characters. Each reader must interpret each role through gestures, facial expression, and voice quality.*

Rehearsing the Script

- *Try out different expressions or gestures—you'll begin to read more fluently until you deliver the lines as an actor would.*

- *A **read-through** is the first time the cast gets together to read the script. Keep going even if someone makes a mistake or has a problem. Remember, you're trying to establish the overall flow of the episode. Details can come later.*

- *Don't rush your lines. A well-placed pause can be very effective.*

- *Handle the rhythm of the lines delicately—don't get into a sing-song voice.*

- *After the read-through, talk about how you think it sounded. If one actor had some trouble reading, other actors could offer advice. Remember that this is an ensemble effort.*

- *As a group, change anything that you now understand differently.*

- *Practise reading the script several times. The emphasis is not on production quality, but rather on dramatic reading and the interpretive quality of the readers' voices and expressions.*

- *Costumes and props are unnecessary; however, adding a few props enhances interest and enjoyment, as long as they don't interfere with the dramatic quality of the reading.*

Staging the Performance

- *Readers' theatre can be presented on a stage or in a corner of the classroom. You stand or sit and read your lines in the script. You must stay in position through the presentation.*

- *Readers hold copies of the script as they read, or scripts can be placed on music stands.*

- *Readers may choose to look at a point over the heads of the audience, unless they decide together to interact in appropriate ways (e.g., looking at another reader while speaking).*

- *The audience members are seated and listen attentively as they use their imaginations to enjoy the readers' interpretation of the script.*

After Participating in Readers' Theatre

- *The group may wish to talk with the class about their interpretation. Comparing views and suggesting alternative interpretations can expand your understanding of the characters and themes.*

Checklist

Presentation	
Do the characters sound as though they are actually speaking, not reading?	❑
Does each character have a distinctive voice?	❑
Is the pace of the reading appropriate to the mood—not too fast or too slow?	❑
While not reading, do the other characters listen attentively?	❑
Interpretation	
Do the actors use facial expressions and body movements to interpret the meaning of their lines?	❑
Do the actors work together to create a whole episode with a single interpretation?	❑
Is the mood consistent throughout the entire episode?	❑
Does the presentation make the meaning of the episode clear?	❑

CHAPTER 3

drama

> In listening to a play on a stage or on film,
> you have to listen as carefully as you do to music.
> *Northrop Frye*

> Drama is life with the dull bits left out.
> *Alfred Hitchcock*

Drama is meant to be seen rather than simply read. Its meaning can only be fully appreciated when actually experienced in performance. This makes it a much more public form than prose or poetry.

The word *drama* comes from the Greek word meaning "action" or "doing." Drama had its beginnings in the religious ceremonies of ancient Greece. Comedy and tragedy, the two fundamental types of drama, both originated with celebrations connected to Dionysus, the Greek god of fertility. Whereas comedy developed from the fertility festivals associated with Dionysus, tragedy came from Dionysian rites dealing with life and death. In Asia, rich theatrical experiences incorporate music, dance, mask, and puppets. The Kabuki and Noh theatre of Japan, the opera of China, and the shadow puppet plays of Indonesia are examples of the more formalized traditions of Eastern theatre.

LEARNING GOALS

- understand the form and structure of the play
- understand the methods used to communicate plot, themes, and issues
- examine stylistic devices
- develop the skills to write short dramatic works
- present an effective drama

CONTENTS

Analyzing and Responding to Drama

» CHECKPOINT: *Assess Your Knowledge*

the fighting days

Place: office of *The Rural Review*, a farm newspaper published in Winnipeg
Time: 1912 or 1913
Characters: Francis, George McNair

Shortly after arriving in Winnipeg, Francis lands a job writing for the women's page of *The Rural Review*. Influenced by Nellie McClung, who is a friend of Francis's sister Lily, she has transformed the women's page into a forum for women's suffrage. Francis's editor George McNair views this transformation with wry amusement. One senses that he tolerates Francis's opinion because he is in love with her; he will later ask her to marry him.

McNair: Let's see what you've got on your page this week. (*He pulls the page out of the typewriter and begins to read aloud*)
"We have too long been contented with the kind of motherhood that can turn its back on mere children toiling incredible hours in factories making bullets and ammunition and uniforms for some faraway war and yet calmly say, 'Thank God it's not my children.' What we need now is a new spirit of national motherhood." And someone who can write shorter sentences. National motherhood. National motherhood? You make it sound like the railway, Miss Beynon.
Francis: (*Deflated*) I quite liked that expression.
McNair: Is it yours?
Francis: Well ...
McNair: It sounds like something off of Mrs. McClung's bat. You seem to have an opinion about everything lately. National motherhood, intemperate husbands, the German war machine, the profession of parenthood, the Boy Scout movement, and suffrage ad nauseum. But I find myself wondering ... what happened to your columns on mothers and babies, ginger snaps and peonies? What about the little crocheted sweaters for the wee ones.

Hmmmm? What about those things? They're important, too.

Francis: Do you think they are more important than freedom from cruel husbands and fathers, from hypocritical ministers, from war-mongering politicians?

McNair: Oh, don't bludgeon me with adjectives. Just say what you mean.

Francis: I'm sorry.

McNair: Unfortunately, the things you mention will always be with us. Scotch broth and shortbread and a garden full of bluebells make them a bit more tolerable. My mother knew that. She would never have bothered herself with voting and chasing men out of bars.

Francis: But was she happy?

McNair: Happy? I don't know. She seemed content. She smiled a lot.

Francis: You mean she just put up with it.

McNair: Perhaps. But the point is, she had enough to do in the home. You'll be wise to keep that in mind.

Francis: If you think that women belong in the home, why did you hire me?

McNair: I had no choice. What self-respecting man would want to write about "women's things"? Unfortunately, you don't seem interested in writing about them either.

Francis: Mr. McNair, are you not finding my work satisfactory?

McNair: Did I say that?

Francis: You imply that.

McNair: I do not. I think that the suffrage question is … interesting, but you take it much too far. Mrs. McClung need only pen one of her silly little verses and it somehow finds its way into your editorials.

Francis: Mrs. McClung is at the forefront of the suffrage cause.

McNair: She is a dilettante and a debutante. And a hypocrite. She's an upper class snob who wouldn't have given my poor mother the time of day.

Francis: That's not true. Nellie McClung is fighting for the vote for women.

McNair: For women who don't need the vote. For women who've got something better than the vote! Influence! And furthermore, the proper lineage!

Francis: No!

McNair: No? Then tell me why your suffrage club list is full of names like Stewart, Titheradge, Ward, Galbraith, Gordon, and not … Lewycky, Schapansky and Swartz?

Francis: Well, maybe their husbands won't let them come.

McNair: They're not there because your suffrage club doesn't want them there. Neither do they want them living next to them on Chestnut Street nor their children sitting beside theirs at school.

Francis: Mr. McNair, I believe in democracy for ALL women. I do!
McNair: Then you're in the minority. Isobel Graham has gone on record saying she's afraid the entire western hemisphere is sinking under the weight of the immigrants.
Francis: Isobel has … a blind spot.
McNair: And Laura McLaughlin, another one of your leading lights, is heading up the fight to eliminate any foreign language in the schoolyard.
Francis: That's because Laura thinks it's important that newcomers learn English.
McNair: That's because she hates the very idea of them.
Francis: I admit there are some members who don't feel comfortable with all the strangers in our midst, but that will change. It takes time to alter attitudes. It takes time to remove the walls of class and privilege and ethnic differences that …
McNair: Oh don't start that again! The fact is the suffragists are an exclusive club. And you'd do well to stay away from them.
Francis: I find it curious how you suddenly spring to the defence of foreign women. Because in the year that I've known you, you have never shown interest in ANY women having the vote, whether their name was Gordon or Schapansky! I'm beginning to think that you just enjoy muddying the waters!
McNair: (*Winking*) I enjoy arguing with you. You argue like a man!
Francis: Well, I am not.
McNair: And I'm glad you're not.
Francis: (*Flustered*) I believe in the vote for women, all women, and I am going to keep fighting for it.
McNair: Now don't get so flustered. It's not that important, is it?
Francis: Mr. McNair, let me try to explain something to you. When I was a child, on the farm, I was constantly asking questions. Does God ever change his mind? Why was he angry all the time? Why couldn't I talk to the Polish children on the next farm? Why didn't my father help them out like the other neighbours? But nobody wanted to answer my questions. There seemed to be a secret fraternity at work that I didn't understand. My father and the Methodist minister and later my teachers thrashed and sermonized and ridiculed me until my spirit shrank and I began to doubt my very worth.
McNair: It doesn't seem to have been a lasting affliction. You seem to have quite an unswerving confidence.
Francis: Well, I don't. I still cower at the voice of authority. Even now, I tense up as you, my editor, come into the room. Do you understand what I'm talking about?
McNair: Yes, I think so, but I'm not sure what it has to do with suffrage.

Francis: Oh, but it's all connected! When I came to the city, I met women fighting for the freedom to think and worship and question for themselves. Women who challenge authority ... who look men in the eye and say, prove you're worthy of respect! I felt like I'd been let out of prison. I felt like a great gleam of sunlight had broken through the fog. And I didn't feel alone any more!

McNair: You're a funny one. You remind me of those little birds found trapped in the house when I was a child. My mother would make me catch them and let them go free outside. And when I caught them, I could feel their little hearts beating in my hands. I wanted to tell them not to be afraid, that I wasn't going to hurt them. You're like one of those little birds. Miss Beynon, I understand you live alone since your sister married. Perhaps you might be needing someone to look in on you once in a while.

Francis: I would like that very much.

McNair: Good, then. I will do that. It's time you associated with someone who still holds womanhood sacred.

Francis: No! I don't need anyone to hold womanhood sacred. I hold womanhood sacred myself. I do!

McNair: Well, you hold it at quite a distance. It might help you—if you applied some rouge to your cheeks occasionally. Good day, Miss Beynon, I'll let you get back to national motherhood.

Wendy Lill

1. What do you learn about the suffrage movement in Canada from reading this scene?
2. Explain how Wendy Lill creates dramatic tension.
3. This scene contains minimal stage directions. Consider the few that are included. Why are they there?
4. Explain what you learn about the two characters in this scene, a) directly, from what they say, and b) indirectly, through inference.

Reading Strategies

As you read a play, keep in mind the total experience of what transpires on the stage. The playwright provides the bones of the play. But the actor's interpretation of character, the director's vision, and the technician's skill in stagecraft are all crucial contributions. So it's important to try to visualize the play—to bring it alive in your mind, to see and hear the action as if you were watching it at the theatre.

Bringing a Play to Life

- *Plan group read-alouds, where everyone is assigned a different part.*
- *As you read, notice not only what the characters are saying, but also what they are doing. If you are working with a group, trying acting out some of the scenes. Use any stage directions that the playwright has provided, as well as what the dialogue itself may suggest to you.*
- *Be receptive to inference; that is, to what you may deduce from the dialogue and stage directions. A great deal of the information provided by dialogue comes from what is not said, or from what is stated indirectly. Silences are often important.*
- *Read the stage directions and character lists carefully. Often they contain important information or clues about the characters, plot, or mood of the play.*
- *Go to plays, if you can. Seeing different plays helps you understand the dramatic conventions used by playwrights.*
- *Listen to audiotapes or watch video recordings of plays.*
- *Research any background information that might help you to understand the script. Your research might focus on the playwright, the time period in which the play was written, and the issue or event on which the play is based.*

Understanding Meaning

Issues and themes are embedded in any play, and you must be able to identify them and see how they are developed. To identify these issues and themes on the basis of plot alone is not enough. *Romeo and Juliet*, for example, isn't simply about two young lovers who try to make a life for themselves and fail. Rather, it is through the interactions of the various characters that Shakespeare weaves a tale of family conflict, rivalry, jealousy, and pride.

The ideas, themes, and issues explored in a play may be expressed directly by the actual characters. Or, they may be presented indirectly, as the issue around which the characters react.

INTERPRETING CHARACTER

We can understand the play's meaning by interpreting what the characters in the play say and do.

Considerations of Character

- *What do the characters say about themselves?*
- *What do others say about them?*

- *How do they speak?*
- *What do they do when speaking (e.g., gestures, facial expressions)?*
- *What do they do when they're silent?*
- *How do they look?*
- *How do their words match their deeds and motives?*

There are two sources for this information in a play: the **dialogue** and the **stage directions** (which are usually italicized and put within brackets scattered throughout the text).

Read the two excerpts that follow. The first illustrates the importance of dialogue in portraying a character, and the second emphasizes stage directions. What do you learn about the theme or issues of the play from each?

G.B.: Well, well, lots o' snow you got out here, eh? Afternoon, Miz' Cochran. Hi Grandpop! Holy gol, what are you doin' in that get-up for Pete sake?
Pop: Awright now, G.B.; awright; say your say and don't be all day over it. I'm busy.
Ethel: Poppa, what a way to talk to a man who's just come in out of the cold. Will you have a cup of tea, Mr. Bailey?
G.B.: Sure, thanks, if you got it handy.
Ethel: Right on the stove; always keep some going.
G.B.: Now then, Grandpop, what's the big idea? Gettin' ready for an Orange Walk, or something?
Pop: If you got to know, I'm listenin' to the op'ry on the radio. I listen every Saturday afternoon. I'm a paid-up member of the Op'ry Radio Guild, same as Miz' August Belmont. This hat is what's called an op'ry hat, but I guess you wouldn't understand about that.
G.B.: (*uproarious*): Holy smoke! And what's the idea of the furnace-man's gloves?
Pop: In New York white gloves for the op'ry are *dee rigger*. That's French for you can't get in without 'em.
G.B.: (*choking*) Well by gollies, now I seen everything.
Pop: No you ain't: you ain't seen nothin', nor been anywheres. That's what's wrong with you and a lot more like you. Now what do you want?

Robertson Davies, *Overlaid*

Edward: Why don't you go for a walk once in a while?
Leopold: Are you mad? Go out?
Edward: Why not?
Leopold: And be a nervous wreck the whole time, not knowing what's going on back here?

Edward: Nothing's going on back here—
Leopold: I know, but how am I going to know that if I'm gadding about somewhere else? What if they came just then?
Edward: They'd find you weren't at home. So what?
Leopold: I couldn't possibly—
(At that moment the doorbell rings. Leopold jumps up in confusion. Edward gets up as well. Leopold goes to the peep-hole and looks through it and then turns towards Edward.)
Leopold: (*Whispering*) What did I tell you!
Edward: (*Whispering*) Is it them?
(*Leopold nods. They pause, at a loss. The bell rings again.*)
Leopold: (*Whispering*) Should I open the door?
Edward: (*Whispering*) Yes, you have to—
(Leopold hesitates a moment, then breathes in, goes to the door and opens it decisively. The newcomers are First Sidney and Second Sidney.)
First Sidney: Good afternoon, sir—
Leopold: Good afternoon—
Second Sidney: Can we come in?
Leopold: Do ...
(First Sidney and Second Sidney come forward a few paces. Leopold closes the door behind them. They all remain standing and looking at each other somewhat at a loss.)
First Sidney: You don't remember us?
Leopold: I can't place you at the moment—
First Sidney: We called on you once before, two years ago. You've obviously forgotten. I'm Sidney and he's also Sidney—
Leopold: How do you do—
Second Sidney: We won't hold you up long—
Leopold: (*Perplexed*) Well, do sit down—

Vaclav Havel (translated by Tom Stoppard), *Largo Desolato*

INTERPRETING SETTING

Stage directions also contain information about the **setting** of the play. A playwright will often describe the placement of furniture; the size, shape, and colour of the props; and even the style and colour of the costumes worn by the characters. There may also be instructions as to the level and shades of the lighting on stage. All these descriptions can provide us with important insights into the themes and issues of the play.

Some playwrights use the play's setting to echo or symbolize what is happening emotionally to the characters. This is called **pathetic fallacy**. A famous example of this is found in Shakespeare's *King Lear*, when the king's anguish and madness is echoed in the fury of the storm raging around him.

Consider this description of a setting:

> *Place: The doorstep and clearing outside Josephina's cabin on the reserve ...*
>
> *As the play opens Martha and Josephina are sitting one on either side of the fire, Josephina on the bench at stage right. From a house off stage comes the sad thin sound of a harmonica very well played ... the unseen player improvises a plaintive tune, slides into some cowboy folk song, then returns to his improvisation. Somewhere in another long house the player, a boy of fifteen, lies on a ragged mattress, looking up at the chinks of light that filter through the roof, and plays his music. The sound recurs from time to time during the play and is never obtrusive, merely a part of the place.*
>
> *Martha wears a dark cotton print dress, almost to her ankles, and heavy shoes. She has a dark shawl or jacket around her shoulders. Her hair is tied back. She is smoking a cigarette. Martha is about 60 years old.*
>
> *Josephina is dressed in a long dark skirt, dark blouse and shapeless sweater. Heavy low black shoes and dark stockings. Her hair is in two long braids and is very black. She is older than Martha. She is broad and stocky with a strong patient face.*
>
> Gwen Pharis Ringwood, *Lament for Harmonica (Maya)*

Note how the playwright sets the mood of the play through the spareness of its setting, the melancholy of the harmonica player and his tune, and the dark shades of the women's clothing.

THE CONCEPT OF SATIRE

Playwrights write about the human condition in society. Sometimes they choose to satirize or make fun of the foolishness of social customs, beliefs, and traditions. Writers of **satire** may mock trivial things like the hypocrisy or artificiality of individuals. They may also use wit to attack larger issues in hope of stirring social change.

When interpreting the meaning of the play, the viewer or reader must be able to identify **satirical tone** if it is present in the script. Otherwise, your interpretation might be the exact opposite of what the playwright intended!

Examine the following scene. The annotations point out the elements of setting, dialogue, and stage directions that contribute to the overall meaning of the play.

the glass menagerie

On the dark stage the screen is lighted with the image of blue roses.

Gradually Laura's figure becomes apparent and the screen goes out.

The music subsides.

Laura is seated in the delicate ivory chair at the small clawfoot table.

She wears a dress of soft violet material for a kimono—her hair tied back from her forehead with a ribbon.

textures: soft
colours: pale
=Laura

She is washing and polishing her collection of glass.

Amanda appears on the fire-escape steps. At the sound of her ascent, Laura catches her breath, thrusts the bowl of ornaments away and seats herself stiffly before the diagram of the typewriter keyboard as though it held her spellbound. Something has happened to Amanda. It is written in her face as she climbs to the landing; a look that is grim and hopeless and a little absurd.

infer that she is hiding the ornaments (doesn't want her mother to see them)

She has on one of those cheap or imitation velvety-looking cloth coats with imitation fur collar. Her hat is five or six years old, one of those dreadful cloche hats that were worn in the late twenties, and she is clasping an enormous black patent-leather pocketbook with nickel clasp and initials. This is her full-dress outfit, the one she usually wears to the D.A.R.

imitation
old-fashioned
black/grey tones
= Amanda

Before entering she looks through the door.

She purses her lips, opens her eyes wide, rolls them upward and shakes her head.

Then she slowly lets herself in the door. Seeing her mother's expression Laura touches her lips with a nervous gesture.

Laura: Hello, Mother, I was—(*She makes a nervous gesture toward the chart on the wall. Amanda leans against the shut door and stares at Laura with a martyred look.*)

Amanda: Deception? Deception? (*She slowly removes her hat and gloves, continuing the swift suffering stare. She lets the hat and gloves fall on the floor—a bit of acting.*)

Laura (*shakily*): How was the D.A.R. meeting? (*Amanda slowly opens her purse and removes a dainty white handkerchief which she shakes out delicately and delicately touches to her lips and nostrils.*) Didn't you go to the D.A.R. meeting Mother?

note Amanda's exaggerated, melodramatic gestures and expressions

Amanda (*faintly, almost inaudibly*): —No.—No. (*Then more forcibly.*) I did not have the strength—to go to the D.A.R. In fact, I did not have the courage! I wanted to find a hole in the ground and hide myself in it forever! (*She crosses slowly to the wall and removes the diagram of the typewriter keyboard. She holds it in front of her for a second, staring at it sweetly and sorrowfully—then bites her lips and tears it in two pieces.*)

Amanda finds the way to make Laura's problems the cause of her shame, creating guilt

Laura (*faintly*): Why did you do that, Mother? (*Amanda repeats the same procedure with the chart of the Gregg Alphabet.*) Why are you—

Amanda: Why? Why? How old are you, Laura?

Laura: Mother, you know my age.

Amanda: I thought that you were an adult; it seems that I was mistaken. (*She crosses slowly to the sofa and sinks down and stares at Laura.*)

Laura: Please don't stare at me, Mother.

Amanda closes her eyes and lowers her head. Count ten.

question surrounded on both sides by silence

Amanda: What are you going to do, what is going to become of us, what is the future?

Count ten.

Laura: Has something happened, Mother? (*Amanda draws a long breath and takes out the handkerchief again. Dabbing process.*) Mother, has—something happened?

Amanda: I'll be all right in a minute. I'm just bewildered—(*count five*)—by life …

Laura: Mother, I wish that you would tell me what's happened.

Amanda: As you know, I was supposed to be inducted into my office at the D.A.R. this afternoon. (**Image: A Swarm of Typewriters.**) But I stopped off at Rubicam's Business College to speak to your teachers about your having a cold and ask them what progress they thought you were making down there.

Laura: Oh …

Amanda: I went to the typing instructor and introduced myself as your mother. She didn't know who you were. Wingfield, she said. We don't have any such student enrolled at the school! I assured her she did, that you had been going to classes since early in January. "I wonder," she said, "if you could be talking about that terribly shy little girl who dropped out of school after only a few days' attendance?" "No," I said, "Laura, my daughter, has been going to school every day for the past six weeks!" "Excuse me," she said. She took the attendance book out and there was your name, unmistakably printed, and all the dates you were absent until they decided that you had dropped out of school. I still said, "No, there must have been some mistake! There must have been some mix-up in the records!" And she said, "No—I remember her perfectly now. Her hand shook so that she couldn't hit the right keys! The first time we gave a speed-test, she broke down completely—was sick at the stomach and almost had to be carried into the wash-room! After that morning she never showed up any more. We phoned the house but never got any answer"—while I was working at Famous and Barr, I suppose, demonstrating those—Oh! I felt so weak I could barely keep on my feet. I had to sit down while they got me a glass of water! Fifty dollars' tuition, all of our plans—my hopes and ambitions for you—just gone up the spout, just gone up the spout like that. (*Laura draws a long breath and gets awkwardly to her feet. She crosses to the victrola and winds it up.*) What are you doing?

Laura's character as revealed in another context

note Laura's response to Amanda's recounting of the story

Laura: Oh! (*She releases the handle and returns to her seat.*)
Amanda: Laura, where have you been going when you've gone out pretending that you were going to business college?
Laura: I've just been going out walking.
Amanda: That's not true.
Laura: It is. I just went walking.
Amanda: Walking? Walking? In winter? Deliberately courting pneumonia in that light coat? Where did you walk to, Laura?
Laura: It was the lesser of two evils, Mother. (**Image: Winter Scene In Park.**) I couldn't go back. I—threw up—on the floor!
Amanda: From half past seven till after five every day you mean to tell me you walked around in the park, because you wanted to make me think that you were still going to Rubicam's Business College?
Laura: It wasn't as bad as it sounds. I went inside places to get warmed up.
Amanda: Inside where?
Laura: I went in the art museum and the bird-house at the Zoo. I visited the penguins every day! Sometimes I did without lunch and went to the movies. Lately I've been spending most of my afternoons in the Jewel-box, that big glass house where they raise the tropical flowers.

places of interest to Laura reveal character qualities

Amanda: You did all this to deceive me, just for the deception? (*Laura looks down.*) Why?
Laura: Mother, when you're disappointed, you get that awful suffering look on your face, like the picture of Jesus' mother in the museum!
Amanda: Hush!

note Amanda's reaction to Laura's explanation

Laura: I couldn't face it.

Pause: A whisper of strings.

(**Legend: "The Crust Of Humility."**)

Amanda (*hopelessly fingering the huge pocketbook*): So what are we going to do the rest of our lives?

importance of this gesture? note change in pronoun (we)

Stay home and watch the parades go by? Amuse ourselves with the glass menagerie, darling? Eternally play those worn-out phonograph records your father left as a painful reminder of him? We won't have a business career—we've given that up because it gave us nervous indigestion! (*Laughs wearily.*) What is there left but dependence all our lives? I know so well what becomes of unmarried women who aren't prepared to occupy a position. I've seen such pitiful cases in the South—barely tolerated spinsters living upon the grudging patronage of sister's husband or brother's wife!—stuck away in some little mouse-trap of a room —encouraged by one in-law to visit another— little birdlike women without any nest—eating the crust of humility all their life! Is that the future that we've mapped out for ourselves? I swear it's the only alternative I can think of! It isn't a very pleasant alternative, is it? Of course—some girls *do marry*. (*Laura twists her hands nervously.*) Haven't you ever liked some boy?

we infer that father has deserted them

note Laura's nonverbal response

Laura: Yes I liked one once. (*Rises.*) I came across his picture a while ago.

Amanda (*with some interest*): He gave you his picture?

Laura: No, it's in the year-book.

Amanda (*disappointed*): Oh—a high-school boy.

why is Amanda disappointed?

(Screen Image: Jim As A High-School Hero Bearing A Silver Cup.)

Laura: Yes. His name was Jim. (*Laura lifts the heavy annual from the clawfoot table.*) Here he is in *The Pirates of Penzance.*

Amanda (*absently*): The what?

Laura: The operetta the senior class put on. He had a wonderful voice and we sat across the aisle from each other Mondays, Wednesdays, and Fridays in the Aud. Here he is with the silver cup for debating! See his grin?

Amanda (*absently*): He must have had a jolly disposition.

Laura: He used to call me—Blue Roses.

(Image: Blue Roses.)

Amanda: Why did he call you such a name as that?

we learn about Jim's character/personality from Laura's account of him (how he responded to her; his interests)

Laura: When I had the attack of pleurosis—he asked me what was the matter when I came back. I said pleurosis—he thought I said Blue Roses! So that's what he always called me after that. Whenever he saw me, he'd holler, "Hello, Blue Roses!" I didn't care for the girl he went out with. Emily Meisenbach. Emily was the best-dressed girl at Soldan. She never struck me, though, as being sincere ... It says in the Personal Section—they're engaged. That's—six years ago! They must be married by now.

Amanda: Girls that aren't cut out for business careers usually wind up married to some nice man. (*Gets up with a spark of revival.*) Sister, that's what you'll do!

Laura utters a startled, doubtful laugh. She reaches quickly for a piece of glass.

Laura's glass a refuge, security

Laura: But, Mother—
Amanda: yes? (*Crossing to phonograph.*)
Laura (*in a tone of frightened apology*): I'm—crippled!

(Image: Screen.)

manda refuses to cknowledge Laura's ifferences

Amanda: Nonsense! Laura, I've told you never, never to use that word. Why, you're not crippled, you just have a little defect—hardly noticeable, even! When people have some slight disadvantage like that, they cultivate other things to make up for it—develop charm—a vivacity—and—*charm!* That's all you have to do! (*She turns again to the phonograph.*) One thing your father had *plenty of*—was *charm!*

focus on charm as a solution and an excuse

Tom motions to the fiddle in the wings.

(The Scene Fades Out With Music.)

Tennessee Williams

Understanding Form

INTERNAL STRUCTURE: PLOT

Dramatic form refers to the way the play is put together—the sequencing and pacing of the action. The playwright is concerned first and foremost with developing audience response. He or she must maintain a pace for the play that captures and holds the audience's interest.

The play must be structured so that it moves the **action** on from one episode to the next. The members of the audience must quickly develop an interest in both the characters in the play and the situation itself. Prior to breaks in the play, when there is an intermission required, the playwright must create high points or moments of crisis. The playwright must constantly challenge the audience by creating expectations and surprise.

The structure of a play usually follows a basic pattern. The elements in this pattern (described below) make up the **plot** structure. One-act plays usually contain only one plot. Longer plays may, and often do, contain one main plot and a number of subplots.

A **subplot** is a secondary arrangement of incidents involving secondary characters who are involved in a situation that poses a second dramatic question. For example, if two of the characters in a murder mystery happened to fall in love—thus posing the dramatic question "Will they live happily ever after?"—the audience would recognize and demand resolution to this subplot.

EXPOSITION

The **exposition** is the section that begins the play, introduces the characters, and provides the background information. In a one-act play the exposition may take just a few pages. In a multi-act play the exposition may take up the complete opening scene.

The way that a play begins is crucial to engaging the audience's attention. A playwright must decide what effect the scene is to have on the audience, and what purpose it serves in the play as a whole.

Purposes of Exposition

- *provides an explanation of the plot so far—background information and details that the audience needs to understand what is going on*
- *creates a setting or background against which the play is set*
- *creates a mood or a tension that captures the audience's attention*
- *introduces characters, situations, and relationships*
- *provokes a sense of intrigue that captures the audience's attention and makes them want to know more*

DRAMATIC INCITEMENT

The incident that provides the starting point for the main action of the play is known as the **dramatic incitement**. Usually a dilemma is presented or a problem is identified that needs to be solved. The dramatic incitement often ends up posing the play's dramatic question.

For example, if the dramatic incitement in a murder mystery is the murder of one of the characters, the **dramatic question** that must be answered is "Will the murderer be discovered?" In a multi-act play, the dramatic incitement often occurs at the end of the first scene.

COMPLICATION

The **complication** usually forms the main action of the play. The characters respond to the dramatic incitement and other developments that may stem from it. Similar to a short story or novel, this part of the play is sometimes called the **rising action**.

CLIMAX

The **climax** or **crisis** usually occurs late in the play. It is the moment when the play's dramatic question is answered.

RESOLUTION

The **resolution** is the final section of the play, in which things are worked out and the conclusion reached. Sometimes this section of the play is called the **denouement**.

EXTERNAL STRUCTURE: CLASSIFICATIONS OF DRAMATIC FORM

While the internal structure of almost all plays is the same, plays receive other designations based on the nature of the action that occurs.

Tragedy is a serious play that dramatizes the disastrous downfall of the central character. According to Aristotle, tragedy must achieve a **catharsis** (purification) in the audience by presenting incidents that arouse both fear and pity. The downfall of the protagonist is the result of his or her own tragic flaw, which takes the form of **hubris**, or excessive pride. The character suffers **divine retribution** or **nemesis** at the hands of the gods or fate. Modern tragedies often depict the hero caught in domestic or social crisis. Willie Loman in Arthur Miller's *Death of a Salesman* is a classic modern tragic figure.

Comedy is a play written chiefly to amuse and entertain the audience members by allowing them to feel a sense of superiority over the characters. Comedies usually represent ordinary life and explore common human frailties. The ending is usually happy for the leading characters. Comedy takes many forms, including romantic comedy, satire, comedy of manners, farce, black comedy, and burlesque.

Tragicomedy is a play that combines elements of tragedy and comedy. The play might provide a happy ending to a potentially tragic story, or it might combine serious and light moods.

Melodrama is a form of sensational drama that first became popular in the 1800s and that we now often see in television and movies. Melodrama provides its audiences with larger-than-life, one-dimensional characters of either pure innocence or great villainy. The conflict is emotionally exaggerated and often simplistic. Batman movies are a good example of modern melodrama.

The opening scene of Shakespeare's play *Hamlet* provides an illustration of the basic elements of form.

hamlet

Act I
Scene I (Elsinore Castle. A Guard Platform.)
Enter Bernard and Francisco, two sentinels, (meeting).

Bernardo: Who's there?
Francisco: Nay, answer me. Stand and unfold yourself.
Bernardo: Long live the king!
Francisco: Bernardo?
Bernardo: He.
Francisco: You come most carefully upon your hour.
Bernardo: 'Tis now struck twelve. Get thee to bed,
Francisco.
Francisco: For this relief much thanks. 'Tis bitter cold,
And I am sick at heart.
Bernardo: Have you had quiet guard?
Francisco: Not a mouse stirring.
Bernardo: Well, good night.
If you do meet Horatio and Marcellus,
The rivals of my watch, bid them make haste.

Enter Horatio and Marcellus.

Francisco: I think I hear them.—Stand, ho! Who is there?
Horatio: Friends to this ground.
Marcellus: And liegemen to the Dane.
Francisco: Give you good night.

short, shouted sentences capture audience attention

setting: guard platform, midnight, cold—eerie, desolate

Francisco describes himself as "sick at heart": Why?

more information on Denmark setting

Marcellus: O, farewell, honest soldier. Who hath
relieved you?
Francisco: Bernardo hath my place. Give you good night.

Exit Francisco.

Marcellus: Holla! Bernardo!
Bernardo: Say, what, is Horatio there?
Horatio: A piece of him.
Bernardo: Welcome, Horatio. Welcome, good Marcellus.
Horatio: What, has this thing appeared again tonight?
Bernardo: I have seen nothing.
Marcellus: Horatio says 'tis but our fantasy,
And will not let belief take hold of him
Touching this dreaded sight twice seen of us.
Therefore I have entreated him along
With us to watch the minutes of this night,
That if again this apparition come
He may approve our eyes and speak to it.
Horatio: Tush, tush, 'twill not appear.
Bernardo: Sit down awhile,
And let us once again assail your ears,
That are so fortified against our story,
What we have two nights seen.
Horatio: Well, sit we down,
And let us hear Bernardo speak of this.
Bernardo: Last night of all,
When yond same star that's westward from the pole
Had made his course t' illume that part of heaven
Where now it burns, Marcellus and myself,
The bell then beating one—

past experience: they have seen a "dreaded sight" on two previous occasions

Enter Ghost.

device to capture audience interest; raises suspense, anxiety

Marcellus: Peace, break thee off! Look where it
comes again!
Bernardo: In the same figure like the King that's dead.
Marcellus: Thou art a scholar. Speak to it, Horatio.
Bernardo: Looks 'a not like the King? Mark it, Horatio.
Horatio: Most like. It harrows me with fear and wonder.
Bernardo: It would be spoken to.

background information: king has died

Marcellus: Speak to it, Horatio.
Horatio: What are thou that usurp'st this time of night,
Together with that fair and warlike form
In which the majesty of buried Denmark
Did sometime march? By heaven, I charge thee, speak!
Marcellus: It is offended.
Bernardo: See, it stalks away.
Horatio: Stay! Speak, speak! I charge thee, speak!

Exit Ghost.

Marcellus: 'Tis gone and will not answer.
Bernardo: How now, Horatio? You tremble
and look pale.
Is not this something more than fantasy?
What think you on 't?
Horatio: Before my God, I might not this believe
Without the sensible and true avouch
Of mine own eyes.
Marcellus: Is it not like the King?
Horatio: As thou art to thyself.
Such was the very armor he had on
When he the ambitious Norway combated.
So frowned he once when, in an angry parle,
He smote the sledded Polacks on the ice.
'Tis strange.

dead king has had history of battle with Norway and Poland; Horatio was there

Marcellus: Thus twice before, and jump at this dead hour,
With martial stalk hath he gone by our watch.
Horatio: In what particular thought to work I know not,
But in the gross and scope of mine opinion
This bodes some strange eruption to our state.

foreshadowing

Marcellus: Good now, sit down, and tell me, he that knows,
Why this same strict and most observant watch
So nightly toils the subject of the land,
And why such daily cast of brazen cannon
And foreign mart for implements of war,
Why such impress of shipwrights whose sore task
Does not divide the Sunday from the week.
What might be toward, that this sweaty haste
Doth make the night joint-laborer with the day?
Who is 't that can inform me?

Horatio: That can I;
At least, the whisper goes so. Our last king,
Whose image even but now appears to us,
Was, as you know, by Fortinbras of Norway,
Thereto pricked on by a most emulate pride,
Dared to the combat; in which our valiant Hamlet—
For so this side of our known world esteemed him—
Did slay this Fortinbras; who by a sealed compact
Well ratified by law and heraldry
Did forfeit, with his life, all those his lands
Which he stood seized of, to the conqueror;
Against the which a moiety competent
Was gagèd by our king, which had returned
To the inheritance of Fortinbras
Had he been vanquisher, as, by the same cov'nant
And carriage of the article designed,
His fell to Hamlet. Now, sir, young Fortinbras,
Of unimprovèd mettle hot and full,
Hath in the skirts of Norway here and there
Sharked up a list of lawless resolutes
For food and diet to some enterprise
That hath a stomach in 't, which is no other—
As it doth well appear unto our state—
But to recover of us, by strong hand
And terms compulsatory, those foresaid lands
So by his father lost. And this, I take it,
Is the main motive of our preparations,
The source of this our watch, and the chief head
Of this posthaste and rummage in the land.

establishing context: Fortinbras, king of Norway, was defeated by Hamlet; Fortinbras's son is gathering an army to regain his lost lands

Bernardo: I think it be no other but e'en so.
Well may it sort that this portentous figure
Comes armèd through our watch so like the King
That was and is the question of these wars.
Horatio: A mote it is to trouble the mind's eye.
In the most high and palmy state of Rome,
A little ere the mightiest Julius fell,
The graves stood tenantless, and the sheeted dead
Did squeak and gibber in the Roman streets;
As stars with trains of fire and dews of blood,
Disasters in the sun; and the moist star

recounts how spirits/ghosts have been seen before; cataclysmic events foreshadow future happenings and build audience anticipation

Upon whose influence Neptune's empire stands
Was sick almost to doomsday with eclipse.
And even the like precurse of feared events,
As harbingers preceding still the fates
And prologue to the omen coming on,
Have heaven and earth together demonstrated
Unto our climatures and countrymen.

recounts how spirits/ghosts have been seen before; cataclysmic events foreshadow future happenings and build audience anticipation

Enter Ghost.

But soft, behold! Lo, where it comes again!
I'll cross it, though it blast me. (*It spreads his arms.*)
Stay, illusion!
If thou hast any sound or use of voice,
Speak to me!
If there by any good thing to be done
That may to thee do ease and grace to me,
Speak to me!
If thou art privy to thy country's fate,
Which, happily, foreknowing may avoid,
O, speak!
Or if thou has uphoarded in thy life
Extorted treasure in the womb of earth,
For which, they say, you spirits oft walk in death,
Speak of it! (*The cock crows.*) Stay and speak!—
Stop it, Marcellus.
Marcellus: Shall I strike at it with my partisan?
Horatio: Do, if it will not stand. (*They strike at it.*)
Bernardo: 'Tis here!
Horatio: 'Tis here!
Marcellus: 'Tis gone.

(*Exit Ghost.*)

We do it wrong, being so majestical,
To offer it the show of violence,
For it is as the air invulnerable,
And our vain blows malicious mockery.
Bernardo: It was about to speak when the cock crew.
Horatio: And then it started like a guilty thing
Upon a fearful summons. I have heard

The cock, that is the trumpet to the morn,
Doth with his lofty and shrill-sounding throat
Awake the god of day, and at his warning,
Whether in sea or fire, in earth or air,
Th' extravagant and erring spirit hies
To his confine; and of the truth herein
This present object made probation.

we wonder why ghost didn't reveal its message

Marcellus: It faded on the crowing of the cock.
Some say that ever 'gainst that season comes
Wherein our Savior's birth is celebrated,
This bird of dawning singeth all night long,
And then, they say, no spirit dare stir abroad;
The nights are wholesome, then no planets strike,
No fairy takes, nor witch hath power to charm,
So hallowed and so gracious is that time.

Horatio: So have I heard and do in part believe it.
But, look, the morn in russet mantle clad
Walks o'er the dew of yon high eastward hill.
Break we our watch up, and by my advice
Let us impart what we have seen tonight
Unto young Hamlet; for upon my life,
This spirit, dumb to us, will speak to him.
Do you consent we shall acquaint him with it,
As needful in our loves, fitting our duty?

suggests future action, i.e., meeting with Hamlet, and Hamlet meeting with ghost

Marcellus: Let's do 't, I pray, and I this morning know
Where we shall find him most conveniently.

Exeunt.

William Shakespeare

Understanding Style

LANGUAGE

When considering a playwright's style, it is important to examine his or her choice of language. It has an enormous impact on the audience's understanding of character, as well as on the mood and pace of the play.

Consider the **formal language** of this excerpt from *The Doll's House* by Henrik Ibsen. What does it tell you about the characters in the play and their relationship to each other?

Helmer: Miserable woman ... what is this you have done?

Nora: Let me go. I won't have you taking the blame for me. You mustn't take it on yourself.

Helmer: Stop play-acting! (*Locks the front door.*) You are staying here to give an account of yourself. Do you understand what you have done? Answer me! Do you understand?

Nora (*looking fixedly at him, her face hardening*): Yes, now I'm really beginning to understand.

Helmer (*walking up and down*): Oh, what a terrible awakening this is. All these eight years ... this woman who was my pride and joy ... a hypocrite, a liar, worse than that, a criminal! Oh, how utterly squalid it all is! Ugh! Ugh! (*Nora remains silent and looks fixedly at him.*) I should have realized something like this would happen. I should have seen it coming. All your father's irresponsible ways ... Quiet! All your father's irresponsible ways are coming out in you. No religion, no morals, no sense of duty ... Oh, this is my punishment for turning a blind eye to him. It was for your sake I did it, and this is what I get for it.

Nora: Yes, this.

Helmer: Now you have ruined my entire happiness, jeopardized my whole future. It's terrible to think of. Here I am, at the mercy of a thoroughly unscrupulous person; he can do whatever he likes with me, demand anything he wants, order me about as he chooses ... and I daren't even whimper. I'm done for, a miserable failure, and it's all the fault of a feather-brained woman!

Nora: When I've left this world behind, you will be free.

Helmer: Oh, stop pretending! Your father was just the same, always ready with fine phrases. What good would it do me if you left this world behind, as you put it? Not the slightest bit of good. He can still let it all come out, if he likes; and if he does, people might even suspect me of being an accomplice in these criminal acts of yours. They might even think I was the one behind it all, that it was I who pushed you into it! And it's you I have to thank for this ... and when I've taken such good care of you, all our married life. Now do you understand what you have done to me?

Nora (*coldly and calmly*): Yes.

Helmer: I just can't understand it, it's so incredible. But we must see about putting things right. Take that shawl off. Take it off, I tell you! I must see if I can't find some way or other of appeasing him. The thing must be hushed up at all costs. And as far as you and I are concerned, things must appear to go on exactly as before. But only in the eyes of the world, of course. In other words you'll go on living here; that's understood. But you will not be allowed to bring up the children, I can't trust you with them.... Oh, that I should have to say this to the woman I loved so dearly, the woman I still.... Well, that must be all over and done with. From now on, there can be no question of happiness. All we can do is save the bits and pieces from the wreck, preserve appearances.... (*The front door-bell rings. Helmer gives a start.*) What's that? So late? How terrible, supposing.... If he should ... ? Hide, Nora! Say you are not well.

(Nora stands motionless. Helmer walks across and opens the door into the hall.)

Compare the dialogue in the preceding scene with the **informal language** used in this passage from Arthur Miller's *Death of a Salesman*. Why would a playwright choose an informal style of conversation over a more formal one? What is the effect created?

Linda (*hearing Willy outside the bedroom, calls with some trepidation*): Willy!
Willy: It's all right. I came back.
Linda: Why? What happened? (*Slight pause.*) Did something happen, Willy?
Willy: No, nothing happened.
Linda: You didn't smash the car, did you?
Willy (*with casual irritation*): I said nothing happened. Didn't you hear me?
Linda: Don't you feel well?
Willy: I am tired to the death. (*The flute has faded away. He sits on the bed beside her, a little numb.*) I couldn't make it. I just couldn't make it, Linda.

The following excerpt is from *The Drum-Maker* by St. Lucian playwright Kendel Hippolyte. Note how the characters' **dialect** and rhythm of speech contribute to the impact of their dialogue:

A low rolling that builds to a crescendo, then the drumming explodes dying to a raging stammer.... Jack comes on, a meditative rhythm on the drum hanging from his shoulder. A young boy (narrator) approaches from the other side. Smiling, Jack fades out the rhythm.
Boy: How you make it sound so strong? Everybody hear you.
Jack: I want everybody hear me. Drums mus' sound strong make everyone hear. And see.
Boy: I wish I could play loud like that.
Jack (*laughing*): Is alright. When you have things to say, you will want to play louder than that. You will want the whole world hear you.

Boy (*laughing*): How the whole world can hear me? Not even in the city out there so they can hear you. And look how loud you playing. See? Is not true.
Jack (*serious*): They doan want to hear me. Is not because I not playing loud enough. The doan want to hear. *(he hits the drum, startlingly)* And it doan matter how loud I hit the drum. They listening to other things. They 'fraid to hear it. 'Fraid what will happen when they hear it.
Boy: You always saying some funny things. When you going teach me to play?
Jack (*smiling*): When you want the whole world hear you. And what you have to say.
Boy: You too smart. You just doan want teach me....
Jack (*serious again*): No, not that. I didn't say when it hear you. I say when you want it hear you. No matter what, is only a few does listen. But when you play, you must want everybody hear, otherwise you will get discourage and want to stop play. I doan want you wake up the drum and then ask it go back go sleep—it won't go back.

PROSE AND VERSE

Plays may be written in either **prose** or **verse**. Because it echoes real speech, prose is by far the most common choice for a playwright. Verse can be used to create a particular dramatic effect.

William Shakespeare wrote all his plays in a combination of verse and prose. While much of his work is written in blank verse, he does make substantial use of prose. The general rule is that **high** or **noble** characters speak in verse and **low** or **comic** characters speak in prose, but there are many exceptions. Sometimes Shakespeare used prose for subplots, or to indicate a character's madness or highly wrought emotional state.

It's important to examine each passage carefully and consider the context of the speech. In every case there will be a good dramatic reason why either verse or prose is used.

PACE AND TONE

The length of the sentences also affects the **pace** and **tone** of the play. Short, brisk dialogue moves the plot quickly forward and builds audience anticipation. A playwright might use this technique to create tension leading up to a particularly exciting or revealing moment. Playfulness and humour are also created through short, snappy dialogue. Sometimes shorter sentences will lead into a longer passage. This creates an effective contrast in pace that focuses the audience's attention on the significance of the longer passage.

The following excerpt from *Joe Turner's Come and Gone* by August Wilson illustrates this technique.

Reuben: Hi.
Zonia: Hi.
Reuben: What's your name?
Zonia: Zonia.
Reuben: What kind of name is that?
Zonia: It's what my daddy named me.
Reuben: My name's Reuben. You staying in Mr. Seth's house?
Zonia: Yeah.
Reuben: That your daddy I see you with this morning?
Zonia: I don't know. Who you see me with?
Reuben: I saw you with some man had on a great big old coat. And you was walking up to Mr. Seth's house. He had on a hat too.
Zonia: Yeah, that's my daddy.
Reuben: You like Mr. Seth?
Zonia: I ain't see him much.
Reuben: My grandpap says he a great big old windbag. How come you living in Mr. Seth's house? Don't you have no house?
Zonia: We going to find my mother.
Reuben: Where she at?
Zonia: I don't know. We got to find her. We just go all over.
Reuben: Why you got to find her? What happened to her?
Zonia: She ran away.
Reuben: Why she run away?
Zonia: I don't know. My daddy say some man named Joe Turner did something bad to him once and that made her run away.
Reuben: Maybe she coming back and you don't have to go looking for her.
Zonia: We ain't there no more.
Reuben: She could have come back when you wasn't there.
Zonia: My daddy said she ran off and left us so we going looking for her.
Reuben: What he gonna do when he find her?
Zonia: He didn't say. He just say he got to find her.
Reuben: Your daddy say how long you staying in Mr. Seth's house?
Zonia: He don't say much. But we never stay too long nowhere. He say we got to keep moving till we find her.
Reuben: Ain't no kids hardly live around here. I had me a friend but he died. He was the best friend I ever had. Me and Eugene used to keep secrets. I still got his pigeons. He told me to let them go when he died. He say, "Reuben, promise me when I die you'll let my pigeons go." But I keep them to remember him by. I ain't never gonna let them go. Even when I get to be grown up. I'm just always gonna have Eugene's pigeons.

ASIDES AND SOLILOQUIES

In order to create a convincing character, the dramatist sometimes needs the audience to understand his or her deeper inner thoughts and feelings at key points in the play. Two dramatic conventions are often used to do this.

The **aside** is a kind of stage whisper, or behind-the-hand comment. It may be directed either to another character or to the audience. Asides tend to be short, single sentences, and sometimes a single word. They are often aimed at getting a laugh from the audience.

The **soliloquy** is used by the playwright to provide the audience with a greater insight into the inner thoughts and feelings of a particular character. It is an expanded, fully developed speech delivered by a character alone on stage. Soliloquies allow the character to reveal his or her true feelings, plans, or motives. They usually occur when a character is experiencing some kind of emotionally or psychologically heightened experience.

DRAMATIC IRONY

The stylistic device known as **dramatic irony** allows the audience to know more about the character's situation than does the character. The audience can thus foresee an outcome that differs from the one perceived by the character.

For example, in the famous scene at the end of Shakespeare's *Romeo and Juliet*, Juliet finds Romeo lying in the tomb. Assuming he is dead, she kills herself. The audience knows he is only sleeping. The poignancy and tragedy of the scene is reinforced for the members of the audience (who, at the moment that Juliet stabs herself, want to leap from their seats and shout "Wait!").

Dramatic irony creates a tension and anticipation on the part of the audience. It helps to focus and sustain their involvement in the action of the play and the characters in it.

» CHECKPOINT: *Reassess Your Knowledge*

account balanced

Characters
Betty: A recent widow of sixty some odd years.
Lucille: Betty's young married neighbour.

Setting
Betty's living room

Betty: More tea, dear?
Lucille: *(Working on some papers.)* No, no tea. I hate tea.
Betty: Another sandwich perhaps? Or a dainty? You haven't had any dainties.
Lucille: You wouldn't happen to have any instant coffee, would you Betty?
Betty: Oh no, I'm sorry. We don't drink—I forgot. There is no "we" any more. It's so hard. Sometimes I feel overwhelmed. What will I do without him?
Lucille: I don't know. Are these all your T5 slips?
Betty: I think so. Walter was always the one who filled out the tax returns. I didn't know what to do about them. I kept putting it off.
Lucille: It's pretty straightforward, Betty. Especially your return. Nothing too difficult. A few simple calculations—
Betty: Oh, it's not that I can't do it. I've never been intimidated by mathematics, dear. After all, I've always handled the cheque book. Kept all our accounts balanced. But you see, we each had jobs to do. He had things that he did and I had things that I did. I balanced the accounts. And Walter did the taxes.
Lucille: That's all right, Betty. I don't mind. After all, this is what I do best.
Betty: Oh yes. It certainly is. You're very successful, aren't you? Built yourself quite a career. Travelling all over the place. How exciting it must be. Where was it you were last week?
Lucille: Chicago.
Betty: And before that?
Lucille: Ottawa.
Betty: You're certainly going places, aren't you?
Lucille: I have big plans for my future.
Betty: But—I can't help thinking, dear—it's all a little hard on Brian, isn't it?
Lucille: Brian?
Betty: Yes, your husband, dear.

Lucille: I know who he is, Betty. But I disagree with you. It's not hard on him at all. We may have to sacrifice a little time together right now but he's willing to do it. He knows how important my job is to me.
Betty: Yes, of course. You mustn't mind me. But with his shift work and all ... speaking of which, he should be getting home soon, shouldn't he? I can't imagine when the two of you find time to even see each other.
Lucille: I wouldn't worry about it, Betty.
Betty: It's no wonder you haven't started a family yet.
Lucille: We aren't going to have a family, Betty.
Betty: No, no children.
Lucille: No. We don't want any.
Betty: Well, I'm not surprised about you, but I thought Brian ...
Lucille: I don't know what business it is of yours.
Betty: Walter and I would've given anything—anything to have had a child.
Lucille: You had foster children.
Betty: Yes, we did.
Lucille: Quite a few of them.
Betty: Twenty-three of them in total. Until the agency decided we were too old.
Lucille: Oh, but then you had all the neighbourhood children to play with, didn't you?
Betty: That reminds me. Have you met our new neighbour?
Lucille: The ones across the street? Brian mentioned something about them.
Betty: I had her over for tea several weeks ago. When you were in, uh, Ottawa was it? She's a nurse you know. Very pretty. Divorced with three young children. But a very nice young lady. Very happy, very bubbly.
Lucille: Well, that's nice. I think I'm about done here, Betty.
Betty: Did I mention I had Brian over to check on the furnace?
Lucille: Yes you did. All I have to do now is get a copy of Walter's Last Will and Testament and then I can mail this for you.

(Starts to pack things up.)

Betty: (*Taking the papers.*) I can do that. (*Pause.*) Did you tell Brian you were going to be here this afternoon?
Lucille: I didn't get a chance to.
Betty: Well, thank you so much, Lucille. It's very good of you to do this for me. Taking time off from work and all. You won't get into any trouble there, will you?
Lucille: Of course not. They don't keep tabs on me.
Betty: So smart. So efficient. That company is so lucky to have you. And I'm lucky to have you as a neighbour.
Lucille: I was happy to do it for you. (*She pats Betty's hand.*)

Betty: (*Holding on to Lucille's hand.*) Oh it's not only this. Look what you did for us when Walter was so ill.

Lucille: What do you mean?

Betty: You were on your holidays those last few weeks in August. Do you remember?

Lucille: Of course.

Betty: Any time I needed to go to the store or the post office or even out for a walk, you were only too happy to come over and sit with my Walter. (*Lets go of Lucille's hand.*) I thought at the time you were doing a marvellous thing for me. I really did. And I felt very bad, too, Lucille. Yes, I did. You know as well as I do, that we didn't always see eye-to-eye on things. Well, take for example, our feelings about children.

Lucille: Betty, that's all in the past. Let's put the past behind us.

Betty: I'm not quite sure I'm ready to do that yet, I feel I still have unfinished business to attend to. (*Nervous laugh.*) My accounts aren't balanced, you could say.

Lucille: (*Stands.*) Look at the time! Well, I'd love to stay and visit …

Betty: Walter and I were together for forty-nine years. Forty-nine years. We loved one another. My Walter. (*Lucille sits again.*) Such a sweetheart. It was horrible seeing him die like that. Slowly, bit by bit …

(*Betty starts to cry softly.*)

Lucille: Should I call someone to sit with you?

Betty: How we wanted a child. I don't suppose you can understand that. Two people longing for children of their own. We never could have any. You spend a lot of time fighting the bitterness, the anger. Sure, we took in children, foster children, children who needed us.

Lucille: I have to get going, Betty.

(*Gets up again to leave.*)

Betty: Nonsense. You can spare some time for a little chat. I want to talk about Walter. Or do you think the people at your work will be angry?

Lucille: (*Sitting back down.*) Certainly not.

Betty: Well then, to continue … After we stopped taking in foster children—

Lucille: I know all of this, Betty.

Betty: We noticed the little children playing in the front street. We invited them all in. "Come, come," Walter would say and he'd bring them into the back yard to the sand box and swing set and the little wooden playhouse he had built so many years before.

Lucille: I've heard the story before.
Betty: I invited the parents over for tea so they could see where their children played. Everyone was happy, Lucille. The children were happy. The parents were happy. Walter was happy.
Lucille: Look, Betty, did you forget to take your pills or something?
Betty: The children were everything to us. They were everything to Walter. Those last days of his when he was still at home. The children were his only source of joy. They knew they were always welcome here. They knew they could come and play whenever they wanted.
Lucille: It wasn't right, Betty. He was a sick man.
Betty: He loved to hear them laugh.
Lucille: No person, especially a sick person should have to put up with that kind of noise.
Betty: Oh surely it couldn't have bothered you that much, Lucille. You never opened your windows all summer long. Surely the sound of your air conditioner was louder than any child's laughter. Surely your pool parties were more raucous than any child playing tag on a hot summer afternoon.
Lucille: I never complained. I never said one word—
Betty: The noise never bothered Walter. Never bothered him at all. It was only when it stopped. (*Pause.*) Only when they stopped coming, when there was nothing but silence that my Walter started dying.
Lucille: That's nonsense.
Betty: (*Accusingly.*) I'm telling you, Lucille, it was the silence that killed him. He refused to go outside. He sat here, right here, by this window and watched for them, but they never came back again.
Lucille: The man was sick. He was dying. (*Stands and gathers her stuff.*) There was nothing anyone could've done. For your own good, you should stop dwelling on it. Put it behind you. Forget it. He's gone. Whatever happened was for the best.
Betty: Please. You're right. Don't leave. Stay a moment. You're quite right. For a second I was—caught up in—it's very hard to live without someone. It's very hard. I'm so sorry if I was rude.
Lucille: That's all right.
Betty: I was only trying to sort it out in my head. So that I can forget it. Be finished with it. Put the past behind me.
Lucille: As well you should.
Betty: It's only, I didn't understand why they were afraid …
Lucille: Betty—
Betty: It was the end of August. Remember? You had three weeks off. You were so kind to me then. You would come over and sit with him.

Whenever I had to go out, you'd sit with him. And the children. Because they were still coming around then. It was so good of you. I mean, I know you never liked children, but you would still come and stay with him ... and the children. I know what children are like. I can understand you not liking them. So noisy, so messy ...

Lucille: Dirty little faces.

Betty: Their hair never combed.

Lucille: Destructive little monsters.

Betty: (*Checks her watch, looks out the window.*) Yes, they would break things.

Lucille: They destroyed your back yard. Traipsed in and out of your house like they owned the place. Trampled your flowers. Absolutely ruined your grass. Screamed and fought the whole time they were here. Why, it's incredible to hear you suggest the little brats were good for Walter. My god—it was the worst thing imaginable. He was a sick person. He should've been in the hospital. But he wasn't. Fine. But to have those filthy little creatures running all over the place. Demanding cookies without so much as a please or thank-you. Sneaking, whispering, whining, plotting god knows what. I put an end to it.

Betty: Did you?

Lucille: I certainly did. I told them the truth. I told them Walter was dying. I told them they should stop coming around.

Betty: What else? (*Pause.*) What else did you tell the little children, Lucille?

Lucille: Nothing—

Betty: Why, here's Brian home. Such a nice man your husband. And so handsome.

Lucille: I really do have to go.

Betty: Not yet.

Lucille: No, I have to.

Betty: You know, I met the little Johnson boy's mother in the store one day. You remember the Johnson boy. Little redhead. Freckles.

Lucille: Not really, no. Would you get me my coat please?

Betty: Of course. It's right here. You must remember the Johnson boy. He used to come every day.

Lucille: Well I don't. And I'm tired of talking about it.

Betty: (*Looking out of the window.*) Oh and here's our new neighbour. Susan. Isn't she lovely? Did I mention I had her over for tea one day?

Lucille: Yes you did. Several times. (*She puts on her coat, looks for her gloves.*) I seem to be missing my gloves.

Betty: As a matter of fact, now that I think about it, it turned out to be the same day Brian was here checking my furnace.

Lucille: My gloves?

Betty: He sat down with us for tea. Yes, now I remember. We had a wonderful time, Lucille. Brian and Susan—that's her name, Susan—they spent the whole afternoon talking and laughing. Oh, they seemed to have so much in common. They talked and talked and then he walked her home.

Lucille: What're you talking about?

Betty: There—there she is. You can see her in her front window. (*Lucille looks out the window. Pause.*) Oh, well Brian must be in there to, uh, help her with her groceries.

(*Betty turns away from the window and begins tidying the room. Lucille remains transfixed at the window.*)

Now where was I? Oh yes. The Johnson boy. I met his mother in the supermarket. Someone had told the boy he could catch Walter's sickness and die from it. They told him he could catch it just by being here. He could catch it and shrivel up and die. Poor little thing. Mrs. Johnson said he had nightmares for months. Who would tell a child something like that? What kind of mean, spiteful—(*Lucille suddenly turns and runs off.*) Why, Lucille—your gloves—(*Betty looks out the window.*) Dear, dear. People really should be more discreet. (*She continues to tidy.*) If they're going to carry on like that, they should really close the curtains. There now. Everything seems to be in order. Now where did I leave my account books … ?

Valorie Bunce

1. What would you say is the central theme of the play?
2. Much of the play's meaning is conveyed through inference. Find three examples of this technique, and explain how it is used.
3. Find an example of dramatic irony in the play, and explain its effect.
4. Who do you think is the protagonist? Explain why.
5. *Account Balanced* contains very few stage directions. The few that do exist, however, are important. Explain why by referring to a specific example.

Creating Drama

Preparing and Planning

Preparing to write a play is very similar to preparing to write a short story. You must have a plan for the plot, the characters, and the setting. You must know your purpose. Is it simply to entertain—to make your audience laugh or cry—or do you also want them to gain an understanding of some larger theme or issue? Deciding on your intent will have a profound impact on the way you write your play.

Aristotle outlined some conventions of playwriting that offer good advice to first-time playwrights. He claimed that a good play should observe what are known as the **three unities**: unity of **action**, unity of **time**, and unity of **place**. A play should represent a single series of interrelated actions that take place within twenty-four hours in a single place. Obviously there are many plays that violate these rules, but amateur playwrights are well advised to consider them.

Planning Decisions

- *What is your purpose in writing this play?*
- *What background information will the audience need to know in order to understand what is happening or to connect with particular characters? How will you provide this information right at the beginning of the play?*
- *What location would work best for the interactions between characters? Is it possible to have the play occur in only one or two places?*
- *Can the characters interact within a short time period? Something that happened in the past and is integral to the play doesn't need to happen live; it can be represented using reported conversation. In fact, it's often more effective dramatically not to actually witness a particular action or event, but to hear about it from a character who has observed it.*
- *Are all the characters, scenes, and dialogue necessary? Unless it contributes in some way to the plot or theme of the play, leave it out.*

Checklist

Creating Drama	
Is every character, scene, and conversation necessary?	❑
Will the description of the characters help a director or audience member visualize them?	❑
Will the stage directions assist the director, actors, and/or readers of the play in visualizing the movement or action that is happening on stage?	❑
Does the exposition of the play provide the audience/reader with enough information to understand what is going on?	❑
Does the audience or reader of the play have opportunities to infer meaning from conversation?	❑
Does the dialogue have a realistic or authentic tone?	❑
Are the themes and issues clear?	❑
Is the pacing of the play appropriate? Will the audience's/reader's attention be held throughout the play?	❑

Revising and Editing

CREATING AUTHENTIC DIALOGUE

Writing dialogue that sounds like natural speech is one of the biggest challenges of the playwright. Natural, or colloquial, language is informal, and uses expressions and structures appropriate to everyday speech. The language used in conversation is very different from the kind of language used to write a formal essay or give a speech in front of an audience.

Characteristics of Everyday Conversation

- *slang expressions*
- *interjections* (uh, like, so, you know)
- *questions*
- *non-sentences and short, single-word responses*
- *silence*

If you were to transcribe a conversation between two friends onto paper, it might look something like this.

Call me?
Yeah.... I have to pick up my brother.
When?
Now
Not that.
Oh, tonight—no wait, I have hockey. Murray's coaching. We'll be late.
Around 11:30.
Too late. My parents would kill me.
Call me then.
If I'm still awake. See ya.
Later.

The added challenge in writing a play is to advance the plot through the dialogue. Imagine if the above exchange were to function as the exposition of a play. The playwright would have to work into this scene any background information the audience would need, as well as a sense of the characters. The playwright must also capture the audience's attention and interest.

With these requirements in mind, the scene might look something like this:

(Two young men are standing at their lockers. It is the end of a school day. Others may wander by during the conversation. Carl Evans is fifteen, of medium height, and wears jeans and a T-shirt. The other boy, Chris Lee, is sixteen. He is also wearing jeans and a T-shirt.)

Chris: (*anxiously*) Call me?
Carl: Yeah.... (*remembering*) I have to pick up my brother. (*He is nervously sorting through some books on the top shelf in his locker, then finds what he wants and shoves it into his bag.*)
Chris: When?
Carl: (*glancing down at his watch*) Now. Ever since that thing last week. My parents have really clamped down. Heard they may have found the guy though.
Chris: (*Pause.*) Not that. (*quietly*)
Carl: (*Pause. He turns toward Chris, but avoiding his stare*) Oh ... tonight—no wait, I have hockey. Murray's coaching. We'll be late. Around 11:30.
Chris: Too late. My parents would kill me. That phone call last week really freaked them out. Now when the phone rings late, they go nuts. (*He adjusts his back-pack, now full of books, onto his back.*)
Carl: (*understanding*) Call me then.
Chris: If I'm still awake ... I'm sure I will be. See ya. (*He exits.*)
Carl: (*Swings his backpack over his shoulder, in an attempt to look offhand*) Later.

Notice that a great deal of meaning is gathered through **inference**. The audience reads meaning into what is not directly stated. It is what is *not* said that creates dramatic tension and suspense. If the conversation between the two boys were explicit, the audience would be far less likely to be engaged. Consider how important it is when writing dialogue not to say everything directly.

GRAMMAR, USAGE, AND MECHANICS

HOMONYMS

You might find yourself writing dialogue based on something you've heard (even if it's something you've heard in your head!). Or, perhaps you are transcibing from a taped, improvised interaction. When moving from oral to written conversation, it's easy to make spelling errors, because it's easy to confuse words that sound and look similar. These are called **homonyms**—words that are pronounced the same but are spelled differently. Here are some examples:

board	to get on a plane or a ship; flat piece of wood
bored	uninterested
boarder	one who pays a homeowner for food and lodging
border	a boundary
brake	a device for slowing or stopping motion
break	to crack or destroy
desert	dry land; to abandon
dessert	a sweet served after a meal
die, dying	to become dead, becoming dead
dye, dyeing	to colour, colouring
forth	forward, onward
fourth	between third and fifth
gorilla	an ape
guerrilla	a revolutionary soldier
hear	to listen to
here	in this place

heard	past tense of *hear*
herd	a group of animals
heroin	a drug
heroine	a courageous woman
plain	simple; flat land
plane	airplane, tool
right	correct; opposite of left
rite	ceremony
write	to form letters
scene	setting; public display
seen	past participle of see
thorough	complete, accurate
through	by way of
wear	to be clothed in
were	past tense of *be*
where	in what place
weather	climatic conditions
whether	if

SUBJECT–VERB AGREEMENT

Something else to watch out for when writing dialogue is **subject–verb agreement**. When the subject and verb are separated in the sentence by a few words, it's easy to lose track of the subjects's *number* (singular or plural).

The subject—which isn't necessarily the closest noun to the verb—always controls the number of the verb.

> The new word processing programs that have every kind of option are the best yet. (modifies the subject *programs*, not *option*)

When the elements of a compound subject are joined by *or* or *not*, the element closer to the verb determines whether the verb is singular or plural. If the element of the subject closer to the verb is singular, the verb is singular. If it is plural, the verb is plural.

> Either Karen or her daughter is going to pick me up.
> Either Karen or her daughters are going to pick me up.

When the subject is a **collective noun** (such as *group* or *team*), the verb may be either singular or plural, depending on the context. Collective nouns are treated as *singular* when the individuals within the group are considered as a group, and as *plural* when the individuals within the group are considered as individuals.

Our band of happy travellers is leaving now.
The class of 2003 are going their separate ways right after graduation.

When the subject is an **indefinite pronoun**, the verb may be either singular or plural, depending on the pronoun and its context. Some indefinite pronouns (such as *both, few, many, others*, and *several*) are plural and take a plural verb.

Someone is going to pay for this.
Many are volunteering, but few are actually showing up.

When the subject of a dependent clause is a relative pronoun, such as *which, that*, or *who*, the verb should be singular or plural depending on the number of the pronoun's antecedent.

The girl suddenly had a great idea, which was to plan a camping trip.
I called up two of my friends, who seem to understand my problem.

Presenting Drama: Dramatic Reading and Full Production

Presenting a play to an audience requires the expertise of many people—and a fair amount of money. Professional productions involve producers, directors, actors, stage technicians, lighting designers, and costume designers. However, for class or school presentation, the task may be slightly less onerous. (Remember that if you are charging admission to a play, you must pay a royalties fee. Royalties information is provided in any script, as well as certain conditions of performance. Usually you must produce the play in its entirety and exactly as written.)

When presenting a script to classmates or to a limited school audience, you have two options. One is to simply do a **dramatic reading**.

Elements of the Dramatic Reading

- *Actors may use their scripts and don't have to memorize lines.*
- *The play is presented using only a few props and costume pieces, and with a minimal set.*
- *Several rehearsal readings should take place so that all participants are familiar and comfortable with their roles.*
- *Each actor might choose one costume piece or prop that helps define the character—a shawl, hat, or pipe, for example.*
- *Movement in the presentation space should be kept to a minimum. No attempt is made to block the play. The actors might do the reading from chairs and occasionally shift the physical arrangement to retain audience interest.*

The second option is a **full production** of a scene or entire play. This requires that actors memorize their parts and present the character through movement and gesture. This preparation obviously requires a great deal of time and hard work.

Elements of the Full Production

- *Usually a director will be assigned to manage the scene. He or she is the one who creates the "vision" for the drama. The director gives the actors suggestions for character interpretation, movement, and gesture.*
- *The individual actor, however, usually creates the character. It is through voice and gesture that the characters take on a life of their own.*
- *The driving force in dramatic presentation comes from the interaction between the characters and the energy created by these interactions. Without that energy, a play will seem lifeless and dull. The interaction of the characters must look as though it's happening for the first time—a freshness and energy that is difficult to sustain through countless rehearsals.*
- *The director determines the physical arrangement of the stage and recruits those people required to manage the set and costumes.*
- *During rehearsals the actors practise not only their lines but also their blocking (see next page).*

- *Costumes help define a character. If a costume is unusual, actors should have a chance to practise in it before presentation. Practise with props also helps with the ease of use.*

- *Prior to the performance a* ***dress rehearsal*** *gives everyone a chance to run through the play as it will be presented on the day of performance.*

BLOCKING

Planning how characters move on stage is called **blocking**. The playwright sometimes provides specific directions for character movement. Often, however, it is the director who must make these decisions.

A stage is traditionally divided into nine areas:

upstage right	upstage centre	upstage left
centre stage right	centre stage	centre stage left
downstage right	downstage centre	downstage left

AUDIENCE

Note that upstage is away from the audience and right and left are based on the actors' position when facing the audience.

Blocking Decisions

- *The director uses the preceding stage areas to denote the actors' position. For example, an actor may cross from* upstage right *to* downstage left *during a particular line of dialogue. The actor would note this blocking pattern and move in this way in all performances.*

- *Directors plan the movement of characters based on what they see as character motivation. In other words, characters move when they have a reason to move. That reason my be physical, like sitting down to eat dinner, or it may be psychological, like moving away from someone who makes them uncomfortable.*

- *Whatever the reason, movement on stage is fairly constant. The actors must be arranged so that they command the focus of audience attention when speaking.*

Checklist

Dramatic Presentation	
Do the actors communicate a sense of character through their voices and gestures?	❑
Does the interaction and dialogue taking place on stage look and sound as though it is happening for the first time?	❑
Does the movement on stage seem natural?	❑
Do the props and costumes add to the dramatic presentation?	❑
Is the timing and pacing of the presentation appropriate?	❑
What will sustain the interest and attention of the audience?	❑

CHAPTER 4

essays

> A good essay must have this permanent quality about it; it must draw its curtains round us, but it must be a curtain that shuts us in, not out.
>
> *Virginia Woolf*

> The essayist … can pull on any sort of shirt, be any sort of person, according to his mood or his subject matter—philosopher, scold, jester, raconteur, confidant, pundit, devil's advocate, enthusiast.
>
> *E.B. White*

The word *essay* comes from the French *l'essaie*, meaning a trial or an attempt. The essay as a genre was formally introduced to the world through the work of Michel Montaigne, whose *Essais* (1580), a collection of personal reflections, gave the genre its name. As the genre developed, writings that conveyed opinions on a wide range of topics also came to be called essays.

Beginning in the seventeenth century, essays were circulated in pamphlets or published in magazines. Today, essays can be found in newspapers, magazines, and online in the form of opinion pieces, editorials, and reviews (book, restaurant, theatre, film); as speeches; and in books, as collections by a particular author or on a particular theme or subject.

LEARNING GOALS

- understand the characteristics of the essay
- examine stylistic devices and organizational methods
- develop the skills to write an argumentative literary essay
- develop the use of particular rhetorical devices
- present an effective seminar based on an essay

CONTENTS

Analyzing and Responding to Essays

» CHECKPOINT: *Assess Your Knowledge*

books a dying art? don't believe it

Every other week someone says that books are dead or dying, that just around the corner is the black hour when they will be curiosities like stereopticon slides of milkstools—probably the same thing they said when radio was invented, when television flickered its way into our living rooms.

To some the phrase means sluggish book sales in the recent and lingering recession; to others it means that the old grey novel ain't what it used to be. Not a few associate the obliteration of distinguished literary houses and imprints in the age of the corporate takeover as synonymous with the inevitable disappearance of books. The house-followers mournfully announce that no one reads these days, can't read, won't read. It doesn't strike them as peculiar that there is a fierce scramble among corporate interests to buy the publishing houses that put out these dying books.

It's possible that the premature obituaries merely cover our confusion about the clouded direction of change in the culture. As the big publishers try for bestsellers at the expense of serious books, it is increasingly the small publishers and university presses that are finding and publishing the books of interesting new writers.

Books once rather scornfully considered grist for the small publisher's mill are catching the reading public's interest. Among the new books published last year were important works of fiction from Arab-Americans, African-Americans, Chinese-Americans, Mexican-Americans, Caribbean-Americans, Native Americans and others. The so-called gay and lesbian novel is beginning to escape the genre closet and stand on book-store shelves alongside traditional works.

Book-groups, an old idea, are everywhere. Books are moving into motel and hotel rooms, where a year ago one could find only a single title in a black binding. Now thousands of copies of Joel Conarroe's *Six American Poets* engage travellers in lonely rooms across the continent. There are guidebooks and used book shops, and a few imaginative independent book-sellers thrive in the shadow of ever-increasing numbers of superstores.

Those who say the book is moribund often cite the computer as the asp on the mat. But the electronic highway is for bulletin boards on esoteric subjects, reference works, lists and news—timely, utilitarian information, efficiently pulled through the wires. Nobody is going to sit down and read a novel on a twitchy little screen. Ever.

In a curious way the computer emphasizes the unique virtues of the book:

The book is small, lightweight and durable, and can be stuffed in a coat pocket, read in the waiting room, on the plane. What are planes but flying reading rooms?

Books give esthetic and tactile pleasure, from the dust-jacket art to the binding, paper, typography and text design, from the moment of purchase until the last page is turned.

Books speak even when they stand unopened on the shelf. If you would know a man or woman, look at their books, not their software.

E. Annie Proulx

1. State the thesis of the essay in your own words.
2. Is this essay expository, narrative, argumentative, or persuasive? Support your decision with reference to the essay.
3. Identify an example and explain the effect of three of the following stylistic techniques: metaphor, simile, allusion, rhetorical question, analogy.
4. What does Proulx mean when she says "Books speak even when they stand unopened on the shelf"?
5. In a couple of thoughtful paragraphs, explain to what extent you agree with Proulx's view of the relationship between books and computers. Draw from your own experience and knowledge to support your position.

Reading Strategies

If you read primarily fiction, you may find essays difficult to follow at first, because they are organized by thoughts or ideas, not by narrative. To become more comfortable reading essays, try reading editorials and opinion pieces in newspapers and magazines. These are relatively short and will start you thinking about how essays work.

Reading Editorials and Opinion Pieces

- *Identify the topic. The title is often—although not always—the first predictor of the topic and may even provide clues to the thesis (the position taken in relation to the topic).*
- *Determine the writer's viewpoint, and ask yourself if you agree.*
- *Consider how the writer supports his or her view. Do you find the evidence convincing?*
- *If possible, underline or highlight and make brief notes in order to help you grasp the structure of the essay and the flow of its ideas.*
- *Consider what you like about the writer's style, and why. How is it effective in conveying the writer's viewpoint?*

Understanding Meaning

The essay's primary function is the clear communication of thoughts, ideas, or information. Yet it is a remarkably flexible genre; people write essays for a variety of reasons, using a variety of forms and writing styles.

Why Essays Are Written

- *to express new ideas or points of view*
- *to teach or explain*
- *to reflect on or express opinions about people, events, or situations*
- *to raise awareness of social issues or injustices*
- *to persuade or influence readers on political issues; for example, by presenting arguments from a particular point of view*
- *to entertain or amuse by presenting topics in original or clever ways*

The key to understanding the essential meaning of any particular essay is to identify its central thesis. This will enable you to grasp how the overall flow of its ideas relate to and support this main idea.

INTRODUCTION (THESIS STATEMENT)

The first paragraph or two of the essay should present the **thesis** and a big-picture overview of what the essay will be about. The thesis is usually expressed in the form of a sentence. This is why it is often referred to as the **thesis statement**. It includes the topic of the essay, as well as the writer's position in relation to this topic. Sometimes the thesis is not explicitly stated, and so you may have to reread the essay a few times to put all the pieces together into a full and coherent thesis statement.

Since the thesis is the lynchpin of the essay, accurately identifying it is critical. Take time to ensure that the thesis you identify is the right one.

Identifying the Thesis

- *Does the thesis include all the material in the essay or only part of it?*
- *Is the thesis restatement in the conclusion similar to what you have identified as the thesis?*
- *Does each topic sentence directly relate to and support the thesis?*

BODY PARAGRAPHS

The **body**, or main section, of the essay follows from the introduction and leads up to the conclusion. The body of the essay is where its thesis is developed: arguments are put forth, evidence is given, and ideas are connected into a cohesive whole.

Each paragraph in the essay must develop some aspect of the thesis. The **topic sentence** is often the first sentence of a paragraph. It states the main idea or argument to be developed in that paragraph. (Be wary though: the topic sentence may also be buried deeper in the paragraph.) The details contained within each paragraph must develop and support the topic sentence. Each of the topic sentences in the essay, when read together, should outline the key arguments or ideas that support the thesis.

Shifts in thought between the key arguments of the essay are usually contained in the first sentence of the paragraph (the topic sentence), and sometimes within a paragraph. Look for **transitional phrases** or connecting words that signal such shifts. These connectives will help you to see the relationships between the **thought blocks** of the essay. Here are some commonly used transitions:

Transitions/Connectives	Relationship Established
because ... then; with the result that	cause–effect
similarly; likewise; in a similar manner	similarity
in contrast; on the other hand; an opposing view; in summary	contrast
therefore; finally; hence; together these	drawing conclusion
chiefly; mainly; the primary ...; especially	emphasis
in addition; also; as well; and	making additional points

Once you have read through the essay once, go back and examine the paragraphs in more detail.

Assessing Individual Paragraphs

- *Identify the topic sentence.*
- *Identify transitions in order to begin to establish relationships of ideas within and between paragraphs.*
- *Identify the large "thought blocks" of the essay (chunks of thought that may fall into single or multiple paragraph blocks).*

CONCLUSION

The **concluding paragraph** should summarize or restate the thesis of the essay and provide some insight or statement of the importance of this topic.

Use this pattern of the formal essay—introduction (thesis statement), body (development of thesis), and conclusion (summary of thesis)—both for reading and writing essays. Working through the essay according to this pattern will help you to identify and understand the development of its thought and/or argument.

The annotations to the following essay illustrate how Chief Dan George develops his thesis.

i am a native of north america

It is hard for me to understand a culture that spends more on wars and weapons to kill than it does on education and welfare to help and develop.

clear statement of author's direct experience of "two distinct cultures"

In the course of my lifetime I have lived in two distinct cultures. I was born into a culture that lived in communal houses. My grandfather's house was eighty feet long. It was called a smoke house, and it stood down by the beach along the inlet. All my grandfather's sons and their families lived in this large dwelling. Their sleeping apartments were separated by blankets made of bull rush reeds, but one open fire in the middle served the cooking needs of all. In houses like these, throughout the tribe, people learned to live with one another; learned to serve one another; learned to respect the rights of one another. And children shared the thoughts of the adult world and found themselves surrounded by aunts and uncles and cousins who loved them and did not threaten them. My father was born in such a house and learned from infancy how to love people and be at home with them.

focus on author's upbringing in the Aboriginal culture

And beyond this acceptance of one another there was a deep respect for everything in nature that surrounded them. My father loved the earth and all its creatures. The earth was his second mother. The earth and everything it contained was a gift from See-see-am … and the way to thank this great spirit was to use his gifts with respect.

I remember, as a little boy, fishing with him up Indian River and I can still see him as the sun rose above the mountain top in the early morning … I can see him standing by the water's edge with his arms raised above his head while he softly moaned … "Thank you, thank you." It left a deep impression on my young mind.

And I shall never forget his disappointment when once he caught me gaffing for fish "just for the fun of it." "My Son" he said, "the Great Spirit gave you those fish to be your brothers, to feed you when you

transition from description of Aboriginal tradition of respect and idyllic communal living to a criticism of other behaviours

are hungry. You must respect them. You must not kill them just for the fun of it."

specific aspects of a culture that cause harm

This then was the culture I was born into and for some years the only one I really knew or tasted. This is why I find it hard to accept many of the things I see around me.

I see people living in smoke houses hundreds of times bigger than the one I knew. But the people in one apartment do not even know the people in the next and care less about them.

It is also difficult for me to understand the deep hate that exists among people. It is hard to understand a culture that justified the killing of millions in past wars, and is at this very moment preparing bombs to kill even greater numbers. It is hard for me to understand a culture that spends more on wars and weapons to kill than it does on education and welfare to help and develop.

examination of the importance of love beyond oneself (of others and of nature) and its apparent lack in "white" culture

It is hard for me to understand a culture that not only hates and fights his brothers but even attacks nature and abuses her. I see my white brothers going about blotting out nature from his cities. I see him strip the hills bare, leaving ugly wounds on the face of mountains. I see him tearing things from the bosom of mother earth as though she were a monster, who refused to share her treasures with him. I see him throw poison in the waters, indifferent to the life he kills there; and he chokes the air with deadly fumes.

My white brother does many things well for he is more clever than my people but I wonder if he knows how to love well. I wonder if he has ever really learned to love at all. Perhaps he only loves the things that are his own but never learned to love the things that are outside and beyond him. And this, of course, is not love at all, for man must love all creation or he will love none of it. Man must love fully or he will become the lowest of the animals. It is the power to love that makes him the greatest of them all … for he alone of all animals is capable of love.

You and I need the strength and joy that comes from knowing that we are loved. With it we are creative. With it we march tirelessly. With it, and with it alone, we are able to sacrifice for others.

There have been times when we all wanted so desperately to feel a reassuring hand upon us ... there have been lonely times when we so wanted a strong arm around us ... I cannot tell you how deeply I miss my wife's presence when I return from a trip. Her love was my greatest joy, my strength, my greatest blessing.

I am afraid my culture has little to offer yours. But my culture did prize friendship and companionship. It did not look on privacy as a thing to be clung to, for privacy builds up walls and walls promote distrust. My culture lived in big family communities, and from infancy people learned to live with others.

My culture did not prize the hoarding of private possessions, in fact, to hoard was a shameful thing to do among my people. The Indian looked on all things in nature as belonging to him and he expected to share them with others and to take only what he needed.

comparison of the values of the two cultures

Everyone likes to give as well as receive. No one wishes only to receive all the time. We have taken much from your culture ... I wish you had taken something from our culture ... for there were some beautiful and good things in it.

author points out the central problem (this is as close as he comes to stating a thesis): absorption of Aboriginal culture by white culture represents a loss for both

Soon it will be too late to know my culture, for integration is upon us and soon we will have no values but yours. Already many of our young people have forgotten the old ways. And many have been shamed of their Indian ways by scorn and ridicule. My culture is like a wounded deer that has crawled away into the forest to bleed and die alone.

The only thing that can truly help us is genuine love. You must truly love us, be patient with us and share with us. And we must love you—with a genuine love that forgives and forgets ... a love that forgives the terrible sufferings your culture brought ours when it swept over us like a wave crashing along a beach ... with a love that forgets and lifts up its head and sees in your eyes an answering love of trust and acceptance.

mutual love and trust is offered as a solution

This is brotherhood ... anything less is not worthy of the name.

I have spoken.

traditional Aboriginal expression indicates the end of author's statements (these words seem to wait for the response of the white culture to the invitation to join in a true brotherhood as equal cultures)

Chief Dan George

Understanding Form

The **form** of a piece of writing refers to how the text is structured. The essay follows a standard structure: the introduction establishes the topic and the positions to be taken in relation to it (the thesis). The body develops the thesis through supporting arguments. The conclusion sums up the key ideas of the essay and leaves the reader with a sense of the importance of the topic. This basic structure is a flexible one, and to suit their purpose writers vary in how they use it.

FORMAL AND INFORMAL ESSAYS

Essays fall into two broad categories: **formal** and **informal**. The informal essay is often called the familiar or personal essay.

It is useful to see the similarities and differences between informal and formal essays, as shown in the comparison chart below.

Characteristic	Informal Essay	Formal Essay
Author's Viewpoint	usually uses first person; directly addresses reader	usually uses third-person pronoun
Subject/Content: Sources of Evidence	frequently drawn from life of the writer and everyday events	more commonly drawn from shared historical events or literature or other forms of knowledge
Tone	frequently more personal and subjective; may be ironic, amusing, thoughtful, angry, or serious	tends to be removed from the subject and appears to be objective; may be ironic, amusing, thoughtful, angry, or serious, but tends to hold emotions in check and express concerns through strong arguments and powerful rhetorical devices
Structure	appears to be more loosely structured	follows a fairly rigid structure that focuses on the development of one clear argument at a time to support a clearly stated thesis
Location of Thesis	may appear anywhere in the essay; may not be explicitly stated	usually stated explicitly, generally located in the first or second paragraph of the essay

Characteristic	Informal Essay	Formal Essay
Style	a number of stylistic devices likely used to engage the reader; vocabulary tends to be drawn from everyday usage	a number of stylistic devices likely used to engage the reader; vocabulary tends to be more academic and may contain some unfamiliar words
Purpose	entertainment; gentle reflection	provokes thought, and sometimes action

Essays may combine characteristics of the formal and informal. However, most essays tend to be predominantly one or the other. A familiar essay can usually be understood and appreciated in a single reading. A formal essay frequently requires several rereadings to ensure a clear and full understanding.

The type of essay you will most frequently encounter is the formal essay. The following diagram illustrates its form. Note how tightly structured the ideas are, and how each relates to the overall thesis of the essay.

Structure of a Formal Essay

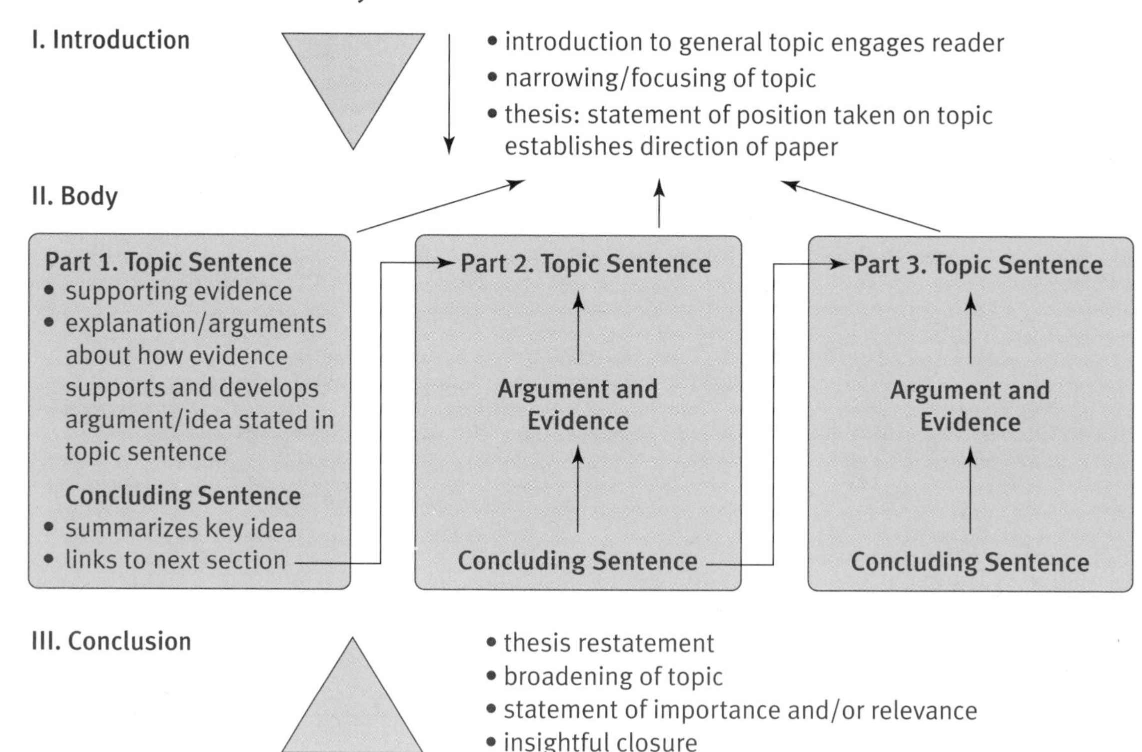
I. Introduction
• introduction to general topic engages reader
• narrowing/focusing of topic
• thesis: statement of position taken on topic establishes direction of paper
II. Body
Part 1. Topic Sentence
• supporting evidence
• explanation/arguments about how evidence supports and develops argument/idea stated in topic sentence
Concluding Sentence
• summarizes key idea
• links to next section
Part 2. Topic Sentence
Argument and Evidence
Concluding Sentence
Part 3. Topic Sentence
Argument and Evidence
Concluding Sentence
III. Conclusion
• thesis restatement
• broadening of topic
• statement of importance and/or relevance
• insightful closure

THE FOUR TYPES OF ESSAYS

Whether they are formal or informal, essays can be divided into four basic types depending on the writer's purpose. These purposes are: to explain, to recount a story, to argue for a position, or to persuade. The line between these purposes can sometimes be blurred (for example, a writer may choose to tell a story in order to explain something).

1. The **expository essay (explanation)** describes or explains a topic. For example, an essay entitled "The Care and Maintenance of a Bicycle" would be an expository essay.
2. The **narrative essay (recounting)** uses a single well-told story as the basis for drawing a conclusion or making a statement of opinion. For example, "My Most Exciting Bicycling Adventure" would be a narrative essay.
3. The **argumentative essay** presents a reasoned series of arguments in support of a position. For example, an essay entitled "Cars or Scooters: Which Is the More Efficient and Safe Method of Urban Transport?" would be an argumentative essay.
4. The **persuasive essay** combines reasoned arguments with the emotion required to persuade the reader to take action. For example, an essay entitled "Save the Ozone and Stimulate Your Heart: Leave Your Cars at Home and Bicycle" would be a persuasive essay.

The purpose of an essay will often determine its form, or structure. In argumentative writing, for example, the author may present both sides of an issue in a measured way before making a judgment, or may be concerned only with building up the evidence on one side.

The information that follows in this chapter specifically applies to the argumentative and persuasive essays, because these are the forms most commonly required in senior English. (Narrative essays—a single, well-told story whose purpose is to support a particular view or insight—are discussed in the Personal Writing chapter.)

STRUCTURAL COMPONENTS OF THE ESSAY

BEGINNINGS AND ENDINGS

Beginnings and endings are the most important parts of an essay.

Significance of Beginnings and Endings

- *The reader remembers these best.*
- *They contain the ideas you most want to emphasize.*
- *The beginning is what draws the reader in.*
- *The ending leaves the reader with a strong final image, thought, or insight.*

Beginning/Ending	Strategy Example
illustrative anecdote: a brief recounting of an incident that illustrates or introduces the point you made or are about to make	In his essay "How to Live to Be 200" Stephen Leacock uses the anecdote of Jiggins, the health nut, to introduce his criticism of the overly health conscious.
shocking statistic	"... powerful industries—the $33-billion-dollar-a-year diet industry, the $20-billion cosmetics industry, the $300-million cosmetic surgery industry, and the $7-billion pornography industry—have arisen from the capital made out of unconscious anxieties, and are in turn able, through their influence on mass culture, to use, stimulate, and reinforce the hallucination in a rising, economic spiral." (Naomi Wolf, *The Beauty Myth*)
bold, direct statement: a simple statement of belief or opinion that frequently challenges a commonly held assumption	"A student often leaves high school today without any sense of language as a structure." (Northrop Frye, "Don't You Think It's Time to Start Thinking?")

DEVELOPING AN ARGUMENT

The development of arguments is the main structural component of the essay. Employing different methods can indicate a sophisticated and lively thinking process.

Development Method	Definition	Example
Analogy	compares something less familiar with something more familiar in order to help the reader understand the former	Comparing a computer circuit board to a superhighway helps those less familiar with computers to understand that the circuit board is a busy communication highway, containing set routes with junctions for going in different directions.
Cause–effect	explains why something happened by showing the direct causal relationship between two or more things	Edward Roussel in "Letter from Prison" argues that "to think that punishment causes redemption is a trap."

Development Method	Definition	Example
Definition	explores in greater depth the significance associated with the term or concept under consideration in order to give as full a picture as possible of its characteristics	Susan Sontag defines "beauty" (in her essay of the same name) by examining the ancient Greek and Christian views of beauty, the language used to describe men's versus women's beauty, internal and external beauty, and the significance of the absence of beauty in the world.
Example	illustrates a point with reference to a personal or shared experience, an allusion, statistics, analogy, or quote from an authority	In his essay "Were Dinosaurs Dumb?" Stephen Jay Gould cites Jack chopping down the beanstalk and David smiting Goliath with a slingshot as examples of metaphors and fairy tales that show how "slow wit is the tragic flaw of a giant."
Comparison	points out similarities and differences between two or more ideas, things, people, etc.; point-by-point comparison is a more effective organization in that similarities and differences are clearly pointed out	Comparing King Lear and Hamlet as tragic heroes reinforces the characteristics of the Shakespearean tragic hero while pointing out specific differences in their tragic flaws.
Contrast	points out differences between two characters or ideas; because this method can sharpen and clarify an argument it is frequently more powerful than comparison	By contrasting the openly discriminatory laws and practices against women with what couldn't be (and isn't) said to any minority, Doris Anderson in "The 51% Solution" argues that women are routinely discriminated against.
Categorize/ Classify	places together under a single heading concepts or things that share sufficient key characteristics as to be considered similar	Kildare Dobbs in his essay "Canada's Regions" classifies the people of each region of Canada by their character.

These features of form are demonstrated in the following essay.

what literature is for

… Our first and most obvious conclusion is that since the expression of individual feelings is central to literature, affective elements are of the utmost importance in all literary writing. In the evaluation of a novel, poem, play, or short story, as well as in the evaluation of sermons, moral exhortations, political speeches, and directive utterances generally, the usefulness of the given piece of writing as a "map" of actual "territories" is often secondary—sometimes quite irrelevant. If this were not the case, *Gulliver's Travels, Alice in Wonderland, The Scarlet Letter*, or Emerson's essays would have no excuse for existence.

essay is a response to the implied question "What is literature for?"

essay is organized by defining literature through contrast with reports and scientific writing

author ironically applies "scientific" language to a discussion of literature's affective language

central point that literature is the expression of "affective elements" or individual feeling

"map" metaphor the first of many comparisons of literature with science

Secondly, when we say that a given piece of affective writing is true, we do not mean "scientifically true." We may merely mean that we agree with the sentiment; we may also mean that we believe that an attitude has been accurately expressed; again, we may mean that the attitudes evoked seem such as will lead us to better social or personal conduct.

transition word signals introduction of second characteristic of literature

literary truth contrasted with scientific truth

The word "true" has many meanings. People who feel that science and literature or science and religion are in necessary conflict do so because they habitually think in opposites of black and white, true and false, good and evil. To such people, if science is "true," then literature or religion is nonsense; if literature or religion is "true," science is merely "pretentious ignorance." What should be understood when people tell us that certain statements are "scientifically true" is that they are useful and verifiable formulations, suitable for the purposes of organized cooperative workmanship. What should be understood when people tell us that the plays of Shakespeare or the poems of Milton or Dante are "eternally true" is that they produce in us attitudes toward our fellow men, an understanding of ourselves, or feelings of deep moral obligation that are valuable to humanity under any conceivable circumstances.

elaborates meaning of "true" by contrasting its significance in science and in literature

transition word signals next thought block of essay

Thirdly, let us consider an important shortcoming of the language of reports and of scientific writing. John Smith in love with Mary is not William Brown in love with Jane; William Brown in love with Jane is not Henry Jones in love with Anne; Henry Jones in love with Anne is not Robert Browning in love with Elizabeth Barrett. Each of these situations is unique; no two loves are exactly alike—in fact, no love even between the same people is *exactly* the same from day to day. Science, seeing as always laws of the widest possible applicability and the greatest possible generality, would abstract from these situations *only what they have in common*. But each of these lovers is conscious only of the *uniqueness* of her own feelings: each feels, as we all know, that he is the first one in the world ever to have so loved. Literature creates the sense of what life feels like in the living.

elaboration of "short-coming" of scientific language

effective placement of topic sentence at end

rhetorical question provides transition

How is that sense of difference conveyed? It is here that affective uses of language play their most important part. The infinity of differences in our feelings toward all the many experiences that we undergo are too subtle to be reported; they must be expressed. And we express them by the complicated manipulation of tones of voice, of rhythms, of connotations, of affective facts, of metaphors, of allusions, of every affective device of language at our command.

as essay builds toward its conclusion, author focuses on the power of affective language

extension of previous paragraph

Frequently the feelings to be expressed are so subtle or complex that a few lines of prose or verse are not enough to convey them. It is sometimes necessary, therefore, for authors to write entire books, carrying their readers through numbers of scenes, situations, and adventures, pushing the sympathies now this way and now that, arousing in turn their fighting spirit, their tenderness, their sense of tragedy, their laughter, their superstitiousness, their cupidity, their sensuousness, their piety. Sometimes it is only in such ways that the exact feelings an author wants to express can be recreated in his readers. This, then, is the reason that novels, poems, dramas, stories, allegories, and parables exist: to convey such propositions as "Life is tragic" or "Susanna is beautiful," not by telling us so, but by putting us through a whole

culminates in precisely worded comparison using parallel structure

final description certainly expressed in the language of the scientist!

series of experiences that make us feel toward life or toward Susanna as the author did. *Literature is the most exact expression of feelings, while science is the most exact kind of reporting.* Poetry, which condenses all the affective resources of language into patterns of infinite rhythmical subtlety, may be said to be *the language of expression at its highest degree of efficiency.*

S.I. Hayakawa

Understanding Style

Style refers to the overall selection and arrangement of sounds, words, phrases, sentences, and paragraphs. Style is affected by regional and cultural variations, by changing standards of usage, by the development of new words and new meanings in the language, and by the fertility of an author's imagination. A good writer chooses and arranges words to convey a particular shade of meaning and to produce a particular effect.

Rhetorical devices include techniques that help persuade the reader to agree with the view presented. Knowledge of the nature and effect of these devices is critical to effective writing. Use rhetorical devices appropriately and carefully, since overuse can result in an unnatural or even unintentionally humorous effect.

Rhetorical Device	Examples
Abnormal Word Order gives variety and emphasis to your writing by changing the usual subject-verb sentence pattern.	normal word order (subject-verb): "The actor's worst nightmares stood laughing at him from the shadows." abnormal word order (verb-subject): "Laughing at him from the shadows stood the actor's worst nightmare."
Allegory is a narrative in which the characters and sometimes the setting represent general concepts and ideas.	fables in which personified animals are used allegorically to teach lessons of human conduct (e.g., "The Hare and the Tortoise")
Alliteration draws attention to a string of words through repetition of their initial sounds.	"As Frankenstein, Boris Karloff **r**ambled, **r**aged, and **r**oared."

Rhetorical Device	Examples
Allusion is an indirect reference to a well-known event, person, thing, place, or quality. By suggestion, it may enhance the significance of a poetic image or prose passage.	T.S. Eliot's *The Wasteland* alludes to the Garden of Eden after the fall (and includes many other allusions to mythology, the Bible).
Analogy helps the reader understand something unfamiliar by comparing it to something well-known.	Comparing an anthill to an urban centre helps to convey the fact that anthills are heavily populated, busy, and have regular patterns of movement.
A **balanced sentence** expresses two or more equal and parallel ideas.	"Many TV actors work hard all through the season; they play in films all through the hiatus."
Climactic Word Order presents several facts in order from least to most important.	"The young politician's career rise was meteoric; after beginning as a municipal councillor, she became mayor, and three short years later a Member of Parliament."
Denotation is the thing or situation to which the word specifically refers; **connotation** is the associated meanings it implies or suggests.	Home **denotes** the place where a person lives, but **connotes** intimacy, privacy, coziness.
Exaggeration (Hyberbole) emphasizes a fact.	"He was going to live the life of a tree or vegetable." (University of Toronto Convocation Address by George Faludy, 1978)
Image/Imagery appeals to one or more of the senses by creating a vivid impression through the use of concrete details, adjectives, and figures of speech (e.g., metaphor, simile, personification).	The beauty of the daisy is conveyed using imagery such as "a nun demure" and "a silver shield with boss of gold." (William Wordsworth, "I Wandered Lonely as a Cloud")
Metaphor compares two things without the use of *like* or *as*; it is more subtle than the simile and thus requires more interpretation.	"Tyger! Tyger! burning bright" (from William Blake's poem "Tyger! Tyger!")
Opposites contrast two opposing ideas.	"Clint Eastwood, a star in front of the camera, has also had a successful career behind the camera as a director."
Onomatopoeia draws attention to the sound of the word by imitating or suggesting sounds that correspond to its meaning.	"buzz," "splash," "slurp"

Rhetorical Device	Examples
Oxymoron places words that mean the opposite of one another side by side so that they create a new meaning.	"jumbo shrimp," "wise fool"
Parallel Structure (Parallelism) repeats specific words, phrases, or clauses in a series, giving emphasis to key words and making them memorable.	Abraham Lincoln's "government of the people, by the people, for the people" (preposition, definite article, and noun are repeated in a series)
A **periodic sentence** withholds an important part of the sentence until the end so that it doesn't make complete sense until the last word is read.	"Whether playing a young wild adventurer, a fugitive from the law, or a U.S. president, there is one actor whose films always make money —Harrison Ford."
Personification gives human traits to an inanimate object or animal.	"The fingers of ice scraped the window."
A **pun** is a play on words with the same sound but different meanings.	"Sticks float. They would."
Repetition is used for emphasis and rhythm.	"It was a strange night, a hushed night, a moonless night, and all you could do was go to a movie."
Reversals (Chiasmus) make a balanced sentence even more memorable by repeating the words in reverse order.	"Ask not what your country can do for you; ask what you can do for your country." (John F. Kennedy)
A **rhetorical question** is one whose answer is already known or implied.	"Can anyone deny that the microchip has revolutionized communication?"
Rhyme makes two or more words memorable by having endings that sound the same.	"With **might** and **right** on his side, he approached the challenge."
Rhythm is the movement implicit in an arrangement of words, e.g., a regular beat deriving from the patterns of stress on the syllables, a rising or a falling inflection, a series of phrases that move quickly or slowly.	"the moment comes ... bringing back all I have recently experienced to be explored and slowly understood, when I can converse again with my hidden powers, and so grow, and so be renewed, till death do us part." (May Sarton, "The Rewards of Solitary Life")
A **sentence fragment** places emphasis on key words to create an overall effect, such as humour or suspense.	"A cold room. A lonely room. A bare room. No place to spend twenty years of a life."

Rhetorical Device	Examples
A **simile** points out a similarity between two unlike things using *like* or *as*.	"The cold stabbed like a driven nail through the parka's fold."
A **symbol** is an object or action that represents something other than what it is.	The green light at the end of the dock in *The Great Gatsby* represents the verdant hope of the new world and is therefore associated with the American Dream.
Understatement (Litotes) creates the reverse effect (and adds a touch of irony) by making the fact seem less significant.	"Bruce Willis's onscreen characters frequently find themselves in a bit of a jam."

TONE

The **tone** of a text is created through a number of features, such as rhetorical devices, diction (word choice or vocabulary), and type of evidence presented. Tone is a major factor in establishing the overall impression of the piece of writing. Tones vary as much as there are emotions and attitudes. The tone of an essay may be ironic, frustrated, sincere, angry, self-mocking, encouraging, or nostalgic, for example.

In reading and analyzing essays, it's important to identify the writer's voice and examine its impact on what is being said. There are times when a writer may adopt a persona—a front character—in order to add another dimension to his or her writing. In other words, there is a split between the surface meaning of the text and the deeper meaning—the writer's real message. This method is particularly useful in writing satirical pieces.

Stephen Leacock uses a variety of methods to create satire in the essay that follows.

how to live to be 200

Twenty years ago I knew a man called Jiggins, who had the Health Habit.

amusing name

capitals suggest irony

He used to take a cold plunge every morning. He said it opened his pores. After it he took a hot sponge. He said it closed the pores. He got so that he could open and shut his pores at will.

Jiggins used to stand and breathe at an open window for half an hour before dressing. He said it expanded his lungs. He might, of course, have had it done in a shoe-store with a boot stretcher, but after all it cost him nothing this way, and what is half an hour?

After he had got his undershirt on, Jiggins used to hitch himself up like a dog in harness and do Sandow exercises. He did them forwards, backwards, and hind-side up.

He could have got a job as a dog anywhere. He spent all his time at this kind of thing. In his spare time at the office, he used to lie on his stomach on the floor and see if he could lift himself up with his knuckles. If he could, then he tried some other way until he found one that he couldn't do. Then he would spend the rest of his lunch hour on his stomach, perfectly happy.

climactic order climaxes in the ridiculous

In the evenings in his room he used to lift iron bars, cannon-balls, heavy dumb-bells, and haul himself up to the ceiling with his teeth. You could hear the thumps half a mile.

He liked it.

He spent half the night slinging himself around the room. He said it made his brain clear. When he got his brain perfectly clear, he went to bed and slept. As soon as he woke, he began clearing it again.

shock of brief, simple sentence

Jiggins is dead. He was, of course, a pioneer, but the fact that he dumb-belled himself to death at an early age does not prevent a whole generation of young men from following in his path.

one-sentence paragraphs are like "one-liners"

They are ridden by the Health Mania.

They make themselves a nuisance.

They get up at impossible hours. They go out in silly little suits and run Marathon heats before breakfast. They chase around barefoot to get the dew on their feet. They hunt for ozone. The bother about pepsin. They won't eat meat because it has too much nitrogen. They won't eat fruit because it hasn't any. They prefer albumen and starch and nitrogen to huckleberry pie and doughnuts. They won't drink water out of a tap. They won't eat sardines out of a can. They won't use oysters out of a pail. They won't drink milk out of a glass. They are

repetition of *they* used to stereotype by humorous exaggeration afraid of alcohol in any shape. Yes, sir, afraid. "Cowards."

And after all their fuss they presently incur some simple old-fashioned illness and die like anybody else.

Now people of this sort have no chance to attain any great age. They are on the wrong track.

evokes personal, conversational tone

Listen. Do you want to live to be really old? To enjoy a grand, green, exuberant, boastful old age and to make yourself a nuisance to your whole neighbourhood with your reminiscences?

Then cut out all this nonsense. Cut it out. Get up in the morning at a sensible hour. The time to get up is when you have to, not before. If your office opens at eleven, get up at ten-thirty. Take your chance on ozone. There isn't any such thing anyway. Or, if there is, you can buy a Thermos bottle full for five cents, and put it on a shelf in your cupboard. If your work begins at seven in the morning, get up at ten minutes to, but don't be liar enough to say that you like it. It isn't exhilarating, and you know it.

irony for humorous effect

Also, drop all that cold-bath business. You never did it when you were a boy. Don't be a fool now. If you must take a bath (you don't really need to), take it warm. The pleasure of getting out a cold bed and creeping into a hot bath beats a cold plunge to death. In any case, stop gassing about your tub and your "shower," as if you were the only man who ever washed.

So much for that point.

Next, take the question of germs and bacilli. Don't be scared of them. That's all. That's the whole thing, and if you once get on to that you never need to worry again. If you see a bacilli, walk right up to it, and look it in the eye. If one flies into your room, strike at it with your hat or with a towel. Hit it as hard as you can between the neck and the thorax. It will soon get sick of that.

exaggeration for humour

But as a matter of fact, a bacilli is perfectly quiet and harmless if you are not afraid of it. Speak to it. Call out to it to "lie down." It will understand. I had a bacilli once, called Fido, that would come and lie at my feet while I was working. I never knew a more affectionate companion, and when it was run over by an automobile, I buried it in the garden with genuine sorrow.

extended metaphor creates humour

(I admit this is an exaggeration. I don't really remember its name; it may have been Robert.)

parentheses suggest intimacy and sincerity

Understand that it is only a fad of modern medicine to say that cholera and typhoid and diphtheria are caused by bacilli and germs; nonsense. Cholera is caused by a frightful pain in the stomach, and diphtheria is caused by trying to cure a sore throat.

Now take the question of food.

conversational, advice-giving tone

Eat what you want. Eat lots of it. Yes, eat too much of it. Eat till you can just stagger across the room with it and prop it up against a sofa cushion. Eat everything that you like until you can't eat any more. The only test is, can you pay for it? If you can't pay for it, don't eat it. And listen—don't worry as to whether your food contains starch, or albumen, or gluten, or nitrogen. If you are a damn fool enough to want these things, go and buy them and eat all you want of them. Go to a laundry and get a bag of starch, and eat your fill of it. Eat it, and take a good long drink of glue after it, and a spoonful of Portland cement. That will gluten you, good and solid.

repetition of "eat" suggests opposite extreme

last two sentences make it clear that this is not an alternative

If you like nitrogen, go and get a druggist to give you a canful of it at the soda counter, and let you sip it with a straw. Only don't think that you can mix all these things up with your food. There isn't any nitrogen or phosphorus or albumen in ordinary things to eat. In any decent household all that sort of stuff is washed out in the kitchen sink before the food is put on the table.

hyperbole for comic effect

And just one word about fresh air and exercise. Don't bother with either of them. Get your room full of good air, then shut up the windows and keep it. It will keep for years. Anyway, don't keep using your lungs all the time. Let them rest. As for exercise, if you have to take it, take it and put up with it. But as long as you have the price of a hack and can hire other people to play baseball for you and run races and do gymnastics when you sit in the shade and smoke and watch them—great heavens, what more do you want?

rhetorical question makes an effective ending

Stephen Leacock

» CHECKPOINT: *Reassess Your Knowledge*

don't you think it's time to start thinking?

A student often leaves high school today without any sense of language as a structure.

He may also have the idea that reading and writing are elementary skills that he mastered in childhood, never having grasped the fact that there are differences in levels of reading and writing as there are in mathematics between short division and integral calculus.

Yet, in spite of his limited verbal skills, he firmly believes that he can think, that he has ideas, and that if he is just given the opportunity to express them he will be all right. Of course, when you look at what he's written you find it doesn't make any sense. When you tell him this he is devastated.

Part of his confusion here stems from the fact that we use the word "think" in so many bad, punning ways. Remember James Thurber's Walter Mitty who was always dreaming great dreams of glory. When his wife asked him what he was doing he would say, "Has it ever occurred to you that I might be thinking?"

But, of course, he wasn't thinking at all. Because we use it for everything our minds do, worrying, remembering, day-dreaming, we imagine that thinking is something that can be achieved without any training. But again it's a matter of practice. How well we can think depends on how much of it we have already done. Most students need to be taught, very carefully and patiently, that there is no such thing as an inarticulate idea waiting to have the right words wrapped around it.

They have to learn that ideas do not exist until they have been incorporated into words. Until that point you don't know whether you are pregnant or just have gas on the stomach.

The operation of thinking is the practice of articulating ideas until they are in the right words. And we can't think at random either. We can only add one more idea to the body of something doing this and this is why there are so few people we regard as having any power to articulate at all. When such a person appears in public life, like Mr. Trudeau, we tend to regard him as possessing a gigantic intellect.

A society like ours doesn't have very much interest in literacy. It is compulsory to read and write because society must have docile and obedient citizens. We are taught to read so that we can obey the traffic signs and to cipher so that we can make out our income tax, but development of verbal competency is very much left to the individual.

And when we look at our day-to-day existence we can see that there are strong currents at work against the development of powers of articulateness. Young adolescents today often betray a curious sense of shame about speaking articulately, of framing a sentence with a period at the end of it.

Part of the reason for this is the powerful anti-intellectual drive which is constantly present in our society. Articulate speech marks you out as an individual, and in some settings this can be rather dangerous because people are often suspicious and frightened of articulateness. So if you say as little as possible and use only stereotyped, ready-made phrases you can hide yourself in the mass.

Then there are various epidemics sweeping over society which use unintelligibility as a weapon to preserve the present power structure. By making things as unintelligible as possible, to as many people as possible, you can hold the present power structure together. Understanding and articulateness lead to its destruction. This is the kind of thing that George Orwell was talking about, not just in *Nineteen Eighty-Four*, but in all his work on language. The kernel of everything reactionary and tyrannical in society is the impoverishment of the means of verbal communication.

The vast majority of things that we hear today are prejudices and clichés, simply verbal formulas that have no thought behind them but are put up as a pretence of thinking. It is not until we realize these things conceal meaning, rather than reveal it, that we can begin to develop our own powers of articulateness.

The teaching of humanities is, therefore, a militant job. Teachers are faced not simply with a mass of misconceptions and unexamined assumptions. They must engage in a fight to help the student confront and reject the verbal formulas and stock responses, to convert passive acceptance into active, constructive power. It is a fight against illiteracy and for the maturation of the mental process, for the development of skills which once acquired will never become obsolete.

Northrop Frye

1. State Frye's thesis in your own words.
2. Explain two arguments Frye gives to support his thesis.
3. Explain concisely how the introduction is effective.
4. a) Identify one rhetorical device used in the third-last paragraph and explain how it develops the thesis.

   b) Identify one rhetorical device used in the last paragraph and explain how it develops the thesis.

   c) Identify two other rhetorical devices used in the essay and explain how each is effective.
5. Make two comments about the overall tone of this essay. Provide direct evidence for each comment.

Creating Essays

Preparing and Planning

Getting started can be difficult. There are, however, ways of thinking and planning beforehand that can help make essay writing easier and more successful.

Try out several methods and then choose those that work best for you. Your choice will depend upon your learning style. For example, some people naturally find it easier to grasp information when it is presented using pictures and diagrams.

ANALYZING THE QUESTION

Read the essay question at least twice. Consider it very carefully. Check that you understand it fully. If not, ask for help or, if possible, choose a question or topic that you feel more confident about.

First, underline, circle, or highlight the key words or phrases in the question or topic, as shown below:

> Toni Morrison's *Beloved*
> Topic: How does Morrison's novel examine the theme of the paradox of freedom?
>
> Arthur Miller's *Death of a Salesman*
> Topic: To what extent is Willy Loman's tragedy also an American tragedy?

Keep the underlined words in mind while you plan and write your answer. Don't forget that the "hidden message" in almost all questions is that you need to write about how the writer has used language to create meaning.

ANNOTATING THE TEXT

Annotating your text can help highlight the main points that you will want to make. This is true whether the text is a poem, novel, or play.

The following annotations to Tennessee Williams's play *A Streetcar Named Desire* have been made with this question in mind:

> Describe and analyze how the male and female characters are presented in Scene 3 "The Poker Night" in *A Streetcar Named Desire.*

To set the scene, Blanche Dubois, a complex woman with much to hide, is staying with her sister Stella and her husband Stanley in New Orleans. Their life is very different from the unrealistic expectations she carries from her girlhood as a "southern belle." Here, she and Stella return from an evening out to find Stanley playing poker with his friends.

scene 3: the poker night

(There is a picture of Van Gogh's out of a billiard-parlour at night. The kitchen now suggests that sort of lurid nocturnal brilliance, the raw colours of childhood's spectrum. Over the yellow linoleum of the kitchen table stands an electric bulb with a vivid green glass shade. The poker players—Stanley, Steve, Mitch, and Pablo—wear coloured shirts, solid blues, a purple, a red-and-white check, a light green, and they are men at the peak of their physical manhood, as coarse and direct and powerful as the primary colours. There are vivid slices of watermelon on the table, whisky bottles, and glasses. The bedroom is relatively dim with only the light that spills between the portières and through the wide window on the street. The sisters appear around the corner of the building.) ...

colours: bold, bright, simple, modern

"raw" suggests uncultivated

brilliant light where the men are

colour of watermelon could suggest raw flesh

where the women will be is "dim": only light from outside

Stella: The game is still going on.
Blanche: How do I look?
Stella: Lovely, Blanche.
Blanche: I feel so hot and frazzled. Wait till I powder before you open the door. Do I look done in?
Stella: Why no. You are as fresh as a daisy.
(Stella opens the door and they enter.)
Stella: Well, well, well. I see you boys are still at it?
Stanley: Where you been?
Stella: Blanche and I took in a show. Blanche, this is Mr. Gonzales and Mr. Hubbel.
Blanche: Please don't get up.
Stanley: Nobody's going to get up, so don't be worried.
Stella: How much longer is this game going to continue?
Stanley: Till we get ready to quit.
Blanche: Poker is so fascinating. Could I kibitz?
Stanley: You could not. Why don't you women go up and sit with Eunice?
Stella: Because it is nearly two-thirty.
(Blanche crosses into the bedroom and partially closes the portières.)

Blanche concerned with her appearanc Stella gives the answers she needs to hear

old-fashioned—she expects courtesy

she doesn't get it!

Stanley takes no account of Stella's wishes. His responses to both women are abrupt, rude

meaning, to look ov someone's shoulde and sit in on their hand of cards

trying to get "in" with the men

Stanley will have none of it

he wants them out of the way—poker is a man's world; women excluded

Stella trying to be reasonable — Stella: Couldn't you call it quits after one more hand?
(A chair scrapes. Stanley gives a loud whack of his hand on Stella's thigh.) — chauvinistic reaction—treats Stella roughly, disrespectfully, as his possession; "loud whack"—Stanley is solid, boisterous

Stella: (Sharply) That's not fun, Stanley.
(The men laugh. Stella goes into the bedroom.) — she dislikes this, and at least she expresses her anger, but gets no support (the men think her annoyance is funny); all she can do is walk out

LISTING KEY POINTS

Make a list of four to six points that you will need to discuss in order to address the different aspects of the question. Try to arrange the points in a logical order, so that you can move easily from one to another as you write. Often, it is best to begin with the most general point, and then move on to more specific ones.

Here is a list of topics that would need to be considered in the answer:

Men: dominant, forceful, violent
Poker: a man's world—women excluded
Women: feminine—much less powerful
Blanche: nervous, flirtatious
Setting: men—"lurid" kitchen; women—"dim" bedroom
Colours: men—bold; women—white, delicate

An answer that included a paragraph on each of these would cover the main points appropriate to the essay question.

ORGANIZERS

USING WEB DIAGRAMS

Try writing your key words or topic headings in the middle of a blank sheet of paper. Write phrases for related ideas around them, working outwards toward more detailed points, as shown in the brainstorming web below. Link the words in as many ways as possible and circle or highlight the ideas of most importance. Some people who use these say that you can begin your essay with any point on your diagram and find a way to work through all your ideas. Others prefer to start from one of the topic headings, for example in this case "Men" or "Women."

***A Streetcar Named Desire*: Scene 3**

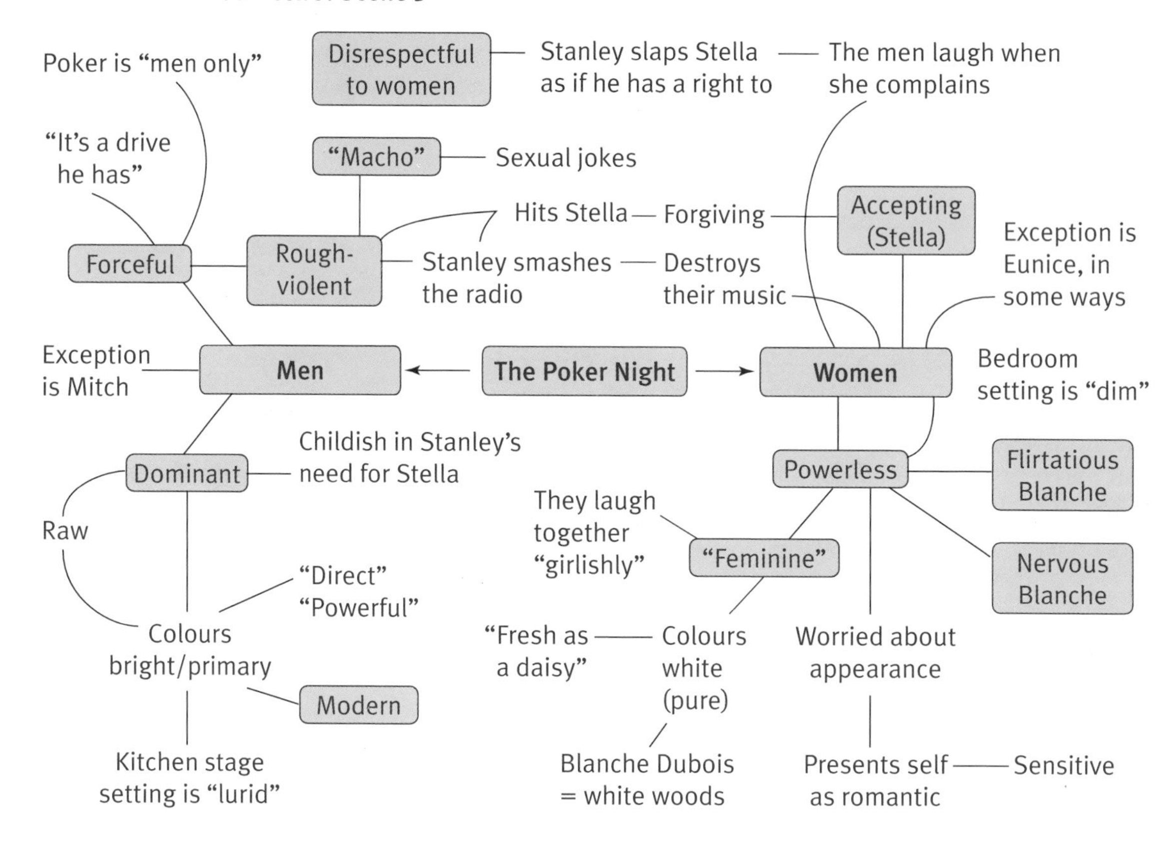

CHARTING INFORMATION

Devise your own ways of arranging information in diagram form. For example, family trees can help sort out complex relationships, or you could use a graph to plot the ups and downs of a character's life.

If the essay question asks you to consider two "sides" argumentatively, or involves a comparison, it could be useful to list the opposing ideas in a two-column chart.

ARRANGING IDEAS ON CARDS

Use cards to write important points and related quotations, or notes for the individual paragraphs you want to include. You can then arrange these, like jigsaw pieces, in different ways until you work out the best order in which to write about them.

FINDING YOUR OWN STRATEGIES

Now that you have some planning strategies, try out a few, using an excerpt from one of your class texts. As you work on each technique, decide how successful it is for you. It's important to remember that the process of writing can be an exploration in itself. At times, it's necessary to throw away all your plans and plunge into the writing before you can find out what your ideas are. Some arguments and ideas take shape only when you have worked them through in the writing process. Some writers work routinely in this way and aren't comfortable planning in advance. If you try this method, you will have to assess your own success with it.

The most important thing is that you discover planning strategies that work for you, and use them so that they become a natural part of your writing process.

WRITING THE FIRST DRAFT

STRUCTURING AN ESSAY

There is no one structure that will work for every essay. Each question will demand a slightly different approach, as the following guidelines suggest.

Introduction

Briefly outline the subject of the essay, referring to the question and its key words and ideas. Sometimes it can be useful to give a very concise introduction to the texts you are writing about. This might include one or two sentences to establish the context of the question. If you are writing about a work of literature, for example, it's important not to tell the story of the work at length. All your time and effort should be devoted to answering the question.

Body

This could take several different forms, depending on the type of question you are answering.

Approaches to Structuring

- *If the question has several key words or ideas, or asks you to explore more than one aspect of the text, you may be able to see a ready-made structure for the main part of your essay.*
- *If you have already made a plan, you can start working through the topics in your list or diagram. Present them in an order that allows you to move easily from one to another.*
- *If the question requires you to consider two sides of an argument before concluding with your own views, you can either: a) present all the arguments on one side first, supporting your ideas with evidence, then repeat the process the other side; b) make a table showing the arguments on each side of the question, then work through them "zigzag" fashion, presenting an argument from one side followed by one from the other side. (This may seem harder to do, but can often have more impact.)*

- *You' ll often find it necessary to explore a side issue or a related topic before returning to your central theme. It' s important to do this without becoming sidetracked. Some of these side issues will contribute to the main argument, while others offer exceptions to it or alternative views. Find ways of incorporating these while maintaining a strong sense of direction and flow in your writing.*

Conclusion

End your essay by briefly summing up your most important points and stating the conclusion that you've reached. Sometimes it's useful to restate the key words and ideas from the original question. Try to express your conclusion clearly—you want to leave your reader with a good impression!

USING EVIDENCE FROM THE TEXT EFFECTIVELY

As you write, it is essential that you provide evidence from the text to support what you say. The quotations you use should be short and relevant. Include quotations only to illustrate a comment or to act as a discussion point. Choose your quotations carefully; instead of putting them in without comment, integrate them smoothly into your writing. For example:

> In the opening scene, Lear shows favouritism to one daughter and to one subject. It is generally observed that the father considers Cordelia "the best, the dearest" (I,i,218), and so it comes as a shock when he banishes her. The people also observe that "the king had more affected the Duke of Albany than Cornwall" (I,i,1-2). Lear, then, is given to prejudice in fulfilling his two life functions.

Note how the brief, relevant quotations from Shakespeare's *King Lear* are integrated into the sentence structure of the essay.

Sometimes a quotation from the text needs to be analyzed in order to show how it relates to the point you are making. For example, if you were to write that a poet "uses a lot of alliteration" in a poem, you would need to follow this statement with some quotations from the poem that contain alliteration. Then you need to go on and analyze the quotation, and comment on the effect created by the alliteration.

Analyzing Quotations

- *State the point you wish to make.*
- *Follow this with your quotation. Make sure the context of the quotation is clear. Briefly explain the situation, or who is speaking and to whom. Quotations should be presented in quotation marks, or set off from the rest of the text by a line space and indented.*
- *Analyze the quotation in detail. Comment on individual words or phrases and explain how and why they are used and with what effect.*

For example, "The Laboratory" by Robert Browning is a poem, in the form of a monologue, spoken by a jealous woman who plans to murder the woman who is her rival. At the time she speaks she is in the laboratory of an alchemist who is mixing some arsenic for her to use, and her words are addressed to him. (Apparently this situation was not that uncommon in Renaissance France and Italy!)

> In stanza three, as the alchemist works on preparing the poison, she comments on his actions, and seems to be enjoying the process. Her words include some alliteration that heightens this effect:
>
> Grind away, moisten and mash up thy paste,
> Pound at thy powder—I am not in haste.
>
> The repeated "m" sounds of "moisten" and "mash" suggest her almost chewing these words with relish, while the "p" sounds not only suggest the actual sound of the pestle and mortar, but, because of their explosive quality, express her spiteful pleasure at the thought of her rival's death.

REFERENCING SOURCES

All sources that you directly quote from, or that you summarize, must be properly footnoted. A proper bibliography must also be included.

Primary sources are the actual texts you are writing about (e.g., *A Streetcar Named Desire*), and all references to them must be properly referenced. In addition, if you use any **secondary sources**—works of criticism, author biographies, or visual material (e.g., film, slides)—you must include these in proper reference format. Your teacher or school may prefer a particular style. If not, the Modern Language Association (MLA) format is widely accepted. (See the Research and Ethics chapter for information about referencing sources.)

FORMALITY OF STYLE

Your essays should be written in a formal style of writing. This can be difficult to define, but there are some things to avoid.

The first person: Avoid overusing the first person in your responses. For example, rather than saying "I think the threat of global warming is serious because …" begin simply with "The threat of …." Back this up with quotations from or references to reliable sources. The occasional use of "I" or "me" to reinforce an important point can, however, be very effective.

Slang: Avoid using slang expressions (unless, of course, they appear in quotations). Colloquial language is the language of informal speech. Try to develop your awareness of the differences between spoken English and written English.

Abbreviations: It is better not to use abbreviated forms in formal writing. For example, write "did not" rather than "didn't" and avoid using "etc."

Numbers: These should be written in word form, for example, "thirty-seven" rather than "37," unless the figure is very large.

THE CRAFT IN YOUR WRITING

As you become more practised in writing essays, you may begin to think of writing as a "craft"—something that most writers think about and work at with great care and attention to detail. Try to think about your own writing in the same way.

Writing Tips

- *Make deliberate choices about the vocabulary you use. Choose the best word for the job, rather than the first one that comes to mind.*
- *Try out different lengths and types of sentences.*
- *Think about the different ideas you wish to include in your paragraphs.*
- *Try to weigh ideas against each other when you are writing argumentatively.*

Reread some of your own recent essays. What are the strengths and weakness of your written style? Think about this carefully yourself and/or ask a teacher for feedback. Choose one weakness (for example, not putting quotations properly in context; changing tense; poor punctuation) and focus on correcting it in your next essay.

During the writing process, work with a partner to read and discuss a partner's work.

Assessing Your Partner's Essay

- *Is it easy to read and understand?*
- *Has the question been answered?*
- *Are quotations used effectively?*
- *Make a note of positive comments and advice about improvements before giving each other feedback.*

Checklist

Creating an Essay	
Is the thesis statement clear and concise?	❑
Is thorough and sophisticated thinking evident in the thesis and supporting arguments?	❑
Are all arguments supported by evidence?	❑
Are arguments developed using several consciously selected methods of development?	❑
Is all evidence clearly connected to arguments?	❑
Is supporting evidence drawn from various parts of the text?	❑
Are all arguments clearly stated and related to the thesis?	❑
Are rhetorical devices appropriately and effectively included?	❑
Are the references to plot events brief and relevant?	❑
Are brief quotations integrated correctly into the essay and into the sentence structure?	❑
Do sentences vary in length, order, and type?	❑
Is the diction carefully selected for precision and conciseness?	❑
Are transitions used to make connections within and between paragraphs?	❑
Is an objective tone consistently maintained, with no use of first-person pronoun?	❑
Does the essay show insight into the text and the topic or question?	❑
Does the essay invite readers in and leave them with a sense of completion?	❑

Revising and Editing

Key aspects of revising and editing include ensuring that your ideas are concisely expressed and key ideas are emphasized.

GRAMMAR, USAGE, AND MECHANICS

CLEAR ANTECEDENT

It is important to be precise. A frequent problem in senior students' writing is the use of "which" without a clear antecedent. Inserting a noun directly preceding the "which" is one way to make its antecedent clear:

Ambiguous antecedent: It was beginning to get dark and the gate was hanging open, which made him nervous. *(Was it just the open gate, or both the darkness and the gate that made him nervous?)*
Clear antecedent: It was beginning to get dark and the gate was hanging open, two facts that made him nervous.

Sometimes it's easier to revise the sentence in order to make the meaning clear:

Ambiguous antecedent: She told a story about the camping trip, which was a real hit. *(Was it the story or the trip itself that was a hit?)*
Revised: The story she told about the camping trip was a real hit.

PARALLEL STRUCTURE

Use parallel structure when you have a number of short points to make in relation to a topic. Write the ideas in a series using the same grammatical structure.

For example, in Albert Camus's "Myth of Sisyphus":

... one sees merely the whole effort of a body straining **to raise the huge stone, to roll it** and **push it up** a slope a hundred times over; one sees the face screwed up, the cheek tight against the stone, the shoulder bracing the clay-covered mass, the foot wedging it, the fresh start with arms outstretched, the wholly human security of two earth-clotted hands.

There are several uses of parallelism in this one example. The two underlined clauses follow the grammatical pattern of pronoun, present-tense verb, and object. The words in boldface follow the pattern of an infinitive followed by an object.

Parallel structure helps to focus the reader's attention only on those words that change. This device is used frequently in speeches because the repetition of the pattern prepares the audience to listen for those words that change. The method gives them special emphasis so that they will be noted and even remembered.

CLIMACTIC WORD ORDER

Climactic word order is helpful in building an emotional effect by piling up phrases from the least to the most important. It is an effective method of persuasion, as both the number and importance of the examples are intended to persuade the reader of the validity of the argument.

She knew she had a chance to win; she was well-rested, in top physical shape, and fiercely determined to make the championship that year.

PUNCTUATION

The correct use of the following punctuation is integral to clear and concise writing.

Colon

1. Use a colon to introduce a list or summary or after certain words, especially *following* and *these*. Note that the items that follow the colon should be written using parallel structure.

   > Many countries have introduced the following laws to reduce highway deaths: setting up photo radar, requiring seatbelts to be worn by everyone in the car, and reducing driving speeds.

2. Use a colon to introduce a phrase or clause that expands on or explains the preceding statement.

   > At the centre of the essay is a statement of the subject with a clear statement of position: the thesis.

3. Use a colon to introduce a quotation that is a full statement in itself.

   > Margaret Laurence introduces the symbol of the stone angel in the novel's first sentence: "Above the town, on the hill brow, the stone angel used to stand."

Semicolon

1. Use a semicolon to connect two or more closely related sentences.

   > He came; he ate; he left.
   > The problem was one of timing; his timing was not the same as everyone else's.

2. Use a semicolon to separate words or phrases in a series, especially when internal punctuation already exists.

   > Attending the national conference were representatives from Red Deer, Alberta; Saskatoon, Saskatchewan; London, Ontario; and Halifax, Nova Scotia.

Presenting Essays: The Seminar

One way of presenting an essay is the **class seminar**. Your job in a seminar is to convince your audience of the validity of your viewpoint—based on convincing evidence, creative arguing, and effective speaking skills. Remember, you are the expert on the topic. You must appear (and be) knowledgeable about it.

During your seminar always remember who your audience is: the students in your class. Although the teacher may be assessing your presentation, it is the students to whom it is addressed. Engage them right from the outset. Involve them actively. At the very least, provide opportunities for them to ask questions.

PLANNING A SEMINAR

1. **Begin by setting a context for your topic** (e.g., make connections to something read in the course or bring in a related newspaper or magazine article). If you are presenting a novel, for example, and a plot summary is necessary, it should be limited to two or three sentences—only what the students must know in order to understand your presentation. The best approach is to introduce information briefly, as needed, throughout the seminar.
2. **Examine your arguments carefully.** Consider whether handouts, blackboard notes, or charts might make it easier for the class to understand particular sections of the paper. Think about how to point out the ways in which your arguments and related evidence support your thesis (e.g., refer frequently to a large-type printout of the thesis on chart paper or an overhead).
3. **Clearly separate the sections of the essay.** Do you want to have a key question or two at the end of each section to ensure the class has understood your main points? What other kinds of markers might you want to use (e.g., transitions, chart or overhead summary) to signal that you're moving from one section or argument to the next?
4. **Ensure that you have a strong conclusion.** You may want to reinforce your conclusion with additional material, such as an excerpt from an appropriate text that reinforces your view, or a summary chart that diagrams how the key points have led you to your inevitable conclusion. Consider how you might use an effective analogy to pull together your thesis, arguments, and conclusion in an unusual and memorable way.

Characteristics of a Good Seminar

- *based on thorough research and careful planning*
- *presented using good oral skills (e.g., make sure you can be heard clearly, use varied tones for emphasis, make eye contact with the students —not just the teacher)*
- *is not read, but is not necessarily memorized either. You should be so familiar with your material that brief outlined phrases (perhaps on small cards) are enough to remind you of the next point or section.*
- *includes visuals (e.g., graphs, charts, overheads) and/or technology (such as PowerPoint)*
- *uses overheads, board notes, or student handouts. These might include a summary of key points or headings so that students can make point-form notes while listening to your presentation.*

- *creates opportunities to engage the audience (e.g., relate an effective anecdote, ask a thought-provoking question, show a clip from a relevant video)*
- *seeks the involvement of the student audience (e.g., indicate when you will accept questions—at certain breakpoints, when you ask the class a question, at the end, or at any time)*
- *uses clear methods of organization (see earlier section on essay organization types)*

Checklist

Seminar Presentation	
Do the opening statements include the thesis and a description of content that supports it? Is the opening brief to ensure that more time is allocated for the arguments?	❑
Is information organized step by step?	❑
Is all information clearly related and supportive of the thesis?	❑
Are all difficult words or concepts clearly explained?	❑
Have you focused on the student audience?	❑
Is delivery clear and audible with varied tones for emphasis?	❑
Are knowledge and confidence displayed in both presentation and class interactions?	❑
Are visuals carefully prepared and supportive?	❑

CHAPTER 5

personal writing

> I never travel without my diary. One should always have something sensational to read in the train.
>
> *Oscar Wilde*

> I have now attained the true art of letter-writing, which we are always told is to express on paper exactly what one would say to the same person by word of mouth.
>
> *Jane Austen*

> It is an awkward thing about autobiography; you can't write it in advance.
>
> *Bertrand Russell*

People have many different reasons for choosing to write, and those reasons may have nothing to do with school or work. The forms of personal writing include journals, diaries, letters, narrative and personal essays, memoirs, and autobiographies. While there are some obvious differences in the way these forms are structured, the common elements of each are the unique, personal voice of the author and the reflective nature of the writing.

LEARNING GOALS

- develop understanding of the form and structure of personal writing
- develop understanding of how to read context clues
- examine the stylistic devices used in personal writing
- develop the skills to write personal texts
- learn how to be an effective storyteller

CONTENTS

Analyzing and Responding to Personal Writing

» CHECKPOINT: *Assess Your Knowledge*

pie-in-the-sky-guy

Let me introduce you to a man who used to live in my head. He is known by many names: The One, Mr. Perfect, but I like to call him Pie-in-the-Sky-Guy. It's got a nice ring to it, doesn't it, Pie-in-the-Sky-Guy? This man, in my mind, is perfect, and I know this to be true because I made him myself. Let me explain.

I'm a six-year-old girl, living in Sudbury, Ontario, and I'm addicted to television. I love television, I love the distraction, mostly, I love how perfect the world of television is, so unlike the real world in which I live. Perfect world, perfect people, perfect relationships.

I am secretly head-over-heels in love with Little Joe Cartwright. Every Sunday night CBC (which was all we got) showed *Ed Sullivan*, and then *Bonanza*. The Cartwright family, three sons and a dad, lived on a ranch called the Ponderosa, and every Sunday meant a new episode of their lives. Nine p.m. was late. I knew it was late, I knew it was bedtime, I knew there was school tomorrow, I knew it all, and still I begged my Mom to stay up, hoping to see Little Joe.

When you're in love, everything seems so perfect, and the object of your deep affection can do no wrong. So it was with Little Joe. He was beautiful to look at, cute as a button, rode a two-toned horse, and seemed to be the only one in his family with a genuine sense of humour. OK, his brother Hoss was funny in his own way, but not like Joe. Occasionally, Hoss and Joe got themselves into funny situations that made their Pa very cross with both of them, but Joe didn't seem to care. Even as their Dad was yelling at them both, Joe seemed to have the most trouble keeping an impish smile off his face. What's not to love? Joe's gorgeous, funny, rides a horse and lives in the TV so I always know where he is. Besides, by the time *Bonanza* went off the air, I had Joe so deeply embedded in my brain, I was happily in reruns for years. That's how Pie-in-the-Sky-Guy got his start.

There's a lot to be said for early childhood development; what and how we learn in our formative years can have far-reaching implications well into our adult lives. Pie-in-the-Sky-Guy was a safe, virtual site in my mind. I knew he wasn't real, I knew I would never meet him, in fact his longevity was due to that very fact; he was the unreal.

So, I went out into the world, met real live men (I *was* even married *to* one for a time), had real live interactions that smacked heavily of real life—and you know how heavy real life can be. In hindsight, I plainly see that in the realm of relationships, my early training came from the vacuum of television, and my preference in men ran toward the unreal. Unbeknownst to me in those past times, I compared the real men in my life to Pie-in-the-Sky Guy. When they didn't measure up (how could they?), my interest in them would come under serious question, and the relationship would end. Of course, I blamed them. Never occurred to me to take any responsibility and that I was, in fact, using Pie-in-the-Sky-Guy as a handy wedge between me and the guy and as a buffer so I could keep one foot out the door.

There's a line in a Blue Rodeo song that says, "It's sad when you discover, that what keeps you going, keeps you all alone." Driving, listening, that line hit home. After much contemplation, soul searching and an honest assessment of my past emotional life, I decided if I wanted to be close to my own happiness, I had to give Pie-in-the-Sky-Guy his walking papers.

He took it well. I explained we were living in two different worlds, and that we had different ideas about relating. I went on to say that I hoped we could stay friends, but that there would be an awkward period of adjustment, and that I just couldn't really see him for a long while. He shuffled a bit, played with the brim of his hat, but he took the parting well. Why wouldn't he, he's perfect.

I'm not quite sure what's left to say. Let's see, have I told you who the perfect man is? Someone told me once that in this life, you get who you are, not what you want. If that's true, and I believe it is, becoming everything you want to see in someone else acts as a kind of beacon, drawing toward you someone who is or will be the perfect mate for you.

Sandra Shamas

1. What do you think was Sandra Shamas's purpose in writing this personal narrative?
2. What techniques does she use to help the reader identify with her perspective?
3. How would you describe her tone? Justify your answer with specific references to the essay.
4. Explain how this essay is organized.

Reading Strategies

Personal writing is strongly imprinted by the writer's own voice. It offers a compelling glimpse into a particular person's state of mind and unique circumstances.

When you approach a work of personal writing, it's important to think about the author's purpose for writing, as well as his or her individual perspective.

Things to Consider as You Read

- *What is the tone of the piece? Even if it was written years ago, in an entirely different context, you may still grasp its core meaning largely through its tone. Ask yourself how the author feels about what he is writing about.*
- *Why do you think the writer has written the piece? Does she want to simply record an event? Does she want to document her musings on a personal dilemma? Does she want to elicit a particular response from her reader?*
- *If it's a journal entry or a letter, note the date and place—these will provide you with an important context for understanding the content. If this information isn't contained directly in the text, you'll have to read carefully to pick up the context clues as you go.*
- *If necessary, do some research to familiarize yourself with the situation referred to in the text. Sometimes just talking and sharing ideas with others will provide you with enough information.*
- *Finally, imagine yourself as the first recipient of the piece of writing. Note your own emotional reaction, and the places in the text where you responded as you did. This will help you determine the techniques used by the writer to evoke a reader response.*

Understanding Meaning

People write letters, journals, personal essays, and autobiographies for any number of reasons. Understanding the **purpose** of a work of personal writing is important for grasping its overall meaning.

Some Purposes of Personal Writing

- *Letters may be written to relate news, to request something, to admonish, to complain, or to communicate a personal response.*
- *Journals, diaries, memoirs, and autobiographies are written to record events and issues in the writer's life and to reflect upon them.*
- *Informal, narrative essays recount personal stories in order to communicate an idea or make a particular point.*

THE WRITER'S PERSPECTIVE

Personal writing conveys a strong sense of how the writer feels about his or her subject. The reader can usually readily identify the author's state of mind and attitude toward the events described. Understanding this perspective is key to understanding the content of the piece.

Consider the following excerpts from Margaret Laurence's personal essay. How would you describe her feelings about her home town?

> A strange place it was, that place where the world began. A place of incredible happenings, splendours and revelations, despairs like multitudinous pits of isolated hells. A place of shadow-spookiness, inhabited by the unknowable dead. A place of jubilation and of mourning, horrible and beautiful.
>
> It was, in fact, a small prairie town....
>
> Summers were scorching, and when no rain came and the wheat became bleached and dried before it headed, the faces of farmers and townsfolk would not smile much, and you took for granted, because it never seemed to have been any different, the frequent knocking at the back door and the young men standing there, mumbling or thrusting defiantly their requests for a drink of water and a sandwich if you could spare it. They were riding the freights, and you never knew where they had come from, or where they might end up, if anywhere. The Drought and Depression were like evil deities which had been there always. You understood and did not understand....
>
> My best friend lived in an apartment above some stores on Main Street (its real name was Mountain Avenue, goodness knows why), an elegant apartment with royal-blue velvet curtains. The back roof, scarcely sloping at all, was corrugated tin, of a furnace-like warmth on a July afternoon, and we would sit there drinking lemonade and looking across the back lane at the Fire Hall. Sometimes our vigil would be rewarded. Oh joy! Somebody's house burning down! We had an almost-perfect callousness in some ways. Then the wooden tower's bronze bell would clonk and toll like a thousand speeded funerals in a time of plague, and in a few minutes the team of giant black horses would cannon forth, pulling the fire wagon like some scarlet chariot of the Goths, while the firemen clung with one hand, adjusting their helmets as they went.
>
> The oddities of the place were endless. An elderly lady used to serve, as her afternoon tea offering to other ladies, soda biscuits spread with peanut butter and topped with a whole marshmallow. Some considered this slightly eccentric, when compared with chopped egg sandwiches, and admittedly talked about her behind her back, but no one ever refused these delicacies or indicated to her that they thought she had slipped a cog. Another lady dyed her hair a bright and cheery orange, by strangers often mistaken at twenty paces for a feather hat. My own

beloved stepmother wore a silver fox neckpiece, a whole pelt, *with the embalmed (?) head still on*. My Ontario Irish grandfather said, "sparrow grass," a more interesting term than asparagus. The town dump was known as the "nuisance grounds," a phrase fraught with weird connotations, as though the effluvia of our lives was beneath contempt but at the same time was subtly threatening to the determined and sometimes hysterical propriety of our ways....

The dead lived in that place, too. Not only the grandparents who had, in local parlance, "passed on" and who gloomed, bearded or bonneted, from the sepia photographs in old albums, but also the uncles, forever eighteen or nineteen, whose names were carved on the granite family stones in the cemetery, but whose bones lay in France. My own young mother lay in that graveyard, beside other dead of our kin, and when I was ten, my father, too, only forty, left the living town for the dead dwelling on the hill.

When I was eighteen, I couldn't wait to get out of that town, away from the prairies. I did not know then that I would carry the land and town all my life within my skull, that they would form the mainspring and source of the writing I was to do; wherever and however far away I might live.

This was my territory in the time of my youth, and in a sense my life since then has been an attempt to look at it, to come to terms with it. Stultifying to the mind it certainly could be, and sometimes was, but not to the imagination. It was many things, but it was never dull.

Margaret Laurence, "Where the World Began"

READING CONTEXT CLUES

Writers of letters and journals generally assume that their reader (particularly if their "reader" is "Dear Diary"!) is familiar with the **context** of what they're writing about. As a result, the context will often not be made explicit. This doesn't always pose a problem for the reader. For example, if you read a letter to the editor in a newspaper about an environmental issue that you've been following, you'll understand the specific references the writer makes and thus will have an informed view of the writer's perspective.

But if you aren't already familiar with the context of a piece of writing, you may have difficulty understanding its meaning. So it's important to be able to pick up contextual clues and create that understanding as you read.

Where can you find these context clues?

DATES, PLACES, AND EVENTS

As mentioned above, both letters and journals traditionally begin with a date. Most letters will also identify the address of the writer.

In order to go beyond these obvious clues, you must sometimes act as a detective. The writer of a journal or letter, for example, may mention specific places, and describe or report on the events that occurred there. These references can help provide you with an understanding of the overall context—or at least a starting point for research.

Consider the clues provided in the following journal entry, taken from the book entitled *Zlata's Diary: A Child's Life in Sarajevo*. How much of the context can you construct? What research would you need to undertake in order to get a full understanding of this context?

Tuesday, October 22, 1991

> Everything really does seem to have turned out all right. Daddy got back yesterday, on his birthday. He's off again tomorrow, and then every two days. He'll be on duty for ten hours each time. We'll just have to get used to it. I suppose it won't last for long. But, I don't know what it all means. Some reservists from Montenegro have entered Herzegovina. Why? For what? Politics, it seems, but I don't understand politics. After Slovenia and Croatia, are the winds of war now blowing toward Bosnia-Herzegovina??? No, that's impossible.

INFERENCE AND SYNTHESIS

Two of the most important skills we bring to reading personal writing is the ability to **infer** and **synthesize**. Once you have exhausted the more concrete context clues, you must read between the lines and put together fragments into a complete understanding of the text.

The notorious trial and conviction of Sacco and Vanzetti in the 1920s in the United States are considered by many to be a gross miscarriage of justice. Prior to their execution in 1927, Bartolomeo Vanzetti wrote the following letter to Dante Sacco, the son of his co-convicted partner, Nicola Sacco. What might you infer from this letter in order to deepen your understanding of this event in history?

> My Dear Dante:
>
> I still hope, and we will fight until the last moment, to revindicate our right to live and to be free, but all the forces of the State and of the money and reaction are deadly against us because we are libertarians or anarchists.
>
> I tell you now that all that I know of your father, he is not a criminal, but one of the bravest men I ever knew. Some day you will understand what I am about to tell you. That your father has sacrificed everything dear and sacred to the human heart and soul for his fate in liberty and justice for all.
>
> That day you will be proud of your father, and if you come brave enough, you will take his place in the struggle between tyranny and liberty and you will vindicate his (our) names and our blood.

> Remember, Dante, remember always these things; we are not criminals; they convicted us on a frame-up; they denied us a new trial; and if we will be executed after seven years, four months and seventeen days of unspeakable tortures and wrongs, it is for what I have already told you; because we were for the poor and against the exploitation and oppression of the man by the man.
>
> The day will come when you will understand the atrocious cause of the above written words, in all its fullness. Then you will honor us.
>
> Now Dante, be brave and good always. I embrace you.
>
> Bartolomeo Vanzetti

Consider the following letter written by the famed English diarist Samuel Pepys to Lady Elizabeth Carteret about the plague that swept the city of London in 1665. Compare this letter to the excerpt that follows from Daniel Defoe's *A Journal of the Plague Year*. In his work, Defoe constructed an account of the plague as seen by a contemporary observer.

How much can you piece together about the London plague from these two accounts?

> Now that by the dispatch of the fleet I am at liberty to retire wholly to Woolwich, your Ladyship shall find no further cause to reproach me my silence, I having stayed in the city till above 7,400 died in one week, and of them above 6,000 of the plague, and little noise heard day or night but tolling of the bells; till I could walk Lumber Street and not meet twenty persons from one end to the other, and not fifty upon the Exchange; till whole families (ten and twelve together) have been swept away; till my very physician, Dr. Burnet, who undertook to secure me against any infection (having survived the month of his own being shut up) died himself of the plague; till the nights (though much lengthened) are grown too short to conceal the burials of those that died the day before, people being thereby constrained to borrow daylight for that service; lastly, till I could find neither meat nor drink safe, the butcheries being everywhere visited, my brewer's house shut up, and my baker with his whole family dead of the plague. Yet, Madam, through God's blessing and the good humors begot in my attendance upon our late Amours, your poor servant is in a perfect state of health, as well as resolution of employing it as your Ladyship and family shall find work for it. I'll go no further in this disagreeable discourse, hoping my next may bring you a

description evokes images of streets in reader's mind

factual details of London plague

pathos of doctor's death, "borrowed" daylight

dead are taken away and buried during the night

shops infected or closed down

reference to wedding of Carteret's son

sense that there is more to say

more welcome account of the lessening of the disease; which God say Amen to.

Pepys

It is true that the locking up the doors of people's houses and setting a watchman there night and day to prevent their stirring out or any coming to them, when perhaps the sound people in the family might have escaped if they had been removed from the sick, looked very hard and cruel; and many people perished in these miserable confinements which, 'tis reasonable to believe, would not have been distempered if they had had liberty, though the plague was in the house; at which the people were very clamorous and uneasy at first, and several violences were committed and injuries offered to the men who were set to watch the houses so shut up; also several people broke out by force in many places, as I shall observe by-and-by. But it was a public good that justified the private mischief, and there was no obtaining the least mitigation by any application to magistrates or government at that time, at least not that I heard of. This put the people upon all manner of stratagem in order, if possible, to get out; and it would fill a little volume to set down the arts used by the people of such houses to shut the eyes of the watchmen who were employed, to deceive them, and to escape or break out from them, in which frequent scuffles and some mischief happened …

more specific focus than Pepys's letter: issue of quarantine and its enforcement

balanced view of issue

topic

Nor, indeed, could less be expected, for here were so many prisons in the town as there were houses shut up; and as the people shut up or imprisoned so were guilty of no crime, only shut up because miserable, it was really the more intolerable to them.

rationale

It had also this difference, that every prison, as we may call it, had but one jailer, and as he had the whole house to guard, and that many houses were so situated as that they had several ways out, some more, some less, and some into several streets, it was impossible for one man so to guard all the passages as to prevent the escape of people made desperate by the fright of their circumstances, by the resentment of their usage, or by the raging

analogy to prison

of the distemper itself; so that they would talk to the watchman on one side of the house, while the family made their escape at another.

example — For example, in Coleman Street there are abundance of alleys, as appears still. A house was shut up in that they called White's Alley; and this house had a back-window, not a door, into a court which had a passage into Bell Alley. A watchman was set by the constable at the door of this house, and there he stood, or his comrade, night and day, while the family went all away in the evening out at that window into the court, and left the poor fellows warding and watching for near a fortnight.

Not far from the same place they blew up a watchman with gunpowder, and burned the poor fellow dreadfully; and while he made hideous cries, and nobody would venture to come near to help him, the whole family that were able to stir got out at the windows one storey high, two that were left sick calling out for help. Care was taken to give them nurses to look after them, but the persons fled were never found, till after the plague was abated they returned; but as nothing could be proved, so nothing could be done to them. — intensifying of pathos

Daniel Defoe

Understanding Form

Letters, narrative essays, journals, memoirs, and autobiographies may be very similar in form if their purpose is to communicate the personal significance of a particular event, experience, or issue.

Common Elements of Form

- *The event (or topic, experience, issue) is recounted in chronological order.*
- *Important events are elaborated upon with detailed description.*
- *Events are often interpreted either symbolically or metaphorically.*
- *Personal reflection is incorporated, either as the important moments of the events unfold or at the conclusion of the recounting.*
- *A concluding comment may summarize the event's most important aspects, evaluate it, or offer insights into its significance.*
- *The reader may be acknowledged or included by being referred to as "you."*

LETTERS

Letters, of course, may have other purposes. Letters to the editor, for example, are written in order to express an opinion about a current event or issue. The following letter, written to the editor of *The Globe and Mail* and appearing on February 6, 2001, is a good example of this form.

> In "Something I'm Passionate About" (The Saturday Essay—February 3), Justin Trudeau reveals a passion for teaching and states that a good teacher is someone who is a "cultural resistance worker," someone who creates thinkers who will themselves "question society, question their parents' values, question authority and make decisions for themselves."
>
> In a glaring inconsistency, Mr. Trudeau subsequently reveals that he does not "read the newspapers" or "watch the news," believing that "if something important happens, someone will tell me."
>
> If you wish to challenge your students to be thinkers, first teach them the vital importance of being informed. An uninformed opinion, however passionate, is nothing more than emotional navel gazing, more likely to serve as a distraction than lead to any real social benefit.
>
> As for your statement, "I don't think I'm ready for politics, and I don't think politics is ready for me"—I agree with the first half of this statement and hope you are sincere. Unfortunately, I think Canadians are all too willing to elect a merely charismatic, famous-for-being-famous politician who has no real informed stances on real issues as a platform (think back to our recent federal election). Please do not confuse celebrity status with political merit.
>
> Tom Honey, *Squamish, B.C.*

Note that this letter has the same structure as that of an essay. What would you say is the writer's thesis? What arguments does he use to support it?

JOURNALS AND DIARIES

Since **journals** and **diaries** are not often written for an audience, their form is based on the discretion of the writer. Journals traditionally recount events or issues in the writer's life, and his or her reflections about them. Since journals are written for entirely personal reasons, they can take any form. The form, in fact, may reflect the author's state of mind at the time of the writing.

Stream of consciousness writing, for example, reflects the thought process of the writer—the ideas are written down as they happen in the writer's mind. The writing doesn't necessarily use correct spelling, grammar, and sentence and paragraph structure. It may be a random series of images or ideas expressed in disjointed and disconnected phrases.

Read this entry from the journal of German writer Peter Handke. How might its form mirror the author's state of mind as he goes through his day?

> May 5
>
> Woke up too late, then jumped out of bed, barely able to function. What happened last night? Nothing; at least I don't remember; stupid way to start a day
>
> The water in the gutter appeared to be flowing rapidly; I threw in a piece of paper and walked along beside it; the water was indeed flowing fast, while I strolled easily beside it
>
> Imagine having to look into such big nostrils first thing in the morning!
>
> Just as a child prefers the meals at other people's houses, so I prefer other people's toothpaste
>
> Read some cheerful poems by an American and now I'm all alone with my bad humor
>
> Chestnut blossoms in a puddle of thick black oil

If, however, the writer were keeping a journal for posterity (or simply as a record that he or she could smile or groan over years later!), the structure of the journal would most likely adhere to traditional principles. The writer would probably set the context for the event; the event or series of events would then be described with appropriate detail; and the writer would include personal reflection or interpretation as part of the recounting.

Consider the following excerpt from the journal of Jack Kerouac, the American writer who gained fame for his wildly exuberant "beat" novel *On the Road*.

> January 3, 1949. San Francisco. *The Sage of the Mist (New York to New Orleans)*. N.Y. across the tunnel to New Jersey—the "Jersey night" of Allen Ginsberg. We in the car jubilant, beating on the dashboard of the '49 Hudson coupe ... headed West. Haunted by something I have yet to remember. Neal and I and Louanne talking of the value of life as we speed along: "Whither goes thou America in thy shiny car at night?" Seldom had I been so glad....
>
> Neal got lost outside of Baltimore and wound up on a ridiculously narrow little tar road in the woods (he was trying to find a shortcut). "Doesn't look like Route One," he said ruefully. It seemed a very funny remark....
>
> I drove in South Carolina, which was flat and dark in the night (with star-shiny roads, and Southern dullness somewhere around). Outside Mobile, Ala., we began to hear rumors of New Orleans and "chicken, jazz 'n' gumbo," bebop shows on the radio, and wild back-alley jazz; so we yelled happily in the car.

"Smell the people!" said Neal at a filling station in Algiers, before going to Bill Burroughs' house. I'll never forget the wild expectancy of that moment—the rickety streets, the palms, the great late-afternoon clouds over the Mississippi, the girls going by, the children, the soft bandannas of air coming like odor, the smell of people and rivers.

God is what I love.

NARRATIVE ESSAYS, MEMOIRS, AND AUTOBIOGRAPHIES

Narrative essays employ a single, well-told story as a basis for personal reflection. The story is used to support the personal point of view or insights of the author.

Consider how the following essay does exactly that.

half-walls between us

For two years, I shared my home with more than 30 children, four freedom fighters, a government bureaucrat, a wife-beater, a Red Cross worker with a taste for liquor, a number of prostitutes, a madman, and all the customers of the tea shop next door. This was not my original intention in moving to the desert, but rather the unexpected circumstances of living in a room with only half-walls.

sets context for narrative

When I decided to work in international development, I imagined living in a small hut of my own, with a palm tree to the side. Instead, when I arrived in town, I found that no housing had been arranged for me. After a few nights sleeping outside on a rope bed, scrounging water from people I didn't know, and living on kilos of bananas, I was anxious for a room of my own. When a townsman finally showed me an empty place, the fact that the walls reached only to the level of my head seemed like a minor inconvenience.

misapprehension elicits empathy from reader

On my first visit to Agordat, a small town in Eritrea, a country in the Horn of Africa, I fell in love with its mystery, its quiet, its soft sandy colors. The searing heat created a lethargy and engendered a lifestyle that seemed more like a snapshot than a moving image. At any hour of the day, one could look out onto the street and see a

establishes unfamiliarity of setting

camel in midstep, a child with a finger in his mouth, a local tribesman carrying baskets suspended from the ends of a pole laid across his bony shoulders.

Traditionally, the desert calls mystics into its presence, and its vast silence allows them to confront the chaos in their hearts. But my half-erected home forced me away from the solitude I found so comfortable and placed me amid the chaos that occurs in the space between people. The liquid ideas of "community" and "neighbor" I had so often espoused—and romanticized—metamorphosed into solid matter, sometimes in the form of a crutch under my arm, other times as thorn dug deep into my skin.

reader identifies with misplaced romanticism

There are no secrets in this kind of community. The air itself, filled with the sounds of anger and laughter and the smells of cooking and fires, moved in and out of our home, bringing messages from one place to another. I soon learned that the rhythmic clattering meant that a young Muslim woman whose husband had left her was teaching her sewing class in order to pay the bills. The moans and grunts meant that an old man who had lost his mind had woken from his nap. The crying of a woman followed by the singing of older women told me that a new baby had been born. Every week or so, the sound of smacks and screams meant that the one-eyed man next door was hitting his wife. And the smell of coffee from my good friend's home, right on the other side of the wall, told me I would soon receive an invitation to visit.

details convey richness of livin[g] circumstances a[nd] dispels previous mindset

reader identifies with first reaction

In this kind of community, there is no time-out when one can take a deep breath, reapply the makeup, brush down loose ends. Whatever rough ends exist become rougher. Honestly, I hated this transparency. It forced me to recognize that I was neither as nice nor as neighborly as I had always assumed. I couldn't maintain an image of perfection. I, too, was judged for my actions. In fact, my activities provided the main attraction of many people's days. Often, after a long day teaching 300 students, my roommate and I would want to vent our frustrations, but we knew that in the tea shop next door, a group of teenagers sat glued to the wall, waiting to practice their English-listening skills. Just by being a foreigner, I provided an endless supply of material. The physical nearness of people imposed vigilance on my speech and actions. It is much easier to be a hypocrite when life can be divided into public and private parts. In a community with half-walls, there is little room for pretense.

transition from alienation to identification

At first I thought I had difficult neighbors. By the end, I counted myself as one of the crowd. After two years of sharing lives with a vast array of characters, I had to admit the similarities between us. I had heard the frustration, irritation, sadness, and jealousy in my voice as well as theirs. I had seen the fighter, the cripple, the prostitute, and the madman in myself. For two years, this proved to be my greatest challenge: to love people through their darkness and, even harder, accept the fact that they knew mine. After all, I was probably the strangest neighbor they ever had.

establishes her inner obstacles to be overcome

Yet from this communion, times of joy and comfort emerged. One of the women who lived next door became my best friend. When the dust storms came and the lights blew out, she would place her candles on top of the wall so that we could share the light. On nights when she worked late, I passed bowls of American-style food over the wall and listened as she and the tea shop customers tried to identify and swallow the strange meals. Each night, after we dragged our rope beds out of the hot rooms into the small courtyards, we would whisper over the wall and wish blessings for the next day. She called me "sister" and her family knew me as a member.

details of the joy of community

concluding reflection sums up point of narrative

Now, living again in America and encapsulated in my own private ghetto, I sometimes revel in, and other times am repelled by, anonymity. I have to remember that I stand before God in a room with no walls. He calls us to reach out to our neighbors over the half-erected walls, and be seen.

Maria Said

A collection of personal essays, based on the personal experiences of an individual, is often called a **memoir** (from the French word *mémoire*, meaning memory). A writer's memoirs may focus only on certain events, or a certain period, or particular people. This form is sometimes distinguished from an **autobiography**, whose purpose is generally to recount the writer's entire life.

Understanding Style

As readers, we know that letters, diaries, and personal narratives focus on things that are of personal significance to the writer. The world he or she describes is interpreted in a completely subjective way. Personal writing also reflects the author's unique writing style. This style can reveal a great deal about him or her. And the more we know about the writer, the more likely we are to make an emotional connection to the text.

Writers of personal texts use stylistic techniques that will help their readers empathize with their particular point of view.

Devices to Enhance Reader Identification

- *first-person point of view* (I *or* we)
- *emotionally charged vocabulary*
- *direct reference to the reader as "you"*
- *imperative and interrogative sentences*
- *interjections*

Consider this excerpt from Nelson Mandela's autobiography *Long Walk to Freedom*. The annotations point out how stylistic aspects give the reader insights into the personality of the writer.

opens with third-person, imperative statement

To survive in prison, one must develop ways to take satisfaction in one's daily life. One can feel fulfilled by washing one's clothes so that they are particularly clean, by sweeping a hallway so that it is empty of dust, by organizing one's cell to conserve as much space as possible. The same pride one takes in more consequential tasks outside of prison one can find in doing small things inside prison.

reverts to first-person

Almost from the beginning of my sentence on Robben Island, I asked the authorities for permission to start a garden in the courtyard. For years, they refused without offering a reason. But eventually they relented, and we were able to cut out a small garden on a narrow patch of earth against the far wall.

repetition of "small"

The soil in the courtyard was dry and rocky. The courtyard had been constructed over a landfill, and in order to start my garden, I had to excavate a great many rocks to allow the plants room to grow. At the time, some of my comrades jested that I was a miner at heart, for I spent my days at the quarry and my free time digging in the courtyard.

overall tone is quiet, reflective, reverential

careful detailing of small tasks conveys modesty and solemnity

The authorities supplied me with seeds. I initially planted tomatoes, chilies, and onions—hardy plants that did not require rich earth or constant care. The early harvests were poor, but they soon improved. The authorities did not regret giving permission, for once the garden began to flourish, I often provided the warders with some of my best tomatoes and onions.

While I have always enjoyed gardening, it was not until I was behind bars that I was able to tend my own garden. My first experience in the garden was at Fort Hare where, as part of the university's manual labor requirement, I worked in one of my professors' gardens and enjoyed the contact with the soil as an antidote to my intellectual labors. Once I was in Johannesburg studying and then working, I had neither the time nor the space to cultivate a garden.

understated irony of juxtaposition

simplicity of language and even tone enhance pathos

I began to order books on gardening and horticulture. I studied different gardening techniques and types of fertilizer. I did not have many of the materials that the books discussed, but I learned through trial and error. For a time, I attempted to grow peanuts, and used different soils and fertilizers, but finally I gave up. It was one of my only failures.

A garden was one of the few things in prison that one could control. To plant a seed, watch it grow, to tend it and then harvest it, offered a simple but enduring satisfaction. The sense of being the custodian of this small patch of earth offered a small taste of freedom.

alludes to reality of prison life

repetition of "small"

In some ways, I saw the garden as a metaphor for certain aspects of my life. A leader must also tend his garden; he, too, plants seeds, and then watches, cultivates, and harvests the results. Like the gardener, a leader must take responsibility for what he cultivates; he must mind his work, try to repel enemies, preserve what can be preserved, and eliminate what cannot succeed.

third-person imperative

I wrote Winnie two letters about a particularly beautiful tomato plant, how I coaxed it from a tender seedling to a robust plant that produced deep red fruit. But, then, either through some mistake or lack of care, the plant began to wither and decline, and nothing I did would bring it back to health. When it finally died, I removed the roots from the soil, washed them, and buried them in a corner of the garden.

words evoke beauty of natural life

honesty about his failure suggests modesty

again, careful detailing evoke[s] an honouring o[f] small things

I narrated this small story at great length. I do not know what she read into that letter, but when I wrote it I had a mixture of feelings: I did not want our relationship to go the way of that plant, and yet I felt that I had been unable to nourish many of the most important relationships in my life. Sometimes there is nothing one can do to save something that must die.

conveys emotional importance of death indirectly

calm reflection suggests wisd[om]

Nelson Mandela

» CHECKPOINT: *Reassess Your Knowledge*

November 22

My Dear Kamla,

I have no news, my dear, none whatever. I have been working very hard, but not as hard as I wanted. A feeling of emptiness is nearly always on me. I see myself struggling in a sort of tunnel blocked up at both ends. My past—Trinidad and the necessity of our parents—lies behind me and I am powerless to help anyone. My future—such as it is—is a full four years away.

My dear girl, my allowance is barely enough for myself. I smoke too much; but don't write home about that. I will do my best to send home £5 for Christmas, but I will only be sure after I have settled with the College Authorities. I am prepared to do some hack writing for anyone who would care to pay for it, and next term

I will write some articles for the *Guardian* and try to get some of my stories published over here. I speak of "some." Actually, I have written only two but I have been engaged on a novel. It is about eight chapters gone—about a hundred and forty pages in any Penguin book; but it is only in a very rough form. I shall not touch it again until the end of next term. I am exhausted. I want new ideas to incubate a bit. I shall have it complete in a year's time. And think what will become of me if it is published! For I am sure of one thing once it is published: it is bound to sell. It is a humorous novel.

And now, about girls. I have conducted two highly unsuccessful love affairs this term. Only yesterday I rounded off one in a romantic way. The first girl—a Belgian and the most beautiful thing you ever saw—tolerated me for three weeks. Then she suddenly told me she couldn't come to tea. I was taken aback and deeply hurt. It appears that one of the stories I had shown her was, in her view, pornographic. Anyway, she packed me up and sent me the most beautiful letter I have ever had from a woman. I shall quote: "My dear Vidia," (she wrote), "I shall never forgive myself for hurting you and for this being the blackest day in my life but do understand it's not only that in society one must not accept your offense, which I myself forgive with all my heart; it is also and above all, as I tried to tell you, that I'm in love with another. I hate myself for the hours of pain I have caused you etc. etc." ...

Good! Not bad, eh? Imagine—your own brother, just turned eighteen but lying to every girl that he is twenty-two, drawing that letter from a girl after whom nearly everybody in the English class is rushing! I think the other chap was a better poet. The other woman, who has been having four-hour teas with me once a week, is English and very stupid and I am relieved to be rid of her.

Goodbye now, my dearest Kamla, and keep well and don't write letters like the one above, because, you see, I *lied* to that girl.

Yours,
Vido [V.S. Naipaul]

1. Why was this letter written?
2. What do you think is V.S. Naipaul's relation to Kamla? How does he feel about her? What details in the letter tell you this?
3. What other information can you infer from this letter? Explain how you came to these conclusions.
4. Comment on how the letter has been structured, and explain how this structure affects your understanding of its content.
5. What stylistic elements provide insights about the writer's state of mind?

Creating Personal Writing

Preparing and Planning

When you set about to create a work of personal writing, your first question to yourself should be "What do I really want to write about?" Is there something in your life that has a particular resonance for you, and that you want to get down on the page? Think about what you're passionate about right now, and that passion will likely find its way into your writing.

Ask Yourself

- *What is my purpose for writing?*
- *What form (letter, journal, narrative essay, memoir) do I want to use to express this?*
- *Am I clear about why this event, issue, or personal experience is important to me? What do I want to say about it?*
- *Am I writing this for someone else to read? If so, who is my audience?*
- *Is there a context for the writing that I must explain?*
- *What is the sequence of events? (You might consider making an outline of this sequence before you start. A flow chart organizer might be useful.)*
- *Are some moments in the sequence more important than others and therefore require a more detailed or descriptive recounting?*

You may be uncertain about which type of writing you'd like to use. Here are some ideas to consider.

Possible Personal-Writing Projects

- *Write a letter to the editor of a newspaper in response to a current issue that you feel strongly about.*
- *Write an e-mail to a friend. Organize the message based a particular purpose, e.g., to ask a favour, to recount an event, to discuss a shared experience, to respond to something he or she has done or said.*
- *Write a narrative essay that recounts an experience and reflects upon it.*
- *Write a memoir of a particular time in your life, or about a particular relationship in the past.*
- *Write a series of journal entries describing a new and ongoing experience, e.g., a vacation, starting a new job.*

Checklist

Creating Personal Writing	
Is the purpose for my writing clear?	❑
Have I incorporated stylistic strategies that will make my reader feel included in my writing? (e.g., referred to him or her directly either by name or as "you"; asked questions)	❑
Are my feelings clear? Have I been honest in representing them?	❑
If necessary, have I explained the context of my writing to my reader?	❑
Have I recounted events in logical sequence?	❑
Have I provided adequate description of the series of events?	❑
Is one part of my story more important than other parts? Would a reader be able to identify which part is more important?	❑

Revising and Editing

AVOIDING CLICHÉS

Clichés are more likely to appear in personal writing than in more formal forms simply because personal writing tends to be more colloquial or conversational in tone. **Clichés** are phrases that have been used so much that their meaning is no longer clear and forceful. Using clichés tends to blunt or obscure your meaning.

Here is a list of common clichés it is best to avoid:

All boils down to
As luck would have it
Beat a hasty retreat
Beat around the bush
Blind as a bat
Crystal clear
Dead as a doornail
Deep dark secret
Growing by leaps and bounds
Light as a feather
More than meets the eye
Nutty as a fruitcake
Playing with fire
Pretty as a picture
Quick as a flash
Sight for sore eyes
Take it for granted
Trials and tribulations
White as a ghost/sheet
Worth its weight in gold

GRAMMAR, USAGE, AND MECHANICS

One of the most common errors that occur in personal writing is shifting verb tense. Because of the reflective nature of the writing, the past tense is most commonly used. Once the tense of the verb is established, generally that tense should be used consistently throughout the piece.

VERB TENSES

The three simple tenses are present, past, and future. The three perfect tenses are present perfect, past perfect, and future perfect. Each of these tenses has a progressive form. They are constructed with the principal parts of the verb, as shown below.

Simple Tenses

The **simple tenses** indicate fairly simple time relationships.

The **simple present** indicates action occurring as it is being mentioned or occurring regularly. This tense uses the infinitive, or for third-person singular, the *-s* form:

	Singular	**Plural**
1st person	I talk	we talk
2nd person	you talk	you talk
3rd person	he/she/it talks	they talk

The **simple past** (the *-ed* form for regular verbs) indicates action completed in the past:

1st person	I talked/swam	we talked/swam
2nd person	you talked/swam	you talked/swam
3rd person	he/she/it talked/swam	they talked/swam

The **simple future** (*will* or *shall* plus the infinitive) indicates action that will occur in the future:

1st person	I will talk	we will talk
2nd person	you will talk	you will talk
3rd person	he/she/it will talk	they will talk

Perfect Tenses

The **perfect forms** indicate action that was or will be completed before another action or time. They consist of a form of *have* plus the past participle:

Present Perfect

	Singular	**Plural**
1st person	I have talked	we have talked
2nd person	you have talked	you have talked
3rd person	he/she/it has talked	they have talked

Past Perfect		
1st person	I had talked	we had talked
2nd person	you had talked	you had talked
3rd person	he/she/it had talked	they had talked
Future Perfect		
1st person	I will have talked	we will have talked
2nd person	you will have talked	you will have talked
3rd person	he/she/it will have talked	they will have talked

Progressive Forms

Each of the six tenses above has a **progressive form** to indicate a continuing action. These verbs consist of a form of *be* plus the present participle.

Present Progressive	**Singular**	**Plural**
1st person	I am talking	we are talking
2nd person	you are talking	you are talking
3rd person	he/she/it is talking	they are talking
Past Progressive		
1st person	I was talking	we were talking
2nd person	you were talking	you were talking
3rd person	he/she/it was talking	they were talking
Future Progressive		
1st person	I will be talking	we will be talking
2nd person	you will be talking	you will be talking
3rd person	he/she/it will talking	they will be talking
Present Perfect Progressive		
1st person	I have been talking	we have been talking
2nd person	you have been talking	you have been talking
3rd person	he/she/it has been talking	they have been talking
Past Perfect Progressive		
1st person	I had been talking	we had been talking
2nd person	you had been talking	you had been talking
3rd person	he/she/it had been talking	they had been talking
Future Perfect Progressive		
1st person	I will have been talking	we will have been talking
2nd person	you will have been talking	you will have been talking
3rd person	he/she/it will have been talking	they will have been talking

Consider the following examples of changing a verb tense to create distinctions as to when something actually occurred.

- He swam yesterday. He had swum the day before that. In fact, he had been swimming every day that summer.
- He was swimming yesterday. He has been swimming every day for the past month.

Identify the verb tenses used in each of the above sentences. Explain what the differences among the tenses are. Based on these examples, try to come up with rules for the use of each tense.

PERSONAL AND REFLEXIVE PRONOUNS

Pronouns are frequently used in personal writing. The most common type, **personal pronouns**, refer to specific people or things.

When used in the subjective case they are:

I	we
you	you
he, she, it	they

These pronouns are used as subjects of a verb.

- I live here.
- She does nothing.

When used in the objective case they are:

me	us
you	you
him, her, it	them

These pronouns are used as the direct object of a verb:

- She saw him.

as the indirect object of a verb:

- I gave him five dollars.

as the object of a preposition:

- Tom came with him to the movie.
- It was divided between him and me.

When used in the possessive case, they are:

my, mine	our, ours
your, yours	your, yours
his, her, hers	their, theirs

These pronouns are used to show possession or ownership:

The dog is mine.
Their dog was kept in a kennel.
The dog kept in the kennel was theirs.

Reflexive pronouns refer to the subject of the sentence or clause. The reflexive pronouns are:

myself	ourselves
yourself	yourselves
himself, herself, itself, oneself	themselves

They are used in a sentence when the subject and object of the sentence are the same:

He cut himself shaving

We also use reflexive pronouns after prepositions:

We'll pay for ourselves.
He lives by himself.

Notice however, that if the preposition indicates place, we use personal pronouns:

Did you take your children with you?
I haven't any money on me.

Reflexive pronouns can also be used for emphasis:

The Grinch, himself, carved the roast beast.

APOSTROPHES

Apostrophes are used to indicate possession.

For singular nouns, add the apostrophe and then *s*:

a week's pay
the valley's residents

When a singular proper noun ends in *s*, the possessive form is written with an apostrophe and *s*.

> James's calendar

For nouns with regular plurals, add the apostrophe after the *s*:

> the teachers' decision
> the buses' fumes

Presenting Personal Writing: Storytelling

So much of personal writing is taken up with **telling stories**. We recount what's just happened to us; what happened to people in our lives; even the strange encounter that we observed on this morning's bus ride. The difference between the stories we write and the stories we relate orally to other people can be summed up in one word: performance.

Telling stories is part of our everyday interaction with others, and is rarely rehearsed. This distinguishes it from **professional storytelling**, which is a formal performance based on careful preparation. Stories are often shared in front of a large audience, whose response is controlled through physical gestures, pacing, and voice inflection.

Consider the following two narratives. You might try reading them aloud. Which of the two do you think is the better-told story?

> So I get to my grandmother's house and ... ah ... Like she's not there. Oh yeah, my mother sent me with some stuff—in a basket—I don't know ... like cookies or something. Maybe a pie. Yeah, it was probably a pie because she baked yesterday. We had one last night. Oh yeah, my grandmother. So I go, "Grandmother, where are you?" and I hear a sound in the bedroom, so I figure she's napping. She does that a lot now. Old people do that—nap, I mean. Where was I? Ah ... so I go into the bedroom and she's in bed all bundled up. So I go, "Grandma, you don't look like you." Like she usually doesn't wear those nightcaps, so it was hard for me to see her face, I guess. But I haven't been over much recently. Anyway, to make a long story short, it's a wolf in bed, this woodcutter runs in and my grandmother's inside— the wolf. Great eh?

Yesterday my mother asked me to take some baking she'd done to my grandmother. When I finally got to my grandmother's house, there seemed to be no one home. It was eerily quiet. I called out and heard a response coming from my grandmother's bedroom. From the doorway, all I could see was this figure all bundled up in the bed. I made some comment about how ill she looked when the figure bolted out of the bed. I screamed and ran for the front door. Standing there was a woodcutter with an axe raised in his hand. It occurred to me that my life was over when I realized that the woodcutter was headed for the wolf and not for me. I managed to get out of the cottage. I could hear the most terrifying sounds coming from inside but I was too afraid to go back to see what was happening. Finally it went quiet and I heard my grandmother's voice calling me. I ran back into the cottage and there she was standing beside the woodcutter. There was blood everywhere and the corpse of one very dead wolf, but Nan was okay. It really was a miracle. What a day!

Preparing a Storytelling Presentation

Your first question, of course, is "Which story?" It's important to make your selection very carefully. The story should have a special meaning for you. If you have no personal connection to it, it will be difficult to tell it well.

If the story is a written one, read the text over many times. Make a mental note of the sequence of the events. What must the listener hear in order for the story to make sense? Are there particular words or phrases that serve as cues that you must remember in order to retell it?

If the story is not in written form, make a point-form outline of the sequence of events on a cue card. Perhaps key words or phrases will be enough to help you remember.

Rehearsing Your Story

- *Practise telling your story out loud. The more often you tell it, the more opportunities you'll give yourself for shaping and fine-tuning your presentation. Rehearse your story as many times as you need to gain confidence.*

- *You might take turns with a partner. Getting feedback is important; you might be doing something during your storytelling of which you're unaware. Sometimes recording yourself will give you this information, but you must listen carefully.*

- *Vary the sentence structures and lengths of sentences as you tell the story. This will help to enliven your presentation.*
- *Vary the pacing of the story. There should be points at which you increase the tempo to enhance the tension and other points at which you slow your pace for dramatic effect.*
- *Avoid using such unnecessary interjections as* ah, like, *and* so.
- *Avoid using slang or clichés.*
- *Avoid the word* goes *(i.e., Then she goes, "...") when quoting dialogue.*
- *Use gestures effectively to help dramatize the story.*
- *Make eye contact with the listener.*

Presenting Your Story

During your presentation you need to be sensitive to the effect your story is having on your listeners. If possible, alter your presentation accordingly.

Monitoring and Adjusting to Audience Response

- *Is your audience attentive?*
- *Does their body language suggest that they're interested?*
- *Is there any form of affirmation upon completion of the story?*
- *If they ask questions, elaborate on parts of the story.*
- *If their interest seems to wane at a certain point, move on quickly to the next part of the story.*
- *If they seem confused or have misunderstood something, backtrack smoothly and qualify or elaborate.*

Checklist

Storytelling Presentation

- Have you chosen a story to tell that has a personal resonance for you? ❑
- Do you have a clear written outline of the story as a basis for rehearsing your presentation? ❑
- Have you varied the sentence structure and pacing of the story? ❑
- Have you eliminated all slang and clichés? ❑
- While you rehearse, have you incorporated gestures to enhance the impact of the story? ❑
- Have you practised your story often enough that you feel confident in presenting it? ❑
- During your presentation, were you sensitive to your listeners' response, and were you able to respond accordingly? ❑

CHAPTER 6

reports

> Non-fiction writers help us to hold onto our truths.
> *Michael Ondaatje*
>
> There is nothing so captivating as new knowledge.
> *Peter Mere Latham*

The report is perhaps one of the most common forms of writing used today. In the world of business and the sciences it is a frequently used mode of communication about current trends, research, and events. A report is written with the purpose of communicating information or explaining something. In this sense it differs from the essay, which is written with the intent of communicating a position, opinion, or point of view and often attempts to persuade the reader of the validity of the writer's perspective. Although a report should be an unbiased presentation of factual information, on occasion it is possible to detect an author's bias. The information that it contains has been selected, sorted, and synthesized to give the reader relevant and important information on a specific topic.

LEARNING GOALS

- develop understanding of the form and structure of reports
- analyze organizational patterns and graphic design
- examine the stylistic devices used in report writing
- develop the skills to write informational reports
- learn how to deliver an effective presentation

CONTENTS

Analyzing and Responding to Reports

» CHECKPOINT: *Assess Your Knowledge*

Sheltering the Deep

Exploring Canada's Marine Protected Areas

From the underwater kelp forests of the Pacific to the ice-free polynyas of the Arctic, from the world famous Grand Banks of the Atlantic to the freshwater Great Lakes, Canada has an incredibly diverse marine environment and the longest coastline in the world. It comes as no surprise, then, that Canada has a rich marine heritage. What is surprising is how slow we have been to protect our watery realms.

The concept of establishing protected water areas may seem a novel idea, yet Canada lags behind many countries in the world. Australia, New Zealand, the Philippines, and the United States have all set up marine protected areas (MPAs).

A litany of threats face Canada's oceans and Great Lakes: the collapse of Atlantic groundfish stocks, the decline of Pacific salmon, and pollution in the Arctic and Great Lakes. Our current approach to marine management focuses on managing individual fish stocks for human harvest. We now realize we need new tools to conserve marine ecosystems.

While marine protected areas cannot solve all of the problems facing the oceans, they do lay an important foundation. Marine protected areas challenge us to consider marine ecosystems, the role of individual species in these ecosystems, and how these different plants and animal species are interrelated.

Over the past few years, concerned Canadians, First Nations, conservation organizations, and governments have promoted marine protected areas as a vital tool to protect marine biodiversity in Canada. In addition, marine protected areas can also provide many recreational opportunities, including kayaking, boating, diving, and whale watching.

What Are MPAs?

Marine protected areas require long-term legal protection. The seabed, water column, plants, animals, and species habitats are all included within an MPA. Size and protection levels can vary. Harvest refugia that are totally closed to all consumptive uses are at one end of the spectrum; multiple use areas are at the other end.

To be effective, MPAs need protection from human activities that can cause long-term, large-scale habitat disruption. At a minimum, Canada should prohibit the following activities in every MPA: oil, gas, and mineral exploration and development, dredging, dumping, bottom trawling, and salmon aquaculture.

A number of fascinating marine areas across the country are being studied for possible protected status. The final decisions are not in, and the processes that will lead to protection can seem to take forever. But all of these sites offer a fascinating glimpse into the varied and beautiful marine realm that surrounds our country.

Race Rocks, B.C.

Perched off the southern tip of Vancouver Island in Juan de Fuca Strait are the subtidal reefs and small islands known as Race Rocks. Strong tidal currents, which reach up to seven knots, ensure a regular and abundant supply of nutrients to nourish the many complex groups of underwater species. Among them, corals, sea stars, kelp, anemones, sponges, and seas urchins adorn the underwater cliffs.

Over 1,500 Northern or Steller and California sea lions haul out on the islets as do hundreds of harbour seals. Other marine mammals, such as the northern fur and elephant seals, porpoises, and grey whales, are occasionally observed. Up to 60 orca whales frequent the waters, foraging on the sea lions, seals, and salmon. The islands provide an important nesting area for many sea birds, including cormorants, guillemots, oyster-catchers, and gulls.

While the primary activities at Race Rocks are research and education, recreational use of the area is growing. The spectacular marine life and highly transparent waters, especially during the winter months, make it a popular diving destination. A thrill for divers is to swim with the sea lions, although caution must be exercised. Experienced paddlers can kayak close to sea lions basking on rocks or bobbing in the rich waters.

Visitors can severely impact the delicate underwater communities by anchoring and can disturb nesting sea birds or resting sea lions and

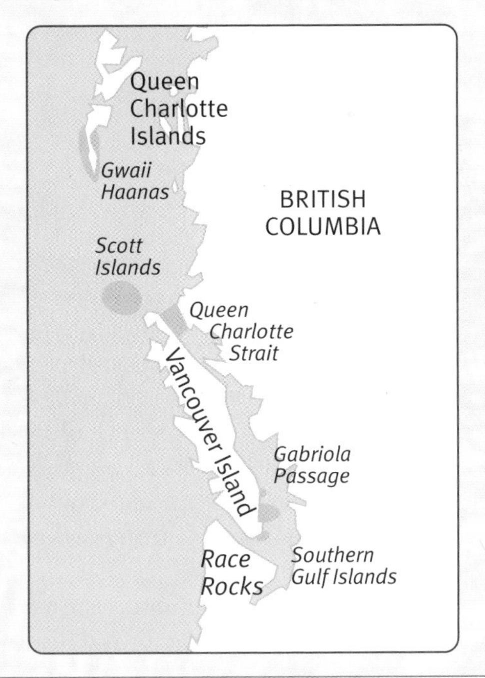

seals by landing or passing too close to the small islets. Scientists and local managers have also raised concerns about the effects of whale watching and other human activities on whales and their foraging.

Race Rocks received provincial ecological reserve status in 1980, and became a pilot marine protected area under Canada's Oceans Act in 1998 to provide better protection and management of the area, including full fishing closures.

Lake Superior, Ontario

East of Thunder Bay along the wild shore of northern Lake Superior lies an incredible area of hundreds of small islands, rocky shoals, channels, and sheltered bays, all dominated by the cold, deep waters of the largest Great Lake.

Lake and speckled trout spawn in the shallow bays, while bald eagles and peregrine falcons are making a comeback after being decimated by DDT pollution. Colonies of great blue herons, ring-billed and herring gulls and double crested cormorants nest on the smaller islands. Raptors and songbirds migrate south through the area in the fall.

Signs of the past remind visitors of the rich geologic and cultural history of the region. The microfossils of Schreiber Channel preserve the earliest life forms on earth. The ancient traces of the first inhabitants, such as cairns and pictographs, highlight the spiritual importance of this area. The numerous shipwrecks, now a magnet for recreational divers, attest to the treacherous waters and well-known fury of Lake Superior storms. Popular recreational activities pursued in the area include boating, canoeing, kayaking, camping, and fishing.

Work began in 1993 to establish a marine conservation area in Lake Superior. Local community representatives and conservation groups working with Parks Canada and the Ontario Ministry of Natural Resources are developing recommendations in the study area for broader public consideration.

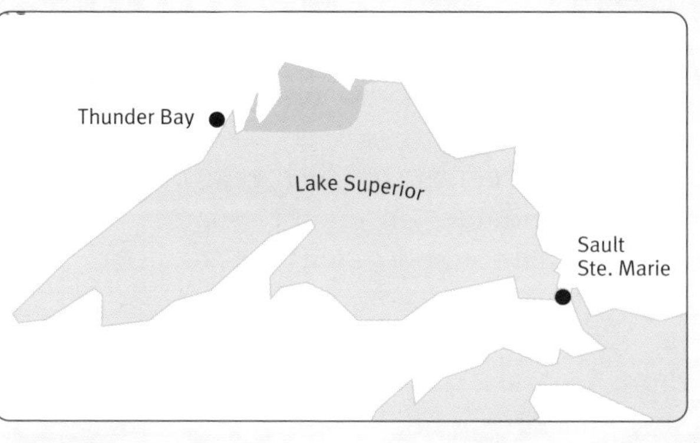

Igalirtuuq, Nunavut

The many inlets, fiords, and bays along the coast of Baffin Island pro-

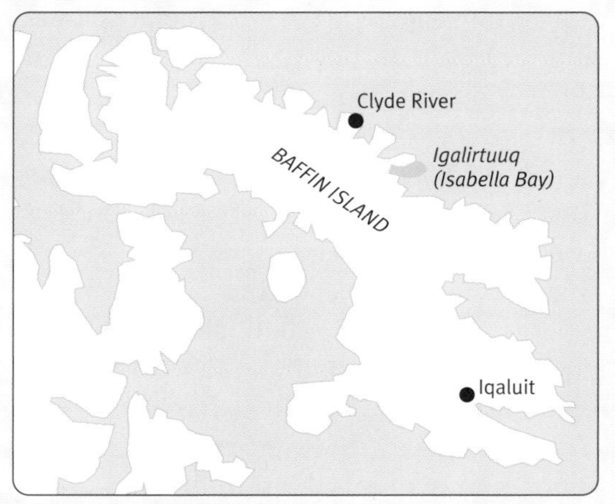

vide important whale habitat for all three of the arctic whales—belugas, narwhals, and bowheads. Narwhals head for deep fiords, bowheads for areas rich with plankton, and belugas for shallow river mouths.

The largest of the arctic whales, the 70-tonne bowhead, is the focus of conservation efforts to establish a marine protected area at Igalirtuuq (formerly Isabella Bay) on the eastern shores of Baffin Island. Led by the local hunters and trappers association, the Inuit community of Clyde River has been trying since 1980 to ensure that this critically important habitat for the endangered eastern Arctic bowhead whale is protected by the Canadian Wildlife Service as a national wildlife area.

Over the past two centuries, unsustainable commercial hunting almost wiped out the bowhead whale population, reducing it to only 1,000 individuals from a former estimate of 11,000. They have been slow to recover, despite a commercial whaling ban on bowheads for over 60 years. With a low reproductive rate and facing threats posed by pollution, boat traffic, and exploration for oil and gas, the bowhead remains endangered.

About 100 bowhead whales come to Igalirtuuq (pronounced *i gal´ er tuck*) in August and September to mate, socialize, and feed in safety from their main predator, the orca whale. Rich in shrimp-like krill—the main source of food for the baleen whale—the bay contains two deep offshore troughs and a shallow shelf at its entrance.

The community of Clyde River is the contact point for travel into the deep fiords of central Baffin that are internationally renowned for their soaring walls and spectacular scenery. Glaciers and icebergs abound in the region.

Whale-watching trips in Nunavut are becoming increasingly popular. However, access to Igalirtuuq is difficult and requires travel along an exposed coastline. A few select groups of tourists may enter the Igalirtuuq area in late summer with a licensed outfitter. Visitors who are lucky enough to make such a trip may also see polar bears, seals, narwhals, and snow geese.

Basin Head, P.E.I.

A shallow, five-kilometre-long coastal lagoon, Basin Head is located on the southeastern tip of Prince Edward Island, near the town of Souris. The lagoon is bounded by agricultural land on the north side and by an extensive system of sand dunes on the south. The beautiful sandy beaches and warm, safe water have long been an attraction in the area.

Many different types of plants and animals live within this unique coastal environment. Of particular interest is a unique strain of Irish moss, found nowhere else in the world.

The lagoon once served as an important fishing port. However, as the entrance to the lagoon narrowed and became shallower, only smaller boats could enter. Eventually, fishers shifted to other local ports.

The Basin Head Fisheries Museum, located adjacent to the lagoon, displays the rich cultural history of the nearby coastal communities. Visitors can view fishing gear, boats, artifacts, and photos that depict the early evolution of inshore fishing. Camping is available at nearby provincial parks. Opportunities for cycling and kayaking from inn to inn are also popular in the area.

Protecting the estuary and its unique Irish moss is the key concern of a local committee. While swimming, scuba diving, recreational fishing, and shellfish harvesting will likely continue, activities such as power boating, harvesting of mussels, bottom trawling and dumping may be prohibited.

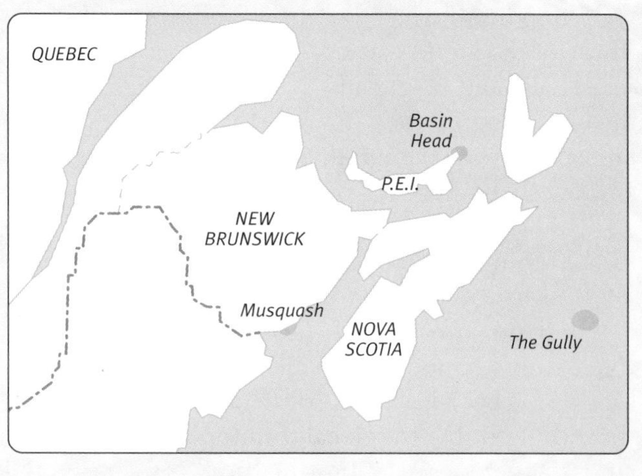

Other Sites

Across Canada, communities, conservation groups, First Nations, and government agencies are working to establish their MPAs. In the Queen Charlotte Islands in British Columbia, the 12-year-old proposal to create a national marine conservation areas in Gwaii Haanas continues to move slowly. Off the northwest tip of Vancouver Island

Too Close and Personal?

The commercial whale-watching industry has grown rapidly around the world. Some communities enjoy significant economic benefits from this growing tourism activity, and local interest in marine mammal conservation has been heightened.

However, scientists are concerned about the potential impact on whale behaviour. Studies of interactions between whale watchers and resident orca whales off northeastern Vancouver Island have shown significant effects of boats on whale swimming and diving behaviour. The long-term impact of such disturbance on the whales remains uncertain....

Fisheries and Oceans Canada administers the regulations protecting whales from harassment, and issues guidelines for both commercial and recreational whale watchers. The regulations prohibit disturbance of whales, with penalties of fines and/or imprisonment....

lie the Scott Islands. The Canadian Parks and Wilderness Society has been urging the Canadian Wildlife Service to protect the ocean area around the Scott Islands for the millions of sea birds that nest on the islands and feed in the rich waters around them. Off the east coast of Nova Scotia, progress remains slow on protecting the Gully, also an MPA pilot site. This deep, underwater canyon is critical to a population of bottlenose whales.

Protecting Canada's spectacular and rich marine environment needs your help. Take the time to visit some of these beautiful places, to learn what makes them special and to understand how you can get involved. Contact the conservation groups and government agencies that are working to ensure a healthy future for our oceans.

Sabine Jessen

Marine Protected Areas in Canada*

Region	Total #	Federal Sites	Provincial Sites	Other
Pacific Coast	110 1,762 sq km	1 national park 2 national wildlife areas 4 migratory bird sanctuaries	15 ecological reserves 86 provincial parks 3 recreation areas	1 municipal site
Central & Arctic	29 2,152 sq km	6 national parks 2 national wildlife areas 17 migratory bird sanctuaries	2 provincial parks 1 territorial park	
Laurentian	19 1,482 sq km	1 national park 2 national wildlife areas 15 migratory bird sanctuaries	1 provincial park	
Maritimes	24 2,764 sq km	1 national park 8 national wildlife areas 6 migratory bird sanctuaries 3 whale sanctuaries	3 provincial parks	
Newfoundland	9 413 sq km	1 national park 3 migratory bird sanctuaries	2 no hunt zones 4 ecological reserves	

Statistics not available for the Great Lakes region.
* Only three sites in Canada meet the minimum protection standards for a Marine Protected Area: Fatom Five national Marine Park, Ontario; Saguenay-St Lawrence Marine Park, Quebec; and Pacific Rim National Park Reserve, B.C.

1. Explain how this report is organized.
2. What is the author's purpose in writing it?
3. What information is provided in the visual text that is not found in the written text?
4. Why did the author choose the examples she did?
5. What stylistic techniques did she use to catch and sustain reader interest?

Reading Strategies

A report requires reading strategies that are different from those of a poem, short story, or novel. Unlike reading a work of literature, you don't expect to be entertained or emotionally involved in the text. Instead, you read a report to gain information. In fact, it's unlikely that you will have any aesthetic response.

Tips on Reading Reports

- *Before you read, consider your prior knowledge about the topic. You might want to jot down what you think you already know.*
- *Consider the reason for your reading. What is it that you want to learn from the text?*
- *Begin by scanning the headings and subheadings. If there are no headings, scan the first sentence of each paragraph.*
- *You don't necessarily have to read the report from beginning to end. There are many gateways through which to enter, including headings and subheadings, illustrations, photographs, graphics, and charts. You might want to read only the introduction, and then select other information you require based on the headings.*
- *"Read" the illustrations and graphics as well as the words, since the images and words together create the meaning. Graphics often provide additional information not included in the print.*
- *Vary the pace of your reading. You may want to skim information that isn't relevant to you or that you already know. Read more slowly during sections on important issues or specific details.*
- *Make notes as you read, using Post-its or a graphic organizer. Determining the organizational pattern first (see "Organizational Patterns" below) will help you decide what type of organizer to use.*

Understanding Meaning

Understanding the **organizational pattern** used in a written report will help you to read and synthesize the information contained within it. Common organizational patterns are found in reports, just as they are in essays. In essays these patterns may be used to help convince the reader of a particular perspective. In reports, however, they are used to communicate information.

TYPES OF ORGANIZATIONAL PATTERNS

ANALYSIS

An **analytical pattern** identifies and explains a phenomenon. It's an objective, after-the-fact analysis of a problem and its solution, or an event and its outcome.

The transitional words and phrases most often found in this type of report are ones that refer to relationships. Common signal phrases include: *adding to the effect, in addition to, related to, just as important as, for example, connected to, supporting, together with, no less important, sometimes overlooked*.

Notice that some of these phrases (e.g., *just as important as* or *no less important*) suggest an opinion or impose a value. Noting the implied value is a good way of detecting bias. For example, a business report might contain the statement, "Just as important as the model provided by the management team was the contribution of the sales staff." Unless this statement were supported by factual data, it could be said to reflect bias.

CAUSE AND EFFECT

This pattern shows a **cause-and-effect relationship** between ideas and events, or events and other events. This relationship may be signalled in a report using the following words: *accordingly, as a result, because, consequently, owing to, since, therefore*.

Newspaper reports often use the cause-and-effect model. They usually identify the initiating event and outline the sequence of events that followed. Consider, for example, the kind of report that would be written under the headline "Transport Trailer Causes Multi-vehicle Pile-up on 401."

CHRONOLOGY

A report that is organized according to time sequence uses a **chronological pattern**. A scientific journal reporting on a research project spanning several months or years might use this organizational structure.

Transitional words found in a report organized chronologically include: *now, then, a little later, immediately, meanwhile, next, finally, earlier, soon, simultaneously, subsequently, previously, at last, afterwards*.

ILLUSTRATION

An **illustrative** report explains by providing one or several examples. A report on clear-cutting forests, for instance, might describe particular locations where this is taking place. The report on marine protected areas at the beginning of this chapter is another example.

Transitional words that signal this structure include: *for instance, for example, that is, namely, in fact, in particular, specifically*.

PROBLEM/SOLUTION

The **problem/solution** report identifies a problem and outlines how it was solved. The first paragraph (or paragraphs) usually identify the problem, and the remainder of the report outlines the steps taken to solve the problem.

Transitional phrases include: *because of, it was necessary to, it became apparent, it was therefore decided, it was determined that, in response*.

USING ORGANIZATIONAL PATTERNS

Although a report may use more than one type of pattern or structure, usually one will predominate.

As mentioned above, if you are planning to make notes while you read a report, it's important to first have an idea of what organizational pattern it uses.

If you determine that a report has a cause-and-effect pattern, for example, you would use graphic organizers like the ones shown below:

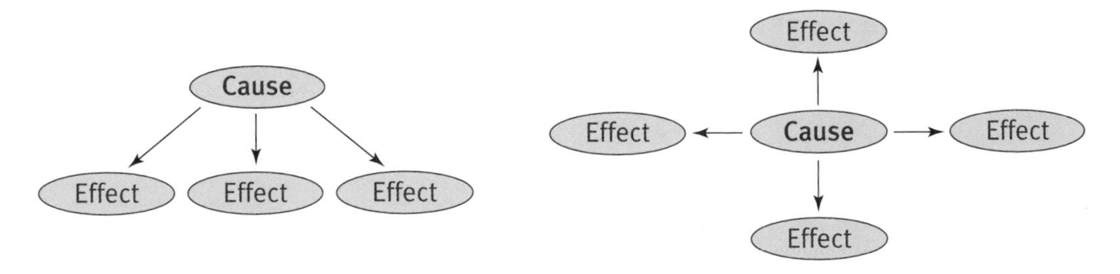

If you know that the organizational pattern is chronological, your organizer might look like this:

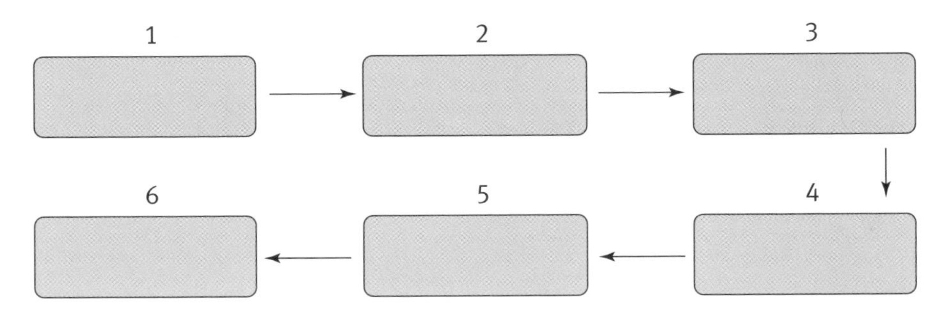

Consider how you might use the following organizers:

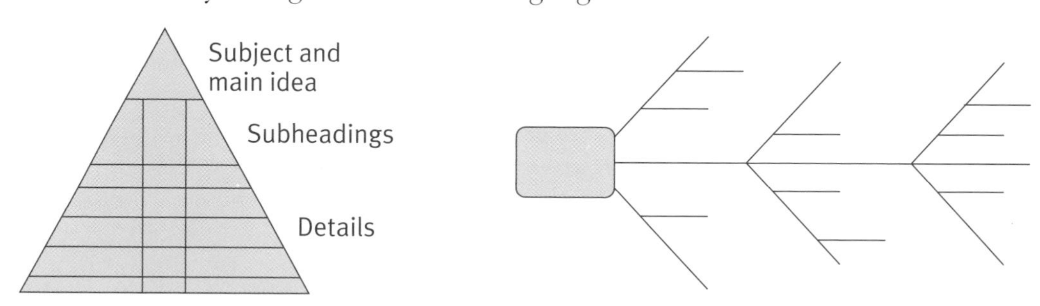

GRAPHIC TEXT

Other important sources of information in a report are illustrations, photographs, graphics, charts, diagrams, sidebars, and boxes.

These may contain additional information, or useful summaries of the written text. So reading this **visual text** is often as important as reading the written text.

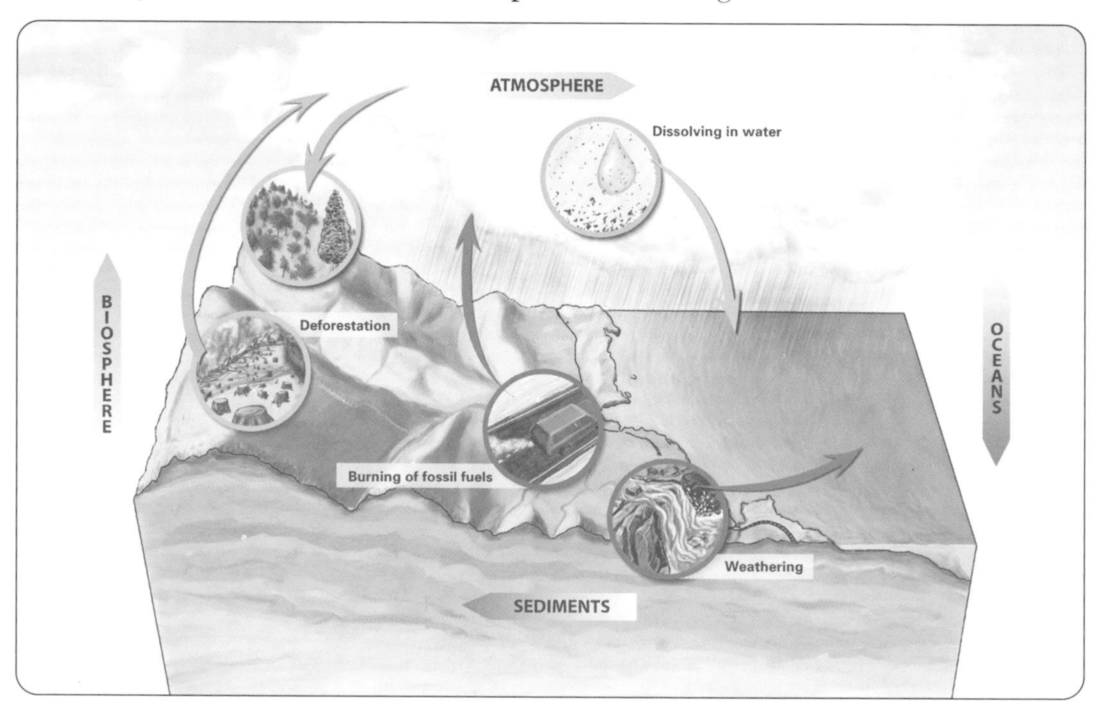

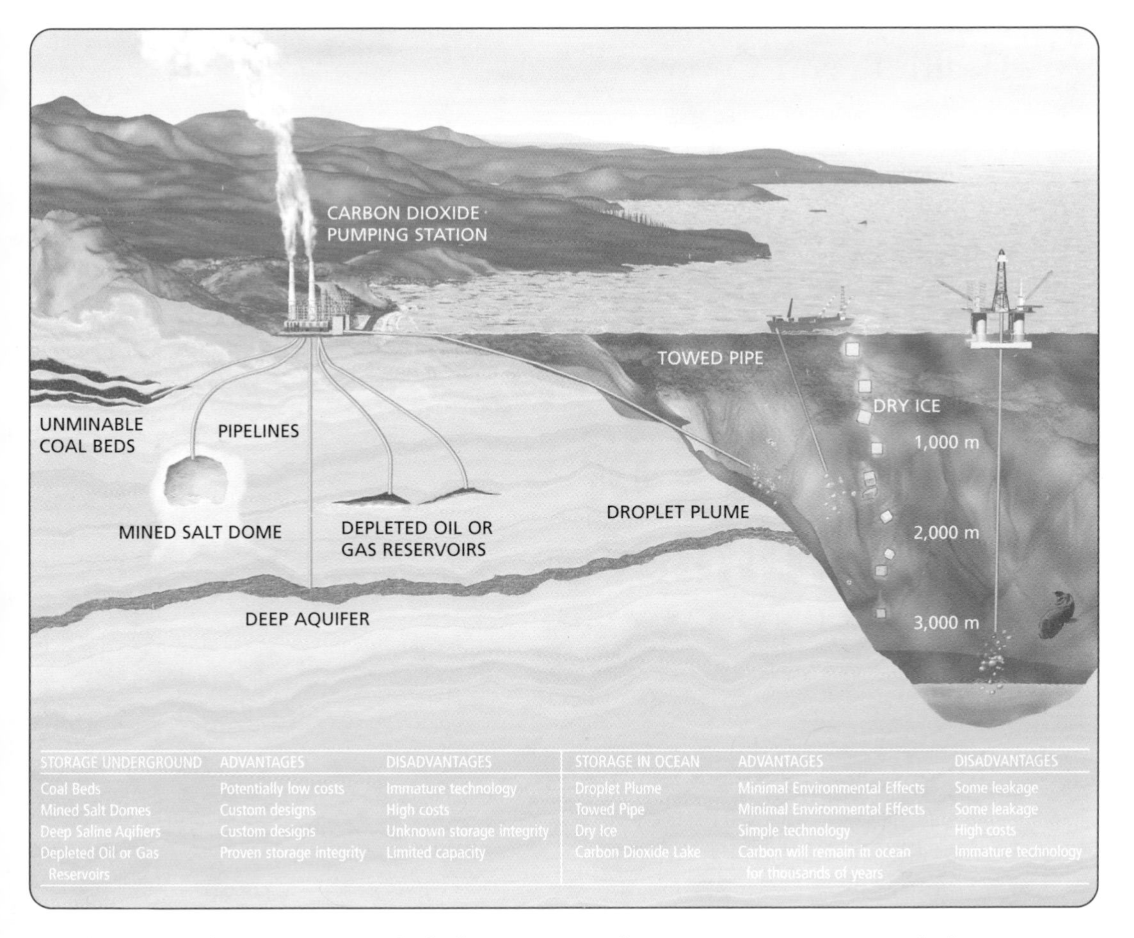

STORAGE UNDERGROUND	ADVANTAGES	DISADVANTAGES
Coal Beds	Potentially low costs	Immature technology
Mined Salt Domes	Custom designs	High costs
Deep Saline Aqifiers	Custom designs	Unknown storage integrity
Depleted Oil or Gas Reservoirs	Proven storage integrity	Limited capacity

STORAGE IN OCEAN	ADVANTAGES	DISADVANTAGES
Droplet Plume	Minimal Environmental Effects	Some leakage
Towed Pipe	Minimal Environmental Effects	Some leakage
Dry Ice	Simple technology	High costs
Carbon Dioxide Lake	Carbon will remain in ocean for thousands of years	Immature technology

These visual texts were included in a *Scientific American* report entitled "Capturing Greenhouse Gases." Note how the illustrations help to communicate information in an accessible way.

Consider also the **typography**, or type features, used in a report. The publisher gives careful consideration to the style, colour, and font used to convey information. Often a change of font or type style will highlight important or key information. **Signposts** such as headings and subheadings, bullets, arrows, boxes, rules, borders, loops, and asterisks, also help the reader's understanding of the report.

Note how the typography and signposts in the following report contribute to your understanding of its meaning:

Health Report Cover

Clusters of Healthiness

Where are the healthiest Canadians? The communities showing the best results over a wide range of health indicators exist in clusters, particularly in and around Vancouver and Toronto. The two left-hand columns of the chart tally the categories in which Statistics Canada has deemed a health region's results to be significantly better (+) or worse (-) than the Canadian norm. (A blank space indicates results close to the norm.) Because the significance of indicators varies considerably (lung cancer, for instance, claims eight times as many lives in a year as bronchitis, asthma and emphysema combined), the totals serve as a broad indicator of overall health and cannot be interpreted as a strict ranking.

Colour codes:

- British Columbia
- Prairies
- Ontario
- Quebec
- Atlantic

Life expectancy: The age to which a person would be expected to live, based on mortality rates in 1996. (Canadian norm: 78.4 years)
Infant mortality: The number of infants who die in the first year of life, expressed as a rate per 1,000 live births. (Norm: 5.7)
Low birth weight: The proportion of live births of infants weighing less than 2,500 g (five pounds, eight ounces). This is a key determinant of infant survival, health and development. (Norm: 5.8 per cent)
Death rates: The rate of death from specific causes per 100,000 population. Lower rates indicate success in disease prevention, detection and treatment. (Norms: lung cancer: 49.2; breast cancer: 28.3; prostate cancer: 29.7; colorectal cancer: 19.4; coronary heart disease: 136.4; stroke: 48.4; other circulatory diseases: 61; pneumonia and flu: 23.3; bronchitis, asthma and emphysema: 6.1; other respiratory diseases: 30.3; unintentional injury: 27.7; suicide: 12.9; HIV: 4)

Source: Statistics Canada data for 1996, adjusted to take account of age differences, from 51 health regions with populations over 100,000, representing 85.5 per cent of the Canadian population. Mortality rates and life-expectancy estimates are calculated from three years of death data (1995-1997).

HEALTH REGIONS	Total better than the norm (+)	Total worse than the norm (
North Vancouver/West Vancouver	12	1
Markham/Richmond Hill, Ont.	10	0
Mississauga/Brampton/Burlington, Ont.	9	1
Vancouver/Richmond	10	2
Toronto	9	2
Victoria	8	1
Kitchener/Waterloo, Ont.	8	2
Surrey/Langley, B.C.	6	0
Ottawa	7	2
St. Catharines/Niagara, Ont.	6	1
Peterborough, Ont.	6	2
Moncton, N.B.	5	2
Saskatoon	5	2
Calgary	5	2
Coquitlam/Burnaby/New Westminster, B.C.	6	3
Hamilton	5	3
Winnipeg	4	2
Edmonton	4	2
Chilliwack, B.C.	4	2
Prince Edward Island	5	4
Fredericton	5	4
Laval, Que.	5	4
London, Ont.	5	4
Windsor, Ont.	3	2
Regina	1	1
Red Deer, Alta.	3	3
St. John's, Nfld.	3	4
Truro, N.S.	4	5
Lévis/Thetford Mines, Que.	4	5
Granby/St-Hyacinthe, Que.	4	5
Owen Sound, Ont.	4	5
Nanaimo, B.C.	2	3
Halifax/Dartmouth	4	6
Saint John, N.B.	3	5
Quebec City	4	6
Brantford, Ont.	4	6
Sherbrooke, Que.	3	6
Montreal	5	8
Kingston, Ont.	3	6
Thunder Bay, Ont.	3	6
Yarmouth/Digby, N.S.	1	5
Lethbridge, Alta.	3	7
Trois-Rivières/Drummondville/Shawinigan, Que.	1	6
North Bay/Huntsville, Ont.	1	6
Prince George, B.C.	1	6
Hull/Aylmer, Que.	1	8
Cape Breton, N.S.	0	7
Joliette, Que.	0	7
St-Jérôme/Ste-Thérèse, Que.	0	7
Chicoutimi, Que.	0	9
Sudbury, Ont.	1	10

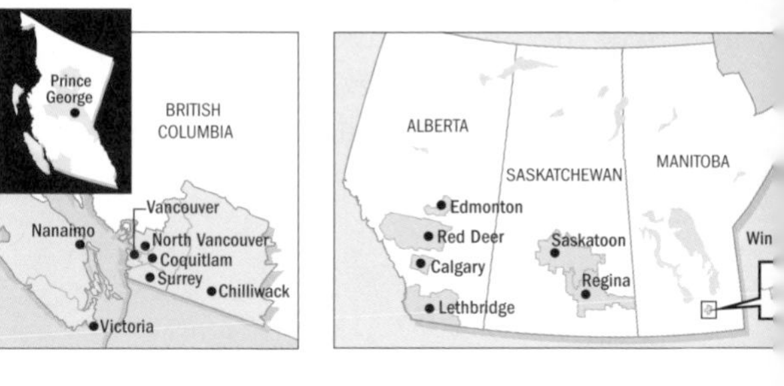

Death Rates													
Low birth weight	Lung cancer	Breast cancer	Prostate cancer	Colorectal cancer	Coronary heart disease	Stroke	Other circulatory diseases	Pneumonia and flu	Bronchitis, asthma and emphysema	Other respiratory diseases	Unintentional injury	Suicide	HIV
+	+	+		+	+		+	–	+	+	+	+	
	+				+		+		+	+	+	+	+
	+	–			+		+	+	+	+	+	+	
	+	+	+	+	+		+	–	+	+		+	–
–	+		+		+		+		+	+	+	+	–
+				+	+		+		–	+	+	+	
+	+				–	–			+	+	+	+	+
				+	+		+				+	+	
			–		–	+	+		+	+	+	+	
	+				–		+	+		+	+	+	
				+	–	–	+		+		+	+	+
			–		+		–	+	+	+			
	+	+	–		+				–	+			
–	+			+	+		–				+		
		+		+	+	–		–	–		+	+	
					–		+	–	+	+	+	+	
					–				+	+	+	+	
–	+			+			–				+		
+		+		+			+	–			–		
+	–	+	–					–		+			+
+			+	+		–	–				–	+	+
	–	–		–			+	+			+	–	
	+	–	–	+	–		+		+			+	
					–			+		+	+		
										+			
	+			+		–		–	+		–		
					–	–	–	+			+	+	
	–			+	+	+	–			–	–		+
		+			+		–	+	–		–	–	+
	–			–	–	+		+	–		+	–	
	+				–			–	+	–	–	+	+
				+	+		–	–	–				
	–	–		+		+	–	–		–	+	+	
	–			+	–		–			–	+	+	
	–			–	+	+		+	–	–	+	–	
				+	–	–	+	–	–	+	–	+	
–		+				+		+	–	–	–	–	
–	–	–	+	–	–	+	+	+	–		+		–
	–				–	–	+	–	+	–		+	
					–	–		+	+		–	–	+
	–				–		–				–		+
	+	–	–					–	–	+	–		+
	–			–				+		–	–	–	
	–				–	–	+			–	–		
	–				+		–			–	–		
	–		–	–	–		–	+		–		–	
	–				–		–		–	–	–		
	–			–	–				–	–		–	
	–			–	–				–	–		–	
	–	–		–		–			–	–	–	–	
	–			–	–		–	–	–	–	–	–	+

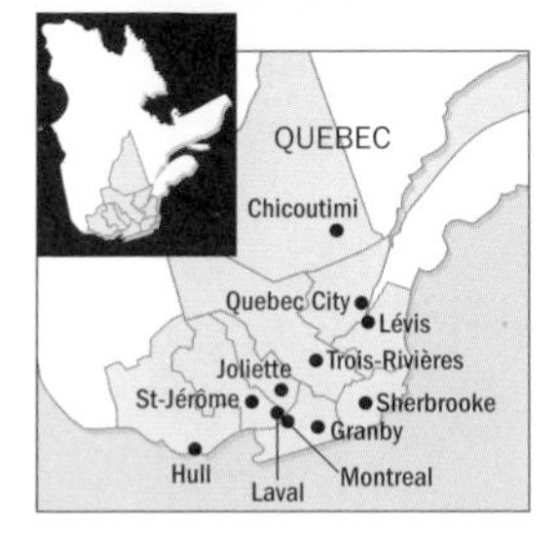

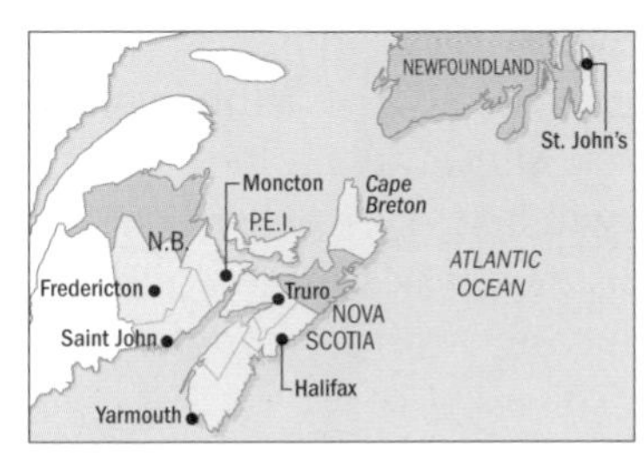

The annotations to the following report show how meaning is conveyed through its organizational pattern and graphic elements.

Struck by Lightning

Primal and powerful, lightning is one of nature's gravest hazards. A new national detection system pinpoints almost every flash.

organizational pattern: problem–solution (with illustration)

CHRISTINE FRAM was struck by lightning on August 6, 1997, while inside a building, which is a relatively safe place, in Vancouver, where there is relatively little lightning. In that split second, she joined the 60 or so Canadians who are struck by lightning each year. She was not among the six or seven who die, but was among those whose lives were, as she says, "rewritten" by the experience.

introductory paragraphs provide specific example

Then 28 and an apprentice auto mechanic, Fram was standing near a metal workbench on the Grandview Tire and Auto shop on Commercial Drive. Lightning struck the power lines outside, surged through to an electrical box on the wall inside, travelled down to the bench, then jumped across a metre-wide gap to her left hand. She heard a bang and saw a blue flash. A man near her saw the bolt. A blue glow filled the room.

Fram felt pain in her left hand. There were holes in her rubber glove, and the rubber sole of her left shoe was melted. Her muscles twitched. Her heart beat irregularly. She was stunned and confused, having weird thought processes, feeling as if she wasn't breathing. Pain spread over her left side, then numbness. She couldn't walk. Her boss drove her to the hospital.

Stupendous bolts of electricity come hurtling from the sky roughly five million times a day worldwide. Considering that each thunderstorm—there are 2,000 in progress at any one time—produces thousands of flashes, it is remarkable that more people aren't injured or killed. Detection systems across Canada and around the world are now helping reduce that risk by sensing almost every bolt, logging its location, direction, timing and frequency, and thus improving our ability to forecast severe storms. We have by no means tamed this force of nature, and we still have much to learn about its impact on humans, but we do know how much damage a bolt can cause and how to protect ourselves.

identifies topic

With its megavolt charges and the explosive effects of its intense heat, lightning can blow apart trees or blast the bricks off buildings. It commonly electrocutes cattle seeking shelter under trees in rainstorms; the current enters the ground through a tree's roots, then travels up the legs of the hapless creatures.

Most skyscrapers, broadcasting towers, bridges and industrial plants have lightning rods. Devised by Benjamin Franklin in the 1750s, the lightning rod is designed to "catch" a bolt and direct its current safely to the ground. Even the steel reinforcing rods inside the concrete CN Tower—which is struck repeatedly during the summer thunderstorm season—are thoroughly grounded. Steel power pylons, obvious lightning attractors, are grounded as well, and their high-voltage lines are protected by lightning arrestors, devices that sense the surges lightning produces, shut down the system, then automatically restart it seconds later. They keep your power on during an electrical storm—and leave your digital clocks flashing.

eady well-established—ocedures

But some things can't be protected. Lightning ignites 4,000 forest fires on average each year in Canada, burning more than two million hectares (an area larger than Lake Ontario). Modern forestry recognizes fire as an important player in the forest cycle, but it remains the enemy in certain stands and near communities. Thus the forest ranger, once a sentinel in a tall tower in the woods, then in a patrol aircraft, is now also stationed in an office scanning computer screens for news from electronic lightning-detection systems.

Two years ago, Canada was outfitted with such a system, by which unmanned sensors can pinpoint ground-striking lightning bolts to within a few hundred metres. There are 81 stations—with sensing antennas, GPS receivers and satellite dishes—distributed from coast to coast. A lightning flash almost anywhere in forested Canada is detected by at least 4 and as many as 10 stations, and its strength, polarity and time to the millisecond are recorded.

new strategies

"They pick up the electromagnetic pulse that lightning produces," says Garry Pearson, who manages the $9.5 million Canadian Lightning Detection Network from an Environment Canada office in Halifax. "It's like your radio crackling when there's lightning nearby."

The sensors transmit the pulses to Global Atmospherics Inc. in

how it works—authority, quotes

A "leader" descends in steps from the cloud
from the ground
"Streamers" rise

Stroke returns up ionized channel formed when leader and streamer meet

A momentary pause ensues

A "dart leader" moves down same channel

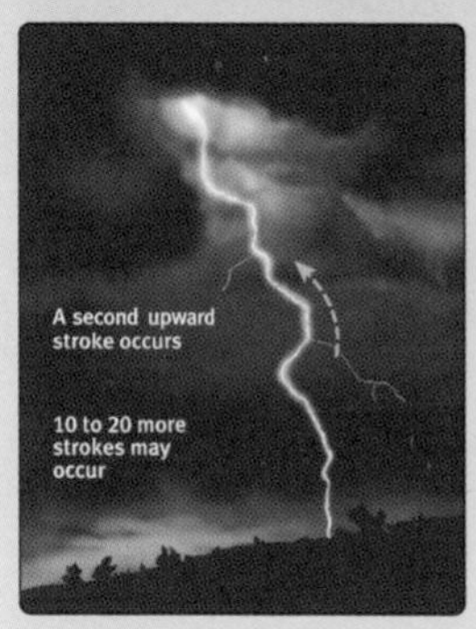
A second upward stroke occurs
10 to 20 more strokes may occur

In a matter of milliseconds, electrons of opposing polarity build to excessive levels, then rush to close the gap between them (*left*), creating mega-charged torrents of electricity that can travel 10 or more kilometres from cloud to ground. Lightning hot spots in Canada (*opposite page*) are found in southern Ontario and the Prairies. Two-thirds of all strikes in the northern hemisphere occur during June, July and August, most of them in the afternoon.

graphics illustrate phenomenon being discussed

how it works—authority, quotes

Tucson, Ariz., where computers locate the lightning by triangulation and send the information back to Environment Canada offices, all in a few seconds. Similar lightning-detection networks operate in 40 countries—covering much of the forested world.

"We get the information as dots on a screen," says Pearson; "usually overlaid with satellite pictures and other information. It gets kind of exciting sometimes—or at least exciting for meteorologists—when there's a lot going on and we can see how things are developing. Formerly, even with radar and satellites, we couldn't always be sure there was a storm in progress. Now if we see there's lightning, that confirms it."

So the lightning reports are of immediate value in weather forecasting and, as all the information is saved, of lasting value as a source of data.

"We archive everything," says Pearson, "the lats and longs of the strikes, amperage, time to the millisecond. It builds up a climatology of lightning, a history of the more vulnerable places."

That information is vital to airlines plotting routes, power companies planning power lines, golf-course designers, construction firms—and insurance companies,

who benefits

If Lightning Strikes ...

If someone is struck by lightning, immediately check for injuries and call for emergency assistance. Victims are not dangerous to touch. The myth that they hold an electrical charge which can shock others has led to unnecessary deaths due to delayed cardiopulmonary resuscitation. If there is no pulse or respiration, CPR should be administered right away. During an active storm, rescuers are at risk as well, so the victim should be moved to a safer area, unless they have fallen or been thrown a great distance.

Cardiac arrest is the main cause of death from lightning strikes. In general, lightning injuries are varied, ranging from vision and hearing loss, tinnitus (ringing ears), memory loss, confusion, cardiac arrhythmia and vascular instability. Serious burns are uncommon. Other residual effects include sleep disturbances, anxiety attacks, pain syndromes, peripheral nerve damage, and diffuse neurological and neuropsychological damage. The study of lightning injury is called keraunomedicine.

which use the archives to verify claims of lightning damage. In a third of the lightning-damage claims that Global Atmospherics was asked to verify for insurance investigators last year, there had been no lightning.

who benefits

Forestry departments are the major clients of lightning-detection systems, both the new cross-Canada network and various provincial counterparts. They all do the same thing: watch for lighting strikes in parched or otherwise high-risk regions and, allowing for smoulder-ing time, send up an aircraft in a day or two to look for smoke.

justifies why we need devices described in report

"Give credit to Environment Canada," says Peter Konopelny, a supervisor with Manitoba's forest-fire program. "For accuracy, reliability and maintenance, the new national system is far better than what we had before. And, bottom line, our ability to detect forest fires is greatly improved."

concludes returning illustratio

In the months after being struck, Christine Fram found herself changed, not totally impaired, but still facing "a whole bunch of little things" she hadn't experienced before—problems with memory, mental quickness and fatigue.

"Sometimes I know I seem dense," she says. "I see an apple in a store, and I can't think of what it's called. And sometimes when somebody says something to me, it takes me longer to figure out what was said. I have trouble with hearing and seeing too, not with the senses themselves but with the brain's interpretation. I can't distinguish conversation from background noise or judge distances so well." ...

"It's a life-changing experience," says Fram. "You have to start over again."

Dane Lanken

Understanding Form

Although reports vary in their organizational patterns, the form of a report always contains certain standard elements.

INTRODUCTION

The **introduction** to a report establishes the general context and identifies the specific topic.

Look at this introduction to a November 2, 2000, *Globe and Mail* newspaper article. Based on these introductory paragraphs, what type of information do you think will be contained in the paragraphs that follow?

> **Chile Faces Rainforest Dilemma**
> by Jimmy Langman
> Puerto Montt, Chile
>
> Every year ecotourists from around the world are drawn to southern Chile's Lake District and northern Patagonia. The region boasts Andean mountains, vast stands of temperate rainforest, rapid rivers, volcanoes and turquoise lakes. It's a perfect place for hiking, kayaking and fly fishing.
>
> The area is also ideal for salmon farming. In less than a decade, Chile has become the world's second-largest producer and exporter of salmon.
>
> Now the U.S. multinational Boise Cascade Corp. has new plans for the district: a controversial project to build what would be the world's largest timber mill in the middle of the region, a project four times larger than current logging ventures in Chile and one that could endanger rare old-growth forest.

BODY

The **body** of the report provides detailed information selected because of its relevance to the topic. These details are sometimes referred to as the five W's—who, what, where, when, and why. The general information provided in the introduction is elaborated on, and important facts about various aspects of the topic are interpreted.

This information is organized into paragraphs that link cohesively in a logical order. Sometimes different aspects of the topic are given headings and subheadings.

CONCLUSION

The **conclusion** may review the main points contained in the body of the report. It may also identify further issues that are relevant to the topic.

The concluding paragraph of the report on the Chilean rainforest, for example, simply states, "The ruling [of an international environmental protection group] will not have the power to force a government agency to act in a particular way."

The annotations to the following report point out the clarity of its structure. This clarity of form helps readers grasp the content.

A Matter of Trust

topic — Water is governed by a patchwork of regulations.

introduction
- states problem
- poses key question
- quotes authority as justification

Fear has been good for Jack McAllister's business. For 12 years, his company, The Water Boys, has delivered spring and distilled water to Hamilton residents. Living in Steel Town, his customers have long been suspicious of the tap water the heavily industrialized city draws from Lake Ontario. But the *E. coli* poisonings in Walkerton, Ont., have added a whole other dimension, doubling sales last week. "It's really scared people," McAllister says. "When you talk death, that's the end of the road."

Canadians across the country are asking whether their water is safe—and wondering who is protecting them and how. Many question the wisdom of having huge factory farms in their communities. And some, like environmental lawyer Elizabeth May, executive director of the Sierra Club, want to know why Ottawa does not set binding regulations for water quality. At the moment, Ottawa's involvement is limited: it is part of the federal-provincial subcommittee on drinking water, which regularly updates guidelines for water safety. But those guidelines are not legally enforceable, and critics say Ottawa has failed to take responsibility, leaving control over water with the provinces whose budget cuts and downloading to municipalities have led to a disturbing lack of uniformity in monitoring, enforcement and public disclosure. "Kids shouldn't have to die," says May, "before governments pay attention to how much they have cut back on the environment."

Others are less critical of Ottawa. Sarah Miller, co-ordinator for the Toronto-based Canadian Environmental Law Association, believes the government of Ontario is to blame for Walkerton. Instead of its current hodgepodge of provincial statutes addressing water quality to varying degrees, Miller says the province should adopt — and administer — a safe-drinking-water act with legally binding regulations. "We need it all to be pulled together in one place," says Miller. "We need the legal authorities to be very clear."

body
- identifies different regulations
- provides example
- dates and statistics support information

There are stark contrasts in how provinces and territories go about trying to keep their water safe. Spring floods in the Yukon usually result in quick action, boil-water warnings issued without waiting for test results for wells. Most governments, however, wait for test results before issuing boil-water advisories. Quebec issues an average of 600 orders a year, by far the most in the country. Other provinces generally issue far fewer directives. In 1999, Alberta was typical, issuing only two orders. (Quebec says its higher numbers are due to the province taking more precautions than the others. It is, however, difficult to compare results because there is no single overseeing body in the country.) Some provinces, including Ontario and Nova Scotia, do not keep a registry of how many times communities are forced to boil water. That, environmentalists say, leaves them with an inadequate picture of their water quality.

There is no standard procedure for sharing test results among different levels of government and the public. When contaminants are found in the water, labs in most provinces report results directly to the provincial government. Only Quebec and Ontario rely on municipalities to inform them when something is wrong. Sometimes, the public is left out of the loop. Last November, Newfoundland Environment Minister Oliver Langdon denied CBC Radio's request for information on trihalomethanes in drinking water, saying it was a cabinet secret. (Carcinogenic THMs are the byproducts of treating water high in organic matter with chlorine.) Two months later, after a series of new reports, Langdon angered Newfoundlanders when he held a media conference to say 63 communities tested between 1985 and 1999 had THM levels above the recommended limit, some as much as four times higher.

Despite their image as centres of pollution, metropolitan areas may have safer tap water than their smaller neighbours. Big cities can afford sophisticated water treatment plants, which effectively guard against microbes, says Barry Thomas, a retired Health Canada official who served on the federal-provincial guidelines subcommittee. "Leaving small towns on their own in handling water treatment, which is so critical to public health, is irresponsible," says Thomas. "You just cannot leave this kind of thing in the hands of people who are not experts."

The federal-provincial guidelines for Canadian drinking water quality set out basic standards for water-testing frequency and minimum contaminant levels. Each province and territory bases its water safety policy on these guidelines, but only Alberta and Quebec have legislation mandating specific standards be followed. There is no set procedure for sharing test results between different levels of government and the public. Most provinces receive results directly from the lab. Governments in Quebec and Ontario, however, rely on municipalities to inform them of positive test results. The guidelines suggest the following schedule for sampling:

Population	Samples per month
up to 5,000	4
5,000 to 9,000	1 per 1,000 population
more than 9,000	1 per 10,000 population and an additional 90

Recent government actions have shaken some Canadians' faith in their elected officials' commitment to protecting water. Last month, federal Environment Minister David Anderson refused to back a NAFTA commission inquiry into large-scale pork operations in Quebec and the waste they produce—and effectively quashed it. Provincial politicians, meanwhile, have taken a go-slow approach on regulating factory farming. Alberta's Agriculture Minister Ty Lund last month backed away from an advisory committee report that recommended tougher rules for the province's hog, cattle and poultry operations. Lund said he does not favour "heavy-handed regulation" and instead prefers voluntary measures, such as a "self-assessment" program in which farmers would be counted on to identify and fix problems. And in Ontario last week, Agriculture Minister Ernie Hardeman defended his recent decision to oppose attempts by municipalities to prevent factory farms from spreading manure on fields. Hardeman, claiming there is a danger of over-regulation hurting business, said he is awaiting a report in the coming weeks by MPPs investigating large-scale farming before addressing how the industry should be monitored and policed.

conclusion
- the future

The last federal budget, however, may promise some hope for cleaner water. It contained provisions for $2.6 billion in funding for municipal infrastructure over the next six years. About $2 billion is earmarked for "green" infrastructure, some of it water treatment and waste-water treatment. But the provinces, territories and the Treasury Board in Ottawa must still negotiate the details—while the provinces and municipalities will have to put in matching funds. And it is up to the provinces, says Michelle Giddings, a Health Canada official who sits on the federal-provincial subcommittee, to ensure watersheds are kept safe from increasingly intense livestock farming, as well as the use of more insecticides and herbicides. Despite Walkerton, though, Giddings feels "the quality of Canada's drinking water remains very high." When asked whether she drinks tap water, she replied: "Everybody asks me that, and yes, I do—I drink it straight from the tap." Given what happened in Walkerton, however, some Canadians are no longer willing to do the same.

ends with simple, strong statement

Danylo Hawaleshka

Understanding Style

Through either research or personal experience, writers of reports have gained insights and knowledge about their topic. Their writing style must reflect this expertise, but also be accessible to readers who may have a limited understanding of the topic. The challenge, then, is to maintain a balance between establishing author credibility and aiding reader comprehension.

Sometimes reports are written for a very specific audience. The *Journal of Medicine*, for example, is intended to be read by medical practitioners. Its reports will likely contain language and terminology that aren't commonly used outside this profession. If a report on a medical issue were published in a newspaper, however, the writing style would have to be accessible to the general reader.

ESTABLISHING AUTHOR CREDIBILITY

Here are some strategies for conveying author credibility in your reports:

USE SUBJECT-SPECIFIC VOCABULARY

Use words and phrases associated with your topic. For example, if you're writing a report about a medical condition, include the appropriate medical terminology. Always make sure, however, that the meaning is clear. Either define the term, or make sure it's explained by the context in which you use it.

INCLUDE AUTOBIOGRAPHICAL INFORMATION

Sometimes it's possible to include information about yourself that will add to your credibility as an authority on the topic. This is feasible only if your report is written from a first-person point of view.

In a travel report on trekking in the Himalayas, for example, a statement like "I met my Sherpa guide on my first trek in 1995, and he's been with me on subsequent journeys in this part of the world" lets the reader know that you're not an amateur hiker, but a seasoned trekker with rich experience. In other words, you are someone who can provide credible information.

USE QUOTATIONS

Quoting authorities on the topic gives the reader a greater sense of trust in the information contained in your report.

RESEARCH DATA

Conducting research is absolutely essential when writing a report. Including specific data provides more depth of detail. It also adds an important element of credibility. You must, of course, ensure that your facts are correct. (See the section on Primary Research below, as well as the Research and Ethics chapter.)

This data may be presented as a chart, graph, map, or diagram. Numerical data in particular lends itself well to visual treatment.

PROVIDE A CONTEXT

Help your reader contextualize the information you provide by including background information. It usually appears at the beginning of the report, or may be included as a chart or graph, for example.

Consider the following overview of the history of seal hunting that appeared with Ray Guy's report on "Seal Wars" in *Canadian Geographic* magazine. The timeline format provides an accessible summary. It also contextualizes the report's focus on present-day seal hunting.

Sealing by the years

2000 BC Archaic Indians on Newfoundland's Northern Peninsula hunt seals on the sea ice.

1880: harp seal featured on stamp.

COURTESY OF CARL VINCENT

Early 16th century Basques, French, Portuguese and British begin sealing for oil and pelts off Atlantic Canada. Early settlers, like today's descendants, hunt seals for income in the fishing off-season.

1750s European demand for oil and skins expands the commercial seal fishery. Oil is used as fuel for lamps, as lubricating and cooking oil, in the processing of leather and jute, and as a constituent in soap.

1818 Beginning of the golden age of sealing as sailing schooners take men to hunt on the whelping grounds. As a record 200,000 seals are landed, the industry grows, bringing foreign investment and work for shipbuilders, carpenters and processors.

1863 Larger, steam-powered vessels with thick sides — called wooden walls — are introduced, raising the stakes in the sealing industry. As the expense of acquiring and operating steamers leads to domination of the industry by wealthy boat owners, employment conditions deteriorate for the men on the ice: they are underfed and given little or no warm clothing or safety gear. Since 1800, some 1,000 men have perished and 400 vessels have been lost, crushed by ice or sunk en route to and from the killing grounds.

1914: in the company of danger on icy killing fields.

NATIONAL ARCHIVES OF CANADA/PA-121934

1899 The century ends with a recorded kill of 33 million seals, primarily whitecoats, the newborn harp seals.

1914 Seventy-eight sealers die stranded on the ice in the Great *Newfoundland* Sealing Disaster, while another 173 men are lost at sea with the SS *Southern Cross*. Despite the dangers, legions of men still go "o'er the side" and march across the ice in search of seals for badly needed extra income.

1921 Aircraft are first used to locate the depleted seal herds. Contemporary critics argue this will ensure the seal's annihilation.

Late 1920s Machinery replaces skinners who remove fat from skin after pelts are landed. In a 10-hour workday, these craftsmen could skin out about 450 young harp pelts.

1933 The SS *Imogene* lands some 56,000 seals, the biggest single-voyage catch.

1920s: St. John's skinners face replacement by machines.

CENTRE FOR NEWFOUNDLAND STUDIES, MEMORIAL UNIVERSITY

1949-1961 After declining during the Depression and the world wars (when sealing ships were pressed into wartime service), the hunt becomes profitable again, primarily due to demand for fur and leather products. An average of 310,000 seals are taken annually off the East Coast.

NATIONAL AVIATION MUSEUM/2285

1920s: Avro used in seal hunt.

1950s Humane society observers first go to the hunting grounds and express concerns about the cruelty involved in the killing.

1965 Spurred by public outrage, the government implements the Seal Protection Regulations, setting annual quotas, dates of the hunt, controls on the methods of killing, and requiring, for the first time, that vessels, aircraft and sealers be licensed.

1969 The International Fund for Animal Welfare (IFAW), dedicated to ending the commercial exploitation of seals, is established by Brian Davies in New Brunswick. In four years, IFAW's global revenue exceeds $500,000.

1974 IFAW hires the same New York advertising firm used by Coca-Cola to coordinate the $100,000 "Stop the Seal Hunt" campaign.

SS IMOGENE LEAVING FOR THE ICEFIELDS BY DAVID BLACKWOOD, 1973

1933: SS *Imogene* steams from St. John's to hunting grounds.

1950-1970 The northwest Atlantic harp seal population declines by 50 percent.

1964 The anti-sealing movement is born and the issue of cruelty to the animals explodes internationally when CBC-TV's French network airs *Les Phoques de la Banquise*, with footage from Îles de la Madeleine, Que., in which a seal is skinned alive. Debate continues as to whether some of the scenes were staged.

1977 Celebrity protest of the hunt takes off as French actress Brigitte Bardot visits the ice in Newfoundland, stirring up anti-sealing sentiment in the French media. As international opposition intensifies, the Newfoundland government launches a global campaign in defence of the hunt.

1979 Activists are arrested for spraying red dye on more than 200 whitecoats on the ice in Canadian waters.

WAYNE LYNCH

Late 1980s: eco-tourist face to face with a whitecoat harp seal.

1983 European Community, which had been importing close to 75 percent of Canadian seal pelts, bans products derived from whitecoats. Sealskin market collapses. Pressure from IFAW and the public leads 570 Tesco and Safeway grocery stores in Britain to phase out all Canadian fish products in protest of the seal hunt.

WAYNE LYNCH

1983: whitecoat products are banned in Europe.

1987 The commercial hunt for whitecoats is banned by the federal government.

Late 1980s IFAW launches seal-watching eco-tours in Îles de la Madeleine, Que., as an economic alternative to the hunt. It now adds $1 million a year to the islands' economy.

1992 The northern cod fishery moratorium begins.

1995 A subsidy for seal meat products is introduced to assist in developing markets. All direct subsidies to the sealing industry are to be eliminated after 1999.

1999 244,552 harp seals are killed in the spring hunt. Only modest gains are made in the status of the cod stocks. Newfoundland fisheries minister John Efford argues harp seals are ravaging the cod stocks. In its 30th year, IFAW has a record 1.8 million members and annual revenues over $60 million (U.S.). Protests against the hunt continue.

December 1999 Sealers await announcement of 2000 quota.

ADRIAN WYLD/CP PICTURE ARCHIVE

1998: protesters at Liberal Party convention in Ottawa.

TEXT BY MARY VINCENT/*CANADIAN GEOGRAPHIC*

EFFECTIVE INTRODUCTIONS

Each of the following excerpts reflects a stylistic strategy that draws the reader into the report.

Introduction	Stylistic Strategy
"We leave St. John's airport at eight in the morning on March 18, 1999, in a small plane bound for St. Antony, 500 kilometres away on the northern tip of Newfoundland. Provincial fisheries minister John Efford has collected several dozen journalists. We are going to be shown why millions of seals must be slaughtered to save what is left of the cod fishery in Newfoundland. The minister is far ahead of even the radio open-line programs in his zeal on the matter." Ray Guy, "Seal Wars," *Canadian Geographic*, January/February 2000	• gives all the pertinent facts: who, where, when, what, and why • first-person narrative helps the reader relate to the issue • matter-of-fact tone introduces a shocking, controversial point of view
"As Simon Whitfield gleefully kicks a soccer ball around with a group of schoolkids, it's hard to imagine anyone fitter or healthier anywhere in the globe, let alone Canada. With his thrilling come-from-behind gold-medal finish in the first-ever Olympic triathlon in Sydney, Whitfield, 25, took his place in the international pantheon of great athletes. Now he is schmoozing with students at a school in the bedroom community of Aurora, north of Toronto. 'I've been to as many schools as I could get to in the two weeks since I got home,' says the busy athlete who grew up in Kingston, Ont., but now lives and trains in Victoria. 'I just think it's important for everyone to talk to kids about surrounding themselves with positive people, setting goals and figuring out how they're going to accomplish those goals.'" Robert Marshall, "Fit for Life," *Maclean's*, October 23, 2000	• personal anecdote juxtaposes athlete's fame with a down-home encounter • inspirational quotations from well-known figure

Introduction	Stylistic Strategy
"The first weather report of the year warning of a cold snap sets homeowners to the task of insulating their most vulnerable water pipes. They know that preventing the water from freezing inside the pipes will avert damage that could happen as the water turns solid and expands. But what many people do not know is that they are also guarding against an even greater pressure generated because the surface of the ice remains liquid." John Wettlaufer and J. Greg Dash, "Melting Below Zero," *Scientific American*, February 2000	• identifies a task to which all homeowners can relate • uses a familiar task to introduce a little-known fact that will be the topic of the report
"These behaviors can be incredibly debilitating. How can you be included in a typical classroom if you can't be dissuaded from banging your head on your desk? How can you make friends if your overriding interest is calendars?" Patricia M. Rodier, "The Early Origins of Autism," *Scientific American*, February 2000	• rhetorical questions encourage readers to identify with the dilemma

The annotations to the following report point out the stylistic elements that help engage the reader.

Halt! Who Goes There?

On the Net, how do you prove who you are? Use an electronic signature.

directly addresses reader—"you"

Every once in a while, you're reminded that signatures play a strangely central role in business.

invitational tone

Take Chevron Canada's B.C. headquarters, for example. Frequently, its gas stations will get into price wars, requiring a speedy response. "If the guy across the street drops his price by one cent, you've got to react quickly," says James Eaton, a Chevron network and security specialist. The top guy at Chevron has to authorize a price cut—now.

quoting credible authority

But even a one-cent price cut can mean a lot of money. So—like any business decision—it involves quite a bit of paper shuffling to and fro, the signing of orders, and the checking of signatures. "You've got to make sure the guy who signs the order has the authority to do so," Eaton notes. By the time they've responded, they might already be losing the price war.

So this summer, Chevron began testing a new system: electronic signatures. Instead of using pen and paper to sign off on the orders, the head honcho will use an electronic signature to approve the cut, and send it instantly (say, via e-mail). The e-signature is encrypted in transit; nobody can alter it. And it moves at the speed of light. "It could really change the way we do business," Eaton notes.

conversational tone

Which is why electronic signatures have recently become a very big thing for e-commerce. They help solve an issue peculiar to the Net—how do you verify the person on the other side is who they say they are? As the old joke goes, "On the Net, nobody knows you're a dog." This is the nut of the issue: How do you make sure that the guy signing your e-contract isn't, well, a dog?

identifies problem—question form

The idea behind electronic signatures is simple. Most use "public key" encryption. In this method, the user and sender of an electronic document each has their own password. Their e-signature software takes both passwords and uses them to encrypt the document—it lets both people in the transaction know who the other is, and makes sure only those two can decode the document and read it.

uses technical terminology/vocabulary

Though several Canadian companies have been developing e-signature software for years, they got a major boost this year when the Canadian and U.S. governments declared e-signatures legally bind-

historical context

Signature Makers

Bill C-6
www.parl.gc.ca/36/2/parlbus/chambus/house/bills/summaries/c6-e.htm
Want to really delve into the murky, legal aspects of electronic signatures? Okay, it's your funeral; the recently passed federal legislation that discusses them is available on-line.

Silanis Technology Inc.
www.silanis.com
Check out the wares of this Montreal-based electronic-signature company—whose clients include no less than the U.S. joint chiefs of staff.

Entrust
www.entrust.com
The industry leader in public-key encryption of secure transactions, Entrust also has a site with solid backgrounders on "e-sign" technology.

Kyberpass
www.kyberpass.com
Check out the Ottawa-based Kyberpass's secure-transaction software, including easy-to-understand illustrations of how security systems work.

ing for general use in business documents. "There's every evidence that this is going to be a major growth area. E-commerce utterly relies on this," says Michael Geist, a University of Ottawa law professor who follows the industry.

One electronic-signature company is Quebec-based Silanis Technology Inc. Its ApproveIt software is currently used by companies like Williams Communications, which has issued 12,000 electronic signatures to speed up internal corporate transactions. Other clients include Allstate, which uses Silanis e-signature technology in-house and is considering using it to sell insurance policies on-line. "Electronic signatures can turn business processes that take several weeks and shrink them to several days," says Silanis president Tommy Petrogiannis.

Still, e-signatures face some serious challenges before they'll be commonly used.

One of the biggest is fraud and privacy. If thieves steal a pass-

provides authoritati[ve] examples-indicates complete research; author credibility establishe[d]

word, they could potentially pretend to be that person—digitally forging documents in their name. Sure, the encryption of digital signatures protects them from being tampered with en route; but good old-fashioned human stupidity can still create security problems on the sending or receiving end. "The weak link is always the human," says Robert Lendvai, vice-president of marketing for Kyberpass, an Ottawa-based maker of e-security software.

One way around it is to use alternate styles of passwords—such as smart cards, or even biometric inputs such as James Bond-style fingerprint and retinal scans. Don't laugh; this stuff is already being rolled out. "We have customers who use smart cards, plus GPS, plus fingerprints. They're about as paranoid as anybody," says Brian O'Higgins, executive vice-president and founder of Entrust Technologies, an industry leader with more than 40% of the electronic-signature market, and customers ranging from New York Life Insurance to Mackenzie Financial Corp.

Still, the first person to successfully fake an identity in a big-money contract could produce some very messy liability issues. "What happens when somebody says, 'I didn't sign that thing'?" wonders John Gregory, general counsel for the Ontario government's Ministry of the Attorney General. Geist, who has studied the legal issues, says there aren't any good precedents yet—the technology is still so new. In the event of a contested signature, anyone could be on the hook, including the e-signature software maker. "The first lawsuit over this will be very interesting," Geist muses.

problem identified as a question

A related issue is "interoperability." Suppose your bank signs your mortgage using an Entrust certificate. Will another institution—say, an insurance company—accept that as valid, if they use different software, such as ApproveIt? Technologically, e-signature companies claim it won't be hard to swap certificates, but it's also an issue of trust. "To stand behind your own certificate is one thing. But it's another thing to stand behind someone else's," Gregory notes.

All the same, none of these concerns change the ultimate lure of e-signatures—making e-commerce move faster. It's likely that companies will accept the risks in exchange for accelerating the hamster wheel. Even in the ether of cyberspace, someone's got to sign on the dotted line.

Clive Thompson

» CHECKPOINT: *Reassess Your Knowledge*

We Are Canadian

The 17th year-end poll finds a confident population shifting its focus towards renovating the social safety net. Tax relief can wait—it is time to fix health care and other problems.

Boring? *Moi*? For being Canadian? I don't *think* so. What's more, fully 70 per cent of my compatriots agree with me. So what that most Americans see us as a giant Minnesota. Or that the world has a long history of dissing Canada—a "few acres of snow," sniffed Voltaire, not even worth having a decent war over. That is not the way we see ourselves. The 17th annual *Maclean's* year-end poll, conducted this year in partnership with the Global Television Network, dared to suggest: "Some consider Canada to be a boring country where nothing exciting happens." And seven out of 10 respondents snorted: "Boring? Not in my backyard." Excitement even verges on the giddy (80 per cent or more rejecting the boring thesis) in New Brunswick, Prince Edward Island and Saskatchewan. And a solid majority of Quebecers (58 per cent), bless their sardonic Gallic hearts, feel that the old shoe they call Canada still has some zip to it.

OK, so maybe we are not all Jim Carreys (though we do seem to produce more than our share of international funnymen). But at the turn of the millennial wheel, Canadians may be excused for a certain amount of collective swagger. Confident about the future? No question, an attitude surprisingly shared by groups that have been shortchanged in the recent past—young people, for instance, who came of age in a time of government cutbacks and a stubbornly jobless recovery.... And the poll finds a population almost vitriolically dismissive of politicians even as it is not quite ready to give up on government as provider and, last month, voted the old gang back in Ottawa.

This is a tough crowd. Tolerant but quirky, its opinions ebbing and flowing with all the subtlety of a lava lamp. Some examples:

- A clear majority would insist that new immigrants adopt Canadian values. But large majorities also believe in affirmative-action programs for visible minorities.
- On the world stage, we still see ourselves as boy scouts, proud of our peacekeeping tradition,

eager to do more—as long as we don't have to expand the military budget.

- On the home front, we are much tougher-minded: 75 per cent of Canadians feel that young offenders, regardless of age, should be tried for violent crimes in adult—not youth—courts, a finding that is consistent across the ages from teens to pensioners.

Call it the contradictory Canuck, the unbearable pragmatism of being Canadian. "Canadians are probably the most non-ideological people in all the world," suggests Allan Gregg, chairman of The Strategic Counsel, the Toronto-based consulting firm that conducted the poll. Pragmatism, however, does not mean there are no grumpy parts.

British Columbia, with an unpopular provincial government and an economy not firing on all cylinders, is noticeably out of sorts. Quebec has a significant number of its citizenry still concerned about jobs. Saskatchewan, with a farm economy in the doldrums, has the most worriers about the future. (Mind you, as noted, they are also among the least bored with Canada.) But asked to look back 25 years, 50 per cent across the country think life is much better today: there is more opportunity, more tolerance, better physical well-being. And the nation's young, the 20-year-olds, feel they have high ethical standards, higher at least than those of their self-indulgent boomer parents.

The flies in the ointment—and they are giant, New Brunswick-sized ones: the sense that health care, the quality of the environment, the education system, feelings of personal safety and ethical standards have all lost ground in the past quarter-century. This is part of a trend. For five years now, social concerns have been creeping up the ladder of what Canadians are fretting about. For two years straight, they have topped the *Maclean's* year-end survey, part of an increasing entrenched belief, says Gregg, that many of the country's key social institutions—hospitals, schools, social services—are broke and need fixing.

So what is the agenda here for federal and provincial governments? And who is driving it?

Restoring the health-care system is clearly at the top of the list, cited by 35 per cent of respondents as Canada's biggest problem....

... But the two-tier idea, the bogeyman of the recent federal election campaign, is clearly gaining ground, dividing Canadians along regional and perhaps generational lines. In three of the four western provinces, a majority of those surveyed are willing to consider a two-tier system. The exception—another Canadian quirk—was Alberta

Subconscious Concerns

Does anyone care about the environment anymore? When asked to identify the major problem facing their country today, only three per cent cite that issue as their top-of-mind concern—a far cry from the 18 per cent who singled it out at its peak in 1989. Since then, economic concerns have pushed environmental questions aside. However, when prompted in specific questions in this year's poll, Canadians make it clear that, even if they don't raise it themselves, the environment is still a fundamental concern.

Q: Is being a leader in environmental protection legislation something Canada should do in the next few years?

83%	**Yes**
89%	**Most likely to say Yes:** residents of the Atlantic region
76%	**Least likely to say Yes:** residents of the Prairies

Support for a clean environment stands up even against the prospect of a tax cut.

Q: Do you want Canada to be a country that has the strongest environmental legislation in the world or that has relatively low taxes?

Environmental legislation	**56%**
Low taxes	**39%**

(60 per cent against), the province that many see as pioneering the idea with its new law to expand the range of private clinics. Fifty-five per cent of Quebecers, who have seen their government shipping cancer patients to New England to alleviate backlogs, are also open to a parallel system. So, too, are those who are least likely to call on its services—the young. While 50 per cent of Canadians reject a private system operating alongside medicare, two-thirds of those in their 20s are prepared to give it a try.

If there is one group that stands out in the survey, it is that Gen X cohort, the one that history and a zigzag economy almost forgot. Now in their late 20s and mid-30s, they graduated high school in the teeth of a recession. Some faced two—in the early 1980s and again in 1990. They were always the last on and the first off the job wheel....

On the national mood, for example, Canadians as a whole are, well, modestly bullish. They are slightly more optimistic about the future this year than last or of the past seven years, when the poll has posed that question. Importantly, they are also much less pessimistic than before. (We are Canadians,

You Dashing Canadian Devil, You

Q: Would you agree that Canada is a boring country where nothing exciting happens?

Agree 19% Disagree 70%

- **Most likely to agree:** 18- to 24-year-olds (**30%**)
- **Most likely to disagree:** Respondents aged over 64, and residents of New Brunswick and Saskatchewan (**81%**) or Prince Edward Island (**80%**)

after all: we hedge our bets.) But those in the under-39-year-old crowd are much more confident still than other Canadians. Fully 67 per cent of those in their 20s and 30s expect their personal prosperity to increase over the next few years, while only 45 per cent of Canadians overall do. And younger Canadians are much more optimistic about their own personal financial situations than they are about the country's: they expect to get ahead.

Younger Canadians, too, are much more tolerant of diversity and much more open to change on the health-care front than their elders: by significant margins, they are the most willing to embrace a two-tier system. And in some respects, they reflect older values: among 20-year-olds, the flame of bilingualism, dimming elsewhere, still commands majority respect; and while 52 per cent of Canadians feel governments are trying to do too much and should be cut back, 51 per cent of those under 30 feel it would be wrong to reduce the size of the government and have it do less.

Is this the writing on the wall, a young person's guide to the Canada

The Canadian Story

The poll respondents' Canada includes the CBC. Only one third want to see the public broadcaster sold to the private sector, with backing for privatization highest in the Prairies (**42%**) and among men generally (**40%**), and lowest in Ontario (**30%**) and among women (**27%**).

A significant majority—**61** per cent, fairly evenly distributed across the country—also approves of rules requiring a high proportion of Canadian content on TV and radio.

But the consensus slips on the issue of foreign ownership of the media. Only **50** per cent say Canada should restrict outsiders' control of the press and broadcasting, with support for restrictions especially low in Quebec at **39** per cent.

Stop or I'll ... Negotiate

Canadian peacekeepers might want to brush up on their diplomatic skills. Contrasting responses to two poll questions suggest Canadians aren't particularly eager to give them better hardware to do their job, given other considerations.

82% Agree that Canada should be a leader in peacekeeping efforts around the world.

But asked to choose between investing in a stronger and more up-to-date military or funding housing for all homeless in Canada, there is no contest:

Stronger military 19%
Housing the homeless 75%

of tomorrow? (Fix the dream, governments, or we do-it-yourselfers will take it on and make you irrelevant.) Perhaps. But this is a country of many constituencies and many quirky contradictions. Fear of a high-tech brain drain, caused in part by a perceived flight from high taxes, tops everyone's to-do list. But ask Canadians how they would divvy up each $100 Ottawa had to spend from government surpluses, and tax cuts come in as a third option ($26), well behind paying down the national debt ($32) and increasing spending on health and other social programs ($42).

Asked to elaborate on the country they want to have in the next few years, Canadians set among their top-ranked priorities: keeping skilled workers, eliminating homelessness and becoming a world leader in environmental protection. More and more of what are called quality-of-life issues—as opposed to bread-and-butter economic concerns—are coming to the fore, demanding attention. And different groups are driving different concerns. Sometimes it's women (the gender gap has been growing on social issues in recent years); sometimes it is the elderly or the young who appear to be leading the charge. What underlies this uptick in Canada's social conscience? Is it simple consideration of others in a time of relative plenty? Or does it stem from a collective desire for stability, a sense that—now that you ask—things are going pretty well right now, let's not rock the boat? (Or go easy on those young offenders who may?) The data can be read either way.

Don't rock the boat. As we officially enter the 21st century, a profound sense of "coping" (as Gregg calls it) is sweeping the land and, with it, sweeping away our sense of ourselves as a dull people in a cold country.... We are Canadian. Hear us roar.

Robert Sheppard

1. What stylistic strategies does the writer use in the introductory paragraphs to capture the reader's interest?
2. Explain how the graphic text supports the information contained in this article.
3. What are the key issues to which Canadians responded most enthusiastically? How do you know this?
4. What is the organizational pattern used in this report?
5. What type of graphic organizer would you use to make notes as you read this report?
6. If you were to include your own graphic text to support this article, what would you create? Explain your choices.

Creating a Report

Preparing and Planning

RESEARCH

It's important to carefully plan how you will gather the information upon which to base your report. Your prior knowledge of the topic may help you determine where to start.

There are two sources of research: primary and secondary.

PRIMARY RESEARCH

Primary research is data that is gathered through first-hand investigation. You conduct this kind of research through observation, surveys, and interviews.

Observation

Before you set up an observation, decide on its purpose—exactly what information you want to gather.

Learn to gather information by using what you see. Let's say you were planning to write a report on the building of a local historical monument. If possible, visit the site. Ask questions of the experts there. Try to keep your data-gathering focused, but take notes on as much as you can. You can always leave redundant information out of the report when you finally write it.

Surveys and Interviews

See the Research and Ethics chapter for information on how to conduct these forms of primary research.

SECONDARY RESEARCH

Printed material and the Internet are called secondary sources. A wealth of information may be found in encyclopedias, handbooks, journals, newspapers, biographies, and Web sites.

Refer to the Research and Ethics chapter for specific information about how to conduct research using these sources.

Planning Tips

- *Who will be reading your report? Do they have any prior knowledge of the topic? Do they have a level of expertise in the area or field? Knowing your audience will help you determine the language you use, and the amount of detail you include.*
- *Plan an organizational pattern for your report.*
- *Choose an appropriate graphic organizer for your notes. Pay particular attention to the order in which you present your information. Select only essential information to present.*
- *Think about what information may be illustrated or extended with the use of graphics.*

Checklist

Assessing Your Report	
Does the introduction clearly define and contextualize the topic?	❑
Does the introduction include any stylistic techniques that will help to engage the reader?	❑
Is there an obvious organizational pattern?	❑
Is the information organized into paragraphs that link cohesively in a logical order?	❑
Does the conclusion present an effective summary of the topic, and does it offer insights or recommendations?	❑
Are linking words used to take the reader logically from one piece of information to the next?	❑
Have you included terminology and vocabulary specific to the topic?	❑
Have you remained objective in reporting the information?	❑
Have you included text features of a report—headings, subheadings, sidebars, etc.?	❑
Have you included graphics or illustrations?	❑
Is the report written in the active voice?	❑
Does the report sound authoritative in tone?	❑

Revising and Editing

GRAMMAR, USAGE, AND MECHANICS

ACTIVE AND PASSIVE VOICE

Writers of reports often use the passive voice because they think it sounds more objective and more formal. Generally, however, the passive voice tends to make your writing sound wordy and flat.

Check carefully to see what voice you have used. A sentence in the **active voice** begins with the subject, followed by the verb, which describes what the subject did. The action is straightforward from the beginning to the end of the sentence:

subject	to **verb**	to **object**
The tornado	struck	the island community

In the **passive voice** the verb explains something done to the subject. The "doer" may or may not be named in the sentence. If it is, the word "by" is used. The flow of the passive sentence is backward:

subject	**having something done to it (verb)**	**by agent (sometimes omitted)**
The island community	was struck	by the tornado.

All passives use a form of the verb *to be* (*am, is, are, was, were, being, been*) plus a past participle.

Passive verbs may be acceptable

- if the agent (the "doer" or actor) of the action is either unimportant or well known:

  Jean Chrétien was elected prime minister in 1996.
  Sidney was buried in the family plot next to his wife.

- if the agent is unknown or if the writer wants to avoid casting blame:

  The bicycle was left on the street all night.

If neither of these two exceptions apply to a sentence in the passive voice, switch it to the active voice. To do this, first identify the agent of the action. Then put the agent into the subject slot and turn the sentence around:

Houses were destroyed by the storm.	The storm destroyed houses.
The cake was eaten by me.	I ate the cake.

MAKING COMPARISONS

In writing your report, you will likely use comparisons to weigh aspects of information. This will give you the opportunity to use the comparative and superlative forms of adjectives and adverbs.

The **comparative** of short adjectives and adverbs is usually formed by the addition of *er*. The **superlative** is formed by the addition of *est*.

fast	faster	fastest
hot	hotter	hottest

Adjectives and adverbs of two or more syllables are usually made comparative with the addition of the word *more* or *less*. The superlative is formed with the addition of the word *most* or *least*.

well	better	best
unusual	more unusual	most unusual
carefully	more carefully	most carefully

Here are several considerations writers should take into account when making comparisons.

1. The two things being compared must be **comparable**.

Non-comparable	Comparable
Compared with Marsha, Sarah's study habits are terrible.	Compared with Marsha, Sarah has terrible study habits. or Sarah's study habits are much worse than Marsha's.

2. A **complete comparison** clearly indicates the two items being compared.

Incomplete	Complete
Dilip is happier.	Dilip is happier than he was last week.
This margarine is better tasting.	This margarine is better tasting than butter.

3. Indicate **degrees of comparison** properly.

   Comparative words ending in *er* and comparative phrases using *more* or *less* are used to compare two items.

   She is smarter than her cousin.
   He is more considerate than his sister.

   Comparison words formed with *est* and comparative phrases using *most* and *least* are used for more than two items.

She is the smartest in the family.
He is the most considerate member of the family.

4. Use *other* with *any* in comparisons.
   The word *other* (or another modifier) must be inserted after the word *any* to clarify that you are comparing a member of a group with other members of that same group.

Misleading Comparison	**Clear Comparison**
This book is better than any book I have read. (*This book can't be better than all books you have read since it is one of that group.*)	This book is better than any other book I have read. or This book is better than any book I've read previously.

5. Use *as* … *as* and *if not* … *than* correctly.
   Remember that the comparison *as* … *as* (*as happy as, as good as*) must always have the second *as*, even when this phrase is combined with *if not* … *than* (*if not hotter than, if not more comfortable than*).

The mountains in Canada are as high as, if not higher than, those in the United States.

6. Check the **case** of the pronoun used when making comparisons.

I am as happy as he. (*The word* is *is understood to follow* he.)
Mary is as happy as I. (*The word* am *is understood to follow* I.)
He is more comfortable than I. (*The word* am *is understood to follow* I.)

Presenting a Report

Reports are often presented at meetings or large gatherings of company or board members. Scientific and medical reports are often presented at conferences. There are several strategies you may consider to ensure a successful oral presentation.

Presentation Strategies

- *Don't just read your report. Know it well enough that you can look away from the paper.*
- *Make eye contact with members of your audience so that everyone feels included.*
- *Vary your pitch and intonation.*
- *Vary the speed or tempo of your speech. Practise where and when your presentation will increase or decrease in speed. Slow the presentation down at points that you want to emphasize. Increase the speed to show excitement.*

- *Enunciate your words carefully. Practise any difficult words and look up those words whose pronunciation you are not sure of.*
- *Make sure you can be heard. Consider your distance from your audience, and the size of the space in which you are speaking. Is there any background noise you must compete with?*
- *What gestures might you use to complement the words? Whether sitting or standing, your body language must suggest authority.*
- *Make large copies of your visuals (charts, diagrams, illustrations). Refer to these directly (e.g., "As you can see..."). There is nothing more frustrating to an audience than a chart or visual that's never explained.*
- *If you're using presentation software, make sure to plan each screen. It should correspond to the sequence of your report. Don't present everything in a visual format—use information, illustrations, examples, and anecdotes to extend what you present on screen.*

Here is a summary of presentation do's and don'ts:

Do	Don't
Stand to present so you can be seen and heard. Even minimal movement makes it interesting for the audience, but you need to be comfortable doing it.	Chew gum or eat candy during the presentation. Don't fidget or carry on repetitive behaviours (e.g., tapping the desk, scratching your head).
Look around the room and establish eye contact at various times with different students.	Look at the teacher throughout. The students are your primary audience. You will be judged on how well you engage them in your presentation.
Speak clearly and formally; this is a formal occasion.	Use colloquial and slang expressions (e.g., *like*, *kinda*, *sorta*, *um*).
Ensure that all the equipment you'll need is in the room for the time you need it.	Think you can do a successful presentation "off the cuff" or by ad-libbing.
Ensure you have enough copies of handouts for all members of the class and the teacher.	Have any grammar or spelling errors on the handouts. Ensure that any visual material can be read clearly and easily.
Be well-rested so that you can "think on your feet."	Panic if you forget a section or a key point. Explain calmly that you want to go back to insert a key point (try to find a logical time and place to do that insertion).
Arrive in enough time to have your presentation papers organized.	Ask for additional time to get organized or start late because you have arrived late to class or your handouts or equipment haven't arrived yet.

Do	**Don't** (continued)
Prepare specific questions for the class.	Ask "So, what do you think?"
Use carefully prepared visuals (e.g., board notes, graphs, multi-media).	Simply talk for the entire presentation with no visual reference point; people's attention span is not that long.
Be enthusiastic, even animated, about your topic. Smile!	Drone on (in a monotonous tone of voice) so that everyone knows your heart just isn't in it. If you don't like what you're saying, no one else will either!

Checklist

Assessing Your Oral Presentation	
Was the content of the report informative?	❑
Was the speaker audible at all times?	❑
Was the pace and tempo of the presentation appropriate?	❑
Did the speaker vary the intonation and pitch of the speech?	❑
Did the speaker use visual aids effectively?	❑
Did the speaker make eye contact with the audience?	❑
Was the speaker's body language appropriate?	❑
Was the attention of the audience engaged throughout the presentation?	❑

You might choose to assess your success in communicating information by asking your audience to respond to the following:

- What was the topic of the report?
- What new information did you get from listening to this report?
- What information that you already knew was presented in this report?
- What questions do you still have about the topic? (i.e., Was there any information you wanted to know that wasn't presented in the report?)
- Summarize what you heard.

CHAPTER 7

business and technical writing

"Since writing is communication, clarity can only be a virtue."

William Strunk, Jr., and E.B. White,
The Elements of Style

The worlds of business and technology are fast-paced and ever-changing. So it is essential that written communication in these spheres be purposeful, well-organized, and concise. There are a wide variety of forms in business writing. They differ according to their purpose, their sender and recipient, and their intended effect. These forms include memos, letters, résumés, proposals, and reports. Technical writing—designed to help people operate and use goods and services—also contains an array of forms. These include instructions, manuals, policies, warranties, contracts, and guarantees.

LEARNING GOALS

- examine various forms of business and technical writing
- develop skills to write business and technical documents
- create and present an effective sequence of directions

CONTENTS

Analyzing and Responding to Business and Technical Writing

» CHECKPOINT: *Assess Your Knowledge*

gettingstarted.net

Building the Web is fun and it isn't hard to do. Gettingstarted.net is here to help you learn the basics through bite-sized tutorials and hands-on interactive lessons. Our tutorials (brought to you by the Web professional's community Project Cool) are easy to follow and in no time you'll be building your own Web pages!

Contents:
Basic Web Development—If you're just beginning to learn or if you don't even know what HTML is, this is the section for you.

Advanced Web Development—For when you're ready to move beyond the basics and into more advanced HTML features, like tables.

Gettingstarted with Web Graphics—A Web page is more than just text. Learn the basics of Web graphics with these bite sized lessons.

Practice!—Practice your HTML with this interactive set of lessons. You don't need anything except a browser to make it work!

What Is HTML?
Hypertext Markup Language (HTML) is the basic building block of the World Wide Web page. It uses a pre-defined set of tags to format text, create hyperlinks to other places, and insert graphic images. When a web browser opens an HTML file, it displays the page based on the tags.

All HTML files begin with an HTML tag. The tag looks like this:
<html>

How Does HTML Work?
Hypertext Markup Language—HTML—is a streaming text markup language that uses tags to format text, create **hyperlinks** to other places, and insert graphic images.

HTML files live on a Web server. Typically the Web server belongs to your Internet Service Provider (ISP) or your company—whoever is **hosting** your pages. The Web server is hooked into the Internet and when people type in the **URL** of your page, they are actually calling the file from that Web server.

When someone requests an HTML page, the Web server sends one long unbroken string of **ASCII** text across the Internet to the reader's computer. The reader's browser turns the long string of text into a viewable page.

The browser displays only your text and the tags that it can understand. Any formatting, extra spaces, or unrecognizable characters that you put into your HTML file will be completely ignored by the browser. It turns anything it doesn't understand into a single spaceband.

It is important to know that HTML is evolving. New additions to HTML are addressing some of the layout control issues and adding new features. For example:

- **Cascading Style Sheets (CSS)** allow you to set specific presentation styles for your page.
- **JavaScript** is a scripting language that lets you add additional interactivity to your page.
- **Dynamic HTML (DHTML)** is a way of displaying the page dynamically, based on the reader's actions.

The browser manufacturers, however, are not completely consistent in their support of the newer standards such as CSS, JavaScript, and DHTML, so once you go beyond basic HTML you'll need to remember that your pages might not look exactly the same in all browsers.

Plug-ins are another way of adding additional functions to your pages. These applications let you incorporate additional features from other programs seamlessly within your HTML pages. Adobe's Acrobat, Macromedia's Shockware and Flash, Apple's QuickTime and QuickTime VR, and Real Audio's streaming audio player are all examples of ways you can extend your site beyond straight HTML to add graphic control, sound, video and other features—but remember, not everyone on the Web has or can use these plug-ins.

Before you start worrying about CSS and plug-ins and any of the other newer features, get a good handle on the basic HTML tags. If you understand them well, it will be much easier to understand the potential of the web and all of its technologies.

HTML Files

Creating an HTML file is pretty simple. You start it with a starting HTML tag, <html>, and end it with a closing HTML tag, </html>. Everything in-between is the content of your file.

The only other requirement for an HTML file is that all HTML documents must have a filename extension of .html or .htm. For example:

basics.html
zoo-visit.htm
spec01-99.htm
atoz.html

The browser looks at the filename extension and knows to interpret the file as HTML tags rather than straight ascii text.

HTML Tag Structure

You **mark up** your HTML pages using HTML **tags**. Each tag describes a certain type of **element**, such as a paragraph. Within each tag you can also set **attributes** for the element, such as aligning the paragraph to the center of the page.

The basic HTML tag has four parts:

1. An opening **delimiter**, the < symbol. This tells the browser that it is encountering a tag.
2. The tag name.
3. One or more attributes (sometimes called "switches") that set variables for the tag.
4. A closing delimiter, the > symbol. This marks the end of the tag.

A typical HTML tag might look something like this:
<p align=center>

In this example, the tag is the paragraph tag and the attribute align says that the paragraph will be centered. Notice that the tag starts with an opening delimiter and ends with a closing delimiter. The tag and attribute are separated with a single space.

Here are a few guidelines for using HTML tags:

- HTML tags are not case sensitive. <p> means the same as <P>.
- When creating a tag, remember to separate each portion—the tag name and each of the attributes—with a single space.
- To use an attribute, type the attribute name, followed by an equal sign and the attribute **value**. Don't put a space between the name, equal sign, and value.
- Sometimes the value is literal text or a value that is passed on to another function. When this is the case, you surround the value with quotation marks. For example, the image tag switch calls a specific file by name, so the filename is enclosed in quotations, like this:

<img src="logo.gif">

- If you don't specify an attribute and its value, the browser uses the default value for that tag. For example, the default value for paragraph alignment is left. If you use the paragraph tag without the align attribute, the paragraph will align left.

Starting Tags and Closing Tags
As HTML evolves, all tags are becoming **containers** that describe some portion of the page rather than tags that stand alone and simply insert an element into the page. As of this writing, we are in a transitional stage, but it is a good idea to start getting used to using tag sets—one tag begins the container and the other ends it.

It might help to think of tags as creating a state that stays in effect until you turn off the tag. For example, the bold tag turns the text that follows it bold. The text stays bold until you enter a bold off tag. In most cases, the closing tag is exactly the same as the ending tag, except that it begins with a slash. For example, the following tags turn bold on and off. The bold tags are highlighted in **color** to make them stand out:

<b>Here's some text I want in bold</b>

Even paragraphs are containers. You begin a paragraph with a paragraph tag. Then, you type the text that makes up the paragraph. At the end of the paragraph, you enter a close paragraph tag, like this:
<p>
Once upon a time there was a frog who lived in a big blue pond. The frog was cursed with intelligence. It was a curse because instead of living like a frog and eating bugs from day to day and just being happy in his pond, he thought about the meaning of life. And he wasn't sure what it meant to be a frog.
</p>

We'll talk more about opening and closing tags as we introduce each of the specific tags....

DevX

1. Who is the intended audience for this Web site?
2. Describe how this document is organized. How does this organization help readers find the information they need?
3. How is the subject-specific vocabulary conveyed to the reader? How is it explained? Refer to specific vocabulary in your answer.
4. Examine the stylistic approach. What aspects of this style are persuasive?
5. Do you think this Web site effectively communicates technical information? Explain.

Reading Strategies

Although business and technical writing take many different forms, there are general strategies that might help you read what can sometimes be rather difficult text.

Approaches to Business and Technical Writing

- *Scan the writing first. Look at headings and subheadings, if there are any. This is a quick way to find out what you are looking for. It will also give you a sense of how the writing is organized.*

- *Look at the accompanying illustrations or diagrams. Visual text helps you to understand the written text, and may provide further information. If you are a visual learner, these graphic elements can be invaluable.*

- *Skim the writing to see if there are words or concepts that are unfamiliar to you. Technical writing may be aimed at an expert audience and contain vocabulary that the non-expert might have difficulty understanding. You may need to skim a computer manual, for example, to determine whether it's at the right level of language for you.*

- *Consider what specific information you are trying to glean from the writing. Focus only on the sections of the text that contain the information you require. For example, if you want to set the clock on your DVD player, you may need to read only that part of the DVD operation manual.*

- *If the writing deals with a single object or a collection of objects to be assembled, have the object(s) in front of you. As you read, stop and connect the written instructions to the real thing. It's much easier to understand technical writing if you use a concrete, hands-on approach.*

Understanding Meaning

PURPOSE

When you read business and technical writing, it's essential that you have a clear purpose in mind.

Let's say that you want to buy a computer. Here are three distinct purposes for reading that will take you through the process:

1. You are about to peruse a catalogue from a major computer manufacturer. You would likely scan the text that describes each of the computers. In this way, you can get an idea of the sort of features that are offered and the range of prices.
2. Now you've decided on the computer you want. You would probably then focus on the descriptions of the peripherals and software that are either included with the computer or available as add-on features.
3. You've bought the computer and carted it home. Now you would read the instruction manual that accompanies it.

SPECIFIC VOCABULARY

Technical and business writing often contains specific terminology that might not be readily understood. If that vocabulary isn't in a regular dictionary, you might need to refer to a subject-specific dictionary. A number of these are available through the Internet. For example, www.yourDictionary.com provides lists of such dictionaries and glossaries.

SEQUENCING WORDS

Instructions or procedures are often explained in a time sequence. In other words, one thing must be completed before the next thing can be done. While many instructions number the sequence of events, some technical writing denotes the sequence through words. So it's important to note such words as *also, besides, consequently, finally, furthermore, incidentally, likewise, moreover, meanwhile, next, similarly, specifically, still, subsequently, then*. These words are called **conjunctive adverbs**.

Some other words and phrases to look for are *after, before, in order to, now that, once, when, so that, since*. Noting the use of these words will help you to understand the sequencing of instructions.

CHARTS AND DIAGRAMS

Formal business reports usually include graphic text to explain or extend the information found in the print text. For example, the "Eggs" report (on pp. 249–254 of this chapter) contains two line graphs. These graphics may also include bar graphs and pie graphs, or line diagrams that show a sequence or organizational structure.

Technical writing also includes visual text, usually in the form of labelled diagrams. These help the reader understand the written instructions.

Read the following excerpt from a set of instructions about how to operate a router (a tool used for cutting grooves). Note how the labelled photograph that accompanies the instructions allows the reader to locate the parts that are described in the text.

task identified in heading

numbers identify sequence

ADJUSTING DEPTH OF CUT

note boldfaced warning

1. **CAUTION:** DISCONNECT tool from power source.
2. Loosen Clamp Screw (A) Fig. 5.
3. While holding Base (E), turn Motor Unit (F) Fig. 5 COUNTER-CLOCKWISE until the tip of the bit is above bottom surface of Base.
4. Set router on flat wood surface.
5. Turn Motor Unit (F) Fig. 5 CLOCKWISE until bit touches the wood surface.
6. Tighten Clamp Screw (A) Fig. 5.
7. Rotate Depth Adjusting Ring (B) Fig. 5 until the Zero-line (C) is opposite the Index Line (D) on the housing.
8. Loosen Clamp Screw (A) Fig. 5.
9. Tip the router so bit is clear of the wood surface. Turn Motor Unit (F) Fig. 5 CLOCKWISE until the Index Line (D) on the motor housing reaches the desired depth indicated on the ring.
10. Tighten Clamp Screw (A) Fig. 5 firmly.

parts are identified in diagram

directional words in capital letters

NOTE: Setting index line to ¼" on the ring means the cutting edge of the bit is exposed ¼" below the base.

labels clearly identify all the named parts

Fig. 5

Understanding Form

When the purpose of technical writing is to describe a procedure, the writing generally follows a standard structure. If the procedure is a simple one, the structure is used only once. If the procedure is more complex, the document may be divided into separate sections. Each section follows the same pattern, but under different headings. In the manual describing the operation of the router, for example, each task is described separately under different headings: Selecting the Bit; Assembling the Motor; Adjusting the Depth of Cut; etc. Under each of these headings the form of the writing is the same.

Some conventions of form are also unique to the business world. Memoranda, letters, and e-mail messages have a prescribed format, as do résumés. Business proposals are meant to persuade the reader, but have a form that varies somewhat from other forms of persuasive writing. Formal business reports have some characteristics that distinguish them from other forms of business writing.

TECHNICAL WRITING

Technical writing may provide the directions required for each step in a process. Examples include what to do after a workplace accident; how to set up your voice-mail message; and how to install a software program.

The **introduction** defines the purpose or goal of the procedure and explains what is to be done. It orients the reader so that the details provided in the method are more accessible.

The **material requirements** to complete the task are outlined. Ingredients, parts, tools, equipment, and utensils are all requirements that may be identified.

The **method** of completing the task is specified in chronological, usually numbered sequence. The instructions are clear and explicit. They often use vocabulary and terminology specific to the task. Diagrams usually accompany the steps in the instructions. If the steps aren't numbered, the procedure is explained using linking words to lead the reader through the process.

Finally, some technical writing includes **criteria to assess** your level of success in completing the task defined.

BUSINESS WRITING

MEMORANDA

Memoranda (**memos** for short) are routinely used to announce policies, request or provide information, identify areas of personal or departmental responsibility, or instruct employees. They serve as the main informational link within a business—and so clear, accurate, and concise writing is essential.

The standard opening of a memo contains the following lines:

- To: [xxx]
- From: [xxx]
- Subject: [xxx]
- Date: [xxx]

The **subject line** serves as an important orientation when the reader first sees the memo. It's also used as the basis for filing and later retrieval.

The **content** of a memo should cover only one subject. The subject is developed in the first sentence of the memo. If readers of the memo are unfamiliar with the subject, you must provide them with the necessary background information in an introductory paragraph. If, however, you are writing a memo to someone familiar with the situation, your introductory sentence need only review the subject, for example, "As we decided in yesterday's meeting, a new set of guidelines will be generated for … ."

It's often a good idea to use **headings** and **lists** in the body of your memo. Headings help the reader identify the information of the greatest personal relevance. Lists prioritize information or identify a functional sequence. (Be careful not to overuse lists, however, particularly if they require the reader to make the connection between each item in sequence.)

Many companies require that the writer of the memo **sign** or **initial** it, to verify that the writer approves of its content.

LETTERS

Business letters are generally divided into types based on the writer's purpose and the reader's anticipated reaction. These purposes include:

- to request something (e.g., a job, information, clarification)
- to respond to a request (e.g., by providing information, by directing the query to the appropriate recipient)
- to persuade the reader (e.g., a sales promotion; a recommended course of action)

Letter Format

You can use the same basic block layout for letters, faxes, and e-mail. Some software programs also provide templates for various kinds of business correspondence.

[Your company]
[Its street address]
[City, province, postal code]

[Date]

[Receiver's name and title]
[Receiver's company]
[Receiver's street address]
[Receiver's city, province, postal code]

[Salutation followed by a comma or colon]

[Body, with each paragraph in a single-spaced block and with a double space after the salutation, between paragraphs, and before the closing. The paragraphs are not indented.]

[Closing followed by a comma]

[Signature]

[Typed name]

[Supplement line(s) for names of enclosed documents]

- **If you use this form for faxes**, be sure to add a cover sheet that names the person you're sending it to, gives that person's phone number, and gives your phone number in case a re-send is necessary. Remember that even with a cover sheet, nothing in a fax should ever be considered private or confidential.
- **If you use this form for e-mail**, omit the first eight lines and begin with the salutation. The message will not include a signature. (Never consider any e-mail you send or receive as private or confidential.)

Job-Application Letters

A job-application letter is a specialized form of persuasion: your letter should persuade the employer to consider you for the position. In it, you want to appear serious, well-organized, and qualified. You want to convey your desire to work at the company and that you will do the job well.

Consider the following job-application letter. The annotations point out the elements of an effective approach.

3344 Grove Street
Saskatoon, Saskatchewan
S7R 8T4

February 12, 2002

Reissman Marketing
2888 Dufferin Road
Saskatoon, Saskatchewan
S8C 3E2

Dear Ms. Renée Chan:

I would like to apply for the marketing assistant position advertised in the *Saskatoon Examiner* on January 26, 2002. I am a recent graduate of the Thompson Technical College program in Marketing and Design. This program focuses on creating marketing campaigns for retail clients, including print, radio, and television ads. My senior year project involved the creation and design of effective direct-mail brochures.

begins by applying for position and naming her best credentials for it

key details prove she has the skills to do the job well

Last summer I worked as an intern at Pask Productions, a marketing agency for non-profit organizations. As well as performing general office duties, I assisted in the production of newsletters, posters, and brochures. This included inputting revisions, contacting clients to confirm scheduling dates, and helping the production team with administrative tasks.

key details about second-best credential

With this background, I believe that I can bring a fair amount of knowledge and experience to the position. I enclose my résumé as well as samples of my course work. I am available for an interview at any time, at your convenience.

emphasis on what she can do for the employer

refers to enclosed résumé and work samples

indicates what she thinks should happen next

I look forward to hearing from you soon.

simple closure

Sincerely,

Jenna Stenopoulis

Enclosures

RÉSUMÉS

A **résumé** is a vitally important part of applying for a job, because it provides your potential employer with a concise overview of what you have to offer.

Your résumé identifies who you are, what you know, what you can do, what you have done, and what your employment objectives are. A résumé should include the following information:

- name, address, and phone number
- immediate and long-range job objectives
- education and professional training
- professional experience, including places you have worked and your responsibilities
- specific skills
- relevant personal information

The information you include in your résumé should be carefully selected based on the job you are seeking. You need to decide what information is most pertinent to that job and your potential employer. For example, the fact that you worked in a bakery might not be worthy of mention in a résumé for a job as a systems analyst!

Résumés should be one or two pages in length. Your name, address, and telephone number are centred at the top of the page. The rest of the information is often organized under the following headings:

- Employment Objective
- Education/Employment Experience
- Special Skills and Activities
- References (optional)

Chronological and Functional Résumés

There are two types of résumés: **chronological** (organized by previous employment listed by date) and **functional** (focusing on the applicant's skills).

Chronological Résumé

JASMINE LAU
18 Elmer Court
Springfield, Ontario
N4N 1T2
(513) 782-8735
coneill@net.ca

Employment Objective

Financial research assistant, leading to a management position in corporate finance

Education

University of Alberta
Bachelor of Business and Commerce (Expected June 2002)
Major: Finance   Minor: Computer Science

Employment Experience

CANADIAN IMPERIAL BANK OF COMMERCE
Research Assistant, June–September 2001
Assisted manager of corporate planning

MARTIN FINANCIAL RESEARCH SERVICES
Editorial Assistant, Intern, June–September 2000
Provided research assistance and developed a design concept for in-house financial audits

Special Skills and Activities

Associate Editor, School of Business Alumni Newsletter
Wrote two articles on financial planning with computer models; edited submissions

References

Available on request

Functional Résumé

Anil Gupta
25 Main Street
Deerbrook, P.E.I.
P5M 3H7
Phone: (874) 892-9387
agupta@home.com

OBJECTIVE I wish to obtain a position as a part-time sales clerk.

EDUCATION Presently attending Grade 12 at Great West Secondary School.

SKILLS AND ABILITIES

Leadership While at Great West Secondary School, I have been captain of the volleyball team, and currently lead small group activities in my business and English classes.

Human Relations	As a delivery person for *The Globe and Mail*, I have dealt with difficult customers and have never lost a customer due to poor service. While babysitting for my neighbours on a regular basis, I have had to interact with children ages two to ten.
Office Skills	In my business course, I have learned to touch key at 20 wpm. I am also comfortable with Windows and Microsoft Office. My telephone manner is pleasant and polite, and I meet all deadlines promptly and completely.

REFERENCES	Mr. S. Sharpe Teacher 3988 North Street Lee, P.E.I. 917-6895	Mrs. R. Harpaul Neighbour 29 Main Street Grange, P.E.I. 922-8506

BUSINESS PROPOSALS

A **business proposal** is written to persuade someone to follow a plan or course of action. Proposals are usually classified as internal or external. An **internal proposal** recommends a change within an organization. It's often written by an individual employee or a department and sent to a person in authority within the organization who has the power to act on the idea. An **external proposal** is written for a reader outside of an organization. The purpose is to present a product or service for sale in the best light possible and explain why the reader should consider it.

The **introduction** of the proposal summarizes the problem you are attempting to solve and its solution. It may identify the benefits or advantages that your reader will gain from your proposal, its total cost, and any background information your reader might need in order to make a decision. It might also include a description of any feasibility studies that have been conducted in connection with the proposal, their results, and their implications. An **executive summary** may also be included if various levels of management must review the proposal before it is considered.

The **body** of the proposal explains in detail:

- how the job will be done
- what methods will be used to do it and what materials (if any) will be used
- when the work will begin
- when the task will be completed
- a cost breakdown

The **conclusion** should (a) emphasize the advantages to the reader of accepting the proposal, and (b) encourage the reader to take action. The tone should be positive, confident, and encouraging.

A **glossary** and **appendix** may be added if technical terms have been used or if certain information requires further explanation.

FORMAL BUSINESS REPORTS

Formal business reports are written accounts of major projects. They often include research, advisability studies, and/or a review of developments within an organization. Most formal reports are divided into three major parts—front matter, body, and back matter. The elements contained in each of these parts are identified in the following chart.

Front Matter	Body	Back Matter
Title page	Executive summary	Bibliography
Abstract	Introduction	Appendices
Table of contents	Detail of summary	Glossary
List of figures	Conclusions	Index
List of tables	Recommendations	
Foreword	References	
Preface		
List of abbreviations and symbols		

Front Matter

The **front matter** of a formal business report usually provides:

- a general idea of the writer's purpose in writing the report
- an overview of the kind of information contained in the report
- a list of chapters, figures, illustrations, and tables, with page numbers

Executive Summary

The **executive summary** condenses the report and explains its significant findings. A typical summary is ten percent of the length of the original report.

Introduction

The **introduction** provides background information and a frame of reference for the information contained in the report. It states the topic, the purpose of the report, the way the topic will be developed, and perhaps its organizational framework.

Body (Detail of Summary)

The **body** is also known as the **detail of summary** of the report. It's usually organized into major sections, which are further subdivided to reflect the logical divisions in each section.

Conclusion
The **conclusion** pulls together the results of the study upon which the report is based. It tells the reader what has been learned and what the implications are. It asks, How did it go? It may also include a post-implementation review.

Recommendations
Recommendations advise the reader of the best course of action based on the results of the study. They are not always included.

References
As in any other form of writing, if you have referred to the work of others you must document these sources. Pictures and/or text taken from a book or from the Internet must be documented. (See the section on Referencing Sources in the Research and Ethics chapter.)

Back Matter
The **back matter** of a formal business report may contain a **bibliography**, an **index**, and a **glossary** that clarifies any specialized terminology used in the report.

Information that requires additional explanation is contained in an **appendix**. This may include long charts, graphs, or supplementary material; questionnaires used in gathering data; transcripts of interviews; relevant correspondence; and explanations too long to be included within the regular body of the report. If a report has more than one appendix, they are numbered or lettered. Each appendix usually contains only one type of information.

Understanding Style

TECHNICAL WRITING

Here are three clear conventions of style associated with procedural writing.

- Use of the **imperative mood**. Most instructions in technical writing are given as commands. If the reader is acknowledged at all, it is only as "you" or "one."
- Use of the **simple present tense**. In the following series of instructions, note that the present tense is used consistently throughout:

> *Preheat* oven to 350°F.
> *Place* pan on central rack in oven.
> *Bake* for 25 minutes.

- Use of **specific, precise language**. Conjunctive adverbs and phrases denoting time sequence are used frequently in technical writing to help the reader move logically and confidently through the process. Notice the use of linking words in this simple instruction:

> *First* clean the surface of the table with a damp cloth. *Next* pour a generous amount of the furniture oil onto a clean dry cloth. *Finally*, rub the oil onto the table surface using a circular motion.

Sometimes it's necessary to clarify *how* something is to be done. It might be necessary to explain a process using specific adverbs for safety reasons or to ensure the best use of the product. For example:

> Apply the glue *evenly* around the perimeter.

Sometimes instructions are also warnings or cautions, and are designated as such in order to alert the reader:

> Caution: *Gently* twist the mouthpiece on. Do not force it or damage may result.

Both procedural and business writing contain **subject-specific vocabulary**, words specific to the area about which they are writing. The use of this terminology gives credibility to the writer and acknowledges the expertise of the reader.

BUSINESS WRITING

The level of formality in language and tone are important considerations in business writing. The level of formality you use depends on your audience. Are you writing to colleagues who have the same position in the company as you do, or are you writing to someone who is in a more senior position? Consider the following two comparisons. Which sentences would you use in a memo to a senior manager?

> I don't agree with your plan because it presents some logistical problems.
>
> *or*
>
> The logistics of moving the department as you suggest may pose certain logistical problems.
>
> I think you'll like what I'm suggesting.
>
> *or*
>
> This proposal offers several advantages.

RÉSUMÉS

Here are the main stylistic conventions of résumés:

- Avoid the use of the pronoun "I." This will help to convey an objective tone that will contribute to the credibility of the information.

- Use point form. This will help to condense the information so that it can be taken in more quickly and seen as a whole.

Original	**Revised**
I was promoted to office manager.	Promoted to office manager

- Use action verbs. Verbs commonly used in résumés include:

administered	managed
analyzed	operated
completed	organized
conducted	oriented
coordinated	prepared
created	programmed
delegated	recruited
designed	started
developed	supervised
directed	trained
evaluated	wrote
increased	

E-MAILS

E-mail is rapidly becoming one of the most common forms of business communication.

E-mail Style Guidelines

- *Always provide a subject line. Since people routinely receive several messages a day, it's polite to let them know what your message is about.*
- *Don't be wordy. Not all e-mail messages can be short, but no e-mail message should be rambling.*
- *Be clear. Remember that your e-mail correspondent may not have all the background on the information you are sending.*
- *Use an appropriate level of formality. Because e-mails are sent instantaneously, they tend to be written in less formal language than that used in letters. Even when a more casual, friendly tone is acceptable, you must still ensure that your tone is objective, professional, and respectful.*
- *Remember that no e-mail that you send or receive can be considered private or confidential.*

The following e-mail message provides an example of a less formal style of business communication.

From: lsunita@imagedynamics.com
To: jacksonp@coolwear.com
Date: March 25, 2002
Subject: XYX logo revisions — subject line summarizes purpose of message

saluation is friendly, casual — Hi Jackson,

It was great meeting with you last week about Coolwear's plans for the new XYX line of sports gear. — introductory paragraph sets context for message

I presented your logo proposal to our design team yesterday afternoon. They liked the overall concept, but had the following concerns about the look of this signature brand:
- the colours—gold with the outlying white stripe—are too similar to ZOZ's athletic shoe
- the inverted, overlapping Y conveys a corporate look that will not appeal to the target 18–24 demographic
- the curvature of the X's does not evoke the edginess critical to the success of this brand

bulleted list highlights specific concerns

criticisms conveyed in neutral, objective tone

technical vocabul[ary] conveys credibilit[y,] assumes recipien[t's] shared knowledg[e] of terminology

As a new player in this market, it's important to establish a distinctive presence. At the same time, we need to maintain a continuity with the Coolwear line. XYX is a solid addition to this line, and we're excited about its prospects.

persuasive language strengthens sender's message

Our design people suggest:
- a charcoal-and-berry palette that would complement the Coolpants logo and so maintain a consistent brand image
- a cleaner look, with subtly overlapping, straight-edged letters, that would help target the 18–24 demographic

I hope this sounds good to you. I'll Fedex the revised samples when our production team has completed the mock-ups. We aim to have them delivered to your office by this Thursday. Looking forward to your response!

indicates next steps in process

ends in an upbeat, collaborative tone

warm, informal closing — Best,
Lulu

» CHECKPOINT: *Reassess Your Knowledge*

eggs

Executive Summary

Imagine a food product consumed by two-year-olds, 102-year-olds, and virtually everyone in between. A product in 93% of fridges. A product familiar and ubiquitous, not to mention nutritious and versatile. And a product that had declined in per capita consumption for 17 straight years, taking $360 million out of the hands of Canadian retailers and farmers. The product is eggs, and in 1996, the situation was dire.

Consumption had fallen for all the wrong reasons. A perception had grown, fueled by misinformed reports via the media and the health-care community, that eating eggs could lead to cholesterol problems in otherwise healthy Canadians. (For 80% of Canadians, eggs do not contribute to increased blood cholesterol.) Unfortunately, facts weren't the issue. Perceptions were. And perceptions are much harder to displace.

To reverse the decline, we looked at the problem in an unprecedented way. Despite years of multi-million dollar budgets spent through the national and provincial egg marketing boards, nothing had stemmed the tide. The answer, as we will show, would be found in the grocery store aisle.

The campaign started in January 1996, with immediate results. AC Nielsen and Stats Canada reported 7% increases in 1996 per capita consumption; stunning when compared to the 17-year decline. This was followed by a 2% increase in 1997, with all major attitudes to eggs improving. Nothing but the new advertising could have caused this turnaround. All other marketing variables were unchanged, with pricing, if anything, edging up.

Situation Analysis

Anthropologists tell us that the Romans began cultivating chickens for their eggs in 404 BC. Eggs were seen as an excellent food for the warrior classes charged with the expansion of Roman civilization. As the population grew, so did chicken farming.

Fast-forward to the early 1900s in Canada. With immigration from the egg-consuming cultures of Europe, egg farming grew by leaps and bounds. Per capita consumption rose every year, peaking in the 1960s at about 22 dozen.

Soon after, with the onset of the fitness craze and health consciousness, eggs came under attack. Per capita consumption began a long decline, and fell to a low of 14.27 dozen a year in 1995. This was one third less than the level in the 1960s, and represented a loss to the egg industry of $12 per Canadian (1995 retail prices), for a total of $360 million in 1995 alone.

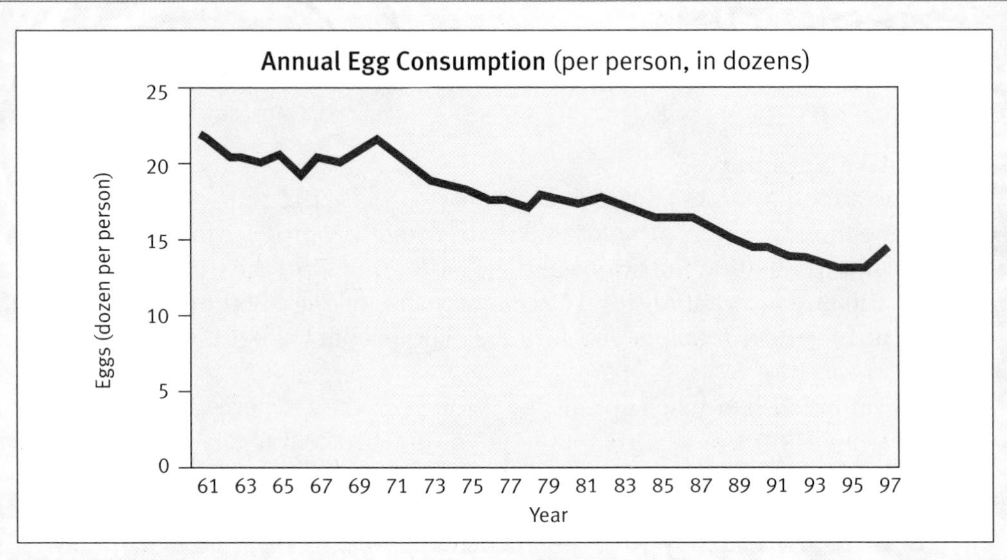

During the decline, 95% of Canadians continued to eat eggs, but less often. Consumption declined for a number of reasons:

- People were eating fewer and smaller breakfasts, and choosing easy-to-prepare cold cereal over eggs.
- More women were going into the work force, radically altering most meal occasions, especially breakfast.
- Most importantly, people began to fear dietary cholesterol.

As the baby boomers reached their 30s and 40s, they heard a proliferation of often inaccurate information trumpeting health causes and concerns. Cholesterol, fat, saturated fat, and oat bran all had their moments in the sun, and the cross-hairs. Eggs took a disproportionate amount of criticism. Although dietary cholesterol had little or no effect on blood cholesterol for 80% of Canadians, the perception grew that cholesterol in eggs was potentially harmful.

The egg industry fought back. It was spending up to $6 million a year at the provincial and federal levels. The strategy was to market versatility and convenience through broadscale advertising, while delivering the health and nutrition message through PR—mainly to the health care community. However, despite one of the most recognized slogans in Canada, "Get Cracking," egg sales continued to decline.

In 1993, the industry took on the challenge of rebuilding sales. The strategy would evolve, as we discuss next, but the business objective could not have been plainer:

Stop the long-term decline in consumption.

Strategy and Execution

Strategy

Advertising had been extolling the convenience and versatility of eggs, but quantitative research showed that this was preaching to the converted. It was evident (from the research and the consumption decline) that this was not the lever for turning sales around. Health concerns were the major barrier. But how should they be dealt with?

The issue: how to convince Canadians, within the bounds of advertising credibility, that increased egg consumption would not adversely affect their health. Many questions faced us, including how to counter the editorial and so-called expert advice that was misinforming Canadians. There were many options. We could intensify PR against the media and the medical community, fueled by the latest scientific research. But the impact would be slow. This strategy could ultimately work, but only after several more years of consumption decline.

We could go directly to the public, and present the medical evidence in a compelling way through advertising. We felt this would be unsuccessful for two reasons.

- Advertising lacked the credibility to overcome the so-called expert opinions bombarding Canadians daily.
- The problem was not factual, but perceptual. Canadians felt that unrestricted egg consumption could be harmful. We had to make them feel, rather than think, that this was not the case.

A final concern was the danger that openly acknowledging cholesterol in advertising might perpetuate the misconceptions. ("Thou doth protest too much," said a certain medieval playwright, who was also an egg farmer.) The solution lay in the strategic thought:

De-fuse don't Dispel

Rather than try to dispel the health concerns directly (unrealistic) we would de-fuse them. And we found how in the grocery store aisle.

Believing in the anthropological method, we intercepted egg buyers in the grocery store, and asked them to free-associate on the subject of eggs. While predictable responses were plentiful (versatile, convenient, etc.) not one person said "natural." Yet, when asked "Are eggs a natural food?" the answer was consistently "Yes."

Following up with qualitative research, we uncovered the overwhelming belief that "Nature doesn't make food that is bad for you." We could use the notion that eggs are "nature's food" as the proxy for "good for you." This would inject credibility into the advertising, to overcome years of negative reinforcement from other sources.

This insight was the basis for the success of the campaign.

Execution

Given the history, we knew that giving people permission to feel better about eating eggs—driven by the "natural" insight—would be a 3-5 year project. But as we explored how to deliver the message creatively, we had to think further. There were two other issues confronting the industry.

First, eating habits would continue to work against egg consumption. Sit-down breakfasts were becoming less and less frequent, and the stove was playing less of a role in breakfast. Second, thanks to the General Agreement on Tariffs and Trade, imported eggs will eventually be available in Canada (likely at a lower cost), so the marketing objective will shift—from increasing consumption to positioning Canadian eggs vs. US eggs.

We needed an advertising property that could act as an "envelope," not only for our immediate message, but for a message that would evolve over time.

We chose real-life egg farmers: credible, honest people who would be the link between nature and the store—and a metaphor for "natural." At a time when people were stressed out, the romanticized perception of simple, honest farm life would communicate the natural health of eggs.

With household penetration at nearly universal levels, we chose to target primary grocery shoppers with families, leaving out empty-nesters and older consumers. Families were the best volume opportunity, particularly because of the stressed-out lives of dual-income couples with kids.

The "Producer Portrait" campaign began in January 1996, when consumption was at its lowest point in recent history. The goal was to frequently refresh the campaign. To date, we have done this with seven different stories in English, and five in French. During the time of this national campaign, the provincial egg boards have run sporadic bursts of advertising, but there have been no major strategy changes at that level.

Results

In 1996 (the campaign's Year 1), the per capita decline finally turned around. We have the luxury of the most thorough quantitative measurement in Canada—Statistics Canada—who reported that egg consumption grew by more than six eggs per person in 1996, the first increase of any kind in 17 years. Consumption grew by another two eggs in 1997, the latest year for which Statistics Canada have data. This brings egg consumption back to levels not seen since 1990. And based on the Canadian Egg Marketing Agency's own tracking, egg consumption has continued up through 1998.

Moreover, per capita consumption of other commodities tainted by concerns about fat and cholesterol, such as red meat and milk, declined during 1996 and 1997, while egg consumption made its remarkable turnaround.

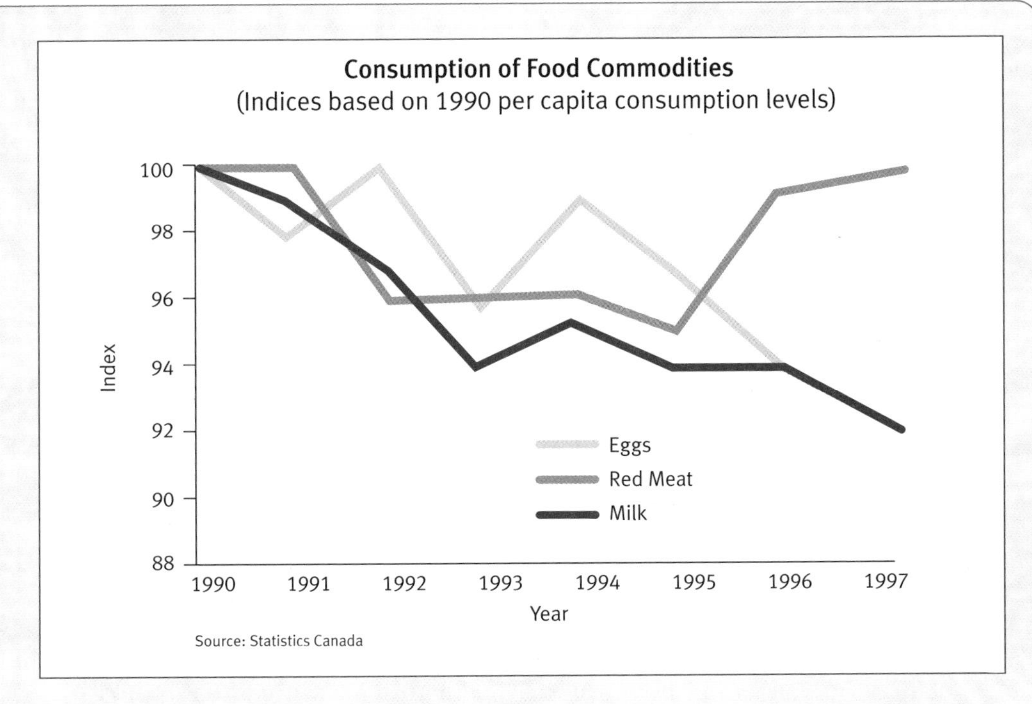

This had been achieved while the retail price of eggs increased (roughly in line with inflation), making the consumption gains that much more surprising and valuable to the industry. Estimates suggest the turnaround in consumption across 1996-97 was worth $70 million at 1995 retail prices.

Isolating Advertising as the Variable

We attribute the increase in consumption to advertising for several reasons:

1. Other marketing variables could not have caused the growth, as packaging and distribution did not change. While in-store promotion budgets did increase over this period, we know from historical performance that this alone could not turn consumption around.
2. Typically, a retail price increase would have suppressed an increase in consumption. This was not the case here.
3. Changes in provincial egg board marketing activities were negligible, and the consumption increases were national, transcending any single province.
4. Quantitative research in September 1996, eight months into the campaign, showed that shifts in awareness and attitudes are correlated to the advertising campaign:

- Past-three-month advertising awareness had jumped by 10 points, reflecting the increased investment behind the new campaign.

- Egg TV advertising recall jumped by 14 percentage points from the pre-advertising wave of research (70% to 84%). Since TV has been the main historical medium for national egg campaigns, this increase, in such a consistently used medium, is highly indicative of the campaign's effect.
- Recall of the advertising message, "Eggs are nutritious," jumped by 18 percentage points to 51% amongst those recalling the advertising. This result is consistent with qualitative evaluation of the commercials by Decima Research, which found them to have excellent credibility, main-message communication, and clutter-cutting ability.
- There was significant improvement in consumer agreement with such statements as "Eggs are good food" and "It's OK to eat eggs"—the areas that pre-campaign research showed were holding consumption back.
- The core message is getting through. A majority say that the main message of the advertising is that "Eggs are healthy and good for you."

In short, the advertising has a research-proven and sales-proven effect.

Note: In addition to the television campaign, many other marketing activities are executed at retail nationally every year for the Canadian Egg Marketing Agency. All provincial egg boards also develop public relations activities as well as print advertising. All of these marketing programs together contribute to the successful promotion of eggs in Canada.

Canadian Egg Marketing Agency—Roche Macaulay & Partners

1. Who do you think is the intended audience for this business report? Explain why.
2. The Canadian Egg Marketing Agency won an award for its campaign. Describe the strategy that earned it this award.
3. Explain how this report is organized.
4. What information is provided in the graphic text that is not found in the written text?
5. How would you describe the style of the language used in this report? Why do you think this style was used? Refer to specific examples from the text to support your answer.

Creating Technical Writing: Sequence of Instructions

Preparing and Planning

Before you compose a list of instructions, make sure that you know your subject thoroughly. For example, if you choose to create a sequence of steps for playing a particular video game, go through the steps yourself several times so that you get a feel for what's required.

Here are some further considerations for planning your written instructions.

Tips for Outlining Your Instruction Sequence

- *Use an organizer to outline the process before you begin. The organizer should note the aim or purpose, the steps required, and any necessary equipment.*
- *Does the process exist in phases or as one unit? Will you divide your writing into process parts? If so, what will be your section headings?*
- *Is there equipment involved in the process? If so, gather that equipment so that you have it in front of you as you write.*
- *What is the age and knowledge base of your target audience? For example, if you were writing a computer software manual for children, you would need to consider their specific age range and their level of technological expertise.*

Revising and Editing

The ultimate test of procedural writing is having someone else carry out your instructions. Ask someone to follow the instructions you have written. Encourage this person to provide feedback on any problem areas, and revise your writing as necessary.

You may wish to ask this person to fill out the following checklist.

Checklist

Assessing Your Procedural Writing	
Is the purpose of the writing clear?	❑
Is the organizational pattern clear?	❑
Have I identified all the equipment required for the process to be successfully completed?	❑
Are all the steps in the process identified?	❑
Are the steps in the right order and is the sequence clear, either through the use of numbers or linking words?	❑
Are warnings or cautions included, if necessary?	❑
Are there diagrams to accompany the visual text?	❑
Is the simple present tense used consistently throughout?	❑
Is the imperative mood used?	❑
Is the vocabulary specific to the topic?	❑
Is the language precise?	❑

GRAMMAR, USAGE, AND MECHANICS

CANADIAN AND AMERICAN SPELLING CONVENTIONS

Many technical manuals that originate in the United States are available in Canada—and these manuals, of course, use American spelling. For example, you may have noticed that the "Gettingstarted.net" excerpt at the beginning of this chapter uses the American spelling of the words *color* and *center*.

Canadian spelling is a mix of British and American spelling. Because of its British influence, Canadian spelling differs from American conventions in the following ways:

Canadian Spelling	American Spelling	Summary
centre metre fibre theatre lustre meagre	center meter fiber theater luster meager	Words ending in **re** in Canadian spelling end in **er** in American spelling.
honour colour favour neighbour odour rigour	honor color favor neighbor odor rigor	Words ending in **our** in Canadian spelling end in **or** in the U.S.
traveller labelling signalled modelled jewellery woollen	traveler labeling signaled modeled jewelry woolen	In Canadian spelling an **l** before a suffix is doubled. In the U.S. it is not.
practise (verb) practice (noun) license (verb) licence (noun)	practice license	Canadian spelling distinguishes between the verb and the noun. In the U.S. there is only one spelling.
storey (as in two-storey building) cheque grey	story check gray	These examples indicate the different standard spellings of these words in the two countries. Similarly, in Britain, *tire* is spelled *tyre*, and *curb* is spelled *kerb*.

Presenting Technical Writing: Giving Directions

Every time we give someone directions or instructions about how to do something, we are presenting technical writing orally. Countless people provide technical assistance through telephone help lines. They may solve a glitch in someone's computer software, or offer medical instructions to someone in distress. In short, their job is to make strategies explicit to someone else. Offering oral instructions is a skill many of us will need.

Try the following exercise with a partner.

Instructing a Partner to Replicate Your Design

1. *On a piece of paper, randomly draw an abstract design using lines, circles, squares, etc. Don't show the design to your partner.*
2. *Provide your partner with a blank sheet of paper and a pencil. Sit back to back so that you can't see what your partner is drawing.*
3. *Instruct your partner on how to replicate your design.*
4. *When finished, compare the two drawings.*
5. *Talk about where confusions arose for your partner. Consider what you needed to say in order to get an exact replica of your original drawing.*

Sequence, Detail, and Precision

The success of oral instructions depends on three main factors:

- sequence of process
- adequate detail
- precision of language

Before you begin to explain a process, consider carefully the sequence of events that must be followed, and any equipment that's required. Make sure that you provide adequate details. Finally, make sure that the directions, locations, sizes, angles, measurements, names, and terms are exact.

To assess your success as an instruction giver, repeat the experiment described above. This time, however, have a third person watch the process. Ask him or her to note which instructions generate an incorrect response. Ask this observer for feedback when the process is complete.

The observer might use the following checklist to assess the success of the oral instructions.

Checklist

Assessing the Success of Oral Instructions	
Were the instructions given in correct sequence?	❑
Did the instructions provide adequate detail?	❑
Did the instructor use specific and precise language?	❑

CHAPTER 8

media

> The vast new borders of electric energy and information created by radio and television have set up world frontiers.
>
> *Marshall McLuhan*

> Whoever controls the media—the images—controls the culture.
>
> *Allen Ginsberg*

What are media texts and why do we study them? When we refer to **media** we usually mean mass media, which include newspapers, magazines, television, film, video, and the Internet. **Media literacy** is the ability to assess and analyze mass media.

Critical analysis of **media texts** helps us understand how meaning is communicated and how techniques of persuasion operate. It also offers us clues to the characteristics and values of our culture. As a result, we are able to become better-informed and more critical consumers of media. In this way we can learn to use media to communicate our own messages more effectively.

LEARNING GOALS

- analyze how different media communicate meaning
- analyze the purpose, values, and conventions of media content
- identify and analyze the authenticity of media information
- learn how to create a storyboard for a video
- develop a multimedia presentation

CONTENTS

Analyzing and Responding to Media

» CHECKPOINT: *Assess Your Knowledge*

1. What are the three central visual features of this ad?
2. Why is the guitar player in the ad not completely in focus?
3. The ad says "power this outrageous." To what does "this" refer?
4. Why was the guitar player's picture shot from below, rather than straight on or from any other angle?
5. What message is the advertiser trying to convey to the audience?
6. Why does the advertiser call the battery e^2?
7. Both the guitar and the battery are pictured on an angle. Why?
8. If you were the advertiser, in what magazines would you place this ad? Why?
9. What intertextual references can you discern (e.g., to other ads, to other genres, to other people)?

Reading Strategies

To begin to look at media critically, ask yourself the following questions.

Encountering Media Texts

- *What is the subject?*
- *What is being said about that subject?*
- *Who created this media text?*
- *What is its apparent purpose? (e.g., to inform, persuade, entertain)*
- *What audience was it created for?*
- *What is the form of media?*
- *What stylistic devices are used?*

Sometimes the answers to these questions are obvious. At other times it may be difficult to pinpoint the answer to any of them.

Go back to the media text, whether it's an ad, Web site, film, or TV program. Note details of presentation and language—not only what's there, but also what's been left out. For example:

- a filmmaker has limited his or her types of shots
- an advertiser has highlighted a specific group of people
- a newspaper reporter has chosen one quotation over another

The choices made by the media creator often tell us much about the underlying meaning, or **subtext**. This subtext is often at the heart of understanding the text.

Understanding Meaning

ACTIVE INTERPRETATION

Active interpretation of media texts involves asking yourself a series of questions.

Text

- *What is the genre and format of the text? (horror movie? newspaper editorial? magazine ad?)*
- *What do you know about this genre and format? (e.g., styles, rules, conventions)*
- *Who is this text aimed at? How can you tell?*
- *To what extent are you part of this intended audience?*
- *What do you think is the preferred response from the intended audience? (to laugh? to buy a product?)*

Context

- *Where are you encountering the text? (alone? what environment? is this the typical place to encounter this text?)*
- *Will this affect your interpretation of the text?*
- *For what purpose are you viewing this text? (entertainment? information? to consider an issue?)*
- *Will your purpose affect what you concentrate on in viewing the text?*
- *How does this text relate to your own life?*
- *What biases can you detect? How do they relate to your own biases?*
- *How was the text introduced? (ad? opening credits? music?)*
- *Were there any interruptions or gaps? (ads? page breaks?)*

Structure and Form

- *What is the overall structure of the text?*
- *How does this text compare to similar texts you've seen of the same type, format, and genre?*
- *What conventions does the text seem to follow?*

Your Own Response

- *What feelings and responses did the text evoke for you?*
- *Why do you think you responded this way?*
- *What elements of the text were primarily responsible for this response?*

TEXT, CONTEXT, AND SUBTEXT

The **text** of a film, print advertisement, Web page, or radio program is its content. The **context** is the environment in which it was created and received. The **subtext** is its underlying meaning, which can often be deliberately obscured.

For example, consider the technique of product placement, in which an advertiser pays to have its product included in a film. In the middle of a scene you might see the cool-looking main character drinking brand X soft drink—and you know it's brand X because the label is so prominent. The text is simply that the character is thirsty. The context is a popular movie designed for entertainment. The subtext is that cool people drink brand X.

MAKING INFERENCES

When elements of the meaning aren't easy to tell at first glance, you might have to **infer** them. You may need to draw on your own experiences and knowledge as well as the information provided in the media text.

Elements of the Media Text	What You Might Infer
Who is performing the action?	When a car zooms up an impossibly steep mountainside in a TV commercial, you can infer that the car is being driven by a professional stunt driver. When a music video shows fans cheering riotously for a band, unless it's actual concert footage, you can infer that these are paid extras.
What's really going on?	A print ad for a perfume shows a man turning to look at a woman; you can infer that he's attracted to her.
What happened before and after?	What happened before and after a news photograph was taken?
What are the relationships between agent and object?	If a television newsperson (agent) is interviewing a politician (object), does he or she seem to be a friend, a stranger, or an adversary?
What were the production circumstances?	Was a scene in a movie filmed in a realistic external setting, recreated in a studio, or digitally enhanced?
What are the causes and effects?	If a Web site publishes material that has been banned from regular media outlets, what is likely to be the effect? If a TV show promotes an alternative lifestyle, what's likely to happen?
Is there an underlying theme?	On the surface, a rock video is simply a dramatization of the song, but it may be making a point about rebellion and individual freedom.

UNDERLYING VALUES, BIAS, AND CONVENTIONS

Values analysis assumes that all media represent cultural values, and in turn influence these values. A two-step approach is used:

1. Identify the values presented through the media text.
2. Interpret what is being said about those values.

When analyzing a media text for **bias**, you need to look at how the presentation slants, or biases, its content.

Let's say you were analyzing a television newscast. You would want to do the following:

Analyzing a Newscast

- *Analyze the newscaster's language for bias, stereotypes, and over-generalizations.*
- *Consider what visuals accompanied the spoken text. What was emphasized? Why was it emphasized?*
- *Examine whether equal time was provided for opposing sides on a given issue.*
- *Investigate the background of the broadcasting station, i.e., its ownership and editorial policies, both stated and implied.*
- *Compare the newscast's treatment of stories to that of other TV stations and to other media.*

SEMIOTICS

Semiotics is the study of "signs"—elements of the text whose meaning is "encoded." When semiotics is applied to media texts, the goal is to try to understand, or "decode," the underlying **conventions** of media.

For example, if you were analyzing a children's animated film, you might ask yourself the following:

Analyzing a Children's Film

- *What type of music is used?*
- *What kinds of characters seem popular?*
- *How does the animator recreate the world (e.g., realistically; fantastically)?*
- *How are we introduced into the world of the story?*
- *What connotes good and evil in the film?*
- *What is possible in the film's world? What isn't?*
- *What are the program's overall assumptions?*
- *What sort of reality does the text construct and how does it do so?*
- *How is the film's world made believable?*
- *What assumptions does the text make about its viewers?*

INDUSTRY CODES AND REGULATIONS

Canadian media and advertising practices are governed by a combination of self-regulated industry codes and government legislation and regulations. These codes influence both the content and the presentation of media.

The major codes and regulations are:

- **The Canadian Association of Broadcasters Code of Ethics**
  The first responsibility of proprietors and managers of broadcasting stations is for the dissemination of information and news, the supply of a variety of entertainment programming to meet the various tastes of listeners, and the necessity for ethical business standards in dealing with advertisers and their agencies.
- **The Canadian Code of Advertising Standards**
  The code is designed to help set and maintain standards of honesty, truth, accuracy, fairness, and propriety in advertising.
- **Advertising Standards Canada Gender Portrayal Guidelines**
  Advertising should strive to provide an equal representation of women and men in roles of authority both for the characters within the actual advertising scenario and when representing the advertiser through announcers, voice-overs, experts, and on-camera authorities.
- **The Broadcast Code for Advertising to Children**
  All children's advertising must conform to the various requirements of this code.

LITERARY TECHNIQUES

Many literary techniques—such as theme, tone, mood, characterization, and rhetorical devices—can be applied to media texts.

In addition, many media texts draw on allusions to literature and literary traditions. A number of novels and plays have been made into feature films. Comparing the print and film versions offers valuable clues to the content and form of each genre. By noting the cuts and changes the film director makes, as well as his or her use of visual symbols, the student can learn about the film as a literary text.

METAPHOR AND SYMBOL

Media creators, like poets, have learned that humans often think in metaphors and symbols. By using the language of metaphor and symbol, the media are often seeking the same emotional connection to the viewer as a poet is.

The **metaphors** in a media text can be **explicit**, for example, "Canada Dry is the Champagne of Ginger Ales." At other times, the comparison is **implied**. For example, when a star athlete promotes a product in a TV commercial, the viewer is meant to associate the product with the prestige of the athlete.

Symbolism in media texts works as it does in literary texts: a concrete object is used to represent an abstract concept. Symbols can be visual or oral. For example, in horror films, an increase in the volume of the soundtrack usually represents imminent danger.

PSYCHOLOGICAL APPEALS

We all have certain psychological needs, and media texts use these to attract and to motivate us. These psychological appeals fall into the following categories:

Psychological Need	Example
need for security	A public service billboard on a busy highway that asks "How fast are you going?" encourages people to slow down.
need for acceptance	Wearing a particular running shoe is associated with being cool. We infer that if we wear it we'll be cool too. This appeals to our need to fit in.
tendency to feel guilt	An appeal to busy parents that plays on the guilt they might feel for not spending more time with their children.
tendency toward boredom	New visual and sound technologies are constantly created in an effort to provide filmgoers with different experiences.

FIGURE AND GROUND ANALYSIS

When you look at an image, some elements seem to come forward while others drop into the background. For example, if you see a photograph of a brightly coloured bird sitting in a uniformly green tree, you might be conscious of the colour of the bird, while you ignore the background.

The elements you are conscious of are called the **figure**, while the other elements are the **ground**. The ground also includes the viewing situation—when and where the text is encountered. It's often the *interplay* between the figure and the ground that is crucial to our understanding.

Media creators try to direct us to certain figures in order to lead us to certain interpretations. For example, the front page of a newspaper usually has five or six different stories on it. Through large headlines and an eye-catching picture, one story may become the central figure on the page. This implies that it is the item we should focus on.

Interpreting Figure and Ground

- *What is being presented as the figure?*
- *What is the background?*

- *What is the foreground?*
- *Why are we being directed this way?*
- *What is being emphasized and why?*
- *Does the figure or ground change at any point? What is the effect on the meaning?*

Understanding Form

Each medium has a unique form, which is very much connected to its content. As Marshall McLuhan famously said, "The medium is the message."

Newspapers and magazines have a long history, with specific conventions. Other forms, such as Web pages and TV programs, are relatively new. Some conventions and styles have emerged, while others are still evolving.

PRINT MEDIA

Although print media texts vary greatly in design, content, and intended audience, they all share certain visual concepts.

Visual Concepts

- ***Balance***: *When we look at a page, we unconsciously seek to find a visual balance. That is, we like to see the visual elements arranged somewhat equally, without any one element predominating. When all the elements are present evenly, this is called* symmetrical balance. *When objects aren' t equal but are balanced as a whole, this is called* asymmetrical balance.

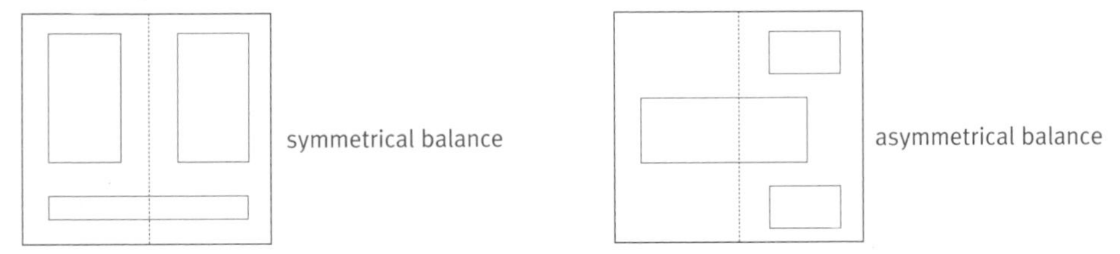

- ***Contrast***: *Contrasting items is a way to draw attention toward or away from them. Sometimes contrasting visual elements are placed together in* juxtaposition *in order to highlight their differences.*
- ***Harmony***: *The opposite of contrast is harmony. The visual elements (fonts, pictures, graphics) are usually similar in style. Some modern publications experiment with deliberate disharmony, choosing elements that clash and contrast.*
- ***Colour***: *The human eye is drawn toward colour. Editors and designers use this fact to direct the eye to information they want stressed.*

NEWSPAPERS

Newspapers have three goals: to **inform**, to **interpret**, and to **entertain**. Of course, they also aim to make a profit by carrying advertising.

Newspapers have become increasingly more visual in their design, as readers demand more information with less reading of print text. This has resulted in shorter stories, more photos, and the addition of graphics, such as charts and graphs.

This front page of the *National Post* illustrates many aspects of newspaper format. The annotations point out ways to analyze the text.

Teasers are designed to make readers buy the paper to get the information inside.

Headline details the story in concise language without using articles (e.g., *the* or *a*)—and the bigger the story, the larger the headline.

Decks are short subheadlines that come between the headline and the body of the story.

The **flag** or **masthead** identifies the newspaper.

The eyes look in toward the flag—Why?

Rules break up print and direct the viewer's eye.

Byline of the person who wrote the story (not all stories

Stories usually cross the **foldline** so that readers have to pick up the paper to read the whole story.

Caption details the photograph. (It's not written by the photographer, who has a small acknowledgment.)

The human eye in our culture tends to scan a page in an inverted "N" pattern. How does this page use this natural tendency to direct the eye?

Lead is written as a quick summary, usually containing the who, what, when, where, and how of the story.

Jumplines are designed to lead the reader to a place inside the newspaper.

Box identifies the ownership of the newspaper. (Does it matter who owns the newspaper?)

Body of the news story. (News stories are written in a style called *inverted pyramid*, in which all major details are presented in the beginning, in case the editor needs to cut the end of the story.)

Picture comes from the **wire service** Associated Press (AP). (Wire services are news-gathering organizations that sell material to many papers.)

Most larger papers have a **Web site**—what effect does this have on news reporting?

Index reveals what features are important to readers. (How many pages seem devoted to each topic?)

cause there is no money in hockey for us otherwise," he said. "But there are ways of doing it and we are looking at various combinations."

CBC executives are looking at an arrangement under which some playoff games would be shifted from the main CBC network to a partner network, where they would be clearly identified as CBC productions. One option is that the CBC would buy a minority interest in CTV Sportsnet, an all-sports cable network CTV will sell early next year. Cable magnate Ted Rogers is seeking regulatory approval to buy a controlling interest in Sportsnet.

"We could carry the weekend playoff games and a weekday game rather than the whole thing," Mr. Rabinovitch said.

The broadcaster will also pull further away from professional sport, he said, likely dumping coverage of Toronto Blue Jays baseball and other events. But it will stick with the Olympics and increase coverage of amateur sport.

"Sports is not that lucrative," he said. "It's OK and we break even. On the French-language side [Radio-Canada] it is not lucrative at all but we have to remember that many Canadians define themselves through sport. We have a responsibility for things like *Hockey Night in Canada* and I don't see anyone else coming to the plate and wanting to take it over."

The CBC's contract with the NHL expires after next season and the network wants to renew, he said.

Mr. Rabinovitch also said he wants CBC-TV to reduce, and ultimately end, its reliance on commercials. *The National* will air without ads by mid-January.

See PRIORITY on Page A6

JEFF MITCHELL / REUTERS (TOP); HARVEY GEORGES / AP (BOTTOM)

In the top picture, Donald Rumsfeld, right, meets reporters yesterday after his nomination as secretary of defence; on the left is Dick Cheney, the Vice-President elect. At bottom, a parallel scene on Nov. 7, 1975, when Rumsfeld was named as Gerald Ford's defence secretary and Cheney was his deputy.

Ford-era defence chief is back in the saddle

By Scott Lindlaw

WASHINGTON · George W. Bush, the President-elect of the United States, completed the uppermost ranks of his Cabinet yesterday, reaching back into the past once again for a key appointment with the surprise nomination of Donald Rumsfeld as secretary of defence.

Mr. Rumsfeld joins such veterans of previous Republican administrations as Dick Cheney, the Vice-President elect, and General Colin Powell, the nominee as secretary of state.

It will be Mr. Rumsfeld's second tour of duty as Pentagon chief. He was the youngest defence secretary in history when he held the position from 1975 to 1977 under Gerald Ford.

The vacancy was the object of intense speculation. Dan Coats, a former Indiana senator, was hotly tipped for the job, with Mr. Rumsfeld, 68, a veteran of four Republican administrations dating back to Richard Nixon, seen as more likely to head the Central Intelligence Agency.

"He is going to be a great secretary of defence — again," Mr. Bush said, adding that he hopes to have his Cabinet completed by the first week in January.

Mr. Rumsfeld said he is looking forward to his second tour. "I have been doing a number of things with respect to national security and foreign policy issues in the intervening years and I look forward to it, I really do," he said.

"It's a fine institution and a wonderful group of people."

Mr. Rumsfeld was elected to the first of four terms in Congress as a Republican from the 13th District of Illinois at the age of 30 in 1962. He had attended Princeton University on a scholarship, served in the Navy as an aviator and became an all-Navy wrestling champion, according to his official biography.

He held more than a half-dozen jobs in Republican administrations. He then spent more than two decades working for companies in pharmaceuticals, banking and high technology outside Washington.

See RUMSFELD on Page A8

David Olive on Bush's Rust Belt choice for Treasury. Page C3

TB to sue Ottawa for letting him in

Seeks $500-million for federal doctor's incorrect diagnosis

By Mary Vallis

An immigrant who exposed hundreds of Canadians to a virulent form of tuberculosis intends to launch a $500-million lawsuit against the federal government for allowing him into the country.

Three people infected by Gaspare Benjamin, including his Canadian wife, also intend to sue the government as part of a class-action lawsuit, according to court documents filed in Hamilton.

Mr. Benjamin, a 37-year-old singer from the Dominican Republic, immigrated to Canada in December, 1999. He was improperly diagnosed with a case of inactive tuberculosis because a doctor working for Citizenship and Immigration Canada misread his X-ray.

Mr. Benjamin in fact carried a contagious and drug-resistant strain of the disease. His ailment went unacknowledged for about nine months, during which time he lived and worked in Hamilton. Some 92 people might have been infected. An estimated 1,500 more were potentially exposed.

"Everybody should have been notified — including Mr. Benjamin — that he was in an infectious state," said David Smye, one of Mr. Benjamin's lawyers.

"They all have a sense of outrage that this occurred. We want to ensure this does not happen again."

Mr. Benjamin and his wife, Hilary Lomas, are in quarantine in Toronto, and are separated from one another.

Mr. Benjamin seeks compensation because he says a quick diagnosis would have brought about earlier treatment. He also claims damages for his personal suffering at being separated from his wife plus his possible medical costs.

See LAWSUIT on Page A7

present advantages to Canadian firms," it says. "If employees absorb those costs through the public tax system, firms will obviously not complain."

The business leaders' underlying concern is the relative slide in Canada's standard of living, said Yves Poisson, author of the analysis and the forum's director of special projects.

The dismissal of quality of life as an economic asset runs counter to findings by Canadian Policy Research Networks, another Ottawa-based group specializing in economic issues.

See SURVEY on Page A6

Millions like to watch naked newscasters

By David Steinhart

A Canadian-based Internet site that features women reading national, international and business news while casually disrobing is attracting about four million viewers a month.

Www.nakednews.com is barely a year old, yet it has already far surpassed the traffic at other Canadian media Web sites, such as that of the CBC, which had 238,000 unique visitors during the Sydney Olympics in September.

"Our first priority is to bring viewers the stories," said Elliott Shulman, writer, director and producer of Naked News. "The nudity makes it visually eloquent ... it certainly gets people's attention, but then they stop looking and tune in for the news."

See NAKED on Page A2

Diane Foster

NAKED NEWS

"Our first priority is to bring viewers the stories."

INSIDE

'IS IT GONE FOREVER?'

When Juliean Nagera arrived in Canada she was too shy to lift her chin and say hello. The bloated tumour on her face had hemmed in her spirit. In a two-page photo essay, Yvonne Berg recounts how a 14-hour operation has set this girl free. Avenue, Pages B6-B7

www.nationalpost.com

INDEX

Published by The Proprietor, The National Post Company, a Hollinger / CanWest partnership, 300-1450 Don Mills Road, Don Mills, Ontario M3B 3R5

canada.com

A newspaper's **editorial page** differs from the news pages in both writing style and layout. By analyzing the opinions presented on this page, you can gain insight into the possible biases and slants of a given newspaper.

Note the differences in content, style, and layout on the following *National Post* editorial page. What conclusions can you draw about the newspaper's audience and its agenda?

NATIONAL POST, FRIDAY, DECEMBER 29, 2000 *A15*

DONALD BABICK PUBLISHER AND PRESIDENT
GORDON FISHER ASSISTANT PUBLISHER
RON CLARK SENIOR V.P. SALES & MARKETING
DENNIS SKULSKY V.P. READER SALES & SERVICE
DAVID SWAIL V.P. OPERATIONS & PLANNING
LYNNE MUNRO V.P. PROMOTIONS
PATRICK BRENNAN V.P. MANUFACTURING

EDITORIALS

KENNETH WHYTE EDITOR-IN-CHIEF
MARTIN NEWLAND DEPUTY EDITOR
HUGO GURDON MANAGING EDITOR
DOUGLAS KELLY EXECUTIVE EDITOR
ALISON UNCLES NATIONAL EDITOR
MARVIN ZIVITZ DEPUTY MANAGING EDITOR

This is a list of the main editors of the newspaper—**the editorial board**. Along with the **publisher,** they decide on what position the paper takes on issues.

Art with an ugly past

The National Gallery of Canada and the Art Gallery of Ontario are taking a laudable, but long-awaited, step today by posting on their Web sites a list of suspect paintings and other *objets d'art* acquired during and immediately after the Second World War. The many works – there are more than 100 suspect paintings at the National Gallery alone – all have serious gaps in their provenance or ownership history; and some may have been looted from Nazi victims during the period between 1933 and 1945, when the Nazi regime dispossessed Jews of their property, both through outright looting and forced sales at extremely low prices.

But while this is a bold move on the part of Canada's leading art museums, more needs to be done, for their efforts lag those of other Western institutions. Two years ago, for instance, the 180 members of the American Association of Museum Directors agreed to investigate works of suspect provenance and return them to the original owners or their heirs. Similar efforts have been made in Europe. In 1996, the Austrian government held an auction of "heirless" art, looted from Nazi victims. The proceeds went to benefit the Austrian Jewish community, decimated during the war. Even in Russia, where researchers have tried for years to gain access to archives, the government recently threw open all formerly classified Second World War records to help recover art looted by the Nazis. More than 50 years after the end of the war, some heirs of the owners of looted works in Europe and the United States are actually seeing the return of their paintings.

In Canada, where museums are publicly funded, there should be full disclosure of, and access to, archival sources that would reveal the history of suspect works. The most important European works hanging in Canadian museums and galleries were acquired in the immediate post-war period, and every attempt should be made to ascertain their ownership history. If the art is looted, all avenues should be pursued to track down the original owner or their heirs.

In some cases, there may be no claimants or heirs to take possession. But even in such cases, museums would do well to at least set the historical record straight. Every suspect painting deserves a plaque revealing its full provenance. If a painting was looted from a desperate Jewish family in Holland during the Nazi invasion in 1940, for instance, the plaque would reflect this. Though a painting is no less beautiful merely because it passed through the hands of Nazi killers and their lackeys, it is a disservice to the victims if we ignore the great tragedy of which these paintings were but a small part.

Ontario protects its kids

OH HI, YES, I'M YOUR NEIGHBOUR TO THE NORTH, AND I WAS JUST WONDERING IF YOU'D LIKE TO BORROW A CUP OF SUGAR?
MANLEY

Editorials are written by the editorial board. Although subjective, they are written in a style similar to formal essays, with an introduction, supporting paragraphs, and a conclusion. The personal pronoun "I" is not used. Editorials represent the views of the newspaper, and so carry no byline.

Editorial cartoons often feature visual symbols (e.g., the U.S. flag), caricature (Mr. Manley), and hyperbole (deliberate exaggeration). These cartoons comment on important issues. They also serve to visually perk up the page.

est, receive medical attention and be treated by social workers. The law has been used 400 times in Alberta, with great success. More than 60 child prostitutes have been reunited with their families, and dozens more meet regularly with social workers trying to wean them off their vicious trade.

Rick Bartolucci, a Liberal Ontario MPP from Sudbury, introduced three private member's bills modeled on Alberta's law. To its credit, Ontario's Cabinet has now adopted Mr. Bartolucci's idea, and, this month, introduced the Protecting Children from Sexual Exploitation Act. The law represents an improvement on Alberta's blueprint: Children may be kept for up to 30 days to receive treatment from the Children's Aid Society. And pedophiles who cruise the streets for child prostitutes will have their driver's licences suspended. Moreover, Ontario has added a desirable legal safeguard to its proposal that Alberta's law originally lacked: Within 24 hours of being seized, a child has the right to appear before a judge who determines whether detention is appropriate. The absence of such a provision was one reason a judge struck down the original version of Alberta's law. In many cases, reunification with families. Thus, it cannot be dismissed by liberals as an example of Premier Mike Harris's "tough on crime" press-release politics.

Unfortunately, if predictably, a chorus of extreme Charter of Rights enthusiasts is decrying the bill because, as one newspaper editorial opined, it "strip[s] youths of their freedom." No doubt a gaggle of lawyers will soon present themselves to sue the government in the name of children's rights. But children do not freely decide to sell themselves into a life of prostitution. They are coerced into it because of extreme duress and terrible circumstances; and they do not have the maturity to understand the gravity of their actions. There is no Charter right to be a 14-year-old prostitute.

Ontario's law is a welcome reform. Our society rightly and traditionally allows children fewer freedoms than adults, because it recognizes that minors are not competent to make some decisions on important matters. A country that legitimately bans children from voting, buying cigarettes and even seeing mature movies should surely protect them from pedophiles and pimps.

Editorials don't necessarily deal with political issues. For example, this one deals with a sports figure. Editorials also don't have to be negative in tone.

Super Mario II

It is a rare and wonderful thing when a great athlete comes back from retirement to breathe new life into his sport. It happened when basketball legend Michael Jordan returned to the NBA in 1995 after giving up the hardcourt in 1993 to pursue a baseball career. He went on to win his fourth, fifth and sixth championships, before his second, "real" retirement in 1999. This week, hockey experienced its own Mike-like phenomenon: To the delight of sports fans, superstar Mario Lemieux returned to the ice after a three-and-a-half year retirement.

Unlike Wayne Gretzky – the Great One with whom Mr. Lemieux was often compared when the two were in their prime – Mario has often battled ill health. In 1993, he temporarily left the Pittsburgh Penguins after being diagnosed with Hodgkin's disease. But he came back and wowed fans before back pain forced him to bow out in 1997 with six scoring titles.

How long before Mr. Lemieux's second retirement? Who knows. He's 35, hardly over the hill. And though some sportswriters suspected his comeback was partly a publicity stunt to benefit the team he now owns, it took Mario only 33 seconds on Wednesday to register an assist and debunk that notion. Before the game was over, he scored another assist and a goal. Even Mike didn't do this well on his first day back from retirement.

Others may say the spectacle in Pittsburgh was yet another attempt by a failing business to recapture some of its past glory. All the king's horses and all the king's men were on hand for the event. The CBC, which has seen its hockey ratings drop steadily for years, broadcast Mario-mania live. The Toronto Maple Leafs were also on hand, not only as the official opposition but to basically watch Mario and the Penguins skate around them to victory. In some instances, the Leafs ensured nothing was going to ruin the second coming by giving the Penguins the puck at just the right time. The outcome of the game was decided long before the puck was dropped in the first period. Even Leafs' goalie Curtis Joseph could not hide his frustration and anger at having to give up a game for the betterment of the sport. He took one for the team.

Mario Lemieux's return can only help the league and the Penguins organization – but one has to wonder for how long.

Guy Pattison, Bracebridge, Ont.

Child rights

Re: Britain may relax Rules on Identity of Sperm Donors, Dec. 28.

The rights of children born through artificial conception is not a reproductive health issue. It is a human rights issue. According to provisions in the United Nations Convention [on the Rights of the Child,] ... deprived of some or all of the elements of his or her identity, states that have ratified the convention, such as Britain and Canada, are legally bound to retroactively "provide appropriate assistance and protection, with a view to speedily re-establishing his or her identity."

These children's rights are inviolable and non-negotiable and it is high time health ministers ensure that in reproductive health, "the best interests of the child shall be a primary consideration," as stated by the Convention.

James Kelly, Legislative Chair, Parent Finders of Canada, West Vancouver.

Art is dead

John Bentley Mays was able to write more than 1,000 words on the evolution of visual arts in the 20th century while politely ignoring the obvious fact that painting and sculpture have become irrelevant (Today is Slipping through our Fingers, Dec. 27).

See how many of your friends can tell you the names of the three most "important" painters and sculptors working today. (I certainly have no clue who they might be). Painting and sculpture were rendered obsolete by motion pictures and have long since degenerated into gimmickry and intellectual humbug.

There are no more Picassos and there never will be again.

Ian Coleman, Edmonton.

[...] ders what they will be willing to suspend the Charter for in the future? I am reminded of the parable: "Beware of the man who would sell his freedom for a few pieces of gold; he deserves neither and will probably lose both."

Kevin Maher, Duncan, B.C.

Eat your words

Having waded through more student papers than I care to remember, I share Mark Kingwell's dismay at the decline in standards of writing (Bad Grammar Drives me to Drink, Dec.27). But it is not only students who make mistakes.

Mr. Kingwell writes, "... we lost a chance to make a valid distinction and correct a small matter of fact – something increasingly rare ..." I read that to mean that it is increasingly rare to miss a chance to make a distinction and correct a fact, which is the opposite of what he seemed to be trying to say. But if that makes him miserable and he seeks company, he will find it in whoever wrote the headline, "Two Canadian Diplomats Defied their Country's Orders to save 225 frightened Chileans caught in the 1973 Coup," (Dec. 27). As that article makes clear, the diplomats were not ordered to save the Chileans, but quite the opposite; they were ordered *not* to save them, and bravely defied that order.

Now, I suppose someone will find an error in this letter.

Anthony Westell, Toronto.

[...] ate for 'Peace,' was cynical in the extreme and left no doubt as to where the *National Post's* sympathies lie.

The leaders of both sides of this tragic conflict, together with U.S. President Bill Clinton, have devoted much effort to putting forth a solution acceptable to both the Jewish and Palestinian people, which is a difficult task given the extremist views in the region.

Yes, there is no doubt President Clinton would take credit for any international settlement agreed upon. What is wrong with that? Any partial solution – which contributes to future generations of Israelis and Palestinians being able to live together in peace – is better than none. Negotiations have never been so close and the parties have a duty to continue. With Bush, Sharon and Arafat in power, what chance is there left for peace?

Your editorials should be espousing a vision for peace, and supporting, not mocking, all efforts made to reach an equitable solution.

Bob Evans, London, Ont.

Letters to the editor give readers an opportunity to express their opinions. By analyzing these positions over a given time, we can make inferences about what people in society are thinking.

Monkey see ...

Ezra Levant errs in blaming the deeply mired Firearms Act on the stubborn pride of Justice Minister Anne McLellan (Canada's Gun Registry: The PR stunt that Flopped, Dec. 28). The monkey is not responsible for the actions of the organ grinder!

R.A. Watt, Nanaimo, B.C.

National Post welcomes letters to the editor by mail, fax or e-mail. Please include name, home address and daytime telephone number. We reserve the right to edit, condense or reject letters. 300-1450 Don Mills Road, Don Mills, Ontario M3B 3R5, Canada. Telephone: (416) 383-2300; fax: (416) 383-2439; e-mail: letters@nationalpost.com

White space, rules, and **headlines** break up the print.

Internet voting: e-foolishness

Howard Fienberg

Is Internet voting the solution to poor voter turnout and costly balloting? A group of high-tech companies think so and are lobbying both Canada and the United States to consider it. But as the business world has recently demonstrated, adding a "dot-com" to something is no guarantee of success. Those who feel Internet voting would be an improvement over the current system could be proven grossly mistaken.

So far, opposition to Internet voting has focused on issues of access, particularly the much-touted but poorly-defined "digital divide" – the assumption that minorities and the poor are much less likely to have a computer and Internet access and would be discriminated against. What good data we have indicates that, if any digital divide does exist, it should evaporate shortly. The real problems lie in issues of security, identification and reliability.

In the United States, the Arizona Democratic party opened this can of worms by enlisting Election.com to conduct part of its March 11 primary election on the Internet. Election.com nonsensically claims this experiment proved Internet voting is safe and that its system is hacker-proof. Like most hacker challenges, this one offered little incentive that would convince a talented hacker to (a) take time off from his well-paid work, (b) risk prosecution and (c) reveal his secrets. Given the minimal stakes involved in the Arizona primary (Bill Bradley had already dropped out, leaving Al Gore the only contender), it is unlikely anyone would have bothered to hack the vote anyway.

Encryption and security measures never outpace the ingenuity of those out to crack them and the Internet is teeming with hackers of all skills and motivations from around the world. But you hardly need basic knowledge to cause trouble. Last February, perpetrators temporarily felled many prominent e-commerce Web sites such as Yahoo! and E-Bay with "distributed denial of service" attacks. Using code readily available on the Internet, they overloaded these sites with junk e-mail, routed through other people's computer systems, until the targeted sites had to shut down. Viruses, a far more dangerous breed of code, are also easy to find in cyberspace.

All software and hardware have bugs, ranging from the innocuous to the thoroughly destructive, which take a while to discover and fix. Many of us have learned to live with the dreaded "Windows has suffered a fatal error" message because we face it so often, but imagine something similar occurring during an Internet vote. Forget about vote boxes being tossed into a river, or Florida's hanging chads: Has your vote been cast or hasn't it? Should you try to vote again, or would that be illegal? Computer systems are anything but infallible, and the Internet gets tangled up on a regular basis. When either do work, they can be slow and plodding.

Our recent election showed up some of the problems in compiling an accurate voter list. Far from helping, the Internet could exacerbate these problems, because assigning and verifying secure voter IDs is difficult. Since Election.com distributes passwords using regular mail, these can be easily intercepted or misrouted. Sure, voters who failed to receive the correct IDs and passwords could probably call a customer service line and be put on hold. But who has the time? And wasn't the point to encourage voting by making it easier?

While Canada's current voting system can be disorganized and messy in pockets, enough checks and balances exist to all but eliminate large-scale fraud and mistakes. Imagine converting to a system open not only to the usual small errors, but also to error, manipulation and fraud on a massive, national scale. Moreover, we're already experienced with almost every kind of fraud in other countries' elections, so we know what to look for and can try to prevent it. But with Internet voting, we open ourselves up to whole new venues of attack. Imagine the U.S. presidential election of 2000 and worse. Of course, we would not be subject to all aspects of the Florida chaos – it is not clear recounts are possible over the Internet. But when an Internet vote goes wrong, we are stuck with the results.

Our national ego would gain little from this kind of trailblazing. Let the Yanks forge ahead over the cliff of Internet voting, while we more carefully consider what awaits us on the other side.

Howard Fienberg is research analyst with the Statistical Assessment Service (STATS), a nonprofit nonpartisan think-tank in Washington, D.C.

Note how this page is designed for the eye to follow a natural flow.

Columns allow for easy reading of the large amount of print text.

MAGAZINES

Magazines are increasingly aimed at small segments of the general public, often called **niches**. Traditional **general-interest** or news magazines have dropped in popularity, while **special-interest** publications have flourished.

Like newspapers, the **page design** of a magazine guides the reader to the information that the editor wishes the reader to view. Magazines use colour, layout, and font styles to provide clues to the unwritten codes connecting the magazine to its audience.

The **magazine cover** is designed to convey the magazine's image, whether it be young and hip or staid and traditional. Most magazines have a distinctive name logo. All these elements can be analyzed to determine the meaning and subtext of the magazine.

Examine this front cover from the Canadian news magazine *Maclean's*. What can you infer about this magazine from its cover?

Logo doesn't change from issue to issue, providing continuity.

Use of **colour** emphasizes a word and draws the eye to the print text.

Text is **superimposed** over the picture in **reverse lettering** (white), and is **wrapped** around the figure in the picture (allowing viewer to connect words and picture).

Teasers are deliberately vague and mysterious—a reader would need to look inside to really know what the story was about (note how they are in black to contrast with the photo background).

Background can give clues to the picture. Wh was this setting shown and not a hospital? Also note the shadows on th doctor's face and on the background mountains. Is this one picture or a **composite**? Why did the editors do this?

Notice the expression and body language of the doctor—how does this reinforce the headline? What **symbols** show us that this is a doctor?

Compare the following two magazine pages. In both cases, the content consists of pictures and many small, separate pieces of information. Note however, the differences in layout and arrangement of the content. How would you describe the differences between these two magazines?

Only one **photograph** is used; its impact is enhanced by extending it the full length of the page.

Page headline is clear and understated.

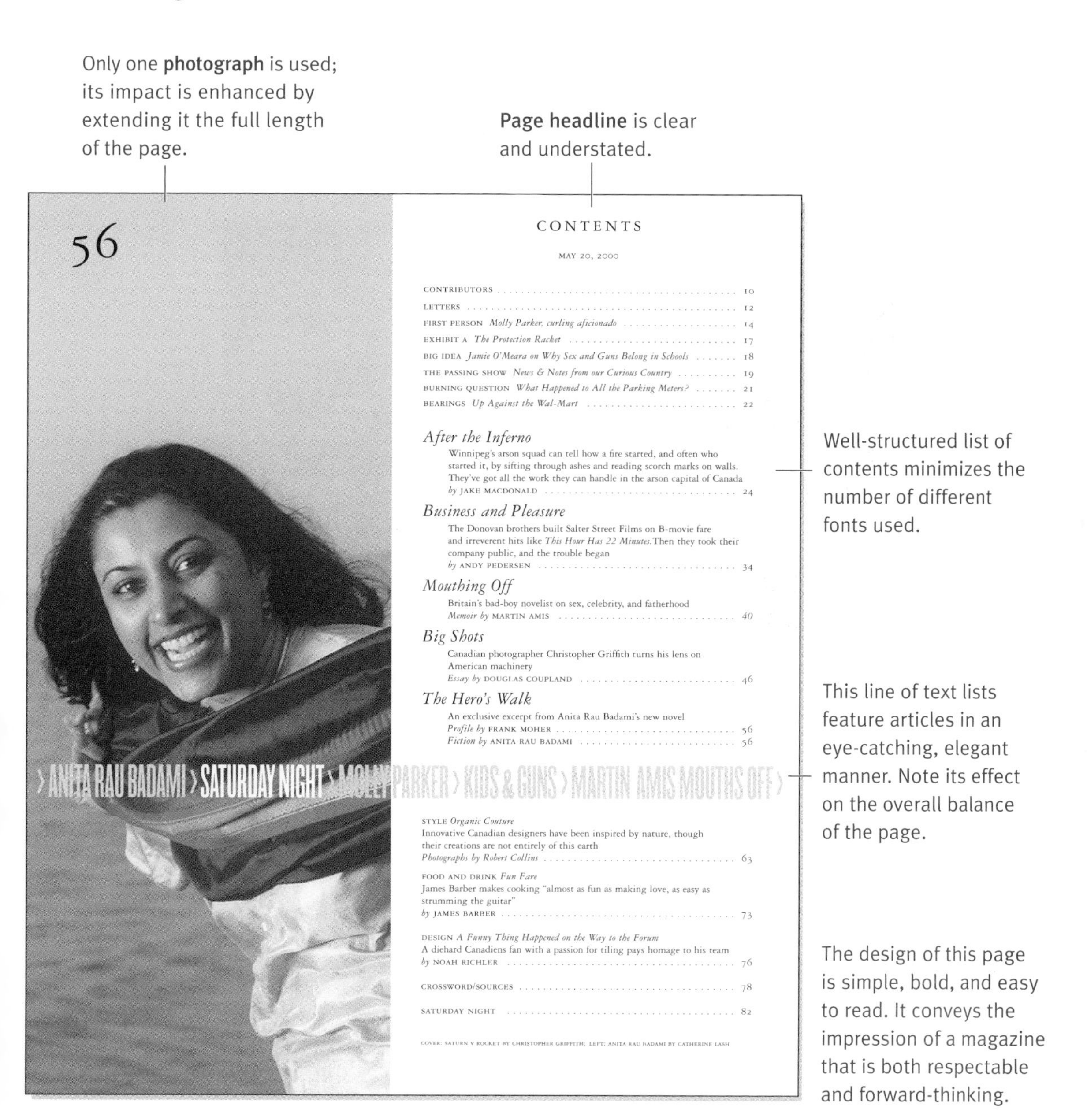

56

CONTENTS

MAY 20, 2000

CONTRIBUTORS 10

LETTERS 12

FIRST PERSON *Molly Parker, curling aficionado* 14

EXHIBIT A *The Protection Racket* 17

BIG IDEA *Jamie O'Meara on Why Sex and Guns Belong in Schools* 18

THE PASSING SHOW *News & Notes from our Curious Country* 19

BURNING QUESTION *What Happened to All the Parking Meters?* 21

BEARINGS *Up Against the Wal-Mart* 22

After the Inferno
Winnipeg's arson squad can tell how a fire started, and often who started it, by sifting through ashes and reading scorch marks on walls. They've got all the work they can handle in the arson capital of Canada
by JAKE MACDONALD 24

Business and Pleasure
The Donovan brothers built Salter Street Films on B-movie fare and irreverent hits like *This Hour Has 22 Minutes.* Then they took their company public, and the trouble began
by ANDY PEDERSEN 34

Mouthing Off
Britain's bad-boy novelist on sex, celebrity, and fatherhood
Memoir by MARTIN AMIS 40

Big Shots
Canadian photographer Christopher Griffith turns his lens on American machinery
Essay by DOUGLAS COUPLAND 46

The Hero's Walk
An exclusive excerpt from Anita Rau Badami's new novel
Profile by FRANK MOHER 56
Fiction by ANITA RAU BADAMI 56

› ANITA RAU BADAMI › SATURDAY NIGHT › MOLLY PARKER › KIDS & GUNS › MARTIN AMIS MOUTHS OFF ›

STYLE *Organic Couture*
Innovative Canadian designers have been inspired by nature, though their creations are not entirely of this earth
Photographs by Robert Collins 63

FOOD AND DRINK *Fun Fare*
James Barber makes cooking "almost as fun as making love, as easy as strumming the guitar"
by JAMES BARBER 73

DESIGN *A Funny Thing Happened on the Way to the Forum*
A diehard Canadiens fan with a passion for tiling pays homage to his team
by NOAH RICHLER 76

CROSSWORD/SOURCES 78

SATURDAY NIGHT 82

COVER: SATURN V ROCKET BY CHRISTOPHER GRIFFITH; LEFT: ANITA RAU BADAMI BY CATHERINE LASH

Well-structured list of contents minimizes the number of different fonts used.

This line of text lists feature articles in an eye-catching, elegant manner. Note its effect on the overall balance of the page.

The design of this page is simple, bold, and easy to read. It conveys the impression of a magazine that is both respectable and forward-thinking.

THE JUMP ON
SPORTS &STUFF

ATHLETE OF THE MONTH

QUEEN *PIN*

Name Diandra Hyman | **Age** 20 | **Hometown** Dyer, IN | **Sport** bowling | **Years bowling** 15 | **Honors** reigning U.S. National Amateur Champion, two-time member of Team USA, three-time gold medalist and two-time silver medalist at Tournament of the Americas, 2000 Bowling Digest College Player of the Year, first place in the girls' masters title at the World Tenpin Bowling Association World Youth Championships 2000 **Gutter Girl** "My grandmother is the one who got me bowling when I was 5. I was into soccer at the time, but when I went with her to the bowling center, I loved it. I quit soccer, and I've been bowling ever since." **On a roll** "Our house is packed with trophies. I've never actually counted how many I have, but I know that it's more than a hundred." **Charmed life** "I miss a lot of school [she's on an NCAA scholarship for bowling at the University of Nebraska], but nothing compares to the knowledge I've gained from visiting other countries while on bowling tours." **Pinhead** "This game is 90 percent mental, but lots of other playing conditions factor into my performance, like the type of oil used on the lanes, the core and surface of the ball, shoes, wrist devices and the temperature of the bowling center." **Roll on** Diandra has bowled a 290 three times. Her highest three-game total is 824, which is the fifth highest three-game series ever recorded by a female under the age of 23. **Strike out** "A lot of people think that bowling is just a beer-bellied men thing, but I'm trying my hardest to change that image." **Bowl me over** "When I was little, I would think about what it would be like to be one of the best. I still can't believe that now I *am* the best." **Lane change** "With two or three tournaments a month, I've still managed to be an Academic All-American. I don't even have time to hang out. If I do have any downtime, I like to bowl." —*TM*

sports&stuff factoid

Women 18–24 are the most active exercisers.
—*Women's Sports Network*

HERE WE ***GO*** AGAIN

You can't keep a good woman down. Women's pro basketball is in its fourth year and pro soccer is in its second year. Even women's boxing is trying its hardest to be taken seriously. So why not women's football? The Women's Professional Football League (WPFL) made its debut last October and, except for a smaller ball and no blocking below the waist, the game is the same. Players range in age from 18 to 38 and most hold regular day jobs since they're only paid about $100 a game plus attendance incentives. Why do they do it? "This was something I always wanted to do but couldn't," says Tampa Tempest center Garlynn Boyd. Will football fans support it? Only time will tell, but cheers to the women who are battling for more female recognition in sports. Check out the official Web site at www.womensprofootball.com. —*TM*

COOL STUFF TO DO

Have a ball this March and watch the NCAA Women's Basketball Final Four. The 2001 Championships will be held in St. Louis, March 30–April 1, 2000. For ticket info, call the NCAA at (913) 339-1906.

Grab your board and slush your way to the U.S. Open Snowboarding Championships, which will be held at Stratton Mountain in Vermont, March 15–28, 2001. For ticket info, log on to www.usopen-snowboarding.com.

PHOTOGRAPHY (right, center): TIM GABRIELSON

24 JUMP | MARCH 2001

The **page headline,** although top and left, is not prominent.

Many different fonts, including colours, bold, ital light, reverse, and raised styles. Prin extends beyond columns, is used vertically and wit no uniformity.

Stories are **boxed and screened,** serving to separate the many stories and visual elements.

Much more visual information is provided, in the form of **photographs, graphics,** and **logos.** No cutlines connect the images to the written text.

This page in many ways resembles a Web page layout, busy and active. Since it is a teen magazine, this is most likely an intentional design.

VISUAL MEDIA

When analyzing visual media texts, it's important to consider the following elements.

Elements of Visual Media

- ***Point of view***: *From what position, camera angle, perspective, or vantage point was the visual created? For example, was the photographer close to or far from the subject? Whose point of view is being represented in the text?*
- ***Subject***: *What is the central focus? Is the subject a specific case or does it represent a general idea (e.g., is the photo of a specific dog, or does the dog represent all dogs)?*
- ***Framing***: *What is isolated in the visual text? What has been left out and why? What happened just before the event was captured? What will happen the moment after? Has anything been cropped? Combined?*
- ***Foreground***: *What is in the foreground? Is it in focus? How does it relate to the subject?*
- ***Background***: *What is in the background? Is it in focus? How does it relate to the subject?*
- ***Lighting and colour***: *Are light and colour used to highlight or focus the viewer's attention? Are they used to obscure some element in the visual text?*
- ***Context***: *What is the location in time and space? What purpose(s) does it serve? What other visual texts are presented along with this one?*

PRINT ADVERTISING

Print advertising can take many forms, from newspaper and magazine ads to billboards, bus signs, and T-shirts. Almost all print advertising uses some form of persuasion. The goal of the ad is to promote a product, a service, an action, or an idea. Like most media texts, print advertising can be analyzed to determine its purpose, its message, and its intended audience.

Most print advertising contains a **headline**, written text called **copy**, and an **illustration**—usually a photograph, logo, or other artwork. By examining the interplay of these elements, you can often interpret the meaning of the text. Also keep in mind the **context** of the ad, i.e., where or when it appears.

Examine the following ad for sports goggles that appeared in *Slam*, a magazine for basketball fans. Consider the individual features and their interplay. How would you say this ad works?

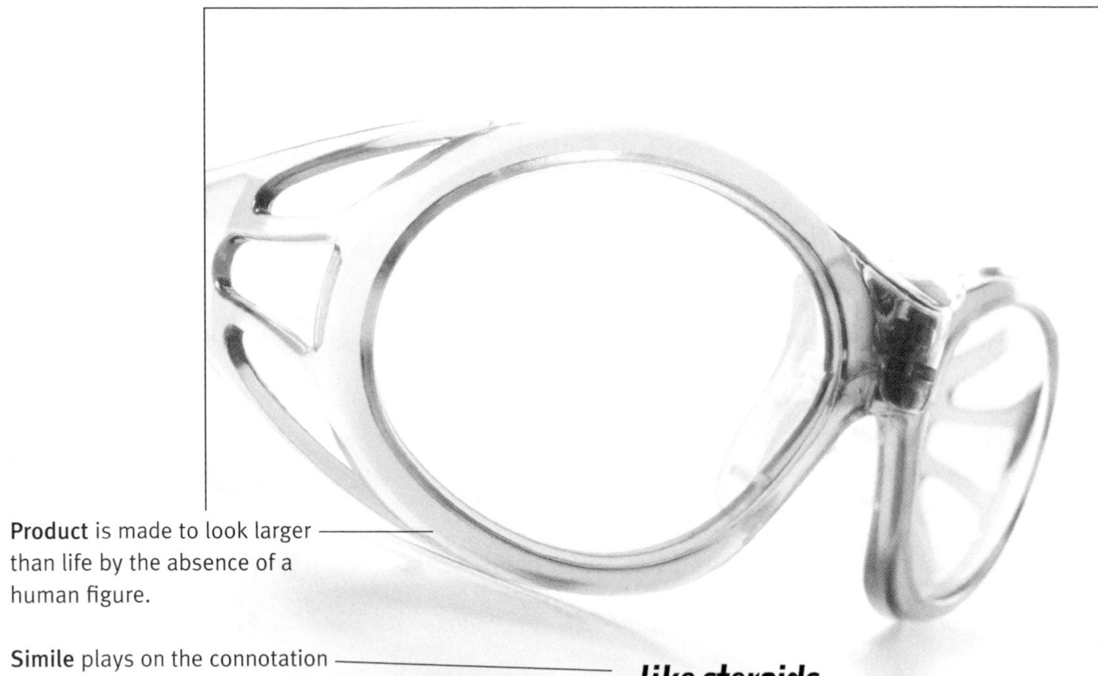

...like steroids
for your eyes
Introducing ZOOM, high performance optics specifically designed for basketball.
This ain't about fashion – we're talkin' pure vision enhancement for ballers looking for 20/20 on the court. Featuring a unique biomorphic design technology that delivers superior optical clarity and a custom fit... an exclusive CLEAR-OUT™ profile for maximum peripheral vision and anti-fog protection... a light-weight POLYAMIDE TP construction for big-elbow-to-the-head impact resistance...
100% Urkle-free styling.
The new ZOOM – boosts your vision to the max, no nasty side effects. Check it out at 1-800-847-2001 and you can win your very own pair.

Product is made to look larger than life by the absence of a human figure.

Simile plays on the connotation of the word *steroids*, implying that these glasses will improve the wearer's performance.

Terms add an **image** of scientific accuracy to the product.

Why did the copywriter change from the scientific to the informal? What does this imply about the audience?

Allusion to a TV show with a nerdish character—what assumptions does this make about the audience and their media habits?

Product **logo** resembles the product—why?

Overall design—from large product photograph at top left, through written copy, down to logo—directs viewer's eye down the page diagonally to the product name.

PHOTOGRAPHS

Photographs are used for a variety of purposes. By examining a photograph carefully, a fuller understanding of its meaning can become clear.

Consider this dramatic news photograph of a winter storm in California. What emotion was the photographer trying to evoke in the viewer, and how is this achieved?

Which is the **subject** of the photograph, the waves or the fishermen?

The photographer chose to leave the men in the **foreground** of the picture rather than the optical centre. This makes them appear smaller than the breaking waves.

At the moment this picture was taken, this man had his back turned to the waves. Was he unconcerned or turning away in fear? The photographer captured a contrast between the two men.

The photographer framed the shot (or cropped it) so that the bottom of the pier or the shore is not shown. Why? Does it increase the drama of the photograph?

COLLAGE

A **collage** is a group of visual images that are placed together to create a uniform message. Images that explore different aspects of the same theme might be placed together (as in the example to the right), or images of a contrary nature might be placed together to express **contrast**. Collages often combine written words with visual elements.

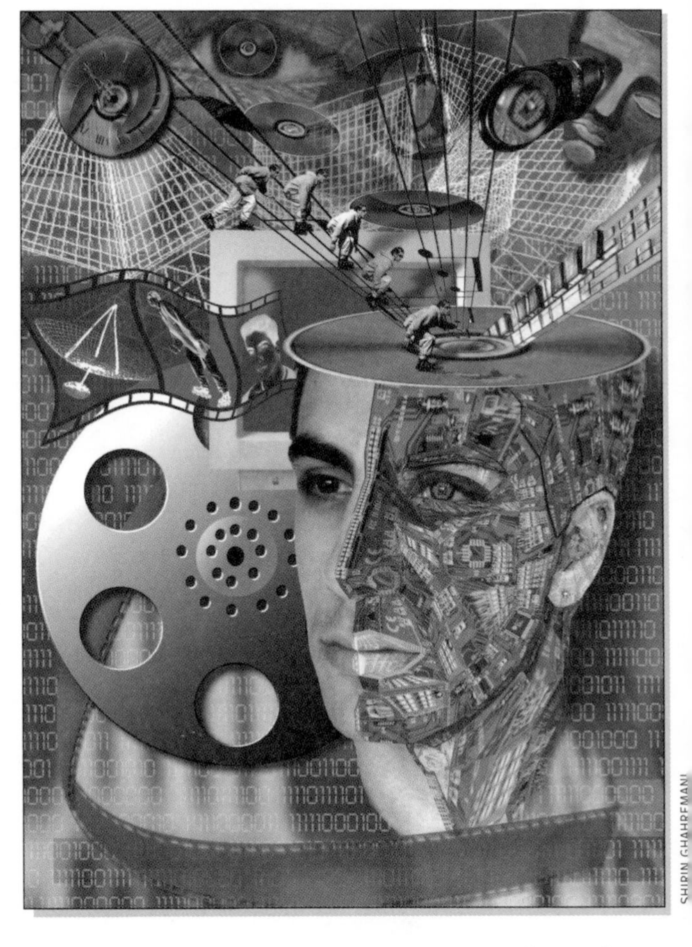

SHIRIN GHAHREMANI

FILM AND VIDEO

After we've watched a film or a video, our initial response is usually some variation on "I liked it" or "I didn't like it." The first step in analyzing these media texts is to move beyond this response. Ask yourself *why* you liked or didn't like it. The next questions to ask yourself are "What was the filmmaker trying to communicate?" and "How did he or she accomplish this?"

As you watch a film, consider what emotions you experience. Try to analyze what is happening on the screen to evoke this emotional response. The following elements all contribute to the overall effect.

Elements of Film and Video

- ***Sound***: *Music and sound can change our perception of a visual scene. The same shot of an actor walking can be made suspenseful, funny, calm, or intense—simply by adding suitable music and sounds. These are always added* after *the scene has been shot and edited.*

- ***Shots***: *The camera angle of the shot can change our perception of what is happening in the scene. The angle of the shot, the distance from the subject, the framing of the shot, and the movement of the camera relative to the subject will all change our perception of what's happening.*

- ***Transitions**: Just as a novel or short story is divided into chapters, paragraphs, and sentences, a film or video is divided into scenes, sequences, and shots. The scenes might cut quickly from one to the next or slowly fade in or out. Often these changes take place so seamlessly that we may not be consciously aware of them.*

- ***Lighting and colour**: These are used to direct our attention to what the creator wants us to see. Changes in lighting also affect our emotional response to the subject and mood of the film.*

- ***Special effects (SFX)**: These can be as simple as slow-motion or as complicated as computer-generated graphics and animation. Explosions and fires are known as* **pyrotechnics**. *If they're done well, special effects can add to our understanding of a film.*

SCREENPLAYS

One way to explore film is to examine the **screenplay**, or **shooting script**. There are two main types: a double-column script and a single-column script.

In a **double-column script**, half of the page details the audio (sound) part of the film, including dialogue, music, and sound effects. The other half provides the video (sight) portion, including camera angles, action, and camera movements.

In a **single-column script**, all the details are listed in the order they occur. This format is usually less detailed. Dialogue appears in upper- and lower-case letters, while information about shots, sound, etc., is in capital letters.

MUSIC VIDEOS

Music videos don't usually follow the traditional narrative structure of initial incident, rising action, climax, and denouement. Instead, they are composed of a series of non-chronological visual shots and sequences. This is called **discontinuous text**. One popular technique that videomakers have borrowed from traditional filmmaking is **montage**: a series of shots that convey either plot or theme. Think of a montage as a sort of moving collage, that is, a collection of related visual elements.

Music videos convey cultural values and symbols. By examining the content and the form of videos, we can gain insights into their subtexts. Issues of gender, race, and violence are often central.

It's important to remember that, although the artist's song may be the original source, the finished music video is the creation of the videomaker. Like TV commercials, music videos often originate in the form of the **storyboard**. A storyboard attempts to convey what the viewer will see in the finished video text.

Consider this storyboard of a montage-style music video by artist Andrea Dietrich:

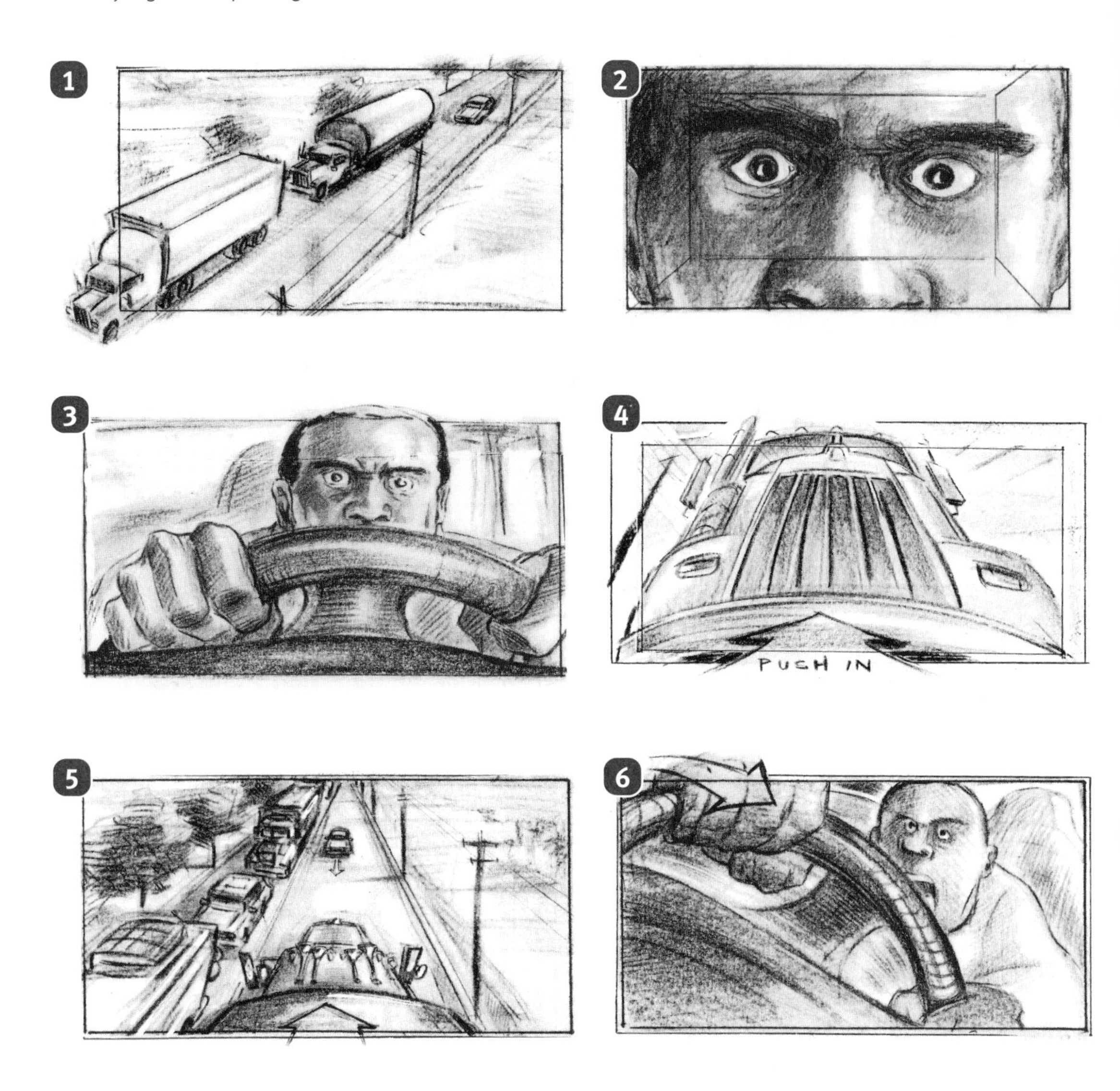

Scene 1: **establishing shot**

Scene 2: **extreme close-up** brings the viewer deep into the action quickly

Scene 3: camera pulls back, enabling us to connect the first two shots—the man is in the car passing

Scene 4: **low angle shot** makes the truck appear larger and more ominous—we assume this is from the car driver's point of view

Scene 6: in six short shots (only seconds on the screen) the video maker has created a story with tension

RADIO

PROGRAMMING

Radio has evolved over a long history, and remains a major form of media. Local radio stations provide a lot of people with their main source of news, and countless commuters listen to radio in their cars on the way to and from work. And today radio has expanded onto the Internet, with many stations now broadcasting to audiences worldwide.

Although individual formats vary greatly, there are two basic types of radio programming:

Foreground: This programming assumes an active listener; it's meant to be central to the listener's focus. Through much of radio's history, this was the main form of radio programming. It includes talk shows, phone-ins, radio plays, public service and news shows, and advice shows.

Background: Most music programming falls into this category. Just as the name implies, it's designed to be in the background, not central to the listener's focus.

In analyzing radio programming, it's useful to keep a log of the station's activities.

Radio Log

- *What kind of music is played?*
- *How many minutes of foreground programming per hour and how many minutes of background does it feature?*
- *How often do the announcers talk?*
- *How long is the news programming and how often is it presented? (hourly? every half-hour?)*
- *How many minutes of commercials per hour does it have, and how are they distributed?*
- *Is the programming produced locally or imported from somewhere else?*
- *Does the station seem to have an editorial policy or any apparent biases?*

RADIO ADVERTISING

Most commercial broadcasters sell advertising **spots** of time to advertisers. A creative advertiser can create illusions on radio through the use of sound.

Consider the intended audience, the message, and the form of persuasion being used. To whom is the advertiser trying to appeal? What is the message (both direct and implied)? What techniques are used to communicate the message?

The standard radio commercial is usually thirty or sixty seconds long. Advertising writers must keep their message simple, short, and creative. Commercials range from simple one-announcer messages to elaborate productions with complex sound effects, music, and dialogue. Successful commercials usually do four things (**AIDA**):

Elements of a Successful Radio Ad: AIDA	
Attention	the commercial grabs the listener's attention
Interest	the commercial generates an interest in the listener for the product, service, or idea
Desire	the commercial generates a desire for the product, service, or idea
Action	the listener is moved to act in the way the advertiser wants. The commercial usually provides information on how this can be done.

Examine the following thirty-second announcement written by the ABC Literacy Campaign to promote family reading:

Give your child a head start.

> The opening line speaks directly to the listener. Clearly, this ad is aimed at parents. **Attention** is generated by offering something, in this case an educational advantage. This appeals to parents' psychological need to protect their children.

If you read with your child, research shows your child stands a better chance of growing into a fully literate adult. Encourage good reading habits by making books and reading a part of your family's daily routine.

> The listener is kept **interested** by the combination of supporting research and advice. The solution to a potential problem is offered. Notice the stress on words that connote family closeness and the direct appeal to the listener (*your* child, *your* family). The tone is that of a concerned friend.

Set aside a shelf for your child's books and make a special place for daily reading.

Make reading time, family time.

> The advice moves from the general to the specific. Reading = family. Since the listener wants a healthy family, the required **action** is implied.

For information about family literacy contact [name of local literacy organization and contact phone number here].

> Very specific direction and a way to follow up is given. The listener's required action is now clear.

Don't forget to book time with your children.

> An easy-to-remember **slogan** reinforces and summarizes the concept of family reading time.

TELEVISION

With the possible exception of the Internet, no other media form has changed the shape of the modern world more than television. From its birth in the 1940s and 1950s, television has seen many changes in style, technology, and programming. But one thing has remained constant: the programs and the advertising both reflect on and help create the culture in which we live.

Analyzing Television

- *What (and whose) view of life is being presented?*
- *At what audience is this view aimed?*
- *What codes are used to convey the message?*
- *For what purposes is this view being used?*

Television, like film, has its own language and grammar. Shots, camera angles, lighting, sound, and editing all form part of this grammar. Learning the basics of television's unique code allows us insights we would not otherwise have.

The recent rise of specialty channels has been made possible by digital satellite transmission. Television used to be described as **broadcasting**—information sent out to large heterogeneous groups. Now television seems to be moving toward **narrowcasting**, with shows aimed at such specialized niches as golfers and science fiction fans.

TELEVISION PROGRAMMING

There are many genres of television program, each having a different set of styles and features. They also have different origins:

Origin	Types of TV Programs
literary genres or other media	dramas, movies, science fiction, westerns
radio	situation comedies, soap operas, sports, game shows, news shows, talk shows
unique to television	children's shows, nature shows, documentary shows; special interest shows like cooking, home renovation shows

By analyzing the programming of a given station or time period, we can understand the assumptions being made about the audience, the values being constructed and represented, the nature of television's impact, and the values of the society it reflects.

Here's an example of a typical night's programming:

News programming is often a local stations' largest generator of revenue. The number of news shows has increased over the past twenty years.

TV programmers are very aware of their competition. One strategy is called **block programming** —scheduling similar shows on the same night, such as the sitcoms noted here.

Prime time is the period between 8 p.m. and 11 p.m. on week nights when more people are watching TV than at any other time. For advertisers, the most expensive time.

6:30PM
7:30PM

Wednesday

Program grid is on page 112
January 17, 2001

16-26-LIF **Real World**
22-13 **Nightly Business** [CC]
23-79-STR **Access Hollywood**
26-70-MM+ **Pop Up Quiz**
27-18-CNN **The Point with Greta Susteren**
30-TLN **Un posto al sole**
33-28 **Suddenly Susan**
34-21-WTN **Men on Women** [CC]
37-35-H&G **Before & After**
42-31-TEL **Sabrina** [CC]
45-32-FAM **Buzz Lightyear** [CC]
48-42-PRI **Bewitched**
55-54-V **Cosby Show** [CC]
63-51-TRE **Pumper Pups**
70-68-ROB **The Close**
74-76 **Jet 7**
BCTV **Canada Tonight**
ONTV WWJ **Welcome to NY** Jim's overprotective older brother arrives for a visit. [CC]
WUHF **Grounded for Life** Sean finds his daughter's fake ID. [CC]

7 PM

2-2 CFCN **Wheel of Fortune** 2369/3611 [CC]
4-4 **On the Road Again** 5475 [CC]
6-6 **News**
7-7 **Friends** 23185
8-8 CICT CISA **Inside Entertainment** 4543/8543/4253
9-9-ACC **Help!tv: Body Help** *1:00* 72982
11-3 13-46 **News** [CC]
12-12 **Virginie** Évelyne refuse de dévoiler son secret à Virginie et Bernard. 8727 [CC]
14-44-YTV **Olsen Twins** 294765 [CC]
15-23-NW **National** *1:00* [CC]
16-26-LIF **Extra** 8360307 [CC]
22-13 **News** *1:00* [CC]
23-79-STR **True Hollywood Story** *1:00* A look at the career of professional wrestler Hulk Hogan.
24 **Jazz** *1:30* Recalling the years from 1935 to 1937, including the emergence of swing music. 97123 [CC]
25-19-A&E **American Justice** *1:00* Victims who were murdered by a member of their own family. (R) 563794 [CC]
26-70-MM+ **BackTrax** *1:00*
27-18-CNN **Larry King Live** *1:00* 528340 [CC]
30-14-CMT **Top 12: People's Choice** *1:00* 997456
30-TLN **Incantesimo** *2:00* 7598340
31-24-SHO **Danger Bay** 658949
32-25-DIS **Predators Week** *1:00* A look at the harpy eagle in Central and South America. [Another episode airs tomorrow at this time.] 430630 [CC]
33-28 **3rd Rock** 4829291.
34-21-WTN **Oh Baby** Tracy faces an ethical problem at work. 39369 [CC]
35-20-TLC **Junkyard Wars** *1:00* 647814
36-27-BVO **MOVIE** – Comedy *1:45* ***Stuart Bliss*** (1998) Paranoia sets in when a man's wife suddenly leaves him. Michael Zelniker, Dea Lawrence. 3017098
37-35-H&G **Martha Stewart** 1182562
38-29-CNB **Rivera Live** *1:00* 2149833 [CC]
39-40-GLF **Viewer's Forum** *1:00* 5672562
40-38-HIS **Escape from Colditz** *1:00* Pasrt 2 of three. Recounting how MI-9 assisted in Allied PoW escapes. 2612861
41-34-COM **Royal Canadian Air Farce** 2887369 [CC]
42-31-TEL **Kids From Room 402** 384833 [CC]
43-39-SPC **First Wave** – Science Fiction *1:00* 2154765
44-33-TBS **WCW Thunder** *2:00* 805036
45-32-FAM **Little Lulu** Tubby tells Alvin a very different version of "Little Red Riding Hood." 386291 [CC]
47-41-SV **Ship Shape TV**
48-42-PRI **Bynon** *1:00* 5674920 [CC]
49-36-FN **Good Eats** 1177630
50-37-OLN **Top Dogs** *1:00* 5676388
51-59-SBK **Star Trek: Voyager** *1:00* Chakotay finds he is the only crew member that can move through a temporal anomaly. 45494 [CC]
52-60-TLA **Sabrina** 2885901 [CC]
53-58-MAX **MOVIE** – Comedy *2:00* ★★★ ***Real Life*** (1979) A filmmaker tries to document a "typical" American family. Charles Grodin, Frances Lee McCain. 869388
54-55-SUP **MOVIE** – Drama *2:00* ★★ ***Boiler Room*** (2000) A young man joins a brokerage house with shady dealings.
Giovanni Ribisi, Nia Long. 7525494 [CC]
55-54-V **Little House on the Prairie** *1:00* 3914388 [CC]
58-52 **Family Law** *1:00* Lynn is violently attacked by a mob of rowdy men. 32340 [CC]
59-45-MM **Damix** *1:00* 708678
62-WPX **Jack & Jill** *1:00* Jill tells Jack that he's planning on popping the question. 904746 [CC]
63-51-TRE **Ants In Your Pants** 1140920
64-66-RDI **Téléjournal/Le Point** *1:00* [CC]
70-68-ROB **Bottom Line** *1:00*
71-64-CLT **Natural World** *1:00*
74-76 **Nouvelles** [CC]
79-73-APT **Indians of North America**
BCTV **News** *1:00*
CITL WDIV **The West Wing** *1:00* The staff bristles when Bartlet offers a key position to a Republican (Emily Proctor). (R) 1104/81272 [CC]
CITY WWJ **MOVIE** – Thriller *2:00* ★★★ ***Breakdown*** (1997) A man desperately searches for his wife, who may have been the victim of foul play. Kurt Russell, J.T. Walsh. 492630/81456 [CC]
CKSA **Friends** 8543 [CC]
ONTV **MOVIE** – Drama *2:00* ***The Man in the Attic*** (1994) An adoring younger man is held captive by a manipulative woman. Anne Archer, Neil Patrick Harris. 401388
WUHF **Temptation Island** *1:00* 2326727 [CC]
WXYZ **Drew Carey** Drew takes a job with Oswald's recently paroled father (Tom Poston). 25543 [CC]

7:30

2-2 CFCN **Jeopardy!** 833/475 [CC]
4-4 **Country Canada** 3712 [CC]
6-6 **Hollywood Squares** 209678
7-7 **Frasier** 48982
8-8 CICT CISA **Entertainment Tonight** 6630/307/5340 [CC]
11-3 CKSA **Frasier** Frasier and Niles must venture into no-man's land — a shopping mall on Christmas Eve. 263920/307 [CC]
12-12 **Caserne 24** Albert est ému par les actions de la directrice d'un centre pour enfants. 5185 [CC]

WEDNESDAY

116 TV GUIDE/EC

Wednesday

7:30PM
8:30PM

13-46 **Entertainment Tonight** 265388
14-44-YTV **Monster by Mistake** 919542 [CC]
16-26-LIF **The Lofters** 1562340
20-22-TSN **Off the Record** 610814
31-24-SHO **T. And T.** 373746
33-28 **3rd Rock** 9770814
34-21-WTN **As Time Goes By** Jean and Lionel decide that they should share living space. 87494
37-35-H&G **Design for Living** 2543659
41-34-COM **New Red Green** 6905185 [CC]
42-31-TEL **Cardcaptors** 180730
45-32-FAM **Timon & Pumbaa** Timon and Pumbaa pose as foreign dignitaries. 885348
47-41-SV **Powerboat TV**
49-36-FN **The Best Of** 2538727
52-60-TLA **Fresh Prince** 6910017
63-51-TRE **Treetown** 6461253
73-65-TV5 **Plaisir honteux** *1:00* Documentaire sur l'inceste, visant à détruire les tabous et les idées préconçues. (R) 205659
74-76 **Piment fort** 9765982
79-73-APT **Beyond Words**
WXYZ **Spin City** 40340 [CC]

7:45

63-51-TRE **Pirates** 83633630

8 PM

2-2 CFCN CITO WDIV **Law & Order** *1:00* An AIDS researcher is killed during an animal-rights attack on his lab. [Viewer discretion is advised.] 9982/7524/7524/90920 [CC]
4-4 58-52 **Fifth Estate** *1:00* 50746/58388
6-6 **Seinfeld** 546611
7-7 **MOVIE** – Drama *2:00* ★★ ***Sweet Nothing*** (1996) A young family man watches his life go down in flames when he becomes addicted to cocaine. Michael Imperioli, Mira Sorvino. 94746
8-8 CICT CISA **Gilmore Girls** *1:00* Lorelai decides to end her relationship with Max. 36104/2456/45814
9-9-ACC **Anything is Possible** 2307
11-3 **Jeopardy!** 524543 [CC]
12-12 **Passeport musique** *1:00* 83098
13-46 **Drew Carey** Drew's flyer advertising free beer falls into the wrong hands. 519611
14-44-YTV **Mona the Vampire** 270185 [CC]
15-23-NW **Antiques Roadshow** *1:00* 3772388 [CC]
16-26-LIF **Birth Stories** 8346727 [CC]
20-22-TSN **Sportsdesk** *1:30* 839272
22-13 **National Geographic** *1:00* Filmmaker Mike deGruy goes underwater to examine various shark species. 563974 [CC]
23-79-STR **Conan O'Brien** *1:00* [CC]
25-19-A&E **Investigative Reports** *1:00* Host Bill Kurtis examines the case of death-row inmate Sean Sellers. (R) 268302 [CC]
26-70-MM+ **Tom Petty** *1:30* The band performs at the Fillmore in San Francisco.
27-18-CNN 38-29-CNB 62-WPX **News** *1:00*
29-16-TNN **18 Wheels of Justice** *1:00* Chance and Cie try to bring a New Jersey mobster to justice. 654104 [CC]
30-14-CMT **Face The Music** 755307
31-24-SHO **Dead Man's Gun** *1:00* 801104 [CC]
32-25-DIS **Discover Magazine** *1:00* Burying an interstate highway below Boston. 456678 [CC]
33-28 **Star Trek: Voyager** *1:00* 3763630
34-21-WTN **Dr. Willoughby** The appearance of Donna's grown son makes people wonder just how old she really is. 48017
35-20-TLC **Junkyard Wars** *1:00* 656562
37-35-H&G **House & Home** 1168982
39-40-GLF **European Tour Weekly** 1124982
40-38-HIS **Miracle on the River Kwai** *1:00* Recounting how doctors kept Allied PoWs alive. 3357551
41-34-COM **SCTV** 2896017
42-31-TEL **What About Mimi?** 360253 [CC]
43-39-SPC **Star Trek: Voyager** *1:00* 2130185 [CC]
45-32-FAM **Gargoyles** 362611
47-41-SV **Powerboating** *1:00*
Competition Offshore event, from Lake Hopatcong, N.J.
48-42-PRI **Prime Business** 1126340 [CC]
49-36-FN **Food Fantasy** 1193678
50-37-OLN **Beyond Borders** Visiting a Nepalese rhino safari. 1151036
51-59-SBK **Frasier** 53949
52-60-TLA **Friends** 2801949 [CC]
55-54-V **Skylight** 1195036
59-45-MM **2Ge+her** 517253
61-WGN WUHF **News** *1:00* [CC]
63-51-TRE **Crazy Quilt** 1126340
64-66-RDI **Maisonneuve écoute** 1588494 [CC]
70-68-ROB **Moneyline** *1:00* [CC]
71-64-CLT **Safari**
74-76 **Poule aux oeufs d'or** 4830307
79-73-APT **Nissum**
BCTV **Wheel of Fortune** 757765 [CC]
CKSA **MOVIE** – Science Fiction *2:00* ★★★ ***Back to the Future Part III*** (1990) Marty guns his time-travelling DeLorean back to the Old West. Michael J. Fox, Christopher Lloyd. 6272
WXYZ **Once and Again** *1:00* Lily attempts to be heard and not just seen at the office. 92388 [CC]

8:30

6-6 **Friends** 565746
9-9-ACC **Dotto's Data Café** 1814 [CC]
11-3 **Wheel of Fortune** 543678 [CC]
13-46 **Home Improvement** 538746
14-44-YTV **Sixth Grade Alien** 282920 [CC]
16-26-LIF **Little Miracles** 8358562
24 **Frame After Frame** Profiling

WEDNESDAY

[CC] Closed-Captioned / (L) Live Broadcast / (R) Repeat

EC/TV GUIDE 117

Blunting is the scheduling of a program similar to the competition's, in this case a movie.

Bridging is a special type of blunting in which a network schedules a special program earlier than a competitor's big event. Here, a new movie is being played at 8 p.m., before a new PBS Ken Burns special on Jazz can begin at 9 p.m.

By analyzing what kinds of shows are being shown, we can make some assumptions about television. How many shows here are sitcoms? Movies? Sports? How many are family-oriented? How many are adult-oriented? What themes are presented?

TELEVISION ADVERTISING

Television revenue is generated through the sale of advertising. Like radio commercials, the standard length of TV commercials is thirty or sixty seconds.

The past decade has seen an increase in the number of **infomercials**—commercials in the form of programming. Unlike normal television shows, in which the show is paid for by sales of advertising time, infomercials are paid programming in which the advertiser buys the entire segment of air time.

We can group the most common advertising strategies used in television. You are probably familiar with most, if not all of these:

Common TV Advertising Approaches	
Use of statistics and numbers	statistics that may or may not have any real value (e.g., "Four out of five doctors recommend...")
Pseudo-scientific names and claims	products and ingredients that have scientific-sounding names (e.g., "new Hypertron with a gluxinate mixture ...")
Testimonial	famous or prominent people (athletes, actors) endorsing the product, service, or idea
Plain folks	"average" people in situations that appear "everyday" to add credibility to their claims
Nostalgia	evoking our love of simpler times (e.g., "Apple pie just like Mom used to make")
False transference	the implied transfer of positive qualities from a person or object to the product (e.g., if actor X is known as (or portrays) an honest person, then product Y he's endorsing must therefore be honest; if orange juice A is shown outdoors next to a running stream in a forest, orange juice A must be fresh)
Bandwagon	making it appear as if the majority are buying the product or using the service, implying that everyone should join in (a variation is the "limited time only," implying that waiting will involve loss)
Weasel words	vague qualifiers or words like *helps, up to, almost, fights, best-selling*, or *freshest-tasting* to imply a product is better than it may actually be (a variation is the dangling comparison, e.g., "Product X works faster ..." —and faster than what isn't specified)
Ideal children	children who are slightly older and slightly more perfect than the target audience, since most children aspire to being older than they are

Common TV Advertising Approaches (continued)	
Snob appeal	featuring upper class and wealthy people in ads in order to associate the product or service with the "good life"
Emotional response	eliciting an emotional response through images of family, children, people in need, etc.
Fear and guilt	consciously exploiting the viewer's normal fears and guilts (e.g., the fear of being unpopular, or the guilt people feel about spending less time with their families)
Sound effects and music	these often trigger an almost unconscious emotional response; dramatic sounds and music can make a static product or service seem lively
Repetition	the simple process of repeating words or phrases (or whole advertisements) to fix an idea in the viewer's mind
Use of mascots or characters	animated or lifelike mascots used to sell a product or service
Humour and irony	creating an illusion of the "inside joke"

Examine the following storyboard for an award-winning Lay's Potato Chip commercial.

"MESSIER":30

1

MUSIC: *scored throughout*
GUY: Messier! Whoa...Hey have you tried these new chips?

2

MESSIER: A chip's a chip.
GUY: But these are Lay's.

3

GUY: Betcha can't eat just one?
MESSIER: And if I lose?
GUY: I get one hour of your time.
V.O.: Lay's. Betcha can't eat just one!

4

GUY: Guys I got a little bit of help for the big game tonight. Say hello to Mark.

MESSIER: Chip?

TEAMMATE: Who are we?
TEAM: The Pilons!
PLAYER: Man, that guy skates like Messier.
GUY: Could have been somehing he ate.

Scene 1: Mark Messier is a famous hockey player. Although this is not a traditional **testimonial,** the advertiser wishes to link the star to the product.

Scene 2, 5: The product always appears prominently in the ad, and transfers from the non-famous person to the famous. **Symbolically,** the product is now connected to the star.

Scene 4: The "guy" is an average person (he doesn't even have a name). As audience members, we connect to this average guy playing hockey with his friends. We share his dream of getting to play with a great player. The **plain folks** approach aims this ad at a large audience of men.

Scene 6: **Humour** is coupled with **false transference** as the "guy" implies that it was the potato chip that aids Messier's skating ability.

THE INTERNET AND EMERGING TECHNOLOGIES

The Internet is expanding and changing so rapidly that it can be a challenge to maintain a perspective on this form of media. In order to develop a critical approach to Web sites, consider the strategy of active interpretation discussed on pp. 263–264. Also refer to the Research and Ethics chapter for more information on evaluating Web sites.

Active Interpretation of Web Sites

- *Who created this media text?*
- *Who seems to be the intended audience?*
- *What clues tell you this?*
- *What seems to be the overall message?*
- *What elements are used to convey this message (design, links, animations, hypertext)?*

WEB SITES

Since there are so many types of Web sites, it's difficult to make generalizations. However, some features are fairly common.

Examine this home page from Big Brothers and Sisters of Canada.

1. Does the site carry advertising?
2. To what sorts of items are there **links**? Are there links to related sites?
3. Is there evidence that the site is changed regularly?
4. Is the site very graphics-oriented or is there a considerable amount of written text?
5. Is there a method to contact the Web site designer or organization?
6. Is there a link or a description on the **home page** that tells about the site's organization or designer?
7. What sort of image or images make up the **wallpaper**, or background of the site? Here, the digital collage emphasizes this is a site connecting men and women and boys and girls in wholesome interaction.
8. The **URL**, or Web site address, provides the first clue. Is it a commercial, educational, or non-profit site?

HYPERTEXT

Hypertext is electronic text that is coded so that it can link to something else, either within the same document or elsewhere. Hypertext may be in the form of a text, a picture, a Web site, or any other electronic document.

Hypertext organizes text *associatively*. In other words, by clicking on a **hyperlink** you can move from one portion of a document to another without following any preset sequence.

Originally a feature of the Internet, hypertext is now becoming part of the mainstream writing and presentation process. Refer to Apendix A for information on how to create hyperlinks.

Hypertext Applications

- *linking to additional information that enhances a text*
- *allowing instant access to Web sites or illustrative examples in a document*
- *electronic footnoting*
- *adding electronic "see-also" features*
- *creating an interactive table of contents for documents*
- *allowing the possibility of added graphics in a plain print text*
- *creating interactive stories and novels*

COMPARING MEDIA TEXTS ACROSS GENRES

It's useful to compare texts from different media that deal with the same issue, topic, or event. By noting the similarities and differences, we can gain insight into the biases, approaches, and form of each medium.

Consider a topic like snowboarding. Although relatively new, snowboarding has received a lot of attention in the media over the past two decades. Originally at the fringes of the mainstream, snowboarding has grown to be a popular pastime and a major business. How is snowboarding represented by different media?

Read the following excerpt from a mainstream news magazine story on "extreme sports."

> Skillful, fearless—and some might say crazy—[Kristen] Ulmer is a leader in an athletic revolution that puts a premium on the wagering of life and limb. Adored by a young America hungry for thrills, these sports, popularly known by the Madison Avenue-created moniker "extreme sports," are popping up on urban streets, off-road trails, and television screens. Heart-racing activities such as downhill mountain biking, backcountry snowboarding, and sky diving are capturing an ever-growing chunk of the $40 billion plus that America spends on sporting goods annually....
>
> Yet the threat of injury or death inherent in navigating furious rapids on a slab of Styrofoam or snowboarding down a 20,000-foot mountain fails to turn away new recruits. Quite the opposite —it is the chance of a catastrophe that makes extreme sports so enticing. A century ago, in *The Will to Believe*, the philosopher William James wrote, "It is only by risking our persons from one hour to another that we live at all." But contemporary America is a nation that seems hell-bent on expunging risk from every aspect of life. "There's always this notion in America that nobody should take risks. The toilets are clean, the hamburger meat is cooked to X degrees, there are a lot of lawyers," says Ulmer. "American culture is real scaredy-cat culture, and people are sick of it."
>
> Michael Bane, author of *Over the Edge: A Regular Guy's Odyssey in Extreme Sports*, agrees. "The trend in society is to eliminate risk. It's gotten to the point where there are no more swings on playgrounds. At the same time, people are saying, 'Where's Indiana Jones?' People need adventure in their lives."
>
> *US News and World Report, June 30, 1997*

We can draw conclusions from this article about how the mainstream media view snowboarding. We can also infer the target audience. The choice of words present snowboarding as an activity that's outside the norm. Snowboarders are not perceived as the audience for this article. The text doesn't treat them as participants, but as subjects to be studied.

We can contrast this media representation with the following one. This Contents page is from *Transworld Snowboarder*, a special-interest magazine for snowboarders.

CONTENTS 14.6

FEBRUARY 2001 _ VOLUME FOURTEEN _ NUMBER SIX

TRANSWORLD

NO TOKEN AMERICANS

ON THE COVER: Try to burn this one.
Flags shot by: ShemRoose.com

Our site has too much funding to go out of business. Check us out at **transworldsnowboarding.com.**

12 TransworLDSNOWBoarDinG.com

Layout is youthful and features pictures of young snowboarders from a variety of countries.

Articles appear to be written *by* people who know snowboarding *for* people who know snowboarding.

Letters from snowboarders imply that the communication between the reader and the magazine is two-way.

Articles on music and other features imply that snowboarders have other interests beyond snowboarding.

Articles, layout, and design all lead the viewer to believe that the magazine is positive toward snowboarding and that its target audience is snowboarders.

For yet another contrast, examine the following Web site:

1. The .com **URL** indicates that this is a commercial site with something to sell.
2. This home page features an assortment of articles similar to *Transworld Snowboarder*, but the layout follows a more traditional format.
3. Although appearing more "adult," the site offers more opportunity for snowboarders to interact (e.g. a chat feature, an e-mail newsletter, an on-line poll). Many Web sites also use that information to track potential customers.
4. This tagline implies that snowboarding is now a business, as mainstream as any other; the audience for this Web magazine is snowboarding consumers.

Understanding Style

THE GRAMMAR OF FILM

Just as written text has a grammar—a set of rules that allows the reader to understand the communicated message—so does film and video. (See pp. 398–399 of the Glossary for a list of film terms and camera angles.)

And just as a novel is broken down into chapters, paragraphs, sentences, and words, a film can be broken down into smaller units of meaning.

SCENES

Similar to the chapter, a **scene** is a segment of the film that tells a portion of the story.

Sequences

A scene is made up of smaller **sequences** of various lengths, just as a chapter is made up of paragraphs.

- Paragraphs have an introductory sentence, body, and concluding sentence, and so must a sequence have a beginning, middle, and end.
- Like paragraphs in a novel, some sequences will be short and full of action, and others may be longer and more in depth. The filmmaker, like the novelist, must be aware of the pacing of his or her story.

Shots

Sequences are made up of a series of **shots**. Shots, like sentences, vary in length and style, but each must contain one complete idea.

- Shots are punctuated by action and dialogue, just as a sentence is punctuated by commas and periods.
- In place of words, the filmmaker uses camera angles and transitions to convey the main idea. Some angles, such as long and extremely long shots, work best for setting the place and time of a scene.
- Usually a filmmaker or television director will want to open a scene with a long shot, called an **establishing shot**, to convey to the reader where the rest of the action takes place.

Types of Shots

Certain shots tend to create certain perceptions in the viewer, just as certain types of sentences (declarative, interrogative, etc.) affect readers differently.

- **High-angle shots** tend to make the subject look smaller and less imposing.
- **Low-angle shots** have the opposite effect, making the subject appear larger and more powerful.
- **Close-ups** and **extreme close-ups** are best for conveying emotion.
- **Oblique-angle shots** place the viewer off-kilter. These shots work well for implying that things are disoriented.

CAMERA MOVEMENTS

Camera movement also shapes the viewer's perception of a shot or scene.

- **Panning** is horizontal movement and **tilting** is vertical movement. Either can provide an illusion of speed or motion.
- **Zooming in** and **zooming out** moves the viewer closer or farther away from the action, depending on which effect is required.

Look back at the storyboard for the Lay's potato chip commercial. Consider the different types of shots that were used, and why. What other techniques were used (e.g., lighting, focus, foreground)?

» CHECKPOINT: *Reassess Your Knowledge*

1. What are the three central visual features of this ad?
2. Why are there no people shown?
3. Who is the "I" in "Out here, I am not alone"?
4. Why is the photograph shot from a low angle looking up into the skyline?
5. What message is the advertiser trying to convey to the audience?
6. Why does the advertiser use the expression "Out here, I am not alone"?
7. Who, specifically, is the ad aimed at? What evidence is there for your answer?
8. If you were the advertiser, in what magazines would you place this ad? Why?

Creating a Storyboard for a Video

Preparing and Planning

Every media text you've ever seen, whether it's a billboard, rock video, or TV commercial, began as an idea. To make sure that you successfully transmit this idea to the audience, you must first have clear answers to the following questions.

Your Initial Idea

- *What is the idea I want to communicate?*
- *Who is my target audience?*
- *What effect do I want this idea to have on the target audience?*
- *What media form would be most effective in communicating this idea?*
- *What techniques would be most effective in achieving the desired audience response?*

CLARIFYING THE IDEA

If the answer to any of the above questions is unclear, further research may be required. The more specific the information you begin with, the more effective the result.

Content, Audience, Purpose, Technique

- *Learn more about the issue itself.*
- *Learn more about the characteristics of the target audience.*
- *Clarify the desired audience response (e.g., to increase awareness; to entertain* and *inform).*
- *Carefully consider your techniques. How can you create the mood you want using the combination of pictures and sound? (This often requires a balancing act between creativity, audience needs, and limited resources.)*
- *Be very clear about your story and how you're going to communicate it. Don't just grab a camera and go out to shoot. This will likely produce a disjointed, meandering, and above all boring video.*
- *Never lose sight of your purpose: to create a text that effectively communicates a specific message to a specific audience using a specific medium.*

TREATMENT

At this point it's useful to prepare a **treatment**: a brief narrative description of the final text. The treatment should take the initial idea and combine it with the desired effect on the target audience.

Check your treatment for the following:

Checklist

Message

- Is the genre of video clearly explained? Is the specific audience for the video described in detail? ❑
- Is the message to be communicated clearly stated? ❑
- Is there a well-described, captivating opening shot? ❑
- Is a clear tone (sad, solemn, joyous, sarcastic, etc.) established early? ❑
- If there is a conflict, is it clearly presented? ❑
- Is there a strong ending? Is it clear to the audience what comes next? ❑

Form

- Are scene changes described clearly? ❑
- Does the chosen form match the message and the target audience? ❑
- Does the treatment contain more action than dialogue? ❑
- Are there several scene changes? ❑
- Are transitions between scenes logical and clear? ❑

Style

- What kinds of visual or aural images will be created? ❑
- Are characters clearly identified and defined? ❑
- Will any special effects or camera angles be used? ❑

CREATING THE STORYBOARD

A storyboard is a visual representation of what the completed video will be. The storyboard details the audio, including dialogue, music, and sound effects. It illustrates the camera angle, the point of view, the camera movement, and the transitions from one shot to the next.

Guidelines for Storyboard Production

- *Keep things simple. It isn't necessary to record every movement or gesture within each shot. If no one in the group is a great artist, stick figures are certainly acceptable for showing the shot.*
- *Communicate the story. Someone who knows nothing about the video should be able to pick up your storyboard and visualize the beginning, middle, and conclusion of your video.*
- *Be complete. The more details about each shot—camera angle, transition, and audio—the easier shooting and editing will be. The more difficult or complex the shot, the more planning and detail will be required.*
- *Make certain the shots flow. Although shots may be filmed out of sequence and changes made while editing, the storyboard should follow the chronological order of the finished video.*
- *Be original. Don't just string together visual clichés.*
- *Establish each scene change. Whenever you change location or time in your video, give the audience a chance to understand where they are and what's going on before moving on to more complex action.*
- *Use the camera and sound to accentuate. When creating your storyboard, think like a director and a cinematographer. Zooms, pans, camera angles, sound, and transitions can all be used for emphasis.*
- *Work in pencil. You'll always find things you'll want to change.*

Checklist

Storyboard	
Transitions are indicated for the beginning and ending of each shot?	❑
The transitions suit the shots and the idea to be communicated?	❑
Camera angles are described clearly?	❑
Sound effects are described clearly?	❑
Music is described, where desired?	❑

Storyboard	
Dialogue is recorded?	❑
Sound, music, and dialogue transitions are described?	❑
Camera movements are described clearly?	❑
Visuals capture the mood of the scene?	❑
Shots are possible? Plausible?	❑

Revising and Editing

Once you have completed your storyboard, take time to ensure that everyone involved in your project is comfortable with the finished result. Allow each person to have some input and incorporate any suggested changes into the storyboard.

Ensuring the Production Team Is in Agreement

- *Does the camera person (or persons) understand what camera work is required?*
- *Does he or she feel competent to shoot the video as described in the storyboard?*
- *Do the actors feel comfortable with the dialogue and actions?*
- *Does the editor understand the sequencing and transitions of the shots?*
- *Are sound cues clear and easy to follow?*

CONSIDER THE STORYBOARD FROM THE AUDIENCE'S POINT OF VIEW

The word *revision* comes from the Latin word meaning "to see again." In no other type of form is this more important than in a visual medium like video.

Examine the storyboard. Try to visualize the completed video as if you were a member of the target audience seeing it for the first time.

Imagining the Video from the Storyboard

- *Would it make sense?*
- *Would there be gaps, where you couldn' t follow the flow of the action?*
- *Would there be parts that would drag on and seem too long?*
- *Would the message be clear?*
- *Would you keep watching?*

Be honest in appraising your storyboard from the audience's point of view, and you will avoid many of the pitfalls of video production.

Checklist

Have I Created a Great Storyboard?	
Is the meaning clear?	❑
Will the audience receive the message I intended?	❑
Will the video I've storyboarded create the mood or feeling that I want in my audience?	❑
Will the audience be persuaded to respond in the way I have planned?	❑
Did I try to use camera angles, movement, dialogue, and sound to full effect? If so, are all the elements consistent?	❑
Did I choose the words I used carefully? Are the word choices I made the best ones possible?	❑
Did I try using visual imagery?	❑
Can this storyboard be transformed into video?	❑

GRAMMAR, USAGE, AND MECHANICS

BREAKING THE RULES IN MEDIA TEXTS

Creators of media texts often bend or break the grammar, usage, and mechanics rules of standard English. This does not mean, however, that when you are writing a media text anything goes. On the contrary; each deviation from standard English must be justified by its appropriateness to the media form, purpose, and audience.

Be certain to clarify in your own mind what audience you are writing for. Decide on what level of formality would be appropriate. This is the **register** of language. Consider a simple description of a car that might be used in a print advertisement. See how the audience changes the register of the description:

Audience	Hip Urban Teens	Middle-aged parents	Wealthy Seniors
Register	Slang	Informal	Formal
Description	"Ain't it a hottie?"	"It looks super!"	"It possesses classic elegance."

In media texts, the purpose and the audience determine the degree to which a change from standard English is allowable, or even desirable. The media text writer must always try to write to the exact level of his or her audience. If the audience speaks in sentence fragments, colloquialisms, or slang expressions, and the writer's goal is to have the audience identify with the text, then the media writer should use them. The media writer often takes on the dialect of the intended audience.

If the occasion calls for a departure from the use of standard English, it is essential that the writer be deliberate and consistent, or the reader will be unable to tell whether the deviant spellings, grammar, and sentence structures are intentional or not. If a writer uses "ain't" for effect in the first sentence and "isn't" in all subsequent sentences, the reader will assume that the first sentence was a mistake, not intentional dialect.

MEDIA FORMS

The nature of particular media forms also tends to guide language usage. Some forms, such as print ads and radio commercials, often rely on conversational tone and frequent use of sentence fragments. Since space (or time) is at a premium, the writing must be succinct:

Formal Persuasive Essay	Print Advertisement	30-second Radio Commercial
We must always strive to work in the best interests of the environment by curtailing excess car exhaust fumes.	CO— No Go!	Cars. Too many. Air. Too smoggy. People. Too precious. Leave the car at home today.

Advertising in general is a form of text that often consciously sacrifices correct grammar, usage, and mechanics in order to create texts that appeal to viewers. **Slogans**, which might appear on bumper stickers, billboards, or newspaper or magazine ads, might have deliberate misspellings, unusual syntax, or missing or odd punctuation:

- "Come to the ocean resort with TL Sea!"
- "Our Lumber is TREEmendous!"
- "essential expressive exquisite enamels"

Television and film scripts use a variety of language types, including abbreviations for technical terms, conversational language (with colloquialisms, fragments, pauses and dialect), and visual description, often all on the same page. Some parts of a script may need to be in perfect standard English, while others may need to be far from it:

Video	Audio
Next day. Camera zooms in on white pickup.	Sound of "Sweet Home Alabama" coming from truck stereo. Music up and under voices:
Int. of truck. Two teens, one boy, one girl. The girl is crying.	Intermittent sobs. Female voice
CU girl's face	Girl: I hate you. Stop the truck!
CU boy's head turns	Boy: I ain't stoppin'
OS boy from girl's view	Girl: Ya gotta!
Med shot. Boy and girl through windshield	Boy: But I love you, Mandy!

WRITING FOR THE INTERNET

When writing for the Internet, several rules of standard English may or may not apply. Due to the immediate and interactive nature of texts like e-mail, abbreviations and sentence fragments are common. "LOL" for "laugh out loud," "BTW" for "by the way," and "FAQ" for "frequently asked questions" are examples of common e-mail abbreviations. The danger of this form of language is that it gives the illusion of speech, but does not allow for the subtleties that voice inflection, body language, and facial expressions can add to communication. In order to determine whether to abbreviate or write a fragment, consider the **context** of your writing.

- Will the reader be able to understand your meaning?
- Have you corresponded before?
- Will the reader be receiving the information immediately, or is it likely time will pass before the message will be read?

If you can answer these questions, then you'll have some guide as to how specific and complete you must be in your message.

Internet writing is often filled with **jargon**, that is, specialized language used for a specific group. Jargon is generally avoided in most writing, but is permissible in Internet writing if you can honestly expect the intended reader to be able to understand.

Another feature of e-mail writing is the use of **emoticons**, sometimes known as **smileys**. These are small graphic representations made with standard keyboard characters that are designed to substitute for facial expressions to convey emotions. Use emoticons sparingly, as you would an exclamation point in a story or essay. Don't use emoticons if you are not sure your reader will understand them. Common emoticons are: :) smile; ;) wink; :-(chagrin; : / sarcasm.

When writing for a Web site, it is essential to keep your text short and to always be aware of its visual as well as written context. Much like any visual media text, such as a magazine or newspaper page, the text can break the general rules of standard English, but only if it is done to clarify, highlight, or create an emotional response for the intended viewer. In short, breaking the rules for their own sake is not good practice in media texts.

Multimedia Presentations

Multimedia presentations are those that include more than one form of communications. A speech accompanied by slides is a simple form of multimedia presentation. Or you can create sophisticated computer-generated presentations using PowerPoint, Hyperstudio, or Corel Presentations software, which allow you to incorporate sound, video, and graphics.

The first step is to choose a form of presentation that is suitable for both the content and the audience. For example, a computer-generated slide show might be a great way to present a historical review of events in World War I. A simple poster with a guided talk might work better for teaching traffic safety to a group of kindergarten students.

Elements of Presentation

- *Purpose: Are you presenting to inform? To entertain? To persuade?*
- *Content: Is your material at the correct level of difficulty for your audience?*
- *Organization: Is your material organized in a way that will be understood?*
- *Media: Does your use of graphics, sound, and technology enhance your presentation?*
- *Flexibility: Have you allowed for audience questions, equipment problems, and time constraints?*

Presentation Tips

- *Know your topic thoroughly and be comfortable with your use of the media you've chosen.*
- *Capture and hold your audience's attention. Use your voice to focus, direct, and motivate your audience.*
- *Pace the presentation of your material in a way that is neither too fast nor too slow for your audience.*

Standing in front of other people and presenting information is never easy. Experience and practice help to reduce your anxiety. If at all possible, practise your material with a friend or peer before you present it to your target audience. Finally, remember that the human element is what usually makes for a good presentation.

CHAPTER 9

research and ethics

> Whoever ceases to be
> a student has never been a student.
> *George Iles*

> Tell me, I will forget
> Show me, I may remember
> Involve me, I will understand
> *Chinese proverb*

Research skills are vital in today's complex world. Months after a research project, you might forget the details about the causes of World War I, or exactly why the Métis rebelled in 1869. But you may have developed the skills to readily locate this information. One of the keys to research is knowing *how* to find out what you need and want to know.

Of course, finding information is only one part of the research process. You also need to know how to evaluate and use the information. These are the tools and talents of a successful independent learner.

LEARNING GOALS

- know the fundamentals of the research process, including planning, defining, researching, organizing, reflecting, and revising
- develop skill in locating, selecting, evaluating, recording, and documenting research sources
- design and carry out an independent research project
- practise using a wide range of information technologies
- be aware of bias and frame of reference
- understand and practise academic ethics

CONTENTS

The Research Process

Selecting a Topic

In major research assignments for independent study, topics may be assigned in the following manner:

- The instructor or teacher assigns the topic. There is little room for revision or amendment.
- Students may select a topic from a previously drafted list. There may be some room for amendment of the project.
- The student is free to choose the topic or research proposal. This type of assignment usually requires very close reporting and conferencing with the teacher throughout the research process.

What to Ask Yourself When Selecting a Topic

- *Do you fully understand the assignment? Restating it in your own words will help you to grasp its purpose.*
- *What do you need to know to successfully master the research challenge?*
- *Is it appropriate for you, your abilities, and your talents?*
- *What prior knowledge or experience do you have that may be useful?*
- *Who is the intended audience?*
- *What should the finished product look like?*
- *What is the required format? length? timeline?*
- *What kinds of help will you need?*
- *How will it affect your social or work schedule?*

Planners

One of the best ways to keep on track is through the use of planners. The best form of planner is probably a large-format calendar modified to fit the specific challenges of your task.

Important Features of Planners

- *large, easy-to-read format*
- *precise dates based on smaller blocks of time, e.g., days, not weeks*
- *major deadlines marked with an asterisk or in capital letters*

- *firm paper or plastic to ensure durability during the research process*
- *Large- or small-format planners or calendars allow you to see deadlines, appointments, and task completion targets at a glance.*
- *Many computer programs provide easy-to-use planners as part of their basic operations.*

Planning Tips

- *Begin your planning immediately. As you work on your project, keep turning to your planner to keep you motivated and organized. Be prepared for significant revision while your research is underway.*
- *Write deadlines, appointments, and tasks clearly. Place the planner in a highly visible place in your study area or on the inside of your research folder.*
- *Write in pencil or, if the planner is coated, a water-based marking pen. This allows for revision, in case you have to shuffle visits to the library, Internet searches, peer editing sessions, for example.*
- *When using a computer program, revision is a cut and paste away.*

KWL AND KNL CHARTS

Another helpful tool is the **KWL** or **KNL** chart. These are three-column graphic organizers with the following headings:

- KWL: What You Know; What You Want to Know; What You Have Learned
- KNL: What You Know; What You Need to Know; What You Have Learned

These charts can be modified to help you keep tabs on your progress. For example, here are headings for a five-column chart:

- What I Know; What I Need to Know; Who Can Help Me?; Where Can I Find What I Need to Know?; What I'm Learning

Personal Dictionary

Once you embark on your research you are sure to encounter new vocabulary and specialized terminology. Try to understand these new terms and incorporate them into your work.

One way to do this is to enter new terms or concepts in a **personalized dictionary (PD)** or a **factfile (FF)** directly related to your research. This will serve as a handy reference source, and will help you understand and use these terms correctly.

Here are some examples of specialized vocabulary:

Subject Area	Colloquial Vocabulary	Specialized Vocabulary
Voting Rights for Women	women's votes	female suffrage
Space	take-off	launch
Art	paint wash	gouache
Music	changes to	segue
Sports	puts the ball in the hoop	slam dunk

How to Keep a PD or FF

- *Use either a small journal or three-ring binder.*
- *Alphabetize the pages by writing one letter on every one to two pages, like a telephone directory.*
- *On each page draw three columns, with the central column being the widest.*
- *In the first column, write the word or phrase as you come across it in your research.*
- *In the middle column, write a complete and precise definition of the term. Try to use your own words as much as possible. This will make the word your own and reduce the need to memorize.*
- *In the final column, use the word(s) in a sentence or phrase to correctly convey its proper use.*
- *Enter the terms and concepts as you work on your research.*

Research Folder

As soon as you begin your research, you'll find yourself dealing with a flurry of information, including assignment sheets, notes, resource lists, news clippings, summaries of discussions, rough drafts, maps, charts, quotations, Internet material, and file cards.

You'll need to have one place where you can find all your research material—and that place is the **research folder**. It may be a three-ring binder with pockets to hold cards, notes, call-slips, etc., or a simple file folder stapled on three sides so that nothing will fall out. Some researchers use a folding file to separate material into different compartments. A research folder may even be a small plastic box that seals all your materials in one safe location.

Uses of the Research Folder

- *It should be close at hand during the entire research process.*
- *It keeps you and your material organized.*
- *It provides a clear record of what you've done and what you've found.*

- *It can be referred to easily when reviewing what you've already accomplished and what still needs to be done.*
- *It can be useful when conferencing with peers or instructors.*
- *It's sometimes part of the evaluation and assessment process.*

Preparatory Reading

Researchers are faced with the challenge of reading a great deal of material very effectively and in a short period of time. There is little opportunity for false starts or getting stuck. You can't afford to spend several hours wrestling with a source that will prove to be of no value to you.

Preparatory reading is the process of identifying valuable sources and weeding out material that is less useful. Before moving to very close reading and recording of information, it's wise to employ one of the following strategies:

Active Reading Strategies

- *Continually ask your sources the following questions: Who? What? Where? When? Why? Direct your reading to those significant questions, which are fundamental to all inquiry.*
- *Employ the well-known SQ4R technique: Survey, Question, Read, Recite, wRite, Review.*
- *Keep the central question of your research topic clearly in front of you. It is the prism through which you analyze your research sources and determine their usefulness.*

Developing a Thesis

Independent research often assumes that a student will select, develop, revise, research, and prove a thesis. Making sure that you clearly understand the term *thesis* is central to research success.

According to *The Canadian Oxford Dictionary*, a **thesis** is "a proposition to be maintained or proved." This usually means a well-written sentence that clearly expresses the essential idea of your research. State your thesis in your first paragraph and continually refer back to it as you develop your supporting arguments. Your conclusion will be a clear restatement of your thesis and a brief summation of your supporting arguments.

Developing a thesis is the central, singularly challenging task of academic research. For as you continue to research, write, and reflect, it's only reasonable that your opinion will change. This is a natural result of intellectual growth and experience. Yet there is obviously a limit to how much change a thesis can undergo. To have a wobbly thesis throughout your research will make it difficult to build a convincing argument.

Stages in Refining Your Thesis

1. *Understanding/analyzing your topic.*
2. *Creating your focus question and possible thesis.*
3. *Conducting introductory research and discussion.*
4. *Refining and restating your thesis.*
5. *Completing your research.*
6. *Building your supporting arguments, and fine-tuning your thesis.*
7. *Committing to your thesis and defending it formally in your final product.*
8. *Evaluation of your thesis by teacher/instructor/peers and final consideration by you.*

Revise, Reflect, Revise Again

The thrill and pace of significant research can sometimes leave little time for careful reflection and revision of your work and ideas. Too often, researchers are so busy finding, recording, organizing, and writing information that they have little time for anything else. The deadline for completion always looms, large and imposing. Reflecting on and revising your work as you go, however, is an important part of any research experience.

Revision involves the willingness to think seriously about what you are doing—to see the big picture, to reconsider opinions and facts, to investigate with fresh eyes and attitudes.

Strategies for Personal Reflection

- *Sharing ideas and work with peers and instructors is a good way to generate reflection and meaningful revision.*
- *Using your research folder or IQ (Ideas and Questions) journal to record your reflections about what you are doing and what has already been accomplished.*
- *Keeping a learning log, perhaps on your personal computer.*

Proofreading Your Work

It's important to carefully proofread your work before submitting it for evaluation. Here are a few suggestions.

Proofreading Tips

- *Use all available technology. Most word-processing programs contain spell checkers, grammar checkers, thesauruses, and footnoting and endnoting options. Just remember that no machine can catch more than the obvious errors. Technology is a starting point, not the end point.*

- *Leave some time, if possible, between finishing your work and proofreading it. If you don' t, your brain may put in material where it isn' t because your intention is still fresh in your mind. Sometimes you see what you want or expect to see, not what's actually there.*
- *Read your work aloud. Just by listening to yourself you may catch such errors as awkward phrasing, incomplete thoughts, and repetition.*
- *Invite a trusted adult or peer to proof your work. Have them note their concerns or questions directly on your draft.*
- *Consider using a ruler to take you line by line through your text. This will make it easier for you to spot errors and omissions.*
- *Review your IQ journal to make sure that your concerns have actually been addressed in your work.*

Checklist

Preparing for Research	
I fully understand the research task and its parameters.	❑
I have a personal dictionary.	❑
I have a research folder.	❑
I have planners and KWL or KNL charts.	❑
I have a clear thesis.	❑
I have started my preparatory reading.	❑

Notation

One of the basic features of the research process is note making. Since you'll be reading, viewing, and interpreting a broad array of information, it's essential that you have a compact, reliable record available for easy reference and use.

The Value of Well-designed Notes

- *They allow you to record the most important parts of research materials.*
- *They provide you with a permanent, authoritative written record that can be referred to when needed.*
- *They help to organize your research and learning in a meaningful, useful manner.*
- *They may help you to remember material ("muscle memory" suggests that writing something down may reinforce our understanding and recall).*

Note-making Methods

Here are the major methods of note making, along with practical, concrete examples. Consider which of these methods you are familiar with, and what are the major strengths and benefits of each approach.

I. OUTLINING

Outlining can be applied in a variety of circumstances, using notepaper, index cards, or a computer. Never write notes on both sides of a paper or card—it's a sure way to get confused or forget to use crucial information. This type of note should feature only the most important information in a clear, organized, and succinct fashion.

Outlining Steps

- *Record the full bibliographic information for your source (author, title, publisher, volume, page numbers). This is critical and will make your writing much easier later in the project. You need to know exactly where your information has come from! Take no shortcuts. Don' t use abbreviations, and write neatly.*
- *On the left-hand side of your paper or card indicate the page reference for the information that you are noting.*
- *Make sure that you' ve indicated the main idea or theme of the note. This might be the central theme of the book, chapter, or section of a chapter. Mark this idea with a Roman numeral.*
- *Using point form and avoiding words such as* a *and* the, *write a brief summary of the secondary ideas, supporting information, or details. Note the subtopics with a capital letter, and use numbers or bullets to identify further details and important information.*
- *It's useful to number your pages or cards consecutively for each source.*
- *Keep your pages and cards in your research folder, separated by source with staples, paper clips, or elastic bands. Computer files must be carefully backed up on a clearly marked disk dedicated to this research project only.*

Consider the two examples of outlining notes below. Assess them for accuracy, utility, and application of the model presented earlier.

(Spotlight History Book)
Alice Munro is one of the best-known short story writers in the world. Many of her stories are set in a small southwestern Ontario town, much like the one in which she was born.

After attending the University of Western Ontario for two years, Alice Munro moved to Victoria, B.C. There she and her husband opened a bookstore, Munro's Books.

Cruxton, J. Bradley and W. Douglas Wilson. *Spotlight Canada*, Fourth Edition. Toronto: Oxford University Press, 2000.
(Page 388)
Canadian Authors: Alice Munro and Margaret Atwood
I Alice Munro
- One of best-known short story writers in world

II Early Life
- Lived and set stories in SW Ont.
- Attended UWO for two years

II. WEBBING

Some people are more visually oriented, and prefer to summarize information in a graphic form. **Webbing** or **mapping** can can be very helpful in recognizing the links among details or facts.

Web-making Steps

- *Place the main idea or topic in the centre of the page and underline or circle it.*
- *Write secondary ideas and subtopics on lines connected to the main idea.*
- *Add the details and supporting information on lines jutting out from the secondary ideas or subtopics.*
- *Make sure that the web doesn' t become too complex or text-heavy.*

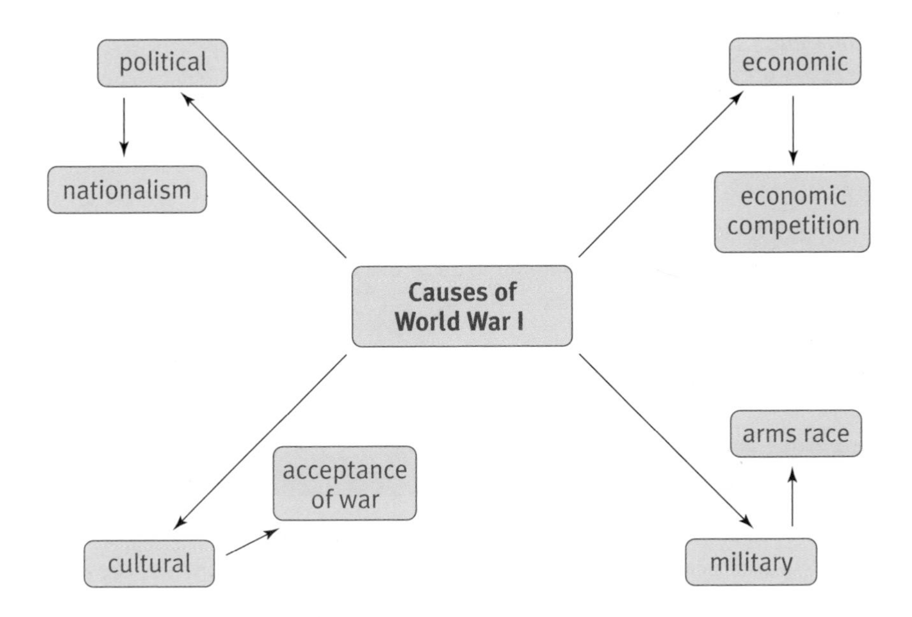

III. POINT-FORM NOTES

This is perhaps the simplest and speediest form of note making, whether you use a computer, index cards, or notepaper. It emphasizes the efficient reading of material and the speedy but accurate recording of important information.

Note-making Steps

- *Place the complete bibliographic form of your resource at the top of the page or card.*
- *Write the topic in large block letters to the left and draw a single column about six centimetres in from the edge of the page. This column can be used later for extra information.*
- *Place your notes to the right, taking care not to overcrowd the lines, use spacing to block out major chunks of your work.*
- *Give each point a new line and open the line with an asterisk or bullet.*
- *As much as possible, use your own words. This reduces the chance of plagiarism* *(see pp. 333–334)* *and helps you actively understand what you are reading.*
- *Use as few words as possible. Focus on the really important details.*
- *Avoid complete sentences, punctuation, and heavy description.*
- *Use standard or even personal abbreviations and symbols—as long as you're confident that they will make sense to you later.*
- *Be as neat and clear as possible and avoid overcrowding. Use white space and blank lines so that your notes are easy on the eyes.*

Cruxton, J. Bradley and W. Douglas Wilson. *Spotlight Canada*, Fourth Edition. Toronto: Oxford University Press, 2000.
Canadian Authors: Alice Munro and Margaret Atwood (Page 388)
Alice Munro:

- One of best known short story writers in the world
- Stories set in town like one she lived in SW Ont.
- Went to UWO for two years
- Moved to Victoria, B.C.
- Opened bookshop with husband

Note-making Forms

There are four major forms of note making: **paraphrasing, summarizing, direct quotation,** and **personal commentary**. While some forms fit certain sources better than others, it's quite possible that you'll use all four in a more complex research project.

The types of notes you make may change as you go. For example, if you find that after a few weeks of work you don't have many direct, specific quotations, you may need to use these more often in your ongoing research. Or, perhaps as you become more experienced in your chosen topic, you may wish to shift from point-form or outline notes to paraphrasing or summarizing material that is now familiar to you.

In short, these approaches are like arrows in a quiver—and it's up to you, the archer, to choose the arrows best suited for your target.

PARAPHRASING

Paraphrasing is the art of saying what a source says but in short form and in your own words. The goal of paraphrasing is to be accurate but brief. Using your own words, expressions, and sentence structure is critical. Poor paraphrasing can easily lead to accidental plagiarism. If you are quoting directly, then use the quotation form of note making (as explained below).

SUMMARIZING

Similar to paraphrasing, **summarizing** is a shortened version of an original text and is written in full sentence and paragraph form. However, rather than a paraphrase of the original text, it is a summary of its key ideas.

DIRECT QUOTATION

Direct quotation is, of course, the direct and accurate repetition of significant facts, views, and statements. Quotations provide authoritative evidence for your work and help you avoid plagiarism. They inform your readers of the quality, depth, and integrity of your research.

Rules for Quoting

- *Enclose the quotation in quotation marks, and make sure that you write down the quotation word for word and with the correct punctuation, exactly as it is found in the original source. Double-check your work!*
- *Indicate the full bibliographic source and carefully note the page number for easy reference later.*
- *Use ellipsis points (...) to indicate any omitted words. Be sure that when omitting words you are not changing the intent of the quotation.*
- *Make sure that your quotations are easy to find. Don't bury them in the midst of other notes, and don't include too many quotations on a single page or card. You might offer a one-word prompt to suggest how this quotation may end up in your final product.*

PERSONAL COMMENTARY

Personal commentary is an active, reflective analysis of your reading, thinking, and research. Writing down personal comments, questions, and statements in an IQ (Ideas and Questions) journal will help you to clarify important issues. It may contain sudden flashes of inspiration or insight that can be followed up later.

These notes can be useful when discussing your progress with instructors, peers, and even friends and family. And long after you've finished your project, they can stand as a valuable personal snapshot of your intellect as it wrestles with a significant challenge.

Using Your Notes

As you finalize your research in either a written, oral, or visual form (or even perhaps a blend of all three), your notes will loom even larger in your work. They now become the building blocks of your final product. It is at this stage that you'll really appreciate their neatness, completeness, and accuracy.

Take time to carefully review the notes you've gathered. You may see new patterns and wish to group your information accordingly. As you draft an outline for your final product, it may be possible to slot your notes into certain arguments. Moving your notes around on a large uncluttered table will give you the freedom and space to direct information to where it can be most effective.

Checklist

Notation	
I have used various note-making strategies: outlining, webbing, and point-form notes.	❑
I have used various note-making forms: paraphrasing, summarizing, direct quotation, and personal commentary.	❑
I have included full bibliographic information with my notes.	❑
I have reviewed my notes and grouped the information according to certain arguments.	❑

Research Strategies

Taking the time to build, develop, and occasionally revise an intelligent research strategy is the mark of a successful researcher.

General Rules for Successful Research

- *Establish your central purpose and your research needs.*
- *Start early and work on a regular basis.*
- *Read and consult widely.*
- *Move from the general to the specific.*
- *Keep an excellent research folder.*
- *Always work with a librarian or teacher-librarian. Consult or conference with your instructor on a regular basis. Record comments in your research folder or IQ journal.*
- *Search browser/card catalogues for print and non-print resources. Consult the Library of Congress Subject Headings for the correct search terminology for your topic.*
- *Maintain a good record of correct call numbers and keep them in your research folder.*
- *Review print and online encyclopedias for a general overview and framework.*
- *Search CD-ROMs and browse hit lists.*
- *Review magazines, newspapers, film and video catalogues (print, CD and floppy), electronic information systems, and databases.*
- *Move out to the wider community and employ telephone, fax, e-mail, interviews, and surveys.*
- *Continue to consult and conference with instructors, librarians, teacher-librarians, and peers, etc., to resolve research problems or clarify issues.*

Research Sources

Human Resources

Connecting with people who are informed and interested about your work is a productive way to carry out your assignments. Fortunately, for most topics there are a range of human sources willing and able to provide information, commentary, and advice. No student should be an island in a sea of research.

THE TEACHER/INSTRUCTOR

Ongoing conferences with your teacher will help to guide your work and steer you clear of major errors. Most teachers will be informed about your topic, as well as the major sources available and the general approaches you can take. They can also spot errors early on and guide you to a more successful approach.

THE TEACHER-LIBRARIAN AND LIBRARIAN

Sooner or later, and sooner is definitely better, you'll need to consult a librarian and/or a teacher-librarian. If possible, try to schedule an appointment and provide a clear description of what you're doing and your central needs. This individual is generally the most informed expert you can consult for available resources, search strategies, and hands-on training using a broad range of technologies.

OTHER SCHOOL-BASED SOURCES

- IT technicians—often the most skilled users of advanced technologies and superb problem solvers
- laboratory assistants
- other teachers in related subject areas (for example, if you are writing about the authors of the Lost Generation in 1930s Paris, it may be helpful to consult with a history teacher about the general historical, political, and social context of the period)
- departmental teachers other than your course instructor (e.g., if you are researching World War I, you may find that another teacher in the history department has a special passion for and knowledge of the topic)

COMMUNITY

Your human search strategy should move outward from your personal contacts in an ever-expanding research circle. You may locate people through the library, newspapers, television, radio, the Yellow Pages, and the Internet. Consider these sources:

- government departments or agencies
- public agencies
- clubs, associations
- service groups
- interest, pressure groups
- educational institutions (schools, libraries, museums, archives)

Multimedia Sources

Fortunately, the range of sources available for most research topics is broad and impressive. You should opt for a blend of personal, print, technological, and other media sources. This relieves the tedium of research, provides balance, and often stimulates insight and synthesis.

PRINT

books, both fiction and non-fiction
handbooks, journals
research studies, abstracts
general and specific topic studies
specialized reference materials, such as atlases, specialized encyclopedias (*Encyclopedia of Chemistry*), biographical dictionaries (*Dictionary of Canadian Biography*), almanacs, dictionaries, yearbooks, bibliographies, book reviews, indexes, government catalogues, microfiche, microfilm, maps, photos, statistics, taped interviews
periodicals and newspapers
vertical or information files

TECHNOLOGY

Internet
- Web sites, search engines, chat groups
- hyperlinks
- online databases and encyclopedias

CD-ROMs
video and laser disks
cameras, videocams
interactive television
audiotapes and disks

OTHER MEDIA

films and videos
film and video catalogues
filmstrips, audiovisual kits
overheads
television and radio broadcasts, archives, and Web sites

Interviews and Surveys

Interviews and surveys are two important forms of primary research. When you conduct an interview or survey, you are relying on your critical listening skills. These skills will help you accurately hear and document what your interviewee or survey respondent tells you.

Active/Passive Listening

Passive listening is ...

- *remaining quiet and inattentive*
- *daydreaming and doodling*
- *slouching, shifting continually in your seat*
- *having little eye contact with the speaker*
- *having no strategy to record or remember what is being said*

Active listening is ...

- *looking directly at the speaker and maintaining eye contact*
- *focusing on what is being said*
- *showing interest through body language such as nods, smiles*
- *sitting straight and leaning in the direction of the speaker*
- *asking questions, and, when appropriate, sharing comments and insights*

Effective Listening Strategies

- *Read ahead, and prepare for the interview, survey, lesson, lecture, etc.*
- *Stay focused. Look at the speaker once in a while.*
- *Make notes as you listen. Use abbreviations or your own personal shorthand.*
- *Leave lots of white space for later notation, answers to questions, or reflective comments.*
- *Note difficult vocabulary or concepts.*
- *Show interest.*
- *Listen for verbal clues, such as word choice, pitch, intonation, summary or introductory statements, phrasing (such as "in the first place," "secondly," "in conclusion").*
- *Write a brief summary based on your notes soon after the interview, survey, presentation, or lecture.*

INTERVIEWS

At its best, an interview is a thoughtful, lively conversation between two people who share a particular interest. It's rooted in respect, close attention, and a desire to learn and share. Most researchers find interviews to be most enlightening, since you can ask questions when you don't understand something (rather difficult to do when poring over a book or article). For interviewees, it's a welcome opportunity to present their views, experiences, and knowledge to an interested listener.

Preparing for Your Interview

- *When you request an interview with someone, clearly explain its purpose, and perhaps the kinds of questions you' ll be asking.*
- *One-on-one personal interviews are the best vehicles for a good conversation. If this isn' t possible, you might consider a telephone interview or a conference call; e-mail or the Internet; or videoconferencing.*
- *You and your subject agree on the interview' s location, time and duration, and recording method (notes, tape recorder, videocam).*
- *Complete some significant research before you meet your subject. That way your questions will be more significant and focused, and you' ll be better able to understand the responses.*
- *Prepare a clear, well-organized set of questions designed to elicit as much useful information as possible. Avoid questions that could generate one-word answers or a simple yes or no. Moving from the general to the specific is usually a good strategy. You might frame your questions with a few comments to make them seem more informal and to generate a more personal response from your interviewee. Create a mix of formal and informal questions, and have a few follow-up questions prepared.*
- *The interview should be a good discussion, not a clinical interrogation. You want anecdotes, personal slogans, and stories to both enliven your account and give it some flesh and bone.*
- *Practise your greeting, listening skills, and presentation of your core questions. If you' re using any technical equipment, know how to use it efficiently. Are power sources available? Do you need batteries?*

Tips for a Successful Interview

- *Arrive on time, neatly dressed, and with all the necessary equipment.*
- *Greet your interviewee warmly and thank him or her again for helping you out with your research.*
- *Briefly restate the purpose of your research and what you are hoping to gain from the interview.*

- *Ask your questions clearly and in an interested manner. Look at your subject, nod your head, smile—be an active listener. Comment briefly about something and be prepared to present follow-up questions or off-the-cuff questions for further clarification and interest.*
- *Keep the interview moving. Avoid wandering far from your purpose, and be prepared to direct your subject once in a while.*
- *Even if you are taping the interview, point-form notes are a good idea because they focus on the heart of the interview and perhaps indicate particularly new or insightful material.*
- *When completed, thank the interviewee warmly, and ask if you may call back to clarify any answers.*

After the Interview

- *Review your notes or tape, highlight or write down significant points, and compose a brief summary. Remember to put this summary in your research folder.*
- *Write a thank-you note and send or deliver it personally to your interviewee. You might also include your summary, just to ensure that you've grasped the material correctly.*
- *Any insights you've gained should be recorded in your personal journal or your IQ journal.*

SURVEYS

Another method of carrying out primary research is through the survey. According to *The Canadian Oxford Dictionary*, a **survey** is a "systematic collection and analysis of data relating to the opinions, habits, etc. of a population based on a representative sample." Surveys are an excellent method for finding out people's thoughts, attitudes, and behaviours.

Designing the Survey

- *Review and analyze other existing surveys to pick up good techniques.*
- *State the purpose of your research precisely and narrowly.*
- *Ensure that you really do have the time to design, employ, collect, and evaluate a good survey.*
- *Choose your audience carefully. Will you need to record age, gender, education, ethnicity, income, etc., as part of your research strategy?*
- *How will you carry out the survey—in person, through the mail or e-mail, over the phone, through an Internet site? Will you focus on individuals or address large groups?*

- *Compose simple, brief questions. You might consider yes or no questions, multiple choice, or rank-order. The less writing required of respondents, the more likely that the results will be clear and easily quantifiable.*
- *Try to guarantee the anonymity of your respondents so that they can feel more independent and truthful.*
- *Before presenting your survey, do a test run with a small group of people. Verify that the survey is clear, and easy to collect and tabulate.*

Conducting the Survey

- *Work quickly to gather a significant number of responses. Supervise the survey as personally as possible. Are the responses accurate and collected correctly?*
- *Keep a good record of all collected surveys and store them carefully in your research folder.*

Analyzing the Results

- *Record the results on a large, easy-to-read tally sheet.*
- *Keep a record of the number and description of the people surveyed. Carefully state and summarize the results, as well as your interpretation of and conclusions about those results.*
- *Include samples of the survey and the full report in an appendix to your final research product.*

Internet Research

Today, skilled and intelligent use of the Internet is one of the foundations of an excellent research strategy. But, like any other research source, the Internet needs to be understood and mastered before it can be really useful.

INTERNET VOCABULARY

Browser: a software program that assists your search by offering links to powerful search engines
Bookmark: a saved URL or Web site address
E-mail: Electronic mail messages sent and received by computers
Home Page: the document first on your screen when you arrive at a site
Hotlists: lists of frequently accessed URLs
Hypertext, Hyperlinks: highlighted words or icons that when clicked on take you to another site

Internet: the vast network linking thousands of computer networks globally and allowing millions of users to connect with each other. The fastest growing communications network in the world

Search Engine: a most useful tool that helps users access Web sites. Search engines search, collect, and organize Web information.

Service Provider: a company or organization that provides access to the Internet, usually for a fee

SIG: Special Interest Group

Surfing: moving from site to site in order to locate information, or as simply a casual tour of the Net

URL (Uniform Resource Locator): address of a Web site. This is the Internet addressing system.

WWW (World Wide Web): the collection of networks and computers on the Internet

Web Site: a virtual location on the Web

SEARCH ENGINES

The goal of Internet research is to generate as many useful hits (URLs) as possible for your particular topic. So it's important to have a good general approach to the use of search engines. Fortunately, most search engines provide guidelines for the most effective use of their search tools. These should always be consulted before using the search engine itself. Many search engines also provide an "advanced search" feature that can offer a more sophisticated, relevant, and exact search for your topic.

Steps to Superior Searches

- *Select a number of key words for your topic.*
- *Brainstorm synonyms or related key words for your topic.*
- *Enter the key word in singular or plural form, or use the singular form followed by an asterisk in order to generate hits (e.g., Canadian poets*).*
- *If you are searching for a person, type in the common form of the name (e.g., William Shakespeare, not Bill Shakespeare).*
- *Try words or terms with similar meaning (e.g., poetry/poetics).*
- *Try expanding, or more likely narrowing, your topic to generate more precise hits.*
- *Use the Boolean features (and/or/not) to more carefully focus your hits.*
- *When you visit a site, pay careful attention to the "hot" sections that are hyperlinks to related sites. Some sites are laden with many useful links.*
- *Bookmark any promising sites so that you can return to them later. If you have a large number of possibilities, consider organizing a series of clearly labelled folders.*

BOOKMARKS

When conducting your research, you may not always have time to fully review a site or download information. Sometimes your goal is to simply make a whirlwind visit to a number of possible sites or work through a number of hyperlinks. These sites should be **bookmarked** for future reference. Simply employ the bookmark command supplied with your browser software. By bookmarking, you will be creating your own personalized URL list organized for the successful investigation of your research topic.

If you have a large number of sites, they should be placed in separate folders for even easier future referral. These folders might be organized by, for example, chronology, subtopic, question, or category.

SAFE SURFING

While you are free to roam the world in search of information, the Web can also be used to track you and any personal information that you share. So it's important to both protect your personal privacy and to stay clear of the commercial applications of the Internet.

- Observe your school, family, or organization's rules for Internet use.
- Keep all passwords, phone numbers, or addresses confidential.
- Never share your account.
- Treat all Internet information as copyrighted material and never plagiarize sources.
- Avoid any links to questionable sites.
- If you receive information or personal contact that seems questionable, inform an adult immediately.

Evaluating Sources

The ability to evaluate the quality of your sources is a critical skill. The last thing you want is to use sources that are outdated, unreliable, incorrect, or biased. Your evaluation "radar" should be turned on as soon as you consider selecting a source. When in doubt, ask a peer, teacher, or informed adult for their comments. One way to protect the integrity of your research is to consult a wide variety of sources, and never rely too much on one source for most of your information or views.

WHO IS PRESENTING IT?

Is the author considered reputable, credible, or an expert? Has he or she published other works in the field? Is the publisher academic, special interest, or mass market? Is it independent or closely allied to a political party or pressure group?

WHAT IS BEING PRESENTED?

Is the account balanced and neutral, or highly subjective and designed to persuade rather than inform? Does the author provide clear evidence to support any claims or arguments? What personal or academic connection does the author have to the material?

WHEN WAS IT FIRST PRESENTED?

Is the information still accurate and relevant? Is it a primary or a secondary source? Is this a reprint or a new edition of a work that has been updated and revised? If older, is it considered a classic? How important is currency of information to the topic?

HOW IS IT PRESENTED?

Does the book have a serious, thoughtful appearance or is it designed more for attention than balanced discussion? Does the text have a table of contents, detailed index, and bibliography, or at least bibliographical notes? Are the unit and chapter titles reasonable in tone or are they sweeping or inflammatory? Is the vocabulary of a high order or is it simplistic and overcharged with generalizations? Is the source largely based on fact, opinion, or argument?

WHY IS IT BEING PRESENTED?

What appears to be the purpose of the source? Is it intended to inform or to persuade? Is there a commercial intent? How much bias and subjectivity does there appear to be in the source? Could it be considered propaganda? Review the foreword or introduction to gain a sense of purpose of the source. Are there any sponsors of the work, such as government agencies, lobby groups, or private corporations?

Bias

The Canadian Oxford Dictionary defines **bias** as "a predisposition or a prejudice." It can be simply a limited view of something or someone; at its worst, it is a clearly slanted, one-sided position.

RECOGNIZING PERSONAL BIAS

In the heat of research and argument, it's natural to become committed to your thesis and supporting ideas. But while a vigorously defended thesis is admirable, it's important to make sure that your point of view is fair and well-informed.

Most people are biased to a certain degree. Bias usually develops out of our particular frame of reference, which is the sum total of our life experiences and personal knowledge. Bias may predispose us to certain opinions and values. It may also blind us to people, ideas, and information that are unfamiliar or that challenge our central notions.

The goal of research is to be critical, but open to new information. So our challenge as researchers is to recognize our biases so that we don't become a prisoner of them.

RECOGNIZING BIAS IN RESEARCH SOURCES

When researching, it's important to recognize bias and prejudice in your sources, whether they be books, Web sites, or resource persons. In some cases bias may be explicit and easy to recognize, but often it is more subtle and implicit.

Just because information is biased, however, doesn't mean that it has no value. For instance, a racist account of the Oka Crisis won't be useful as an informed analysis of the event, but the inflammatory, biased words of the source might be a good example of the highly charged atmosphere surrounding the event.

Features That May Indicate Bias

- *The ratio of fact versus opinion. Facts can be proven and demonstrated to be true. Opinions are statements that cannot generally be proved; they are personal beliefs and assessments that may or may not be informed and balanced.*
- *The amount of simplification and generalization. If the resource offers sweeping, simple answers to complex questions, be wary.*
- *The tone of the source. Screaming titles, wild claims, and emotionally charged language may be interesting to read, but may mask a seriously prejudiced position. If the source appears to be too persuasive, it's probably biased.*
- *Who and what is included or excluded from the text and documentation. A narrow frame of reference will imperil a balanced account.*

Evaluating Internet Sources

The Internet is a free, democratic structure. There is little regulation of its content, and so information may be inaccurate. Web sites can be set up for personal reasons, or intended primarily for commercial purposes. Sites may have a political perspective or represent a particular lobby or interest group. As a result, researchers must be careful about evaluating the credibility of information found on the Net.

Tips for Assessing Web Sites

- *Who is the sponsor, if any, of the site? A government, cultural organization, or educational site generally presents more reliable information than a commercial, political, or personal one. Remember the following address tags when viewing new sites.*

gov	*a government site*
edu	*an educational site*
org	*an organization or advocacy site*
com	*a commercial or business site*
ca	*a Canadian site*
~	*a personal Web page*

- *Who has authored the site? What qualifications does the author(s) have? Is the author a professional or an amateur? Does it matter?*
- *When was the information compiled and presented? Does the site show signs of ongoing revision or updating?*
- *What appears to be the purpose of the site? For whom is the site presented? Is it appropriate or useful for your purposes?*
- *How is the material presented? Is it reasonable and balanced or simplistic or inflammatory?*
- *Is the site logically organized, and is it well-written? (Web sites with obvious grammatical and spelling errors should be avoided as research sources!)*
- *Are there hyperlinks to other sites? What do these other sites reveal about the reliability, accuracy, and purpose of the original site? (For example, a site on the causes of World War I that provides links to commercial sites for memorabilia or travel to battlefields might be less than accurate in an academic sense.)*

Citing Sources

One of the final but most challenging and important parts of the independent research task is the correct listing of your sources.

Tips for Citing Sources

- *Record your sources properly as early as possible in your research. This will reduce confusion and error as you rush to complete your work.*
- *Always check the assignment description and with your instructor to learn the details of the style to be employed. Variations do exist, and individual teachers or institutions sometimes have their own particular approach.*

MLA and APA Styles

The two main styles of documenting sources are the **MLA** (Modern Language Association) and the **APA** (American Psychological Association).

For a detailed analysis of these two approaches, you might consider the following references:

Books

Publication Manual of the American Psychological Association, 4th ed. (Washington, DC: APA 1994).

MLA Handbook for Writers of Research Papers, 5th ed. (New York: Modern Language Association, 1999).

Web Sites

For further information about the APA style, visit:
www.wisc.edu/writing/Handbook/ DocAPA.html

For further information about the MLA style, visit:
www.english.uiuc.edu/cws/wworkshop/ mlamenu.htm

Here is a brief summary of the MLA and APA referencing styles for major categories of sources that you are likely encounter in your work.

Reference Source	MLA	APA
In-text Citation	Author's surname and page number in parentheses at the end of the sentence, e.g., (Smith 24)	Author's surname, year of publication, page number in parentheses at the end of the sentence, e.g., (Smith 2001, p. 24)
Bibliography	"Works Cited"	"References"
Books	Bliss, Michael. *Confederation: A New Nationality*. Toronto: Grolier 1981.	Bliss, Michael. (1981) *Confederation: A New Nationality*. Toronto: Grolier.
Newspapers	Walkom, T. "Conflict at the Core." *The Toronto Star* 13 January 2001: B1, B4.	Walkom, T. (2001, January 13) Conflict at the Core. *The Toronto Star*, pp. B1, B4.
Audiovisual Material	*Water: A Precious Resource*. Videocassette. Washington: *National Geographic*. 23 min. 1980.	*Water: A Precious Resource*. 1980. Videocassette. Washington: *National Geographic*. 23 min.

Reference Source	MLA	APA
Electronic Sources —CD ROM	*Myst*. CD-ROM. Novato: CA: Cyan Inc. and Broderbund Software, 1993.	*Myst*. 1993 (CD-ROM) Novato: CA: Cyan Inc. and Broderbund Software.
Government Publication	Canada. Ministry of Industry, Trade and Technology. *Canada Yearbook*. Ottawa: Statistics Canada. 1991.	Canada. Ministry of Industry, Trade and Technology. 1991. *Canada Yearbook*. Ottawa: Statistics Canada.
Interview	Macdonald, John, Personal Interview. 1 July 2001	Macdonald, John, 2001. Personal Interview. 1 July.
Internet	Ivarone, Mike. *Armory: Gas Warfare*. Home Page. Updated 12 Nov. 1999. 31 Nov. 1999. ‹www.worldwar1.com/arm006.htm›	Ivarone, Mike. *Armory: Gas Warfare*. Home Page. Updated 12 Nov. 1999. 31 Nov. 1999. ‹www.worldwar1.com/arm006.htm›
Periodical or Magazine	Fulford, Victoria. "Time to Remember" *Legion Magazine* Vol. 76, Number 1 Jan./Feb. 2001: 10–12.	Fulford, Victoria. 2001 "Time to Remember" *Legion Magazine* Vol. 76, Number 1 Jan./Feb.: 10–12.
Encyclopedia	Berton, Pierre. "Heritage Canada Foundation" in *The Canadian Encyclopedia*. Edmonton: Hurtig Publishers. 1988	Berton, Pierre. 1988 "Heritage Canada Foundation" in *The Canadian Encyclopedia* Edmonton: Hurtig Publishers.
Film	Zemeckis, Robert, dir. *Forrest Gump*. Perf. Tom Hanks, Sally Fields, Robin Wright. Paramount, 1994.	Zemeckis, Robert. (Director) 1994. *Forrest Gump*. [Film]. Hollywood, CA: Paramount Pictures.

Checklist

Research Strategies and Sources	
I prepare, review, and follow through on an intelligent research strategy.	❑
I am committed to using a variety of excellent sources in my research.	❑
I employ good human resources on a regular basis in my research.	❑
I find and employ many school-based resources.	❑
I find and employ community-based resources.	❑
I use multimedia resources in my research.	❑

Research Strategies and Sources

- I practise active listening skills. ☐
- I know how to prepare and carry out a successful interview. ☐
- I am able to design, employ, and analyze a survey. ☐
- I know how to conduct an effective Internet search. ☐
- I have a procedure for careful evaluation and validation of my research sources. ☐
- I have a strategy for detecting bias. ☐
- I have accurately cited all my sources. ☐

Academic Ethics and Values

Fundamental honesty plays a central role in academic endeavours. **Academic ethics** is a set of moral principles that guide and inspire student work. There are three major areas where these ethical issues come into focus.

Plagiarism

Although plagiarism comes in many forms, it is essentially an academic crime that results in penalties. It is an offence to teacher-instructors, employers, readers, and yourself.

Here are two definitions:

> take and use (the thoughts, writings, inventions etc. of another person) as one's own
>
> *The Canadian Oxford Dictionary*
>
> Failing to cite a source, either intentionally or unintentionally, is called plagiarism. It is a form of stealing because it involves pretending that another person's work is your own.
>
> Michael L. Keene and Katherine H. Adams, *The Easy Access Handbook*

INTENTIONAL AND UNINTENTIONAL PLAGIARISM

Plagiarism can be either intentional and unintentional, but both are wrong and both will result in sanctions and punishments.

Intentional plagiarism is the deliberate and dishonest use of another's work. It is academic theft and is judged harshly. In a society that prizes itself on individual effort, fair play, and openness, plagiarism is a serious moral, academic, and legal issue.

Plagiarism is more often **unintentional** than intentional. However, this is still regarded as a serious error. So it's critical for researchers to fully understand the nature of the problem and be constantly on guard against its practice. For example, if you forget that a sequence of words came from another source and claim them as your own, that is still plagiarism. It's also plagiarism if you use a source's line of argument or reasoning without any recognition of its origin—even if not one line of text was directly copied.

Review the following examples and determine whether you believe an act of plagiarism has taken place. If plagiarism has occurred, how would you handle the issue, and why?

> John and Varsha wanted to write several poems for a Senior English anthology but were running out of ideas and time. They found some poems in an old book in John's attic and decided to use two of the poems. They did change the titles.
>
> Mikhael was not a strong student. He was still learning the English language after living in Canada for three years. He had little or no experience in doing research. When researching his essay on Nuclear Fission, he pasted together ideas from two major sources but added his own opinions at the beginning and end of the research paper.
>
> Selma was an "A" student who had strong writing and research skills. She always read widely and made careful notes while completing major assignments. She was very impressed with one difficult book that she read on the background causes of World War I. As she wrote her essay, she followed the general thinking and unique line of argument in this source. However, all direct quotes were noted and correctly cited.
>
> James had to write a script for a movie in his Media Arts course. He wrote an excellent screenplay that was accidentally based on a movie he had seen ten years before and had forgotten. The instructor, however, had seen and remembered the film.

THE PENALTIES FOR PLAGIARISM

- receiving zero on an assignment
- automatic failure in a course
- suspension or expulsion from an educational institution
- dismissal from the workplace
- public exposure and ridicule
- proceedings in court with the threat of financial penalties or even imprisonment

COPYRIGHT

Passing off copyrighted material as your own is not only a serious moral and academic issue, but a legal issue as well. Copyright laws exist to protect the moral, legal, and economic rights of creators.

The general rule is that copyrighted material is protected for fifty years. Creators and their lawyers have been increasingly zealous in protecting intellectual property. There have been several high-profile cases involving authors, scriptwriters, computer program designers, and reporters that have been settled at great cost and humiliation in courtrooms around the globe. For material taken from the Internet, it is best to assume that it has been copyrighted.

Strategies for Avoiding Plagiarism

- *Always record all your sources when making notes.*
- *Document direct quotations, original ideas, or unique lines of thought, arguments, maps, charts, statistics, pictures, diagrams, etc., as well as information that is not widely known in the subject field.*
- *As much as possible, make notes using your own words. This reduces the chance of copying, enlarges your vocabulary, and ensures deeper comprehension of what you are reading.*
- *Research widely. Never rely on only a few sources.*
- *When in doubt, offer a reference. It's better to cite too much than not enough.*
- *When making notes, use quotation marks and indents and carefully note the exact wording. Some researchers write direct quotations in another colour pen or different font if using a computer.*
- *When following someone's arguments or line of thinking, indicate this clearly in the text, for example, "According to Lu Wen ..." or "as Nicola Smith has so aptly stated ..."*

Group Work: Rights and Responsibilities

We are often thrust into situations where we have to work efficiently and productively with a diverse group of people on a multifaceted project. Collaboration and cooperation are increasingly seen as significant life skills.

The task for group members is to overcome differences and turn diversity into a strength. In other words, to build bridges, not walls. To help you accomplish this, each group member has basic rights and responsibilities:

RIGHTS OF EACH GROUP MEMBER

- to be heard/listened to
- to be valued
- to be respected and appreciated
- to be free to present your own opinion
- to be free from putdown or harassment

RESPONSIBILITIES OF EACH GROUP MEMBER

- to do your own fair share
- to work to your strengths
- to contribute to group success
- to be supportive and enhancing
- to offer honesty of effort
- to complete reasonable tasks on time

ROLES OF GROUP MEMBERS

Group dynamics refers to the way members of a group interact and the kind of roles they play in the functioning of the group.

Review the following role descriptions. Which ones are positive for group dynamics, and which are negative? Which roles have you played?

Role	Description
Recorder	Keeps a record of the group's ideas, decisions, plans.
Clown	Makes jokes, fools around, claims it's important to stay loose and not be uptight.
Blocker	Continually raises objections. May be argumentative. May have good ideas and believes it is important to debate.
Encourager	Is supportive of all. Remains positive during difficult moments and respects and rewards all group members.
Presenter	Enjoys the task of being spokesperson. Prepared to represent the group's work in a public forum.
Sparkplug	Full of energy. Generates a range of ideas of varying quality. Never stumped.
Materials Manager	Reliable and organized. Finds and safeguards group papers, disks, etc.

Role	Description
Chairperson	Manages meetings. Keeps group moving forward and on task. Arbitrates disagreements.
Ghost	Makes few contributions. Uninterested. Often absent.
Worker	Quietly cooperative. Responsible, supportive, reliable member of group.

STRATEGIES FOR GROUP SUCCESS

The central issues to be resolved in collective work experiences are the pressure of tight timelines and the division of labour. These demands may sometimes pose a significant challenge!

Tips for Effective Group Work

- *Work hard, consistently, and responsibly.*
- *Be an active listener.*
- *Be invitational, not confrontational.*
- *Respect the opinions, experiences, and skills of others.*
- *Identify weaknesses, but focus on individual and group strengths.*
- *Be organized—develop a strategic plan early.*
- *Divide the work; share and consult.*
- *Evaluate your effort honestly and try to upgrade your performance.*

Checklist

Academic Ethics	
Academic honesty is important to me.	❑
I fully understand the term plagiarism.	❑
I know my school's policy and penalties for plagiarism.	❑
I understand and respect copyright.	❑
I have strategies to help me avoid plagiarism.	❑
I play a useful and helpful role in group situations.	❑

CHAPTER 10

history of the english language

> We are walking lexicons. In a single sentence of idle chatter we preserve Latin, Anglo-Saxon, Norse; we carry a museum inside our heads, each day we commemorate peoples of whom we have never heard.
>
> *Penelope Lively*

> English is the great vacuum cleaner of languages: it sucks in anything it can get.
>
> *David Crystal*

What is language? The word *language* is derived from the Latin word *lingua*, meaning "tongue." So **language** can be simply defined as a system of sounds. In more developed languages, of course, it also includes written symbols. Language, most broadly defined, is what we use to communicate with one another. And as its history proves—and as you've probably experienced in your own lifetime—language is never static.

LEARNING GOALS

- understand the major steps in the development of the English language
- appreciate the influence of other languages on English
- gain awareness of how power plays a role in the development of languages
- understand how the English language has spread across the globe

CONTENTS

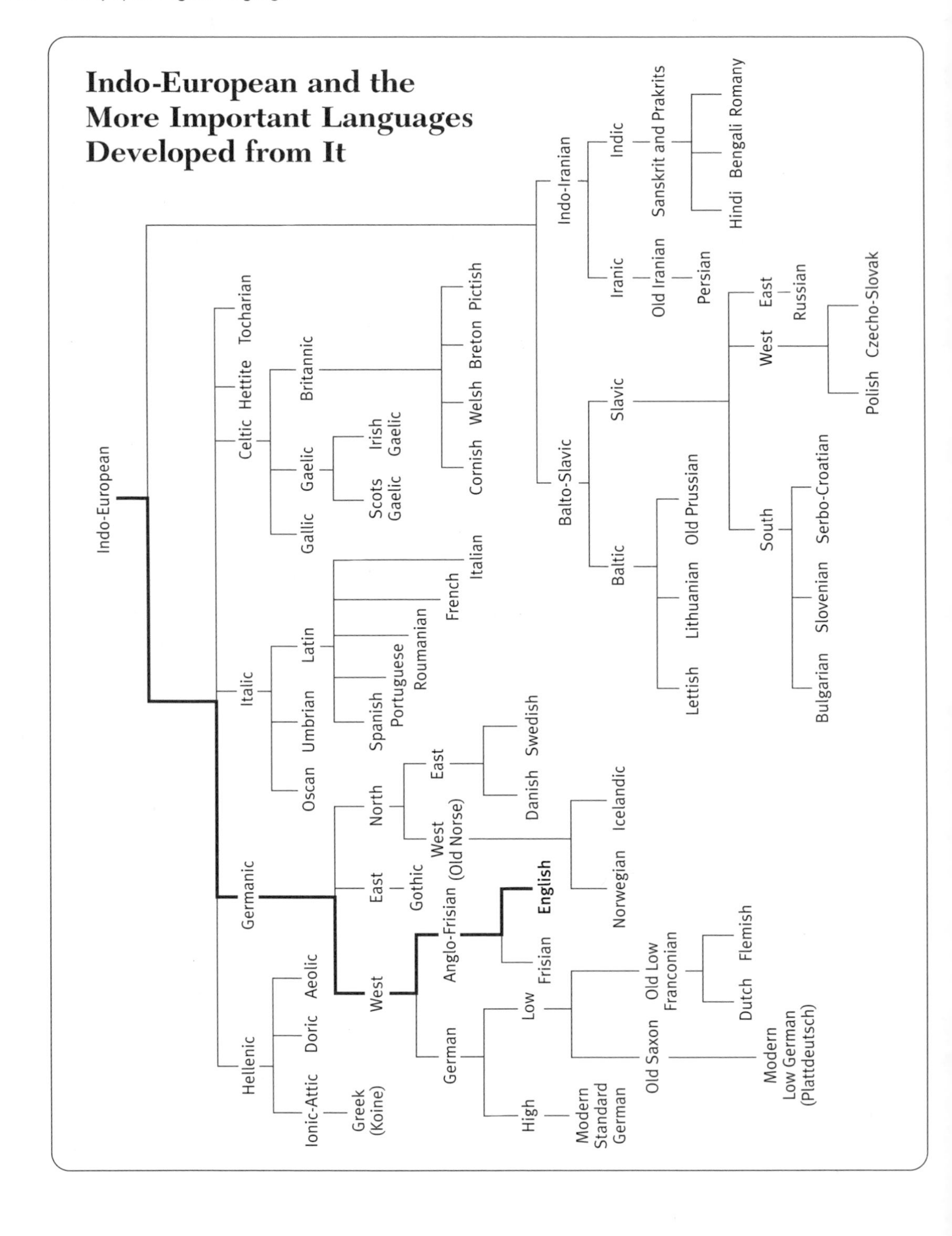
Indo-European and the More Important Languages Developed from It
Indo-European
Indo-Iranian
Indic
Sanskrit and Prakrits
Hindi
Bengali
Romany
Iranic
Old Iranian
Persian
Balto-Slavic
Slavic
East
Russian
West
Polish
Czecho-Slovak
South
Bulgarian
Slovenian
Serbo-Croatian
Baltic
Lettish
Lithuanian
Old Prussian
Tocharian
Hettite
Celtic
Gallic
Gaelic
Scots Gaelic
Irish Gaelic
Britannic
Cornish
Welsh
Breton
Pictish
Italic
Oscan
Umbrian
Latin
Spanish
Portuguese
Roumanian
French
Italian
Germanic
East
Gothic
North
East
Danish
Swedish
West (Old Norse)
Norwegian
Icelandic
West
Anglo-Frisian
English
Frisian
German
Low
Old Saxon
Modern Low German (Plattdeutsch)
Old Low Franconian
Dutch
Flemish
High
Modern Standard German
Hellenic
Ionic-Attic
Greek (Koine)
Doric
Aeolic

The following list is just a sampling of how new words have entered the English language:

Word Source	Examples
French	*theatre, hors d'oeuvre*
space exploration	*satellite dish*
scientific research	*ozone*
medical discoveries	*genome, cloning*
slang	*rip-off*
international politics	*glasnost, apartheid*

Where Did Language Originate?

One of the largest early language families is known as the **Indo-European**. This group of languages was never written or recorded. It was spoken 5000 years ago by tribes that wandered through areas stretching from Europe to India. For various reasons, groups of these tribes left the original body and migrated to other parts of the world. Over the years these wandering groups became increasingly isolated from the original group. As a result, their language slowly changed into different dialects.

A **dialect** describes the regional differences of a language. These differences may be in pronunciation (stress and intonation), grammar, words and expressions, or the meanings of words and expressions. When these differences become distinct from the original language, a new language comes into being.

To get an idea of the interconnectedness of distinct languages, look at the following chart to see how the words *mother*, *nose*, and *three* exist in twenty-nine different languages from the Indo-European family and fourteen different languages from other families.

Indo-European Language	mother	nose	three
Bengali	mata	nak	teen
Czech	matka	nos	tři
Danish	moder	naese	tre
Dutch	moeder	neus	drie
French	mère	nez	trois
Gaelic (Scots)	màthair	sròn	tri

Indo-European Language	mother	nose	three
German	Mutter	Nase	drei
Greek	mitera	miti	tria
Gujarati	baa	nak	tran
Hindi	mata	nasika	teen
Icelandic	móthir	nef	thrir
Irish	máthair	srón	trí
Italian	madre	naso	tre
Latin	mater	nasus	tres
Lithuanian	motina	nosis	trys
Norwegian	mor	nese	tre
Punjabi	ma	nak	tin
Persian (Farsi)	mādar	bini	se
Polish	matka	nos	trzy
Portuguese	mãe	nariz	tres
Romanian	mamă	nas	trei
Russian	mat'	nos	tri
Sanskrit	mātā	nāsā	trayas
Spanish	madre	nariz	tres
Swedish	moder	nasa	tre
Urdu	ma	naak	teen
Welsh	mam	trwyn	tri
Yiddish	muter	nos	drai

Other Language Families	mother	nose	three
Arabic	'umm	anf	thalatha
Basque	ama	südür	hirur
Chinese	muchin	bizi	san
Finnish	äiti	nena	kolme
Hausa	uwā	hanci	uku
Hungarian	anya	orr	harom
Indonesian	ibu	hidung	tiga
Japanese	haha	hana	mittsu

Other Language Families	mother	nose	three
Somali	hooyyo	sān	sadde
Swahili	mama	pua	tatu
Turkish	anne	burun	üç
Twi	mame	hwen	miensa
Vietnamese	mẹ	mũi	ba
Yoruba	ìyá	imun	mẹ́tà

Where Did English Begin?

The original Indo-European language speakers, who lived mostly in northern Germany and the Scandinavian countries, spoke **Germanic**. Several dialects developed from the original Germanic, one of which evolved into English.

Major Stages in the Development of the English Language

OLD ENGLISH: 450–1100

Before the first century B.C.E. England was inhabited by the **Celts**. (Only a few words survive in English from Celtic origins, and they are mostly place names, e.g., Kent and Cumberland, and the Thames river.) Julius Caesar invaded part of England in about 55 B.C.E. A hundred years later the Romans invaded again, and finally settled. Although they controlled Britain for almost four hundred years, the Romans never fully subjugated the Celts.

The most important historical event for the beginning of the English language came in the middle of the fifth century. That was when **Germanic** tribes—the Angles, Saxons, and Jutes—invaded Britain and drove the Celts into Wales, Scotland, and Ireland. England, in fact, derives its name from the Angles. The land and its people were originally called Angelcynn (*Angle-kin* or "race of the Angles"), which eventually became Englaland ("land of the Angles"). Many of our everyday words, such as *house, woman, man, farm,* and *love*, come to us from this period.

The eventual blend of dialects that resulted from the Germanic invasions is called **Anglo-Saxon** or **Old English**. Although Old English is the ancestor of modern English, to the modern reader it appears as unfamiliar as a foreign language! In fact, only about one-fifth of the modern English vocabulary is derived from Old English. And not only was the vocabulary different, but so was the grammar, spelling, and pronunciation.

Here's an example: In modern English we show relations between words in a sentence by using prepositions (*of, to, for*) in front of nouns, and auxiliaries (*will, have, had*) in front of verbs. But in Old English, the functions of words were indicated by *changing the words themselves*.

Read the following rules for reading Old English:

1. The sound that modern English represents with the letters "th" (as in *thin*) was represented in Old English by two letters: þ and ð. Thus, the word for *with* is **wiþ** and the word for *then* is **ða**.
2. The sound that modern English represents with "a," as in *hat* or *mat*, was represented in Old English by the character æ. Thus, the word for *bath* is bæð.
3. A long vowel was indicated by a mark over the letter, as in **ūre**.
4. The modern English sound of "sh" was represented in Old English by the letters **sc**, as in **sceāp**.
5. The Modern English "k" sound was represented by **c**, as in **cynn** (*kin*) or **nacod** (*naked*).

Now try pronouncing the following words. What are their equivalents in modern English? Check your answers in a dictionary that shows word origins.

þaet	(that)
þorn	(thorn)
bæc	(back)
scip	(ship)
folc	(folk)
helpan	(help)

Try pronouncing each of the following words. What does each one mean?

mann	hearpe
wīf	hæt
cild	gyrdel
hūs	glof
mete	etan
lēaf	drincan
horn	slāepan

The development of English was also influenced by the **Latin** and **Scandinavian** languages. Beginning with the arrival of St. Augustine and his monks in 597, Latin words were introduced into the language as monks converted England to Christianity. Not surprisingly, these Latin words were associated with religion, and include *bishop*, *candle*, *angel*, and *wine*.

Many Latin prefixes and suffixes were also introduced into English. Here is a sample:

Latin Prefix	Meaning	Example	Definition
ante	before	antecedent	going before
de	from, down	depose	put down
extra	beyond	extraordinary	beyond ordinary
in	in, into, not	insane	not sane
per	through, thoroughly	perfect	thoroughly made
re	back, again	reconsider	consider again
trans	across, beyond	transgress	step beyond
Latin Suffix			
able, ible	capable of being	portable, credible	
ant, ent, er, or, ian	one who, or pertaining to	servant, president, waiter, navigator, custodian, librarian	
ion, tion, ation, ment	action, state of, or result	opinion, direction, conversation, embarrassment	
ous, y	full of	precipitous, miscellaneous, bounteous, bushy, husky	
Latin Verb Root			
capio, capitum	take, seize, hold	captive	one taken
fluo, fluxum	flow	fluent	flowing
jungo, junctum	join	junction	a joining
pello, pulsum	drive, urge	expel	drive out
scribo, scriptum	write	scribe	a writer
venio, ventum	come	convene	come together

In the eighth and ninth centuries, the **Vikings** invaded Britain. (Danish kings even held the British throne for twenty-five years.) As the Vikings (who spoke Old Norse) intermarried with the Anglo-Saxons, they eventually adopted the language of their new home. In the process they introduced words from Old Norse such as *sky, egg, cake, leg, get, give,* and *die*.

Although Old English was mainly a spoken language, it had a highly developed poetry and prose. You may have heard the name *Beowulf*—and you may have thought this was some long-ago writer. Actually, *Beowulf* is the earliest and one of the greatest English epic poems. It was written around the beginning of the eighth century by an unknown poet. And because the exploits of its hero, Beowulf, take place in Scandinavia, the poem reflects the customs and traditions of these early ancestors.

Here's another interesting fact: Anglo-Saxon or Old English poetry had several distinct characteristics, including the use of kennings. **Kennings** are metaphors created by hyphenating two existing words to create a third word with a new meaning. Because the Anglo-Saxons didn't have the number of words we do now, they had to make use of the ones they had by combining them in new ways (*whale-road*, meaning "sea," is one lovely example).

MIDDLE ENGLISH: 1100–1450

Although there isn't a clear dividing line between Old and Middle English, by the medieval period the language had become much more similar to what it is today. In 1066 England was successfully invaded by William the Conqueror from Normandy. This would prove to be the greatest historical influence on Middle English.

The **Normans**, who spoke French, brought many new words to enrich the English language. Unlike the Vikings, the Normans weren't assimilated. It might surprise you to learn that for two centuries French was the official language of England! But, although French became the language of the court and the upper classes, English was still spoken by the native population.

It's estimated that about 10 000 words were added to English by the Normans. Because the Normans were the ruling class, many of the words they introduced (for example, *castle*, *prison*, and *court*) reflect their position of power. Another interesting result of the Norman influence is that, in the English we speak today, a word of Anglo-Saxon origin and one of French origin will frequently exist for the same thing.

The following chart gives you a taste of this phenomenon.

Old English (Anglo-Saxon) Origin	French Origin
smell	*odour*
ask	*request*
yearly	*annual*
freedom	*liberty*
might	*power*

English was reduced to being the language of the masses and Latin was the language of the Church. This is also why one-syllable words generally come from Old English and most words of more than one syllable come from French or Latin.

By the end of the fourteenth century, however, English was once again the official language of England. It was a much-changed language, as you can see from the following excerpt from the prologue to *The Canterbury Tales*, written by the great English poet Geoffrey Chaucer.

Of Engelond to Caunterbury they wende,
The hooly blisful martir for to seke,
That hem hath holpen whan that they were seeke.
Bilfil that in that seson on a day,
In Southwerk at the Tabard as I lay
Redy to wenden on my pilgrymage
To Caunterbury with ful devout corage,
At nyght was come into that hostelrye
Wel nyne and twenty in a compaignye,
Of sondry folk, by aventure yfalle
In felaweshipe, and pilgrimes were they alle,
That toward Caunterbury wolden ryde.
The chambres and the stable weren wyde,
And wel we weren esed atte beste.

Notice some of the changes from Old English:

- Old English symbols, such as the letter ð, are gone.
- The alphabet looks a great deal more like the modern one.
- Endings (e.g., -en) that showed word relationships have disappeared.
- The word order is much like that of modern English.
- There is evidence of words of French origin.

MODERN ENGLISH: 1450 TO THE PRESENT

In the fifteenth century Johannes Gutenberg invented the movable-type printing press in Germany. The printing press was only fifty years old when, in 1476, William Caxton printed the first books in England. Over the course of fourteen years he printed more than seventy books, including Malory's *Morte d'Arthur* and Chaucer's *The Canterbury Tales*.

Why is this important? It was Caxton who first began to standardize spelling and syntax (word order and arrangement). There were many dialects of Anglo-Saxon, but because Caxton printed in the East Midlands dialect, it became the dominant one—and ultimately became known as Standard English.

Until this time books were rare, and education was limited to the privileged elite. But the advent of the printing press made reading materials cheap and accessible. Mass publishing meant a wider access to the printed word, and made it possible for widespread literacy. This meant the beginning of a popular literature in English.

With the ascendance of Henry Tudor (Henry VIII) to the British throne, the modern age began. The Tudors, and particularly Elizabeth I, launched England's first explorations and began its empire-building. And as its empire spread, so did its language.

The Influence of Other Languages on English

The history of any language is also a history of the political and economic might of its speakers. Not only did the English language begin to dominate other lands, but it was also affected by them. Words were added to English as a result of trade, exploration, and colonization of other parts of the world.

This chart lists some examples of how other languages have left their imprint on the English vocabulary:

Word	Language	How It Came into English
tea	Chinese	from trade with China
bungalow, cot	Hindi	from the time Britain ruled India
tomato, chocolate	Nahuatl (a Mexican language)	these foods were introduced to Europe by the Spanish, who had colonized Central and South America
hurricane	Carib	from the time Britain colonized the Caribbean

Today you need look no further than your own computer screen for evidence of English as the language of economics and power. For the computer software industry depends on the fact that, today, English is indeed the international language of communication.

The Remarkable Spread of English

By the end of the seventeenth century, there were an estimated five to seven million English-language speakers—almost all of them living in the British Isles. More than three hundred years later, at the beginning of Elizabeth II's reign in 1952, this figure increased to about 250 million—the vast majority living outside the British Isles.

What follows is region-by-region account of just how this astounding spread of the English language came about.

THE UNITED STATES

There were three waves of settlement from different parts of England to the United States:

- The first expedition came to Roanoke Island in 1584.
- The first permanent English settlers came in 1607 and settled in Virginia (named after Elizabeth I, the Virgin Queen).

- The *Mayflower* brought the next wave of English settlers to Plymouth, Massachusetts, in 1620.

Settlers to these areas came from different parts of England with different ways of speaking. The New England settlers moved north; the Roanoke moved into the midlands; and the Virginian settlers moved south. And as each group migrated across America, their dialects were retained.

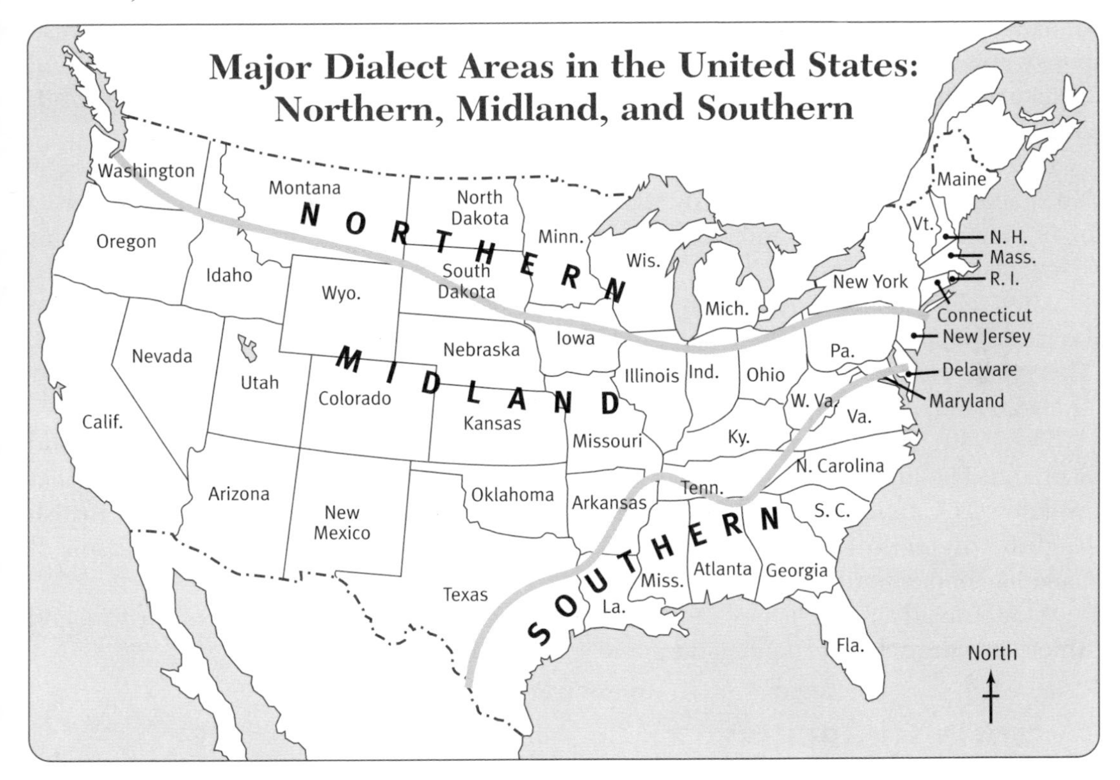

The seventeenth century brought immigrants from a variety of areas, and so the sharp regional divisions began to blur. The eighteenth century saw a vast immigration from Northern Ireland and from the Scots-Irish. The merging of these accents with the existing dialects forms the speech of the "Sunbelt" (from Virginia to California), and is the accent most recognized as American. Other influences came from the Spanish, the French, the Dutch, and the black southern population brought from Africa as slaves.

Massive immigration from Europe occurred in the nineteenth and twentieth centuries. In 1900 the population of the United States was 75 million, and just fifty years later it had *doubled*. Much of this increase was due to immigration from non–English-speaking countries. In order to survive in this new country, immigrants learned English, which, of course, meant a stupendous growth in the use of the language.

CANADA

The fact that Canada has two official languages, English and French, makes it unique. These two languages of course reflect the fact that Canada was settled by both the French and the English.

John Cabot first arrived in Newfoundland in 1497 and was followed by British settlers attracted by farming, fishing, and fur-trading. In 1520 Jacques Cartier began to explore Canada for France, and was followed by French settlers. When Canada became a British possession in 1763 it had almost no English-speaking settlers. The foundation of Canadian English lies in the North American English spoken by the settlers of the 1780s and 1790s.

In the 1780s thousands of French settlers were deported from Acadia (now known as Nova Scotia) and were replaced by settlers from New England. There were many waves of immigrants from England, Ireland, and Scotland. *Nova Scotia*, for example, means "New Scotland" in French.

After 1776 and the American Declaration of Independence, the United Empire Loyalists, supporters of Britain, fled the United States to Nova Scotia and New Brunswick. This group was followed by the so-called "late Loyalists," who were attracted by the offer of cheap land, especially in Upper Canada, which would become known as Ontario.

The 1830s and 1840s brought huge waves of immigrants from England, Ireland, and Scotland. The influxes from the United States were the ones that began to establish what we know as **Canadian English**, which has similarities with both American and British English. (Refer to the Business and Technical Writing chapter for a comparison of Canadian and American spelling conventions.)

What Canadian English is most distinctively known for is the mix of British and American vocabulary, pronunciation, and spelling.

CANADIAN VOCABULARY

As J.K. Chambers notes in *The Canadian Oxford Dictionary:*

> Even before Canada had a significant and widespread population, many distinctive features of the Canadian vocabulary came into being. Explorers and adventurers learned the names of all the places they visited from the [Aboriginal] peoples, and in many cases the [Aboriginal] names stuck. Our place names resound with words from the [Aboriginal] language stocks, from Pugwash and Bouctouche to Wawa, Squamish, Nanaimo, and Tuktoyaktuk. Some places have more than one name because the indigenous name contended with the [British] imperial one: Toronto was called York after the [English] duke who was George III's second son, but in the end—since 1834—the Mohawk name prevailed.

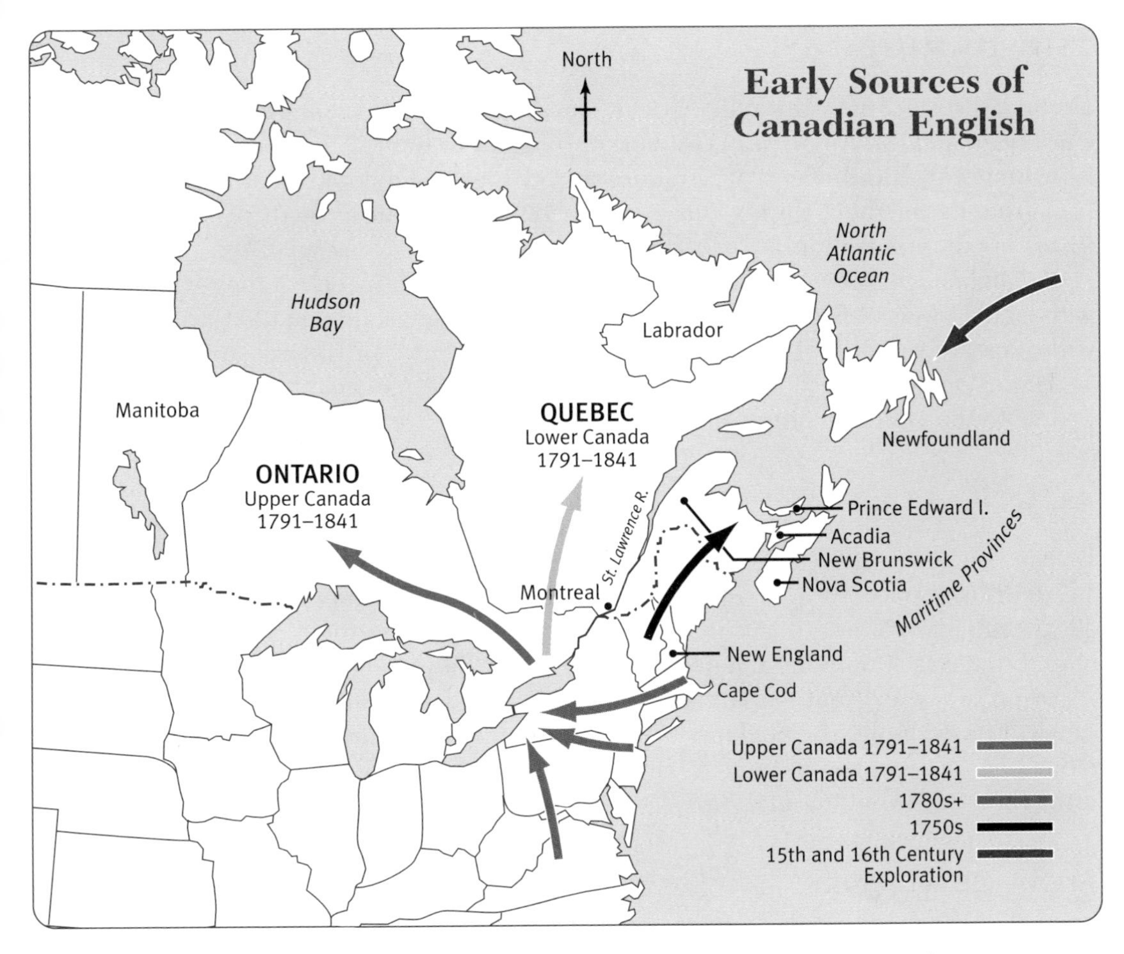

> Indigenous plants and animals usually kept their native names, such as *tobacco, tamarack, skunk, raccoon, moose*, and *caribou*.... [From the Aboriginal peoples], European adventurers learned to use foodstuffs such as *pemmican*, weapons such as *tomahawks*, watercraft such as *kayaks*, and apparel such as *anoraks, mukluks*, and *moccasins*. Because the first explorers were often francophones, a number of French terms attached themselves permanently to forest and plain: *prairie, portage, bateau, snye*.

Today's multicultural Canada demands a broadening vocabulary. Most often we take the foreign words and adjust them to suit our sound system. Sometimes we change the function of words from other languages. For example, *teriyaki* is an adjective we use to modify nouns such as steak or chicken; *cappuccino* is pluralized as *cappuccinos*. By accommodating foreign words of all kinds, we are simply continuing an age-old tendency.

THE CARIBBEAN

From 1517 on, Spain brought African slaves to work on plantations in the western Caribbean and the American West Coast. In order to limit communication (and therefore limit rebellion), the slave-traders mixed together people of different language backgrounds on their ships. This practice resulted in the growth of several **pidgin** forms of communication.

Pidgin became known as **Creole**, the first Black English speech of the region. It mixed with creole forms of French, Spanish, and Portuguese developing in the Caribbean, along with standard varieties of English, to create a diverse range of English speech.

These West Indian speech varieties spread with the movement of large numbers of people to the United States, Canada, and England.

AUSTRALIA

Britain began to explore the Southern Hemisphere at end of the eighteenth century. In 1770, British explorer Captain James Cook established the first penal colony in Sydney to alleviate the overcrowded jails in England. The first "free" settlers arrived shortly thereafter, but it wasn't until the nineteenth century that they would arrive in large numbers.

Some of the distinct Australian speech characteristics originated with these prisoners. For example, the cockney twang originates from the many convicts who came from London; and the brogue "r" originates from the Irish prisoners who were jailed after the Irish rebellion of 1798.

NEW ZEALAND

Captain Cook and the European whalers arrived in New Zealand in the 1770s, and by 1840 New Zealand was a British colony. New Zealand English features these linguistic traits:

- a stronger British accent than Australians (since the people have generally felt a closer relationship with Britain and its values)
- a distinctive New Zealand vocabulary (to support a growing national identity distinct from Australia)
- an increased number of Maori words and expressions in English (resulting from the desire to take account of New Zealand's aboriginal people). For example, *mana* means personal power and influence and is more substantive than *charisma*; *kaupapa* means the way things are conducted, as in the *kaupapa* of a meeting.

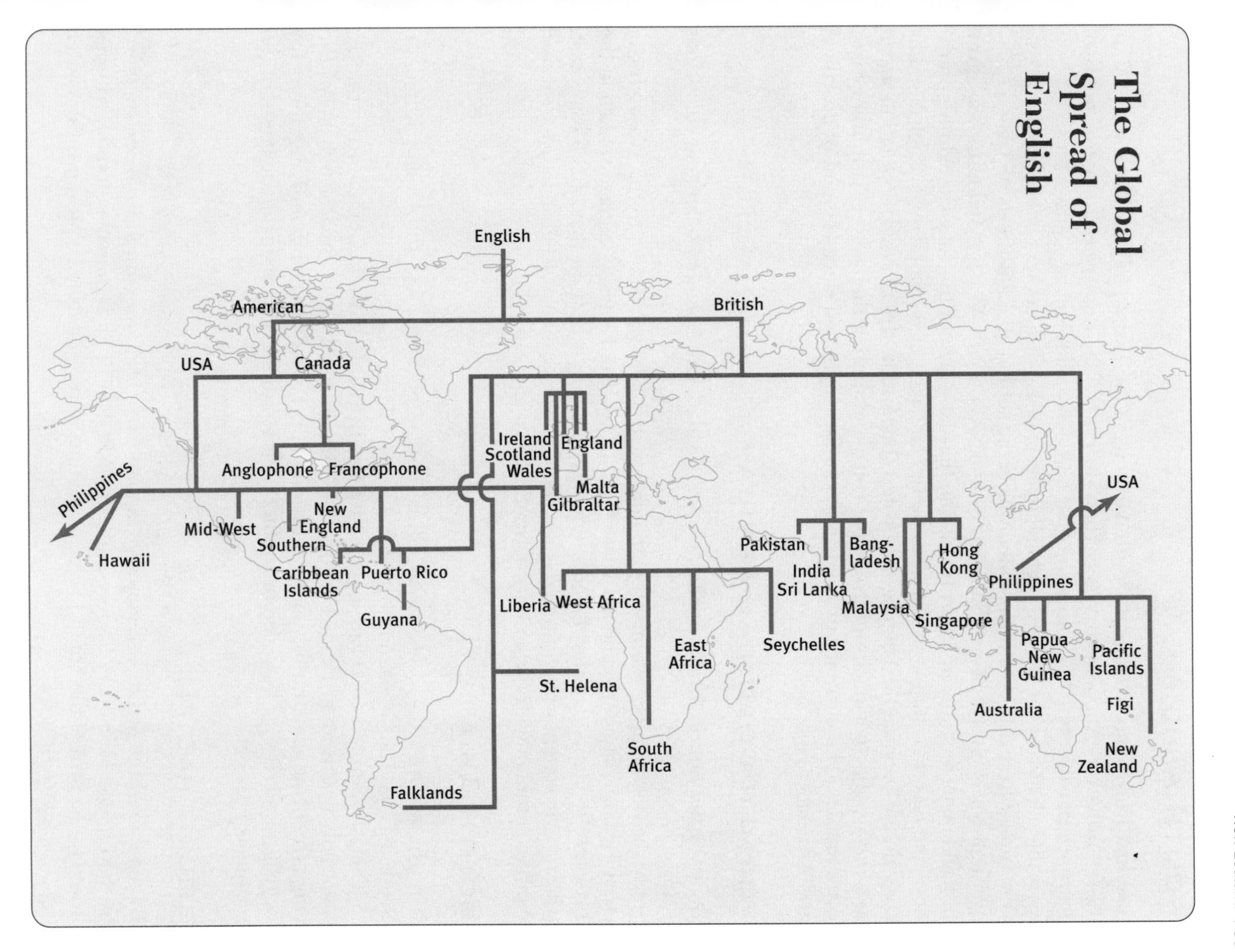
The Global Spread of English
English
American
British
USA
Canada
Anglophone
Francophone
Ireland
Scotland
Wales
England
Malta
Gibraltar
Philippines
Hawaii
Mid-West
New England
Southern
Caribbean Islands
Puerto Rico
Guyana
Liberia
West Africa
St. Helena
Falklands
East Africa
South Africa
Seychelles
Pakistan
India
Sri Lanka
Bang-ladesh
Malaysia
Singapore
Hong Kong
Philippines
USA
Papua New Guinea
Australia
Pacific Islands
Figi
New Zealand

SOUTH AFRICA

The first Europeans to come to South Africa were the Dutch, followed by the British in 1795 during the Napoleonic Wars. Then, in the 1870s, there was a massive influx of Europeans, who came to explore the gold and diamond mines of South Africa.

Although at first there were regional dialects of English, an accent emerged that was very similar to that of Australia, which was being settled at about the same time.

English has always been a minority language in South Africa. **Afrikaans** was given official language status in 1925. It was the first language of the majority white population, and was therefore considered to be the language of the oppressor. English, oddly enough, has become the language of protest: the South African black population sees it as a means of achieving an international voice and uniting themselves with other black communities. The currency of English has in fact increased since the end of apartheid and Afrikaaner rule.

FORMER COLONIAL AFRICA

By 1914 the entire African continent was divided into colonies belonging to various European countries.

By the beginning of the nineteenth century, England was drawn to the West African coast for both commerce and anti-slavery activities. The English language spoken in the British settlements that developed there was very different from that of the east coast, whose environment was less suited to settlement. The east coast English had a great deal more in common with the accents of South Africa and Australia.

SOUTH ASIA

It might surprise you to learn that, after the United States and the United Kingdom, South Asia has the largest number of English speakers.

That's because in 1600 Elizabeth I gave the British East India Company the trading monopoly in this area. From 1765 to 1947 Britain ruled India. Since English was the language of administration and education, it provided a strong unifying force for British power. It was, however, in conflict with Hindi and the regional languages of the conquered people.

SOUTH PACIFIC

By the end of the eighteenth century Captain Cook and other English sailors, followed by the London Missionary Society, had established an English presence in the territories in and to the west of the South Pacific. The Americans established a presence there after the Spanish-American War. After World War II, several islands formerly owned by Japan were won by the United States. As a result of these developments, English has had a strong presence in the South Pacific for two centuries.

SOUTHEAST ASIA

There is no single Southeast Asian English. As elsewhere, England established a strong presence in various protectorates and areas, such as Hong Kong, Singapore, Malaysia, and Papua, New Guinea. English became the language of education and advancement.

In Hong Kong, where Chinese and English have been the two official languages since coming under the control of Britain. Some other protectorates in this area are now administered by New Zealand or Australia for Britain.

REFERENCE SECTION

grammar, usage, and mechanics

This reference section has been designed to provide you with a practical and succinct guide to key areas of grammar, usage, and mechanics particularly relevant to senior students. As senior students, you will be familiar with the basics of grammar such as definitions of the parts of speech. If you need a quick review, you have the skills to find the information in other reference guides, including those you have used in previous years. This section therefore focuses primarily on areas that will help you improve your writing, editing, spelling, and vocabulary development skills at the senior level. It is meant to supplement the Grammar, Usage, and Mechanics sections that are integrated into the previous chapters.

This section also includes a glossary. Terms related to language, literature, critical thinking, logic, and media are defined with examples. The glossary does not include all terms already defined within previous chapters. It is meant as a supplement. You may find the definitions of terms commonly used in essay and exam questions particularly helpful, for example.

Two appendices focus on areas of media and technology. Appendix A is a how-to guide to hyperlinking in word-processing programs. This is a practical skill you can apply in many forms of your writing. Appendix B provides an overview of the film and video production process, along with a list of careers in media.

LEARNING GOALS

- troubleshoot common usage problems to improve writing
- apply conventions of common usage
- recognize and apply spelling rules and strategies
- develop and apply vocabulary-building strategies
- use a glossary for definitions of specialized terms

CONTENTS

Grammar and Usage

NOTE: This section assumes that you have a working knowledge of the parts of speech and the correct use of punctuation. The terms and rules on the following pages highlight the grammatical and stylistic issues with which you are most likely concerned at the senior level.

Parts of a Sentence

Sentence – a group of words that expresses a complete thought and that contains a subject and predicate

Subject – who or what the sentence is about, consisting of at least one noun or pronoun and any modifiers

Predicate – the verb of the sentence, plus its objects, complements, and modifiers

Clause – a group of words that includes a subject and a predicate

A **main clause** is a group of words that makes sense as a sentence on its own. A **subordinate clause** contains a subject and predicate, but does not make sense on its own. It must be linked to a main clause. Subordinate clauses take the place of a part of speech, and therefore cannot function as a sentence.

MAIN CLAUSE: The dog bit me.

adjective clause

SUBORDINATE CLAUSE: The dog *that bit me* had white spots.

adverb clause

SUBORDINATE CLAUSE: The dog bit me *anywhere it could.*

noun clause

SUBORDINATE CLAUSE: The dog bit *anyone it could reach.*

Phrase – a group of words missing either a subject, a predicate, or both. By definition, a phrase cannot be a main clause. We identify a phrase by the most important word in it, though sometimes an entire phrase will function as a single unit.

NOUN PHRASE: the *Leaning Tower of Pisa*

PREPOSITIONAL PHRASE: *in the morning*

GERUND PHRASE: *playing the piano*

Sentence Structures

Simple Sentence – a sentence consisting of a single main clause with no subordinate clauses

Subject Predicate

EXAMPLE: I waited until the last possible moment before sounding the alarm.

Compound Sentence – a sentence consisting of two or more main clauses, with no subordinate clauses

Main clauses can be joined in the following ways:

- by a coordinating conjunction and a comma

main clause — conjunction — main clause

EXAMPLE: Our rabbit chewed the plywood to tiny chips, *but* her teeth kept growing.

- by a semicolon

main clause — semicolon — main clause

EXAMPLE: I felt sad when the couple broke up; the scene reminded me of my own break-up just a few weeks before.

- by a conjunctive adverb and a semicolon

main clause — semicolon — conjunctive adverb — main clause

EXAMPLE: Bill has come to class every day; *however*, I will not guarantee that he will pass.

Complex Sentence – a sentence consisting of a single main clause and one or more subordinate clauses

subordinate clause — comma — main clause

EXAMPLE: Although he had submitted the job application weeks ago, he had not yet received a reply.

Compound-Complex Sentence – a sentence consisting of two or more main clauses and one or more subordinate clauses

subordinate clause — comma — main clause

EXAMPLE: Even though Vern is my best friend, I can give you several examples of unfriendly

main clause (cont'd) — conjunction — main clause

behaviour on his part, *and* I can tell you a few stories in which I was unfair to him.

Sentence Types

Declarative Sentence – a sentence that makes a statement

EXAMPLE: Every Thursday, the newspaper arrives half an hour late.

Imperative Sentence – a sentence that gives a command

EXAMPLE: Pass your papers to the left. [The subject "you" is understood.]

Interrogative Sentence – a sentence that asks a question and ends with a question mark

EXAMPLE: What is the capital of Andorra?

Exclamatory Sentence – a sentence that expresses strong feeling and ends with an exclamation mark

EXAMPLE: That man stole my purse!

Loose Sentence – a sentence in which the subject and verb appear early in the sentence—contrasts with the periodic sentence

EXAMPLE: The party never formally ended, though eventually there were more people asleep than awake.

Periodic Sentence – a sentence in which the subject and verb are postponed until near the end of the sentence—contrasts with the loose sentence. Periodic sentences have the effect of creating suspense and provide variety in a piece of writing.

EXAMPLE: After rushing to catch the train and picking up the package at the station, Stephanie made it just in time for her appointment.

Voice in Sentences – A sentence in active voice has the performer of the action as the subject, while a sentence in passive voice has the receiver of the action as the subject. Writers and editors generally agree that most sentences should be written in active voice, and that passive voice should be restricted to occasional use, for effect. Note, however, that the passive voice is used extensively in reports.

EXAMPLE: A hurricane struck the town. [active voice]

EXAMPLE: The town was struck by a hurricane. [passive voice]

Crafting and Revising Sentences

As you write and revise your work, be aware of the following common sentence problems.

Comma Splice (also called Comma Fault) – a sentence in which two or more main clauses have been joined with a comma. A comma splice can be corrected by replacing the comma with a period and capitalizing the first word of the second clause, by replacing the comma with a semicolon, by placing a conjunction between the clauses, or by subordinating one of the clauses.

COMMA SPLICE: I waited for Juan to return, he never did.

REVISED: I waited for Juan to return. He never did. [period – capital]

REVISED: I waited for Juan to return; he never did. [semicolon]

REVISED: I waited for Juan to return, but he never did. [coordinating conjunction]

REVISED: Although I waited for Juan to return, he never did. [subordinate clause]

Faulty Parallelism – a sentence in which a list appears, but the items in the list do not appear in the same form

FAULTY PARALLELISM: He spends his weekends *working, gardening, and with his partner.*

REVISED: He spends his weekends working, gardening, and spending time with his partner.

FAULTY PARALLELISM: You can either *do research in the library* or *on the Internet*.

REVISED: You can do research either in the library or on the Internet.

Faulty Pronoun Reference – a sentence in which the antecedent of a pronoun is unclear or missing

MISSING ANTECEDENT: I often wonder if he is telling the truth, but *this* is not productive.

REVISED: I often wonder if he is telling the truth, but such thinking is not productive.

Incorrect Subordinate Clause – a sentence in which an adverb clause is substituted for a noun, a noun phrase, or a noun clause. This common error can most easily be avoided by not using phrases such as "is because," "is when," and "is where," or their past tense equivalents.

INCORRECT SUBORDINATE CLAUSE: The reason the tire was flat *was because* Lena had driven over a large spike.

REVISED: The tire was flat because Lena had driven over a large spike.

ERROR: An example of Rafael's sense of humour *is when* he announced he had been abducted by aliens.

REVISED: An example of Rafael's sense of humour is his announcement that he had been abducted by aliens.

Misused Conjunctive Adverbs – adverbs that relate main clauses to each other. Conjunctive adverbs are frequently used in formal writing, but they are often misused, since many of them can also function as regular adverbs. Some common conjunctive adverbs include:

accordingly, also, besides, certainly, consequently, finally, for example, furthermore, however, in addition, incidentally, indeed, in fact, instead, likewise, moreover, nevertheless, nonetheless, now, otherwise, similarly, then, therefore, undoubtedly

HOWEVER AS CONJUNCTIVE ADVERB: Jacob believes the driving age should be fourteen; however, his parents disagree.

HOWEVER AS ADVERB: However much Jacob pleads, his parents will not let him drive until he is sixteen.

Dangling Modifier – a sentence in which the word or phrase to be modified is unclear or missing

DANGLING MODIFIER: *Desperately hoping for sunshine*, the morning was rainy again.

REVISED: Though I was desperately hoping for sunshine, the morning was rainy again.

Misplaced Modifier – a sentence in which the relationship between the words is confused by the word order

MISPLACED MODIFIER: Maria hopes to go home for the holidays to visit her parents in her new car. [who is in the car—Maria or the parents?]

REVISED: Maria hopes to go home for the holidays in her new car to visit her parents.

Squinting Modifier – a sentence in which a modifier could be modifying either of two words or phrases

SQUINTING MODIFIER: Elaine's proposal of marriage *after careful consideration* was turned down by Marco. [either Elaine or Michael was considering]

REVISED: Marco turned down Elaine's carefully considered marriage proposal.

REVISED: After carefully considering Elaine's marriage proposal, Marco turned it down.

Run-on Sentence – a sentence containing two or more main clauses that would be more effective if the clauses were combined or made into separate sentences

RUN-ON SENTENCE: My brother barely arrived on time for his job interview he had missed the first bus he had to take, then he was so nervous he couldn't answer some of the questions.

REVISED: My brother barely arrived on time for his job interview because he had missed the first bus he had to take. As a result, he was so nervous he couldn't answer some of the questions.

Sentence Fragment – a phrase or clause lacking a subject, a predicate, or both

FRAGMENT: *Walking through the woods last December.*

REVISED: Walking through the woods last December, I was struck by the beauty around me.

FRAGMENT: He made three New Year's resolutions. *To work harder, get more sleep, and slow down.*

REVISED: He made three New Year's resolutions: to work harder, get more sleep, and slow down.

FRAGMENT: She had resigned herself to being late for the exam. *When the bus finally appeared down the road.*

REVISED: She had resigned herself to being late for the exam, when the bus finally appeared down the road.

Shift in Number – a sentence that introduces a singular noun, then shifts to the plural, or vice versa

SHIFT IN NUMBER: I would like a subscription to this *magazine*, but *they* cost too much.

REVISED: I would like a subscription to this magazine, but it costs too much.

Shift in Person – a sentence that begins in one person (first, second, or third), then shifts to another person

SHIFT IN PERSON: As *I* walked down the beach, *you* could tell it would be a beautiful day.

REVISED: As I walked down the beach, I could tell it would be a beautiful day.

Shift in Tense – a sentence that begins in one verb tense then needlessly shifts to another

SHIFT IN TENSE: I *was walking* home last Wednesday when a car suddenly *swerves* across the street and *crashes* into a signpost.

REVISED: I was walking home last Wednesday when a car suddenly swerved across the street and crashed into a signpost.

Shift in Voice – a sentence that begins in one voice (active or passive), then shifts to the other

SHIFT IN VOICE: I *ate* all of my vegetables before dessert *was eaten*.

REVISED: I ate all of my vegetables before I ate dessert.

Split Construction – a sentence that needlessly separates a helping verb from its main verb, a subject from its verb, a preposition from its object, or a verb from its object. Inserting single words is less awkward than inserting long phrases

SPLIT CONSTRUCTION: Smith has, *for the last twenty years*, worked as a doctor. [helping verb separated from main verb]

SPLIT CONSTRUCTION: Smith, *for the last twenty years*, has worked as a doctor. [subject separated from verb]

REVISED: For the last twenty years, Smith has worked as a doctor.

SPLIT CONSTRUCTION: Joel has been writing under, *for the last twenty years*, an assumed name. [preposition separated from object]

REVISED: For the last twenty years, Joel has been writing under an assumed name.

SPLIT CONSTRUCTION: Joel has consistently declined, *for the last twenty years*, offers from his publisher. [verb separated from object]

REVISED: For the last twenty years, Joel has consistently declined offers from his publisher.

Split Infinitive – a sentence in which a word or phrase is inserted between the two parts of an infinitive

SPLIT INFINITIVE: He hoped to *as quickly as possible* complete the exam.

REVISED: He hoped to complete the exam as quickly as possible.

Transitions – words and phrases that smoothly guide the reader from sentence to sentence, paragraph to paragraph, and idea to idea. The following are examples of common transitional words and phrases, but you should not be content to use only these; sophisticated writers may write entire sentences or paragraphs that link ideas.

TO COMPARE: also, and, as well, furthermore, in addition, like, moreover, similarly

TO CONTRAST: although, but, conversely, however, instead, nonetheless, otherwise, though, whereas

TO ESTABLISH CAUSE AND EFFECT: as a result, because, for this reason, since

TO PLACE IN SEQUENCE: before, during, after, now, then, later, meanwhile, until, first, second, next, eventually, finally

TO PROVIDE AN EXAMPLE OR PARAPHRASE: for example, for instance, in the following, as follows, such as, in other words, that is, namely

TO QUALIFY: often, generally, specifically, especially, occasionally, usually

TO CONCLUDE: as a result, consequently, hence, therefore

Ensuring Correct Agreement

SUBJECT–VERB AGREEMENT

The subject and verb of a sentence must agree in number (singular or plural). There are many errors that can occur through lack of agreement.

NO AGREEMENT: The employees [plural] is [singular] satisfied with the new contract.
AGREEMENT: The employees are [plural] satisfied with the new contract.
AGREEMENT: The employee [singular] is satisfied with the new contract.

NO AGREEMENT: There is [singular] enough books [plural] for everyone.
AGREEMENT: There are [plural] enough books for everyone.

Subjects including the conjunction *and* are plural and require a plural verb.

NO AGREEMENT: Bill and I [plural] am [singular] looking forward to Friday.
AGREEMENT: Bill and I are [plural] looking forward to Friday.

Two singular subjects including the conjunctions *or* and *nor* require a singular verb.

NO AGREEMENT: Either Tina or Ted [singular] are [plural] hopelessly lost.
AGREEMENT: Either Tina or Ted is [singular] hopelessly lost.

A singular and plural subject including the conjunctions *or* and *nor* require a singular or plural verb, depending on which subject is closest to the verb. To avoid awkward constructions, switch the plural subject to the second position, and make the verb plural.

NO AGREEMENT: Either Hanif [singular] or his friends [plural] usually visits [singular] on Monday.
AGREEMENT: Either Hanif or his friends usually visit [plural] on Monday.

NO AGREEMENT: Neither the prisoners [plural] nor the guard [singular] know [plural] how the fire started.
AGREEMENT: Neither the guard nor the prisoners [plural] know [plural] how the fire started.

Some indefinite pronouns (another, anybody, each, either, everybody, everyone, everything, neither, nobody, one, somebody, someone) are singular. It is helpful to remember that subjects cannot occur in prepositional phrases.

NO AGREEMENT: Each [singular—subject] of the rocks [plural—not the subject] were [plural] formed by sedimentation.
AGREEMENT: Each of the rocks was [singular] formed by sedimentation.

Some indefinite pronouns (all, any, half, most, none, some) can be either singular or plural. Their number can be determined from the number of the noun in the prepositional phrase that follows them.

NO AGREEMENT: Some [singular because of "tape"] of the tape [singular] were [plural] erased.
AGREEMENT: Some of the tape was [singular] erased.

NO AGREEMENT: Some [plural because of "flower"] of the flowers [plural] is [singular] blooming.
AGREEMENT: Some of the flowers are [plural] blooming.

Collective nouns (such as committee, team, crowd) are singular when treated as a group and plural when treated as individual members.

AGREEMENT: The jury [singular] was [singular] unanimous [of one mind] in its verdict.
AGREEMENT: The jury [plural] were [plural] split [of two minds] on the question of guilt.

Some nouns (measles, news, physics) are treated as singular, even though they end in *-s*.

NO AGREEMENT: Measles [singular] are [plural] a contagious illness.
AGREEMENT: Measles is [singular] a contagious illness.

PRONOUN–ANTECEDENT AGREEMENT

A pronoun and its antecedent (the noun or pronoun it replaces) must agree in number.

NO AGREEMENT: The mayor [singular] left their [plural] notes in the chamber.
AGREEMENT: The mayor left her [singular] notes in the chamber.

Some indefinite pronouns (another, anyone, each, either, everybody, everyone, neither, nobody, one, somebody) are always singular. Pronouns that refer to them must also be singular.

NO AGREEMENT: Everyone [singular] forgot to pack their [plural] toothbrush.
AGREEMENT: Everyone forgot to pack his or her [singular] toothbrush.

Subjects including the conjunction *and* are plural and require a plural pronoun.

NO AGREEMENT: Bill and I [plural] lost his [singular] passports.
AGREEMENT: Bill and I lost our [plural] passports.

Two singular subjects including the conjunctions *or* and *nor* require a singular pronoun.

NO AGREEMENT: Neither Kate nor Karla [singular] will complete their [plural] homework.
AGREEMENT: Neither Kate nor Karla will complete her [singular] homework.

A singular and plural subject including the conjunctions *or* and *nor* require a singular or plural pronoun, depending on which subject is closest to the pronoun. To avoid awkward constructions, move the plural subject to the second position, then use a plural pronoun.

NO AGREEMENT: Neither Doyle [singular] nor his friends [plural] said he [singular] would take the bus here.
AGREEMENT: Neither Doyle nor his friends said they [plural] would take the bus here.

NO AGREEMENT: Neither the ministers [plural] nor the premier [singular] will uphold their [plural] responsibility.
AGREEMENT: Neither the premier nor the ministers [plural] will uphold their [plural] responsibility.

COMPARISONS

In grammatical terms, comparison refers to the degree of quality expressed by an adjective or adverb. There are three degrees: the positive, the comparative, and the superlative. The comparative degree is used to compare two subjects; the superlative is used to compare more than two subjects.

When an adjective or adverb has one syllable, the comparative is usually formed by adding *-er*; the superlative by adding *-est*.

ADJECTIVE EXAMPLE: large [positive], larger [comparative], largest [superlative]
ADVERB EXAMPLE: soon [positive], sooner [comparative], soonest [superlative]

COMPARATIVE EXAMPLE: Vancouver rain is colder than Toronto rain. [two subjects]
SUPERLATIVE EXAMPLE: Vancouver rain is the coldest rain on the planet. [more than two subjects]

When an adjective has two syllables, the comparison is usually formed the same way, though there are more exceptions.

ADJECTIVE EXAMPLE: angry, angrier, angriest
EXCEPTION: spiteful, more spiteful, most spiteful

When an adjective has more than two syllables, or when an adverb ends in *-ly*, the comparative is usually formed by adding *more*, the superlative by adding *most*.

ADJECTIVE EXAMPLE: beautiful, more beautiful, most beautiful
ADVERB EXAMPLE: happily, more happily, most happily

Some adjectives and adverbs show comparison in irregular forms.

ADJECTIVE EXAMPLE: good, better, best ADVERB EXAMPLE: well, better, best
ADJECTIVE EXAMPLE: bad, worse, worst ADVERB EXAMPLE: badly, worse, worst

Other Issues in Writing

INTEGRATING QUOTATIONS

Integrating quotations is one of the most valuable skills in writing essays, other persuasive texts, and reports. An argument has no force without support, and quotations are the most powerful form of support. Here are some principles for integrating quotations.

- Long quotations can and should be shortened.
- Anything in a quotation that you replace with ellipses (...) is gone. Your reader will not go back to the primary source to see what it originally said. Use ellipses only to remove irrelevant phrases.
- Always integrate a quotation into a sentence of your own. Quotations presented as complete, detached sentences have no syntactical connection to what precedes and follows them.
- Place quotations in the middle or at the end of your sentences. This follows the model of "claim—support." If the support is presented before the claim, what is it supporting?
- Two or more brief quotations integrated into a single sentence can be effective, if used sparingly.
- Always punctuate your integrated sentence as you would if there were no quotation in it (the exception is the quotation marks, of course).
- Any changes or clarifications you make within a quotation must be put inside square brackets.
- When quoting more than one line of poetry, show the line divisions with a right slash (/).
- Close paraphrasing also requires a citation; if you have only tinkered with someone else's words, the original writer still deserves the credit.

NON-DISCRIMINATORY AND INCLUSIVE LANGUAGE

Non-discriminatory and inclusive language is language that neither discriminates against nor excludes a particular group. Writing inclusive language requires only the habit of looking for discriminatory language both as you write and as you proofread. Here are some of the criteria to test for discriminatory language in your writing.

GENDER: If someone's gender is not relevant, don't mention it.

Use *Ms*. rather than *Miss* or *Mrs*., unless the woman in question has expressed to you a preference for another term. When referring to a married couple when the wife has assumed her husband's surname, include the wife's first name if the husband's first name is used.

> NON-INCLUSIVE: Mr. and Mrs. James Witkowski
>
> INCLUSIVE: Mr. and Mrs. Witkowski
>
> INCLUSIVE: James and Janice Witkowski [or "Janice and James"]

Avoid "man" words; alternatives are not difficult to find.

> NON-INCLUSIVE: mankind, man-made, foreman, chairman
>
> INCLUSIVE: humanity, synthetic ["artificial"], supervisor, chair

Avoid feminine suffixes.

> NON-INCLUSIVE: waitress, actress, stewardess
>
> INCLUSIVE: server, actor, flight attendant

Reword sentences that require masculine or feminine pronouns.

> NON-INCLUSIVE: Everyone should plan his own career.
>
> INCLUSIVE: People should plan their own careers.
>
> INCLUSIVE: Everyone should plan his or her career.
>
> INCLUSIVE: Everyone should have a career plan.

RACE: If someone's race is not relevant, don't mention it. Don't tell or write jokes that are critical of particular races or ethnic groups. Recognize that even telling jokes about your own ethnic group is discriminatory; self-deprecation is no excuse for racism.

Strike racist words and phrases from both your formal and informal diction.

> DISCRIMINATORY: He jewed me out of ten dollars. [critical of Jews]
>
> NON-DISCRIMINATORY: He ripped me off to the tune of ten dollars.

SEXUAL ORIENTATION: If someone's sexual orientation is not relevant, don't mention it. Your writing should not deny the existence of a wide range of partnerships. The word "partner" is a useful substitute for "boyfriend" or "girlfriend."

> DISCRIMINATORY: When a guy gets a call from his girlfriend, who says, "We need to talk," he knows there is a problem.
>
> INCLUSIVE: When you get a call from your partner, who says, "We need to talk," you know there is a problem.

PHYSICAL AND MENTAL DEVELOPMENT: If someone's abilities are not relevant, don't mention them. Avoid terms that stigmatize or classify a group by their abilities. Rather than referring to "the disabled," use the phrase "people with disabilities."

> DISCRIMINATORY : The Para-Olympics are for the disabled.
>
> NON-DISCRIMINATORY: The Para-Olympics are for people with disabilities.

Spelling Rules and Strategies

Anyone who wishes to spell well in English faces many obstacles. For example, English spellings are not consistently phonetic; that is, there are many words you cannot sound out to spell correctly. The spellings of words such as *mortgage* or *subtle* cannot be derived phonetically. In addition, advertisers and other purveyors of popular culture often deliberately misspell words for various effects. *Thru*, *Lite*, and *Reddi-wip* are examples of this phenomenon.

Canadians face a particular challenge in that we are confronted with much writing that uses American spelling, and much writing that uses British spelling.

Spelling Strategies

Read: If you want to spell well, *read*. The best spellers are usually the most avid readers. Most of their spelling success comes from seeing a word printed correctly hundreds or thousands of times.

Keep a dictionary with you as you write: You can spell many words correctly by applying the rules provided later in this section. However, most of those rules have exceptions, and some rules are rather long and difficult to remember. Using a dictionary enables you to resolve most spelling questions quickly.

Use spell checkers wisely: The spell checking routines included in word-processing programs are useful for catching most typing errors. However, if you type *from* when you meant *form*, your spell checker will not identify the error, as both are acceptable English words. Therefore, use the spell checker as a first pass through your writing, then read your writing yourself in a second (and third) pass.

Proofread your work carefully: Successful proofreading requires you to forget what you have just written, and to read it as if for the first time. While you are looking for misspelled words, always look for *missing* words as well. If you can, have other people proofread your writing.

Keep a list of words you frequently misspell: If you can never remember how many *a*'s there are in *separate*, write it down, along with other troublesome words, and keep that paper with your writing materials. Make yourself use these words in your writing, with the aim of eventually taking them off the list.

Identify your weaknesses; learn the rules that govern them: If you continually find yourself stumped by one specific problem, for instance, whether to double the final consonant when adding suffixes, learn that rule and use it often enough to keep it fresh in your mind.

Break difficult words into their constituent parts: There are several ways in which the ability to take a word apart can help you. Breaking a word into syllables can reveal patterns (such as the difference between *ac-cept* and *ex-cept*) and opportunities to apply rules. Breaking a word into morphemes (units of meaning) can reveal different patterns and rules. For example, the word *misrememberings* consists of two prefixes, one root, and two suffixes (*mis-re-member-ing-s*). Examining the word in this way also leads to a richer understanding of its meaning.

Say difficult words aloud, pronouncing silent or unstressed letters and sounds: Many people are auditory learners; they learn by hearing. If you deliberately pronounce the *h* in exhausted or the *p* in psychology, you may find those words easier to spell.

Test yourself on difficult words: Look at the word, then cover it. Say it aloud. Consider its syllables, its prefixes, roots, and suffixes. Write it down. Check the spelling. Repeat if necessary.

Spelling Rules

PREFIXES

General Rule: When adding a prefix to a root word, attach the prefix without adding or dropping any letters.

EXAMPLES: a + moral = amoral
dis + similar = dissimilar
pre + scribe = prescribe

Exceptions: There are four situations in which a hyphen may be required.

1. Use a hyphen to avoid doubling vowels.

EXAMPLES: co + operate = co-operate
re + elect = re-elect
re + enter = re-enter

NOTE: This use of the hyphen is disappearing; for instance, many people write "cooperate."

2. Use a hyphen to separate prefixes from proper nouns.

EXAMPLES: anti + Fascist = anti-Fascist
pre + Raphaelite = Pre-Raphaelite
pro + Marxist = pro-Marxist

3. Use a hyphen to avoid confusion between words.

EXAMPLES: re + creation = re-creation (to make again; not recreation, leisure activities)
re + form = re-form (to form again; not reform, to change)
re + sort = re-sort (to sort again; not resort, a vacation site)

4. Use a hyphen with the prefix *self-*.

EXAMPLES: self + esteem = self-esteem
self + knowledge = self-knowledge
self + respecting = self-respecting

ROOTS

Use of ie or ei

NOTE: The following well-known rhyme is still the best guide to these troublesome words:

"Use *i* before *e*,
Except after *c*,
Or when sounded as (ā)
As in *neighbour* and *weigh*."

EXAMPLES:	mischief	(*ie*)	receive	(*ei* after *c*)
	relief	(*ie*)	eight	(ā)
	review	(*ie*)	vein	(ā)
	ceiling	(*ei* after *c*)	weight	(ā)
	deceit	(*ei* after *c*)		

Exception 1: Unfortunately, not all words follow these rules. You will have to memorize the exceptions below, all of which have *e* before *i*.

EXAMPLES:	caffeine	heifer	sleight
	codeine	height	stein
	counterfeit	heir	surfeit
	eiderdown	leisure	their
	either	neither	weir
	Fahrenheit	protein	weird
	foreign	seize	
	forfeit	seizure	

Exception 2: When *c* is pronounced *sh*, *ie* follows the *c*.

EXAMPLES:	ancient	efficient	quotient
	conscience	patient	sufficient
	deficiency	proficiency	

"SEED" WORDS

Rule: When a word ends with the sound "seed," spell that syllable *-cede*.

NOTE: This rule does not apply to words actually using the root word *seed*.

EXAMPLES: accede
concede
secede

Exception 1: There are three words that end with *-ceed*.

EXAMPLES: exceed
proceed
succeed

Exception 2: There is one word that ends with *-sede*.

EXAMPLE: supersede

SUFFIXES

Adding suffixes in English is more complicated than adding prefixes. Various rules apply, and most rules have exceptions.

Words ending in y

Rule: When a word ends with a *vowel* and *y*, the *y* does not change when adding most suffixes.

EXAMPLES: boy + hood = boyhood
delay + ing = delaying
pay + ment = payment

Exception: Certain words do not follow this pattern.

EXAMPLES: day + ly = daily
gay + ly = gaily
lay + ed = laid

Rule: When a word ends with a *consonant* and *y*, the *y* changes to an *i* when adding most suffixes.

EXAMPLES: angry + est = angriest
fallacy + ous = fallacious
happy + ness = happiness

Exception 1: Certain words do not follow this pattern.

EXAMPLES: shy + ness = shyness
sly + ly = slyly

NOTE: The word *dry* changes as a comparative adjective (*drier*), but not as a noun (*clothes dryer*).

Exception 2: The suffixes *-ing* and *-like* do not change the *y* to *i*.

EXAMPLES: apply + ing = applying
fly + ing = flying
baby + like = babylike

Words ending in silent e

Rule: When a word ends in silent *e*, and the suffix begins with a consonant, keep the *e*.

EXAMPLES: hope + less = hopeless
love + ly = lovely
spite + ful = spiteful

Exception: Many words do not follow this pattern.

EXAMPLES: argue + ment = argument
awe + ful = awful
due + ly = duly
humble + ly = humbly
nine + th = ninth
true + ly = truly
whole + ly = wholly
wise + dom = wisdom

NOTE: Both judgment and judgement are acceptable spellings.

Rule: When a word ends in silent *e*, and the suffix begins with a vowel, or with *y*, drop the *e*.

EXAMPLES: berate + ed = berated
give + ing = giving
rose + y = rosy

Exception: Some words do not follow this pattern to avoid confusion with other words or to maintain the pronunciation of the root word.

EXAMPLES: dye + ing = dyeing (not dying)
singe + ing = singeing (not singing)
eye + ing = eyeing
mile + age = mileage

Words ending in ce, ge, ee, or oe

Rule: When a word ends in *ce* or *ge*, and the *e* is needed to keep the soft *c* or soft *g* sound, keep the *e* when adding suffixes.

EXAMPLES: advantage + ous = advantageous
manage + able = manageable
notice + able = noticeable

Exception: Words ending in *ce* change the *e* to *i* before adding the suffix *-ous*.

EXAMPLES: grace + ous = gracious
malice + ous = malicious
vice + ous = vicious

Rule: When a word ends in *ee* or *oe*, keep the *e* when adding suffixes.

EXAMPLES: agree + able = agreeable
agree + ment = agreement
hoe + ing = hoeing

Exception: When the suffix begins with *e*, drop one *e*.

EXAMPLES: free + er = freer
free + est = freest

Words ending in l or n

Rule: When the root word ends with one *l*, and the suffix is *-ly*, keep both *l's*.

EXAMPLES: beautiful + ly = beautifully
cool + ly = coolly
regretful + ly = regretfully

Rule: When the root word ends with two *l's*, and the suffix is *-ly*, drop one *l*.

EXAMPLES: dull + ly = dully
full + ly = fully

Rule: When the root word ends with *n*, and the suffix begins with *n*, keep both *n's*.

EXAMPLES: mean + ness + meanness
sudden + ness = suddenness

Doubling of the final consonant

NOTE: Generally, you do not double the final consonant of a word before adding a suffix. There are cases in which you do, though.

Rule: When a one-syllable word ends with a single vowel and a consonant, double the consonant before adding a suffix that begins with a vowel.

EXAMPLES: get + ing = getting
knot + ed = knotted
skit + ish = skittish

Exception: When the root word ends with *w*, *x*, or *y*, don't double the final consonant.

EXAMPLES: sew + ing = sewing
flex + ed = flexed
spray + ed = sprayed

Rule: When a polysyllabic word ends with a single vowel and a consonant, don't double the consonant before adding a suffix that begins with a vowel, unless the stress in the root word falls at the end of the root word.

EXAMPLES: refer + ed = referred (show stress on second syllable)
metal + ic = metallic (show stress moving from first to second syllable)
refer + ence = reference (show stress moving from second to first syllable)

Exception: The final consonant of some words is doubled when adding a suffix that begins with a vowel, even though the stress is on the first syllable.

EXAMPLES: handicap + ed = handicapped
kidnap + ing = kidnapping
worship + ed = worshipped

The suffixes -able and -ible

Rule: When the root word is recognizable as a word, use the suffix *-able*. When the root word is unrecognizable as a word, use the suffix *-ible*.

EXAMPLES: recognize + able = recognizable
inflate + able = inflatable
marriage + able = marriageable
permiss? + ible = permissible
irasc? + ible = irascible
tang? + ible = tangible

Exceptions: There are exceptions to this rule. You must memorize them or use a dictionary.

EXAMPLES: inevit? + able = inevitable
irrit? + able = irritable
prob? + able = probable
sense + ible = sensible
defence + ible = defensible
contempt + ible = contemptible

The suffixes -ant, -ance, -ancy, and -ent, -ence, -ency

NOTE: The only rule that apparently governs the use of these suffixes is that once you know whether the *a* or *e* is used, that use is consistent through the forms of that word. Consult a dictionary.

EXAMPLES: discrepant = discrepancy
observant = observance
competent = competence = competency

Suffixes that change the roots

Rule: Some words ending in *er* drop the *e* when adding certain suffixes.

EXAMPLES: remember + ance = remembrance
hinder + ance = hindrance
disaster + ous = disastrous

Rule: Some words ending in *ous* drop the *u* when adding *-ity*.

EXAMPLES: curious + ity = curiosity
generous + ity = generosity
viscous + ity = viscosity

Rule: Some words ending in a hard *c* sound add *k* before the suffixes *-ed* and *-ing* to maintain the pronunciation.

EXAMPLES: panic + ed = panicked
picnic + ing = picnicking
shellac + ing = shellacking

COMPOUND WORDS

NOTE: Compound words can be written as separate words (*filing cabinet, school year, home run*), hyphenated words (*red-headed, empty-handed, mother-in-law*), or single words (*lighthouse, downstairs, bedroom*). This feature of English has no consistent rules; when in doubt, use a dictionary.

PLURALS

General Rule: To form the plural of most nouns, add *-s*.

EXAMPLES: flag = flags
image = images
surprise = surprises

Exception: Nouns ending in *ch, o, s, sh, x,* or *z* form their plurals by adding *-es*.

EXAMPLES: arch = arches
potato = potatoes
cross = crosses
lash = lashes
sex = sexes
buzz = buzzes

Exception: Nouns ending in *o* that are borrowed from foreign languages or are abbreviated words form their plurals by adding *-s*.

EXAMPLES: kimono = kimonos
piano = pianos
photo = photos

NOTE: There are some words ending in *o* that can be made plural either way:

EXAMPLES: cargo = cargoes or cargos
mosquito = mosquitoes or mosquitos
zero = zeroes or zeros

Words ending in consonant + y

Rule: When a noun ends with a consonant and *y*, the plural is formed by dropping the *y* and adding *-ies*.

EXAMPLES: lady = ladies
proxy = proxies
spy = spies

Words ending in f or fe

Rule: When a noun ends in *f* or *fe*, the plural is formed by dropping the ending and adding *-ves*.

EXAMPLES:
calf = calves
half = halves
elf = elves
knife = knives
leaf = leaves (but: *The Toronto Maple Leafs*)
life = lives
shelf = shelves
loaf = loaves
thief = thieves
self = selves
wife = wives
sheaf = sheaves
wolf = wolves

Exception: Some nouns ending in *f* or *fe* form their plurals in the usual way:

EXAMPLES:
cliff = cliffs
giraffe = giraffes
roof = roofs

NOTE: Some nouns ending in *f* can have either plural form: *-s* or *-ves*. Use a dictionary to check.

EXAMPLES:
hoof = hoofs or hooves
scarf = scarfs or scarves
wharf = wharfs or wharves

Irregular Plurals

NOTE: Some nouns with Greek or Latin roots have irregular plural forms.

1. *-is* ending becomes *-es*

EXAMPLES:
analysis = analyses
axis = axes
crisis = crises

2. *-us* ending becomes *-i*

EXAMPLES:
alumnus = alumni
fungus = fungi
radius = radii

Exception: Some words do not follow this rule.

EXAMPLES:
campus = campuses
genius = geniuses
genus = genera

3. *-a* changes to *-ae*

EXAMPLES:
formula = formulae
vertebra = vertebrae
larva = larvae
alumna = alumnae

4. *-on* and *-um* change to *-a*

EXAMPLES:
phenomenon = phenomena
medium = media
datum = data

5. *-ex* and *-ix* change to *-ices*

EXAMPLES: appendix = appendices
index = indices

NOTE: In some contexts, *appendixes* and *indexes* are acceptable. Consult a dictionary.

There are other irregular plural forms in English; you must memorize these or use a dictionary.

EXAMPLES:

child = children	die = dice
ox = oxen	louse = lice
man = men	mouse = mice
woman = women	fish = fish
foot = feet	moose = moose
goose = geese	sheep = sheep
tooth = teeth	aircraft = aircraft

Rule: The plurals of letters, numbers, and initialisms are formed by adding *-s* or *-'s*.

EXAMPLES: A = A's (as in letter grades)
1980 = 1980s
RRSP = RRSPs

Rule: The plurals of compound words are formed by applying the rules above to the main word of the construction.

EXAMPLES: lady-in-waiting = ladies-in-waiting
passer-by = passers-by
sister-in-law = sisters-in-law

POSSESSIVES

Singular Nouns

Rule: To form the possessive of a singular noun not ending in *s*, add *'s*.

EXAMPLES: dog = dog's
Bob = Bob's
love = love's

Rule: To form the possessive of a singular noun ending in *s*, add *'s*.

EXAMPLES: Dickens = Dickens's (as in *Dickens's novels*)
Jones = Jones's (as in *Mrs. Jones's house*)
boss = boss's (as in *my boss's car*)

Exception: For words that contain more than one *s* sound, only the apostrophe is used.

EXAMPLES: Jesus = Jesus' (as in *Jesus' life*)
Ulysses = Ulysses' (as in *Ulysses' journey*)

Plural Nouns

Rule: To form the possessive of a plural noun not ending in *s*, add *'s*.

EXAMPLES: men = men's (as in *men's room*)
children = children's (as in *children's clothing*)
sheep = sheep's (as in *sheep's wool*—note that *sheep* can be singular or plural; the possessive is the same in both cases)

Rule: To form the possessive of a plural noun ending in *s*, add '.

EXAMPLES: ladies = ladies' (as in *ladies' shoes*—shoes for ladies)
months = months' (as in *two months' wages*—wages for two months)
boys = boys' (as in *the boys' adventure*—the adventure of the boys)

Compound Words

Rule: To form the possessive of a compound word, add the appropriate ending to the final word.

EXAMPLES: my brother-in-law's career
the Prime Minister of Canada's announcement
Atkinson, Baker, and Carroll's law practice

NOTE: The number and location of apostrophes in compound words can change the meaning of the word or phrase.

EXAMPLES: the husband and wife's marriage (the marriage they shared)
the husband's and wife's stories (they told separate stories)
the husbands and wives' meeting (a meeting for husbands and wives)
the husbands' and wives' parties (separate parties for husbands and wives)

Possessive Pronouns

Rule: Possessive pronouns never require apostrophes, as they already indicate possession.

EXAMPLES:

my	her	theirs
mine	hers	their
your	its	whose
yours	our	
his	ours	

CONTRACTIONS

General Rule: When forming contractions, the apostrophe takes the place of the missing letters.

EXAMPLES: cannot = can't
it is = it's
we will = we'll

Exception: There is one exception to this rule.

EXAMPLE: will not = won't

HYPHENS

General Rule: In addition to their use in adding prefixes to roots, hyphens are also required in adjectival phrases concerned with age, size, weight, and length of time.

EXAMPLES: a ten-year-old boy
a three-metre wave
a six-kilogram trout
a two-minute warning

NUMBERS

Write out numbers from zero to nine; use numerals for numbers greater than nine.

EXAMPLES: four
eight
14
63 360

Exception: If there are few numbers in a piece of writing, those with shorter names can be written out.

EXAMPLES: one thousand
sixty-two
twelve million

Exception: Don't mix written numbers and numerals applied to the same subject in the same sentence.

EXAMPLES: between the ages of eight and forty-eight *or*
between the ages of 8 and 48

Exception: Don't start a sentence with a numeral.

EXAMPLE: One hundred people were arrested.

CANADIAN SPELLING

NOTE: A dictionary of Canadian English, such as *The Canadian Oxford Dictionary* or *The Canadian Oxford High School Dictionary*, is your best source for Canadian spelling and usage conventions. Some major differences between Canadian and American spellings are outlined below.

Words ending in our/or

The typical Canadian spelling is *our*; the typical American spelling is *or*.

EXAMPLES: colour
humour
neighbour

NOTE: The *u* is often dropped when a suffix is added to the root word.

EXAMPLES: humour + ous = humorous
in + vigour + ate = invigorate
labour + ious = laborious

Words ending in re/er

The typical Canadian spelling is *re*; the typical American spelling is *er*.

EXAMPLES: centre
metre
theatre

Words ending in se/ze

The typical Canadian spelling is *ze* as in American spelling.

EXAMPLES: analyze
criticize
paralyze

Words ending in ll/l

When adding suffixes to words ending in a single *l*, the typical Canadian spelling is *ll*; the typical American spelling is *l*.

EXAMPLES: counsel + or = counsellor
label + ed = labelled
travel + ing = travelling

Different spellings

Most Canadian writers use *cheque* rather than the American *check*, *catalogue* rather than *catalog*, *grey* rather than *gray*, and *storey* (as in part of a building) rather than *story*. Check a dictionary of Canadian English for other different spellings and Canadianisms.

EXAMPLES: I cashed the cheque as quickly as possible.
Home delivery of Sears' catalogue used to be a Canadian tradition.
She had enchanting grey eyes.
The cat was unharmed after its fall from a twelfth-storey balcony.

Vocabulary-Building Strategies

The English language includes hundreds of thousands of words. Still, we sometimes struggle to find just the "right" word in our writing and speaking. Obviously, the larger your vocabulary, the more likely you are to find the word you want. You can probably use and correctly pronounce between 5 000 and 10 000 words. Yet even with these thousands of words at your disposal, you may still find it difficult to express to others your thoughts, feelings, memories, hopes, and so on. The best way to decrease the difficulty is to increase your vocabulary.

Read: The more you read, the faster your vocabulary is likely to grow. Good readers can extract the meaning of an unfamiliar word from the context in which it is used. Your first contextual definition of a word may be approximate, but the more often you encounter that word in your reading, the more exact your working definition will become.

Use a dictionary: Look up unfamiliar words in the dictionary as you encounter them in your reading. Similarly, you can gain the confidence to use a new word in your writing by checking the dictionary first.

Use a thesaurus as you write: A thesaurus is a reference book that lists synonyms (words with similar meanings) for the word you look up. You must be careful in using a thesaurus, though: the synonyms listed are close in meaning, not exact.

Learn words from their context: It is often possible to get a good sense of a word's meaning from the way it is used in someone else's writing.

Sometimes words are defined in a sentence.

EXAMPLE: On TV last night I saw somebody get a *tracheotomy*: the doctor cut a hole in the patient's windpipe so he could breathe.

Sometimes a number of examples are provided.

EXAMPLE: The essay was filled with *split infinitives*, including "to boldly go," "to frantically beg," and "to endlessly fail."

The writer may provide a synonym in the same or a nearby sentence.

EXAMPLE: It was an *egregious* movie; it was awful.

There may be a word that contrasts with the meaning of the unfamiliar word.

EXAMPLE: Bats are normally *nocturnal*, but in the story "Stellaluna," a bat learns to sleep by night and be awake by day.

A word's meaning may be implied by the cause or the effect of it.

EXAMPLE: Investigators determined that the *effluent* from the factory had poisoned the fish.

Keep a list of new words you would like to use: Keep a section of a notebook in which you write down new words, their meanings, and a sample sentence in which the word is used correctly. Regular review of this list will increase your reading vocabulary, as well as your writing and speaking vocabulary.

Analyze the structure of new words: Most English words consist of a *root* that is possibly preceded by one or more *prefixes*, and may be followed by one or more *suffixes*. For instance, the word *connection* is formed from a prefix, *con-* (together), a root, *-nec-* (bind), and a suffix, *-tion* (which makes a verb a noun). Some further examples are provided in the chart below.

Common Morphemes and Their Origins

Prefix	Variations	Meaning	Example	Origin
ambi-		both around	ambidextrous ambiance	Latin
ante-		before in front of	antebellum anteroom	Latin
be-		to make covered	befriend bedecked	Old English
bio-		life	biology	Greek
cata-	cat-	down	catastrophe	Greek
chiro-		hand	chiropractor	Greek
demi-		half	demitasse	French
dis-	dif-	apart	disintegrate	Latin
en-	em-	to cause to place in to restrict	enrich embalm enclose	Latin

eu-		good	euphoria	Greek
for-		away; off	forbid	Old English
hyper-		too much	hyperactive	Greek
inter-		between; among	international	Latin
intra-		within	intraspecies	Latin
meta-		beyond	metaphysics	Greek
mono-		one	monologue	Greek
ob-	oc-, of-, op-	against	obstacle opposition	Latin
para-	par-	beside beyond defective helping	parallel paradox paranoid paralegal	Greek
re-		move backward undo perform again	recede revoke return	Latin
sub-	su-, suc-, suf- sug-, sum-, sup- sur-, sus-	beneath	submarine	Latin
sur-		in addition	surcharge	French
syn-	sym-, sys-, syl-	together	synchronicity symphony system syllable	Greek
trans-	tra-	across change go beyond	transplant transform transcend	Latin

Root	**Variations**	**Meaning**	**Example**	**Origin**
-acr-	-acer-, -acid-	sharp; bitter	acrimonious	Latin
-ali-	-allo-	other	alien	Latin
-bell-		war	belligerent	Latin
-bene-		well	beneficent	Latin
-cad-	-cas-	fall	decadent	Latin
-cede-		withdraw	secede	Latin
-ceive-		get	conceive	Latin
-cred-		believe	incredible	Latin
-cur-	-curs-	happen	curriculum	Latin
-dece-		correct	indecent	Latin

-doc-		teach	doctrine	Latin
-duc-	-duct-	to lead	educate	Latin
-fac-	-fec-, -fic-	do; make effect fiction	manufacture	Latin
-flect-		bend	reflection	Latin
-gen-		race; birth	congenital	Greek/Latin
-graph-	-gram-	written	cartography	Greek
-here-		cling	coherent	Latin
-hetero-		different	heterogeneous	Greek
-homo-		same	homonym	Greek
-lab-		work	collaborate	Latin
-log-		word; speech	dialogue	Greek
-men-		mind	mentality	Latin
-migr-		move	migrant	Latin
-mis-	-mit-	send submit	omission	Latin
-nec-	-nex-	bind	disconnect	Latin
-nom-		custom; law	economy	Greek
-oper-		work	opera	Latin
-ord-		fit	insubordinate	Latin
-phys-		natural order	physician	Greek
-quer-	-quir-, -ques-	seek; ask	conquer	Latin
-rect-		guide; straight	correct	Latin
-sci-		to know	conscience	Latin
-sect-		cut	intersect	Latin
-sess-		stay	obsession	Latin
-soc-		partner	association	Latin
-trude-		push	intrude	Latin
-urb-		city	suburbia	Latin
-vac-		empty	vacuous	Latin
-vade-		go	pervade	Latin

Suffix	**Variations**	**Meaning**	**Example**	**Origin**
-able	-ible	having the quality of	despicable	Latin
-ance	-ant, -ancy	quality of one who does	brilliance servant	Latin
-ary		connected with	honorary	Latin

-eer		producer of an action	engineer	French
-ence	-ent, -ency	quality of	independent	Latin
-fy	-ify	to make	simplify	Latin
-ic	-ice	the quality of	sophomoric prejudice	Middle English
-ine		characteristic of	equine	Latin
-ion		action or condition	union	Latin
-ise	-ize	to render to change into to subject to	sterilize dramatize terrorize	Greek
-ism		the practice of	communism	Greek
-ness		the state of	wistfulness	Old English
-ory		relating to providing	sensory satisfactory	Middle English
-ster		one who does	prankster	Old English
-tion	-sion	state of	action	Latin
-tious		the quality of	pretentious	Latin

Homophones and Commonly Misused Words

Being aware of homophones and commonly misused words can help you both to use words more accurately and to spell them correctly. Homophones are words that are pronounced the same, but have different meanings.

Scan the list below. If you don't know the difference between the pairs of words, check definitions in a dictionary and use each one in a sentence. Keep a personal list of troublesome words and refer to it as needed in your writing or speaking assignments.

a lot/allot
a while/awhile
ability/capacity
accept/except
adapt/adopt
adverse/averse
advice/advise
affect/effect
aisle/isle
all together/altogether
allowed/aloud
allude/elude
allusion/illusion
alternate/alternative
among/between
amoral/immoral
amount/number
any body/anybody
any more/anymore
any one/anyone
as if/like/as though
as/like
assistance/assistants
aural/oral
backward/backwards
base/bass
bath/bathe
beat/beet
beside/besides
biannual/biennial
can/may
canvas/canvass
capital/capitol
censor/censure
choose/chose
chord/cord

climactic/climatic
clothes/cloths
coarse/course
compare to/compare with
complement/compliment
conscience/conscious
continual/continuous
criteria/criterion
data/datum
decent/descent/dissent
desert/dessert
device/devise
different from (not different than)
discreet/discrete
disinterested/uninterested
emigrate/immigrate
eminent/imminent/immanent
ensure/insure
envelop/envelope
especially/specially
every body/everybody
every day/everyday
every one/everyone
farther/further
fewer/less
flaunt/flout
for/fore/four
formally/formerly
good/well
gorilla/guerrilla
groan/grown
hanged/hung
have/of
heal/heel
healthful/healthy
hopefully/it is to be hoped
human/humane
if/whether
imply/infer
in/into
ingenious/ingenuous
is when/is where
it's/its
kind of—sort of/somewhat—rather
knight/night
later/latter
lay/lie
learn/teach
lessen/lesson
lightening/lightning
loan/lend
luxuriant/luxurious
maybe/may be
medal/metal
media/medium
miner/minor
moral/morale
nauseated/nauseous
of (inside of, off of, outside of)
pair/pare/pear
passed/past
patience/patients
peace/piece
percent/percentage
personal/personnel
phenomena/phenomenon
pore/pour/poor
precede/proceed
presence/presents
principal/principle
prophecy/prophesy
quiet/quite/quit
quote/quotation
rain/rein/reign
raise/rays/raze
read/reed
real/really
regardless
respectfully/respectively
reverend/reverent
right/write/rite
ring/wring
scene/seen
seam/seem
seas/sees/seize
sensual/sensuous
shone/shown
side/sighed
sighs/size
sole/soul
some time/sometime/sometimes
stationary/stationery
statue/stature/statute
straight/strait
sundae/Sunday
taught/taut
that/which/who
their/there/they're
thorough/though/through
threw/through
track/tract
try and/try to
use to/used to
waist/waste
wait/weight
warn/worn
way/ways (to go)
wear/we're/were/where
weather/whether
which/witch
who's/whose
who/whom
woman/women
your/you're

Glossary

Language and Literary Terms

Abbreviation – a word formed by shortening a longer word. There are four main kinds of abbreviations: *acronyms*, *blends*, *clippings*, and *initialisms*. These terms are defined below.

Abstract Language – words that identify qualities, attitudes, and ideas that cannot be seen, heard, smelled, touched, or tasted—contrasts with concrete language

EXAMPLES: courage, love, despair, perfection

Acronym – a word created by taking the first letter or letters of each word in a phrase. Acronyms differ from initialisms in that acronyms are pronounceable.

EXAMPLES: scuba (self-contained underwater breathing apparatus), AIDS (Acquired Immune Deficiency Syndrome), imho (in my humble opinion)

Affix – a morpheme added to a root to change or clarify its meaning. There are three kinds of affixes: *prefixes*, *infixes*, and *suffixes*.

Allegory – a narrative work in prose or poetry in which characters, actions, and settings have both a surface and a symbolic representation

EXAMPLES: *The Pilgrim's Progress* by John Bunyan, *The Faerie Queene* by Edmund Spenser

Ambiguous/Ambiguity – language that has two (or more) possible meanings. In essays and business writing, you should avoid ambiguity; however, in fiction, and especially in poetry, ambiguity can be a powerful tool for compression.

EXAMPLE: *Question*: Is the author concerned with plot, character, or setting? *Answer*: Yes. [The fact that the answer is ambiguous suggests that the question is, too. A clearer question would be With which of the following elements is the author most concerned: plot, character, or setting?]

Anachronism – an event, person, or object appearing in a literary work set in a time in which the event, person, or object did not occur or exist

EXAMPLE: In William Golding's *Lord of the Flies* (1954), it would be anachronistic if Ralph had a laptop computer, as they had not yet been invented.

Anagram – a word or phrase created by rearranging the letters of another word or phrase

EXAMPLE: Writer Vladimir Nabokov once created a character named Vivian Darkbloom, an anagram of his own name.

Anecdote – an account of a single incident without any of the elaboration (character development, figurative language, symbolism) of the short story

Antithesis – a phrase or clause in which parallel structure is maintained while the meaning is contrasted

EXAMPLE: "Ask not what your country can do for you, ask what you can do for your country."

Antonym – a word with a meaning opposite to another word. You can add variety to your writing by occasionally replacing a word with the negative form of its antonym.

EXAMPLE: *Big* and *small* are antonyms. Instead of writing "I had only a small chance of success, you could write, "My chances of success were not big."

Aphorism – a brief statement expressing advice or a perceived truth. The aphorism is more serious in tone than the *epigram*.

EXAMPLE: "Art is long, life is short."

Archaic Language – words that are seldom used anymore, having been replaced by more modern words. You can use archaic language in your writing, but doing so may lead the reader to find your writing pretentious.

EXAMPLE: In formal writing, there is no call to write, "I would lief wot what ails ye" when you could (more clearly) write, "I would really like to know what's bothering you."

Audience – The artist's audience is the people to whom she intends to expose her work. A writer or speaker (the artists with whom this text is concerned) should always be aware of her audience, so that she may tailor her work to their needs, expectations, and abilities.

Autobiography – an account of a person's life written by that person

Back-formation – the process of making a new word by shortening a longer word. Back-formation differs from clipping in that back-formation changes the part of speech.

EXAMPLES: *edit* [verb] from *editor* [noun], *back-form* [verb] from *back-formation* [noun], *liaise* [verb] from *liaison* [noun]

Biography – an account of a person's life written by someone else

Blend – a word formed from parts of other words. Blends (also called portmanteau words) are always pronounceable.

EXAMPLES: brunch (breakfast + lunch), infomercial (information + commercial), guesstimate (guess + estimate)

Body – the portion of an essay between the *introduction* and the *conclusion*. The body typically contains the development of the argument through the presentation of evidence supporting the thesis, or the main part of the exposition.

Body Language – nonverbal communication using movement, position, orientation, gestures, and facial expressions. Much of our face-to-face communication takes place in such nonverbal ways.

Cliché – a phrase that has lost its effectiveness due to overuse. It is a cliché to say, "Avoid clichés like the plague."

OTHER EXAMPLES: "bright and early," "it goes without saying," "last but not least," "without further ado"

Clincher – a sentence, usually at the end of the essay or paragraph, which succinctly expresses the focus of the entire essay or paragraph. A clincher may also be a powerful and unexpected example; you achieve extra forcefulness by presenting it last.

Clipping – a word created by keeping part of a larger word and discarding the rest. Clippings are always pronounceable.

EXAMPLES: phone (telephone), demo (demonstration), math (mathematics)

Colloquial Language – language used in everyday conversation. We assume that the language one uses while talking to friends, writing in one's diary, or communicating in other informal ways will be less precise than the language one uses in formal writing. The terms *colloquial language* and *informal language* can be used interchangeably.

COLLOQUIAL LANGUAGE: Bill couldn't make up the test because he'd skipped class.
FORMAL LANGUAGE: Because of his truancy, Bill was not allowed to write the test he had missed.

Concise – Writing that is concise uses the smallest number of words to convey accurately the intended meaning. Conciseness is important in prose; it is indispensable in poetry. Synonym: *succinct*.

Conclusion – typically the last paragraph of an essay, though it can be longer in the case of extended essays. Because the conclusion is the last part of the essay your readers (and markers) will read, you want to leave them with a strong impression. Providing a concise summary, making a general statement, and making a call to action can all be features of an effective conclusion.

Concrete Language – words that identify things that can be seen, heard, smelled, touched, or tasted—contrasts with *abstract language*

EXAMPLES: desk, noise, pungent, smooth, grapefruit

Connotation – the associations triggered by a word; such associations are not explicit in the dictionary definition (called the *denotation*). Connotations can be identified as positive and negative. Good writers carefully choose words with the connotations they desire, both to describe and to persuade.

EXAMPLES: The words *slender, slim, lean, thin, gaunt, skeletal, emaciated* all have similar denotations when applied to people, yet they range in connotation from the positive, *slender*, to the negative, *skeletal*.

Dead Metaphor – a metaphor that has been used for so long we no longer recognize it as such

EXAMPLES: the tongue of a shoe, the leg of a chair

Denotation – the dictionary definition of a word—contrasts with *connotation*

EXAMPLE: the denotation of "dog" may be "a domesticated canine," but the word also has many connotations, including companionship, trustworthiness, and unconditional affection.

Dialect – the use of a language in a particular place or among a particular group. Dialects may differ from the core language in pronunciation, vocabulary, or idiom.

EXAMPLE: Whether you call the central piece of furniture in the living room a *couch, chesterfield,* or *sofa* largely depends upon where in North America you live. The variation you use is part of your dialect.

Diction – the choice of words in speech and writing. Effective speakers and writers adapt their diction to the purpose and audience of their speech and writing. We often speak of levels of diction; here are three possible responses to an invitation, and the levels of diction that they illustrate.

FORMAL: I would be delighted to attend. [This is an appropriate level for a written response to someone you don't know well.]

INFORMAL: I'll be there. [This is an appropriate level for a written or oral response to someone with whom you are well acquainted.]

NONSTANDARD (SLANG): I am so there. [This is an appropriate level for an oral response to only your closest friends.]

Didactic Literature – works of prose or poetry whose purpose is to instruct. Such works usually include a moral, either explicitly or implicitly.

Epigram – a short witty statement in verse or prose. The epigram is less serious than the *aphorism*.
EXAMPLE: Once bitten, twice shy.

Epithet – any item that characterizes a noun and is regularly associated with it
EXAMPLE: Sir Robin the Brave [both "Sir" and "the Brave" are epithets]

Etymology – the study of the history and evolution of words
EXAMPLE: The Old English word *saelig* meant "happy or blessed" 1300 years ago. Five centuries ago, it had evolved to the Middle English word *seely* meaning "innocent." Our word *silly* meaning "foolish" evolved from *seely* some 400 years ago.

Euphemism – a mild or evasive phrase used in place of a harsh or explicit one
EXAMPLES: Bill *passed away* [rather than "died"]; the company is *downsizing* [rather than "firing lots of people"].

Expletive – an exclamatory word or phrase, sometimes obscene or profane. Generally, there is no call for profanity in your writing; there is always a more appropriate word or phrase available. The only exception is that when writing dialogue, your characters must use the language real people like them would use.

Genre – a type of literature. There are many ways of subdividing literature into genres.
EXAMPLE: division by form—poetry, prose, drama
EXAMPLE: division by length—novel, novella, short story
EXAMPLE: division by attitude toward subject—pastoral, existential, Romantic

Glossary – an alphabetical list of the terms used in a special field
EXAMPLE: You're reading a glossary now.

Grammar – the rules governing a language, including its sounds, words, and sentences

Graphology – the study and structure of the writing system of a language

Homophones – words with the same pronunciation but different meanings
EXAMPLE: *their/there/they're*

Idiom – a phrase whose meaning cannot be deduced from its parts. Idioms are by nature confusing for ESL students.
EXAMPLE: It would be difficult to recognize that the phrase "Put a sock in it!" means "Be quiet!" One either understands the idiom or puzzles over the antecedent of "it" and why a sock should be put wherever that is.

Infix – a morpheme added inside a root or word to change or clarify its meaning. Some languages make extensive use of infixes. In standard English, there are no infixes; however, examples can be found in colloquial English.
EXAMPLE: *absolutely* [adverb meaning "with no doubt"] + *bloody* [adjective with slang meaning of "damnable"] = *absobloodylutely* [emphatically with no doubt]

Initialism – a word created by taking the first letter or letters of each word in a phrase. Initialisms differ from acronyms in that initialisms are not easily pronounceable.
EXAMPLES: HIV (Human Immunodeficiency Virus), ISBN (international standard book number), TV (television)

Introduction – typically the first paragraph of an essay, though it can be longer in the case of extended essays. The introduction may be the most critical part of the essay, as readers (and markers) have often made a judgement of the quality of the thinking and the writing by the end of the introduction. A well-written introduction makes writing the body easier, as the means by which the thesis will be developed have already been established.

Invective – a means of insulting someone by the use of *epithets*.

EXAMPLE: Kent's verbal assault on Oswald in Shakespeare's *King Lear*: "A knave, a rascal, an eater of broken meats; a base, proud, shallow, beggarly, three-suited, hundred-pound, filthy worsted-stocking knave...."

Inverted Sentence – a sentence in which a clause or phrase from the middle or end of the sentence has been moved to the front, preceding the subject. Using inverted sentences provides variety in your writing.

EXAMPLE: Because all my clothes were clean, I had a hard time deciding what to wear.

Jargon – words and idioms used by a group or profession, often to the (intentional or unintentional) exclusion of outsiders. When writing for a general audience, you should avoid the use of jargon.

EXAMPLES: *Anticipatory set*, *PLO's*, and *summative evaluation* are examples of teacher jargon.

Latin Terms – several phrases from Latin have become fixtures in literary writing, often as abbreviations. Some of these terms are presented below, to help you understand the contexts in which they should and should not be used.

cf. – abbreviation of *confer* (compare). This term is often used in indexes and glossaries to direct the reader to contrasting entries.

EXAMPLE: hyperbole—deliberate exaggeration *cf.* understatement, litotes

et. al.– abbreviation of *et alia* (and other things/people). *Et al.* can be used when a citation has many authors: at the first mention, you provide the complete list, in subsequent use, you give the first writer's surname, then *et al.*

EXAMPLE: [first use] Smith, Wesson, Colt, Derringer; [subsequent use] Smith et al.

etc. – abbreviation of *et cetera* (and so on). *Etc.* can be used after two or three items in a list, but in formal writing, it is better to use the phrase "and so on." It is even wiser to provide the entire list, as the reader might assume that the etc. may be just a bluff: we may have already seen all your support.

e.g. – abbreviation of *exempli gratia* (for example). While e.g. may not be appropriate in formal essays, it certainly has a place in writing that follows the explanation/example model (such as this glossary: every instance of EXAMPLE could be replaced with *e.g.*).

i.e. – abbreviation of *id est* (that is). If used at all, this abbreviation should be used prior to a clarification. *I.e.* and *e.g.* should not be used interchangeably.

EXAMPLE: my mother's brother's children *i.e.*, my cousins

NB – abbreviation of *nota bene* (note well). This phrase is used as a warning that what follows will qualify or provide an exception to the preceding statement.

EXAMPLE: Iambic pentameter is lines of ten syllables with the even-numbered syllables stressed. *NB* Occasional lines of nine, eleven, and twelve syllables are acceptable.

PS – abbreviation of *post scriptum* (after the writing). Writing added to a letter after the closing is prefaced by PS. Subsequent additions add an extra "P" each time (PPS).

q.v. – abbreviation of *quod vide* (for which see). Used in cross-referencing, *q.v.* directs the reader to other relevant entries.

EXAMPLE: metaphor q.v. simile, personification

sic – a word meaning "as it was." Use *sic*, placed inside square brackets, within quotations to indicate that the error found there was present in the original.

EXAMPLE: According to his diary, "I am fourty-for [*sic*] years old today."

verbatim – a word meaning "word for word." The reader assumes that any citations in your essay are transcribed *verbatim*, and that any changes will be presented in square brackets. If your quotations are not *verbatim*, you have claimed that your words are someone else's, which is the opposite of plagiarism, but arguably just as deserving of punishment.

vice versa – a phrase meaning "the other way around." Use vice versa when the reverse of a long statement is also true, though there are English phrases that are just as effective.

EXAMPLE: The "chicken/egg" problem can be stated as follows: In order to have an egg, one must first have a chicken, and vice versa. [or substitute "the reverse is also true"]

viz – abbreviation of *videlicet* (that is to say). This phrase indicates that what follows is an explanation of the preceding statement.

EXAMPLE: Widespread job dissatisfaction among high school vice-principals likely stems from one factor more than any other, *viz.* they spend much more time with the troubled students than with the successful ones.

Lexicon – the words of a language, or the vocabulary of a speaker

Malapropism – the accidental substitution of one word for another in a phrase, often with humorous effect

EXAMPLE: I resemble that remark. ["resemble" substituted for "resent"]

Morpheme – the smallest unit of meaning in a language. In English, there are two main categories of morpheme: *roots* and *affixes*.

Morphology – the study and structure of words in a language

Neologism – the creation of a new word out of existing elements

EXAMPLES: *E-mail* [from electronic + mail], *fax* [from facsimile], *camcorder* [from camera + video-cassette recorder]

Orthography – the study of the use of letters and the rules of spelling in a language

Palindrome – a word or phrase spelled the same backwards as forwards

EXAMPLES: *madam, Ogopogo, "Able was I ere I saw Elba."*

Paraphrase – a statement that expresses the essence of another author's statement in words you have chosen. The intent of a paraphrase is to maintain the original meaning while employing your own words. When paraphrasing, you must follow the same citation format as in quoting: not to do so is plagiarism.

Phonology – the study and structure of sounds in a language

Prefix – a morpheme added to the beginning of a root to change or clarify its meaning

EXAMPLE: *re-* [prefix meaning "again"] + *-new-* [root meaning "not existing before"] = *renew* [make new again]

Pun – a humorous or clever use of words that employs either different meanings of similar-sounding words or minor changes to the pronunciation or meanings of other words

EXAMPLE: To make dandelion biscuits, you need to start with two cups of flower. [not flour]

Rhetoric – the study of effective or persuasive speaking and writing

Rhetorical Question – a question asked when no response is expected. You can make occasional use of rhetorical questions in your writing, but overuse of them creates an unpleasant effect.

EXAMPLES: "Why?" "Need I continue?" "How much longer can this go on?"

Root – a morpheme that can or did exist as a word without the application of affixes

EXAMPLES: *-blue-*, *-cat-*, *-take-*

Semantics – the study of the meaning of words and phrases. If there is any difference in meaning between the statements "She left me" and "She broke up with me," the difference is a semantic one.

Slang – informal or nonstandard language in which either new words are created or existing words are given new meanings. Do not use slang in your formal writing.

EXAMPLES: *dinkum* [new word (Australian) meaning "true or genuine"], *harsh* [new use (as an adverb meaning "extremely"), as in "That test was harsh hard."]

Source – In writing about something you have read, you must make reference to the source. If you are discussing the theme of a poem or story, for instance, that poem or story becomes your *primary source*. When you are expected to write a paragraph or more, you must make reference to or use quotations from the primary source; otherwise your response amounts to nothing more than unsubstantiated opinion. Sometimes in a longer paper, you may wish to include what others have written about the primary source, its author, its historical context, or its relation to the rest of the author's work. Such writings are called *secondary sources*.

Spoonerism – the switching of sounds between words, generating a new and often humorous meaning

EXAMPLE: Dumb and Mad [for "Mom and Dad"]

Stereotype – a prejudiced or simplistic opinion of something or someone. To say, "All men are self-centred" is to stereotype men, since the writer has not met all men, or even most of them.

Suffix – a morpheme added to the end of a root to change or clarify its meaning

EXAMPLE: *-rain-* [root meaning "liquid precipitation"] + *-y* [suffix meaning "having the quality of"] = *rainy* [weather with the quality of rain]

Syllable – the smallest unit of rhythm, consisting of a *nucleus* (usually a vowel) with or without initial and final *margins*. The initial margin is called the *onset*, and the remaining portion (the *rhyme*) consists of a peak ending with a *coda*.

EXAMPLE: In the word *dog*, the margins are "d" and "g"; the nucleus is "o." The onset is "d," the peak is "o," and the coda is "g." The rhyme is "*-og*."

Synonym – a word with a similar meaning to another word. Effective use of synonyms can add variety to your writing, but you must use them with caution, because two words seldom have identical meanings, and the differences in connotation or usage can be critical.

EXAMPLE: *Fluorescent* and *luminous* both describe objects that give off light, but you should only use the latter to describe your partner's eyes.

Syntax – the study and structure of sentences in a language

Thesaurus – a book of words or phrases grouped on the basis of their meaning

Titles – When referring to the titles of other works, observe the following rules: Titles of long works that were (likely) published by themselves are underlined or written in italics.

EXAMPLES: Macbeth or *Macbeth*, Lord of the Flies, Paradise Lost, Beethoven's Third Symphony

Short works that were (likely) published along with other such works have their titles placed in quotation marks.

EXAMPLES: "The Destructors," "Dover Beach," "Hey Jude"

Logic and Critical Thinking Terms

Every time you argue a point, you are trying to use a logical argument. The brief introduction to logical reasoning that follows should help you construct valid arguments in your own speech and writing, and recognize flaws in the arguments of others.

Analogy – a statement of relationship, in the form "*a* is to *b* as *c* is to *d*." Analogies can be very powerful teaching tools, as they can explain the unfamiliar in terms of the familiar. However, they must be used carefully in logical reasoning. Time and again in Plato's dialogues, Socrates got people to admit one similarity between two things, then two; soon, they were astonished at the things to which they had apparently agreed.

EXAMPLE: Begin with the analogy "Gasoline is to cars as food is to humans." You would probably agree. However, the analogy doesn't need to be stretched very far to take us to the point of conceding that people should only eat every five to fifteen days, that people should only consume liquids, and that people should eat outdoors at communal places.

Bias – a preference for one thing over something else. Objective writing is supposed to be free of bias.

Critical Thinking – a notion that is currently enjoying tremendous attention in education. It has been defined in countless ways. It may be most useful to see critical thinking as an attitude one brings to a topic. Rather than blindly accepting as true, good, and valid everything that is presented, a critical thinker considers what is explicit, what is implicit, and what the context is. Is there an argument? Is it sound? Critical thinkers also monitor their own thinking and reactions (this is called "metacognition").

Conclusion – a statement that includes both a subject and a predicate. In a valid argument, the premises precede the conclusion and logically lead to it.

Deductive Reasoning – combines general statements with specific statements to reach a specific conclusion. Unlike *inductive reasoning*, conclusions reached by deductive reasoning in a valid syllogism based on true premises are absolutely certain.

Double Negative – the use of more than one negative word or morpheme in a clause. In general, you should avoid using double negatives in your writing, but they can be effective if used infrequently and deliberately.

EXAMPLE: The statement "I ain't got none" uses a double negative [*ain't* and *none*] and shouldn't be used because it is nonstandard English and means the opposite of what was intended ["I have some," when the intention was "I don't have any"].

EXAMPLE: The phrase "this incident is not dissimilar" uses a double negative [*not* and *dis-*], but is standard English and does say what is intended. However, the phrase "this incident is similar" is less wordy and easier to understand, and is therefore preferable in most contexts.

Explicit – a term indicating that which is actually stated. In essays, it is generally advisable to be explicit; in fiction or poetry, it can be a flaw.

EXAMPLE: "Class dismissed" explicitly signals the end of class.

Fact – information that can be proven to exist or to be true, or an event that can be proven to have happened

EXAMPLE: Canada consists of ten provinces and three territories. [fact]

Fallacy – faulty reasoning. When an argument is not valid, or one or both of the premises are not true, a fallacy has been committed. A list of logical fallacies appears later in this section.

Implicit – a term indicating that which is implied in the text. The connotations of a word are implicit in that word, even though they are not stated.

EXAMPLE: "Your homework for tomorrow is ..." implicitly signals that class is almost over.

Inductive Reasoning – is reasoning from specific cases to general conclusions. Inductive reasoning is closely related to the scientific method. If you have measured the boiling temperature of water at sea level four hundred times, and each time the temperature has been one hundred degrees Celsius, you can reasonably conclude that at sea level, water boils at one hundred degrees Celsius. It is important to understand, though, that inductive reasoning can never lead to absolute certainty. Even if the boiling temperature of water at sea level has been constant for a million trials, you can not be absolutely certain that it will never boil at ninety-nine or one hundred and one degrees.

Objective – a term that refers to writing that is uninfluenced by emotions or personal prejudices. Objective writing relies on evidence and logic for its strength. In terms of questions, objective questions have one right answer; all other answers are wrong.

Opinion – a belief or conclusion held without the benefit of proof

EXAMPLE: Canada is the greatest country in the world. [opinion]

Premise – a statement that includes both a subject and a predicate. There are two kinds of premises in deductive reasoning: the major premise and the minor premise. Typically, the major premise makes a general statement, while the minor premise makes a specific statement.

Syllogism – a formal argument consisting of a major premise, a minor premise, and a conclusion

Subjective – a term that refers to writing that is influenced by emotions or personal prejudices. There is a lesser burden of proof in subjective writing than there is in objective writing, as the strength of the former resides in the personal bond it builds between writer and reader. In terms of questions, subjective questions may have more than one acceptable answer, but students should remember that even for the most subjective questions, there are answers that are clearly wrong.

True – a statement that is demonstrably true in the external world. Note that statements that are not true need not be false.

EXAMPLE: Nova Scotia is a province of Canada. [true]

EXAMPLE: There will be an earthquake tomorrow. [not demonstrably true, since tomorrow has yet to arrive]

Valid – an argument in which the premises logically require the conclusion. Note that a valid argument need not be true.

EXAMPLE: The following argument is valid, though we would agree the major premise is not true:
All politicians are extraterrestrial beings.
My neighbour is a politician.
Therefore, my neighbour is an extraterrestrial being.

Fallacies and Other Errors of Logic

Ad hominem – a fallacy in which you attack the person rather than his or her writing or statements (the phrase is Latin for "to the man")

EXAMPLE: No wonder "Hills Like White Elephants" is an awful story: everyone knows Hemingway was an alcoholic.

Ad populum – a fallacy in which you appeal to the reader's devotion to country or family (the phrase is Latin for "to the people")

EXAMPLE: North American cars are better than imports because our cars are built right here by our own people.

Appeal to Fear – a fallacy in which you attempt to persuade by playing on the reader's fears

EXAMPLE: If you allow this alleged murderer to go free, your own children will be in mortal danger.

Appeal to Ignorance – a fallacy in which you assert that since something has never been proven, it must not be true

EXAMPLE: Since we've never found evidence of life on Mars, there must not be any.

Appeal to Pity – a fallacy in which you attempt to persuade by substituting sympathy for logic

EXAMPLE: One look at these malnourished children should convince you to give all your money to our charity.

Bandwagon – a fallacy in which you assert that something is right or acceptable because everyone is doing it

EXAMPLE: Cheat on your taxes; everyone I know already does.

Begging the Question – a fallacy in which you present an opinion as a given fact

EXAMPLE: Homeless people contribute nothing to society. They should be denied welfare. [Questions: Do homeless people contribute nothing? Why should they be denied welfare?]

Complex Question – a fallacy that forces the reader to admit something that may not be true, because the question asked contains an unproven assumption

EXAMPLE: Have you quit smoking? [To say yes is to admit you used to smoke; to say no is to admit you still smoke. This question is unfair if directed at someone who has never smoked.]

Enthymeme – not a fallacy, but a common form of informal argument in which either one of the premises or the conclusion is missing (the phrase is Latin for "in the mind")

EXAMPLE: Mowing the lawn is a waste of time because the grass never stops growing anyway. [This argument overlooks the fact that regular mowing maintains an attractive lawn.]

False Dichotomy – a fallacy in which you deny the possibility of more than two alternatives.

EXAMPLE: There are two kinds of teacher: bad and awful.

Hasty Generalization – a fallacy in which you deny exceptions

EXAMPLE: All teachers are overpaid, uninspiring, boring time-servers.

Non sequitur – a fallacy in which the conclusion does not logically follow from the premises (the phrase is Latin for "it does not follow")

EXAMPLE: All men are mortal.
Gloria is not a man.
Therefore, Gloria is immortal. [The mistake arises from assuming that the first premise also means "Only men are mortal."]

Overgeneralization – a fallacy in inductive reasoning. Jumping to a general conclusion based on a small number of observations can lead to some surprising conclusions.

EXAMPLE: If you know two people who are tall and who are bad drivers, it is an overgeneralization to conclude that all tall people are bad drivers.

Oversimplification (also called the "reductive fallacy") – a fallacy in which effects are attributed to actions that may not be the complete causes, or may not be causes at all

EXAMPLE: To get rid of crime, get rid of all the drug users.

Post hoc, ergo propter hoc – a fallacy in which an effect is attributed to an action simply because the action came first (the phrase is Latin for "after this, therefore because of this")

EXAMPLE: The escalation of baseball players' salaries is responsible for the recent melting of the polar ice caps.

Red Herring – a technique in which you try to distract the reader from your argument by introducing something unrelated

EXAMPLE: Of course, the team's owner is losing millions of dollars. However, the team has won four games in a row, and the owner would never sell or move the team when it's winning. [The winning streak is the red herring; if the owner loses enough money, he or she will sell or move the team, regardless of its performance.]

Slanted Language – a fallacy in which you use the connotations of words to portray similarities as substantial differences

EXAMPLE: I am a strong conservative, eager to protect the state and its people by limiting immigration and introducing racial segregation. My opponent, however, is a fascist.

Tautology – technically not a fallacy, but an argument that proves nothing, since something is just defined in different terms (also called "circular argument")

EXAMPLE: All unmarried men are bachelors.
Hanif is an unmarried man.
Therefore, Hanif is a bachelor.

COMMENT: Bachelorhood is the defining feature of unmarried men, it is not a quality such as mortality, greed, generosity, and so on.

Testimonial – a fallacy in which an expert in one field offers his or her opinion in another field

EXAMPLE: We should all drive the new Honnisoyota SUV because Jaromir Jagr drives one.

Undistributed Middle – a fallacy that holds that because two agents perform some action, they share each other's qualities. This fallacy is used extensively by advertisers.

EXAMPLE: Successful people drive SUVs. If you drive an SUV, you'll be a successful person.

Terms in Exam and Essay Instructions

Certain verbs are repeatedly used in writing questions for paragraph and essay responses on both tests and take-home assignments. The following is a list of the most common verbs, and what they actually require you to do in your response. Familiarity with this list will reduce the likelihood of writing well yet not answering the question.

Agree or Disagree – an instruction that invites you to choose one side of a statement, and support your answer by promoting the strengths of your side and exposing the weaknesses of the other side. You should avoid the "I agree and disagree" response: students are seldom rewarded for fence-sitting.

EXAMPLE: Hamlet's indecision was his undoing. Agree or disagree.

Assess – an invitation to evaluate something. It may be useful to present criteria, then test the topic being assessed against them.

EXAMPLE: Assess the validity of the claim "Better to have loved and lost than never to have loved at all."

Compare – an instruction to either "identify similarities between" or "identify similarities and differences between" two or more subjects. In practice, students should assume that "compare" asks for similarities, and that if both similarities and differences are desired, the phrase "compare and contrast" will be used.

EXAMPLE: Compare Iago and Richard III, as Shakespeare has portrayed them.

Contrast – an instruction to "contrast" two or more subjects. Unlike *compare*, *contrast* directs students to identify differences only.

EXAMPLE: Contrast Macbeth and Macduff.

Classify – an instruction to divide into groups or to assign to a category. In essay writing, this often takes the form of "There are *x* kinds of *y*."

EXAMPLE: Classify the deaths in *Hamlet* according to categories of your own devising.

Define – an instruction to provide a clear and concise meaning of the concept provided. In a longer essay, you can place the concept in its context, discuss its importance, and possibly share your attitude toward it.

EXAMPLE: Define the tradition of "courtly love."

Describe – an instruction that requires you to provide a detailed account of a person, object, event, or trend. Figurative language can be a powerful tool for description.

EXAMPLE: Describe Pip's reaction to the news of Joe and Biddy's wedding.

Discuss – an invitation to fully explore a given subject by examining it thoroughly. Discussion questions often lead to lengthy answers.

EXAMPLE: Discuss the juxtaposition of wedding and funeral images in *Romeo and Juliet*.

Evaluate – an instruction to make a value judgement of the topic. Statements and actions can be evaluated morally, logically, contextually, and so on.

EXAMPLE: Evaluate Ralph's decision not to join Jack's group.

Explain – an instruction that requires you to reveal what something is, how it works, or how it got to be the way it is

EXAMPLE: Explain the process of photosynthesis.

Identify – an instruction that asks you to label something or describe its boundaries. Many students make the mistake of providing an example instead of a label. *Identify* is often linked to *explain* in questions.

EXAMPLE: Identify and explain one example of irony in *Macbeth*. [Don't forget to label the irony you identify: verbal irony, dramatic irony, and so on.]

Illustrate – an instruction to provide one or more examples of a term or idea

EXAMPLE: Provide three examples that illustrate the author's existentialist concerns.

Justify – an instruction to provide persuasive evidence that supports the given claim or shows the necessity of the claim

EXAMPLE: Justify Macbeth's murder of Duncan.

List – an instruction requiring you to provide a number of items belonging to the class in question. List questions sometimes ask you to rank the items and *justify* their inclusion.

EXAMPLE: List the eight characters who die in *Hamlet*, in order of the audience's discovery of their deaths.

Outline – an instruction to provide a list or summary of the most important points of the subject. A point form presentation may be sufficient.

EXAMPLE: Outline the treatment Lear receives at the hands of his three daughters.

Prove – an instruction to establish the truth of your claim by using evidence. In most cases, the claim cannot be proven, but your burden is to make the most compelling case you can.

EXAMPLE: Prove that Hamlet knew that Polonius and Claudius were spying on him during his confrontation with Ophelia.

Show – a general instruction to support a proposition by the use of facts, examples, anecdotes, and so on

EXAMPLE: Show that Romeo is ultimately responsible for all the deaths in *Romeo and Juliet*.

State – an instruction to reproduce something already known. "State" is often linked with another instruction.

EXAMPLE: State Newton's *First Law of Motion* and show its relevance to *Macbeth*.

Suggest – an invitation to offer possible reasons for or solutions to the question. While there may be more than one acceptable answer to a "suggest" question, there are many answers that are demonstrably wrong. A subjective question is no excuse for a wrong answer.

EXAMPLE: Suggest three reasons why Hamlet doesn't kill Claudius while the latter is praying.

Support – an instruction that is similar to *Agree* (see above), without the option to disagree. When confronted with this kind of question, it is dangerous to argue the opposite point of view. Remember that arguing something you don't believe is a valuable intellectual exercise.

EXAMPLE: Support the claim that Lear faked his madness.

Trace – an instruction to present, in order, every instance of something. There is likely an expectation that you will comment on the pattern, having traced it.

EXAMPLE: Trace Steinbeck's use of animal imagery in his descriptions of Lennie.

Media Terms

GENERAL MEDIA TERMS

Advertisement – a paid-for promotion of a product, service, or company. Advertisements can take many different media forms.

Art Director – the individual responsible for the overall look of a professionally created media text. An art director might be in charge of preparing initial planning sketches or storyboards, set designs, and possibly hiring artists and creative talent to create the media text (film, video, print advertisement, or commercial).

Audio – sound in a media text, which could include music, spoken words, or sound effects

Audience – the group of people to whom the media text is targeted. Media texts can have specific or broad audiences. A media text can be aimed at more than one audience.

Byline – in a newspaper or magazine, the acknowledgement of the author

Caption – a written description of the content of a photograph or illustration, which may or may not include additional details about the graphic

Collage – an arrangement of images, objects, and occasionally written text placed together to create a visual statement

Commercial – an advertisement created for broadcast on radio or television

Copy – the written text of a newspaper or magazine article, book, or advertisement

Copywriter – the person responsible for writing the text of an advertisement

Contrast – the placing of two elements, visual or audio, in close proximity so as to highlight their difference

Costume Designer – the person who prepares the costumes worn by subjects (models or actors) in a media text

Demographics – the study of population statistics, such as age, gender, and income. Demographics is used by media text creators to determine the characteristics of the target audience.

Endorsement – the recommendation of a product, service, or idea

Feature Film – a film, usually of longer duration, shown at theatres for paying audiences

Headline – the title of a newspaper or magazine article

Icon – any image that has a symbolic meaning

Image – the idea presented by a person, organization, or object

Jingle – a portion of a song used to promote a product, service, or idea

Lead – the introductory paragraph of a newspaper story. It usually contains the who, what, where, when, and sometimes the why of the story.

Masthead – in a newsletter, newspaper, or magazine, the banner across the top of the front page giving the name and date of the publication

Narrowcasting – appealing to a specific audience

Periodical – a publication that appears regularly

Storyboard – a visual representation, using frames, of the video and audio information for a film, video, television show, or commercial

Symbol – a concrete object that represents an abstract idea or concept

Target audience – the specific group at which a media text is aimed

Video – the visual portion of a film, commercial, or other motion picture media text

FILM TERMS AND CAMERA ANGLES

Backlighting – illumination coming from behind the actors or objects being filmed. Used to increase the presence of the object or person in a dramatic way.

Close Shot (CS) – a shot whose view is close to the action. Not as close as a *close-up*, but not as far back as a *medium shot*.

Close-up (CU) – a shot in which we see the head and shoulders of the actor. In a *tight close-up* we see only the head, and in an *extreme close-up* only a portion of the face (eyes, mouth, etc.).

Crane Shot – a shot (usually a *pan* or *tilt*) in which a crane is used to lift the camera above the action

Cutaway – a shot inserted into the *master* or *establishing shot* (see below) in order to focus on some elements of the scene. For example, a cutaway from a medium shot of a fight scene to a close-up of an actor in order to show his or her emotions.

Defocus – to deliberately take a shot out of focus. An effect usually used to make a transition from one scene to another.

Dissolve – the gradual fading out of one shot while simultaneously fading in on another. Often used to make a transition from one scene to another.

Dolly Shot – a shot in which the whole camera is moved to follow the action

Dutch Angle or Oblique Angle Shot – a shot in which the camera is tilted off the normal vertical axis. This shot tend to give the view an off-kilter or odd look.

Establishing or Master Shot – a shot used to show the overall view of a location and/or all the actors involved in a scene. It's usually a wide or *long shot*, used to orient the viewer to the scene. Other shots are often edited into the master shot.

Exterior – a shot taken outdoors, usually with natural lighting

Fade – the gradual increase or decrease of light at the beginning or end of a shot. For example, a fade-out has the shot going to black at the end of the scene. Often used as a transition if a dissolve is not used.

High Angle Shot – a shot taken from above. This tends to make the objects look smaller and less imposing.

Interior – a shot taken indoors, usually with artificial lighting

Jump Cut – a cut (edit) that visually jars or disturbs the viewer, most often by making a break in the continuity of a scene

Long Shot (LS) – a shot in which the subject is at a great distance

Low Angle Shot – a shot whose subject is shot from below. Tends to make objects appear bigger or more imposing.

Medium Shot (MS) – a shot between a long shot and a close shot. It usually includes most of a person's body.

Objective Camera – when the scene is shot from the viewpoint of a spectator watching from outside the scene. The opposite of *subjective camera*.

Panning – moving the camera in a horizontal direction from either left to right or right to left. Often used to follow the action in a scene.

Sequence – a series of scenes edited together that is somewhat complete. A shot is like a sentence; a scene is like a paragraph; and a sequence is like a chapter.

Super – to overlay one shot (often graphics or a title) over another shot

Tilt – moving the camera in a vertical direction either up or down. Often used to follow action in a scene.

Two-shot – a shot in which two actors are framed together

Zoom-in – moving the camera closer to the object being filmed

Zoom-out – moving the camera farther away from the object being filmed

Appendix A

How to Hyperlink in Word-Processing Programs

NOTE: Some variation will be required for some software

- First ensure that all the documents you wish to link together have already been saved, and that you know the location and file name of the documents.
- Ensure that you have access to the WEB /INTERNET/HYPERTEXT TOOL BAR.
- Start with the main document you wish to hyperlink. Select and highlight a word or phrase you wish to connect to. For example, you might highlight the word Shakespeare if you were planning to link it to a picture or text biography of William Shakespeare.
- Click on the HYPERLINK/HYPERTEXT ICON or BUTTON. The hyperlink window should appear.
- If you know the exact location and name of the file you wish to link, type it into the DIALOGUE WINDOW. If you're not sure or don't know, click BROWSE.
- If you wanted to link only to another document and not a specific place in the document, you're done.
- If you wish to link to a specific location in a document, such as a word, image, or presentation, fill in the NAMED LOCATION IN FILE/BOOKMARK. This will enable you to jump to a specific place in the document.
- In the main document your link should appear in small blue print to indicate that it's a working hyperlink.

How to Hyperlink to a Web Site

- Open the Internet site you wish to link.
- Copy the URL (location) of the site.
- Go back to your main document, and highlight the word or picture you wish to link to the Web site.
- Click on the HYPERLINK/HYPERTEXT ICON or BUTTON.
- Paste the URL into the DIALOGUE WINDOW.

Tips for Using Hypertext

- Always try out your hyperlinks once they are completed. If they don't work, edit or delete them and start again.
- Limit the number of hyperlinks so that you don't confuse or frustrate your reader.
- Understand that a given piece of text or image can't be linked to two separate locations.
- It is generally helpful to save all the related documents you're linking together in one folder.
- Always open the original document in the program in which it was created before opening the destination documents for your links.
- If your hyperlinks are to an Internet site, remember that URLs often change or go dead. If a fair length of time has passed since you first set up your hyperlinks, you may need to update the links.
- Keep in mind that you can also add links to the destination documents, directing your reader either back to the original document or on to other information.

Appendix B

Film/Video Production Process

Film and video production seldom follows an exact process; each film or video will have its own history and way of getting made. In general, however, films and videos will follow the same basic progression towards completion. The process of creation can be roughly divided into three phases: pre-production, production, and post-production. All three are collaborative, requiring many different skilled people. Depending on the size of the production, it is rare for any one person to be involved in the entire process, with the possible exceptions being the producer and director.

The following flow charts provide an overview of the process, and the people involved in pre-production:

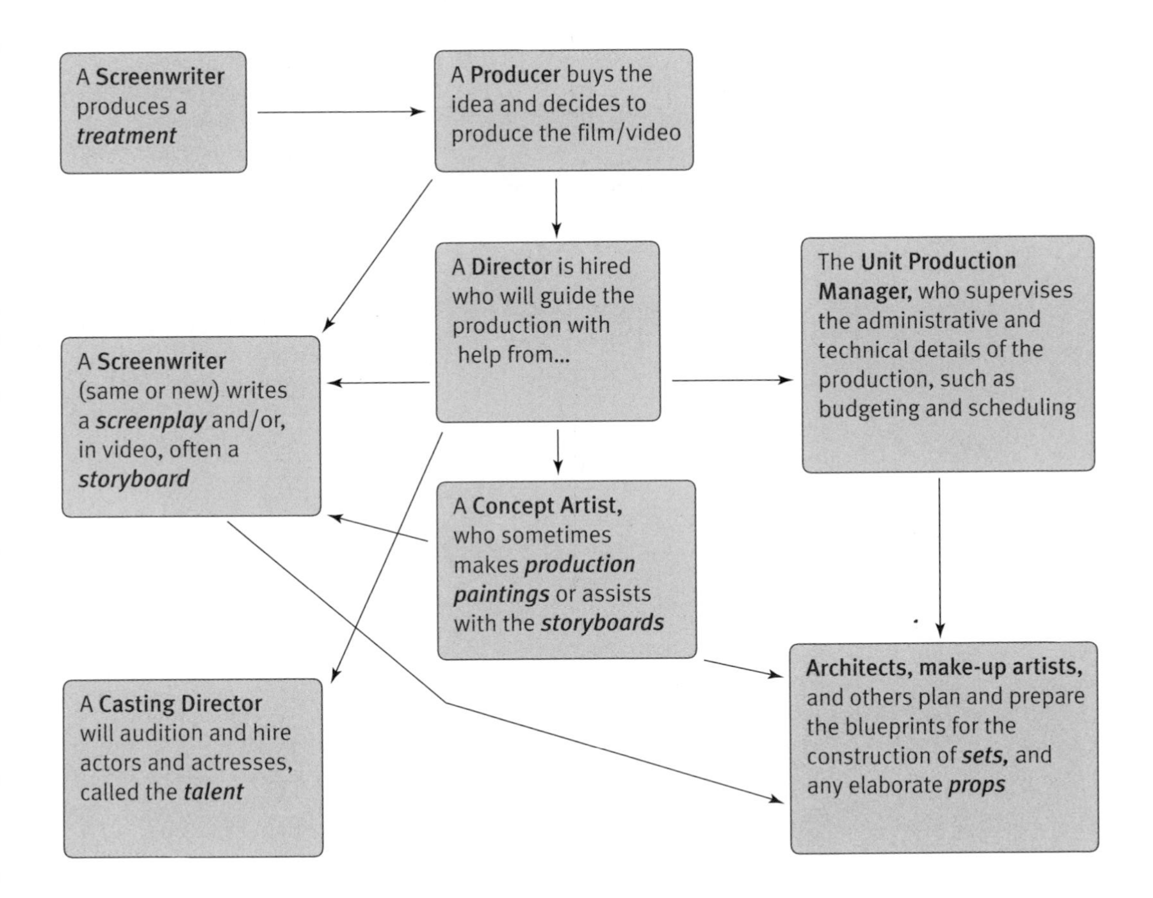

Many people refer to film or video as "director's media," implying that it is the director who guides the artistic vision. In fact, film or video making involves many people at the production phase. As you might imagine, much of the actual production phase of a film or video occurs simultaneously, yet there is still a discernible order in the process:

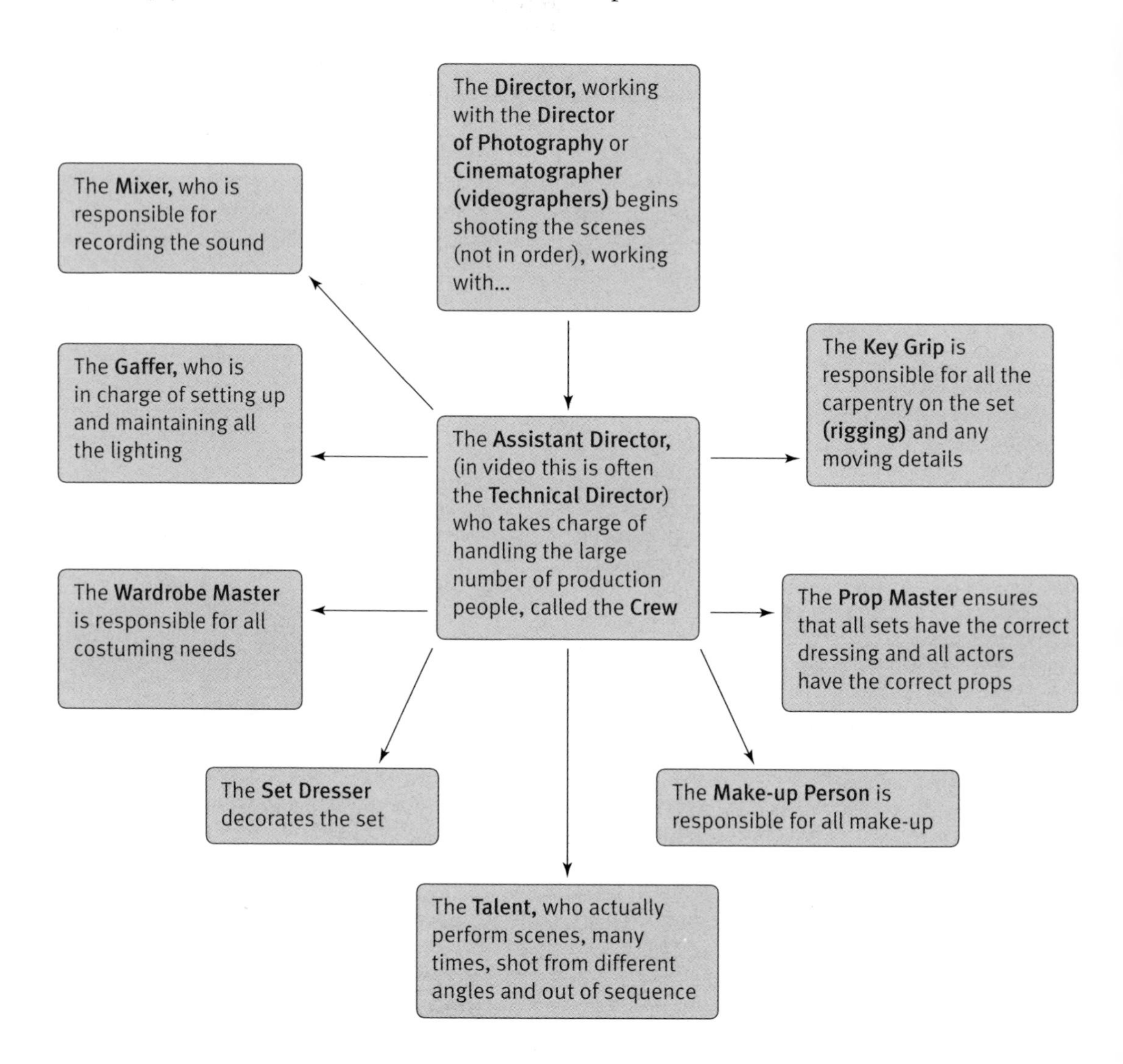

The Director, working with the Director of Photography or Cinematographer (videographers) begins shooting the scenes (not in order), working with...
The Assistant Director, (in video this is often the Technical Director) who takes charge of handling the large number of production people, called the Crew
The Mixer, who is responsible for recording the sound
The Gaffer, who is in charge of setting up and maintaining all the lighting
The Wardrobe Master is responsible for all costuming needs
The Set Dresser decorates the set
The Talent, who actually perform scenes, many times, shot from different angles and out of sequence
The Make-up Person is responsible for all make-up
The Prop Master ensures that all sets have the correct dressing and all actors have the correct props
The Key Grip is responsible for all the carpentry on the set (rigging) and any moving details

The final phase of film/video production, post-production, is the one that varies most from film to video. In general, it is the process of taking the raw film or video and assembling it into the final form that will be seen by the viewer. Since the technologies to do this are so different between film and video, the process is different. However, basic post-production shares certain features:

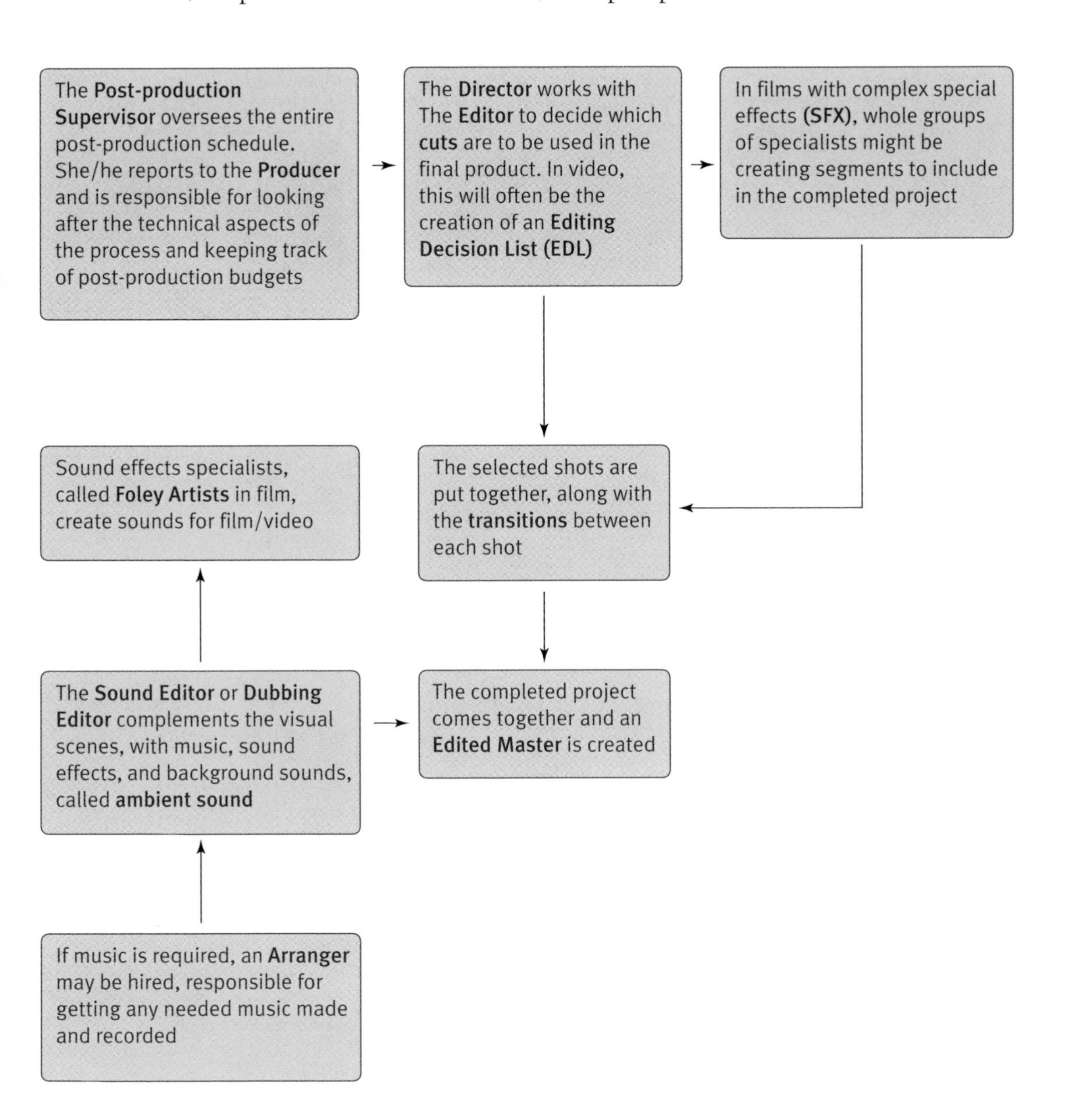

index

Q

R